LEARNING, EARNING, AND INVESTING FOR A NEW GENERATION

COUNCIL FOR
**Economic
Education**

Teaching Opportunity®

AUTHORS:

M. Scott Niederjohn
Charlotte and Walter Kohler Associate Professor of Economics and Business
Director, Center for Economic Education
Lakeland College
Sheboygan, Wisconsin

Mark C. Schug
Professor of Curriculum and Instruction Emeritus
University of Wisconsin-Milwaukee
Milwaukee, Wisconsin

William C. Wood
Professor of Economics
Director, Center for Economic Education
James Madison University
Harrisonburg, Virginia

This publication was made possible through funding provided by Discover.

ISBN: 978-156183-572-0

CONTENTS

Foreword iv

Acknowledgments v

Gen i Revolution Integration Guide vi

Downloading Slides, Activities, and Related Materials xiii

Correlations to National Standards xiv

    Voluntary National Content Standards in Economics xiv

    National Standards in Personal Finance xv

Lesson 1   Why Save?. 1

Lesson 2   Invest in Yourself 11

Lesson 3   What Is a Stock? 27

Lesson 4   Finding Financial Information Online. 41

Lesson 5   What Is a Bond? 65

Lesson 6   What Are Mutual Funds?. 89

Lesson 7   What Are Stock Markets? 107

Lesson 8   Buying on Margin and Selling Short. 119

Lesson 9   Building Wealth over the Long Term 137

Lesson 10   Financial Institutions in the U.S. Economy 167

Lesson 11   Researching Companies 185

Lesson 12   Credit: Your Best Friend or Your Worst Enemy? 199

Lesson 13   Why Not Save? 213

Lesson 14   How Are Stock Prices Determined? 227

Lesson 15   The Role of Government in Financial Markets 251

Lesson 16   The Stock Market and the Economy: Can You Forecast the Future?. 271

Lesson 17   Lessons from History: Stock Market Crashes 285

Lesson 18   Managing Risk 307

Lesson 19   Investing Internationally. 321

Lesson 20   The Language of Financial Markets 335

Lesson 21   Planning Your Financial Future 379

How to Win a Stock Market Game 395

Glossary 397

FOREWORD

In these uncertain times, it is more important than ever for students to learn the fundamentals of money management, saving, and investing. Schools can play a critical role in helping parents and others to provide our young people with a comprehensive program of economic education and personal finance—including investor education. For maximum benefit to young people, investor education must be taught early, often, and well.

Learning, Earning, and Investing for a New Generation introduces students to the world of investing, with its abundant opportunities and ever-present risks. The focus is on strategies for investing for the long term, as part of an overall approach to financial planning that empowers young people to take control of their own financial futures. Lessons cover basics such as the language of financial markets, gathering information on investments, and the nature of financial institutions in the U.S. economy. There are lessons on stocks, bonds, and mutual funds. The 21 lessons provide active learning experiences to help students master the basics of investing.

Learning, Earning, and Investing for a New Generation builds on the success of its 2004 predecessor, *Learning, Earning and Investing*. The new title reflects our effort to update the content and integrate it with the Council for Economic Education's free online personal finance game, *Gen i Revolution*. Every part of the *Gen i Revolution* game is linked to corresponding content in *Learning, Earning, and Investing for a New Generation*.

New content in this edition includes the following:

* New material on the financial crisis of 2008 and the recession of 2007-2009

* A new lesson on short selling and margin transactions

* A new lesson on financial institutions, fully updated with a case study on Apple Computer

* A revised lesson on the relationship between government and financial markets

* A new, comprehensive lesson on managing risk

* A thoroughly revised lesson on international investing

* A revised capstone lesson on financial planning

In 2004, stock and bond markets had achieved a formidable record of providing high returns with minimal observed risk. Declines in the markets, even steep ones, were seen as temporary. Since that time, financial distress and systemic risk have become much more prominent. This revision incorporates what has been learned in the recent financial turmoil. Even with these significant changes, however, the new edition reflects fundamental principles of wealth building that have held up well over time.

CEE gratefully acknowledges Discover, whose generous support made *Learning, Earning, and Investing for a New Generation* possible. The students who learn from these materials, and the nation where they earn and save and invest, will benefit for years to come.

Council for Economic Education

Acknowledgments

The Council for Economic Education expresses its thanks to the many individuals who were involved with this project.

Project Director:

William C. Wood
Professor of Economics
Director, Center for Economic Education
James Madison University
Harrisonburg, Virginia

Project Editor:

Richard D. Western
Florence, Wisconsin

Project Administrator:

Rosanna Castillo
Council for Economic Education
New York, New York

Field-Test Teachers:

Andrea Caceres-Santamaria
Seminole Ridge High School
Palm Beach County School District, Florida

Dawn Framstad
Washington Park High School
Racine Unified School District, Wisconsin

Robert Heinrichs
Spanish River High School
Palm Beach County School District, Florida

Veronica Karas
Santaluces High School
Palm Beach County School District, Florida

Charlie Lemberger
Valders High School
Valders Area School District, Wisconsin

Elizabeth Ramsey
Rockbridge County High School
Rockbridge County School District, Virginia

Donna Wallace
Rockbridge County High School
Rockbridge County School District, Virginia

Special thanks are also due to the authors of lessons in the 2004 predecessor of this project: Jean Caldwell, University of Central Oklahoma; James E. Davis, Colorado Social Science Education Consortium; Suzanne M. Gallagher, Virginia Commonwealth University; Jane S. Lopus, California State University-East Bay; John S. Morton, Arizona Council on Economic Education; Mark C. Schug, University of Wisconsin-Milwaukee; Mary Suiter, Federal Reserve Bank of St. Louis; Phillip J. VanFossen, Purdue University; Donald R. Wentworth, Pacific Lutheran University; and William C. Wood, James Madison University.

GEN i REVOLUTION INTEGRATION GUIDE

The lessons presented in this book are designed to take full advantage of the Council for Economic Education's free online game, *Gen i Revolution*. At the same time, all the lessons are free-standing and may be used without any mention of the game.

In *Gen i Revolution*, each student assumes the role of a secret agent, assigned by the mysterious Monique to help people with financial problems. *Gen i Revolution* is divided into 15 missions. Each mission begins with a briefing from Monique and the selection of computer-based characters to form a team. Then students participate in interactive exercises and tutorials related to the financial problem that has been posed. Each mission concludes with students making financial recommendations, which are then scored according to their effectiveness in solving the financial problem.

Teachers may enroll their classes for participation in *Gen i* missions by applying for a teacher ID at http://genirevolution.org. Each teacher ID enables the teacher to enroll classes, manage access to missions, and monitor student progress.

The print lessons in *Learning, Earning, and Investing for a New Generation* have two specific connections to the online game. At the end of each lesson, you will find a recommendation (Gen i Connection) for a *Gen i Revolution* mission to reinforce the lesson's key points. In cases where the online missions do not correspond directly to a print lesson's key points, the lesson provides other references to Council for Economic Education online resources. Each Gen i Connection is followed by a Gen i Reflection, an in-depth question that invites students to reflect on what they have learned about personal finance and their own investing goals.

Below is a chart showing the correspondence between *Gen i Revolution* missions and the print lessons in *Learning, Earning, and Investing for a New Generation:*

Lesson Number and Title	Key Concepts	Related Gen i Missions
1. Why Save?	Compound interest Consumption Income Rule of 72 Saving Simple interest	1. Help Angela build wealth over the long term.
2. Invest in Yourself	Human capital Income Investment in human capital Opportunity cost	2. Help Veronica chose a tentative career. 3. Help Matt decide whether to continue formal education after he graduates from high school.

3.	What Is a Stock?	Dividend	8.	Help Uncle Louie learn the basics about stocks.
		Income		
		Saving		
		Stock		
4.	Finding Financial Information Online	Closing price		Tutorials on reading financial tables in Missions 8, 9, and 10.
		Dividend		
		Net asset value		
		Price/earnings ratio (P/E ratio)		
		Stock symbol		
		Trading volume		
		Yield		
5.	What Is a Bond?	Bond	9.	Teach Tyrone and Felicia how to invest in bonds.
		Bond rating		
		Coupon		
		Coupon bond		
		Coupon rate		
		Face value		
		Maturity date		
		Par value		
		Risk		
		Zero-coupon bond		
6.	What Are Mutual Funds?	Diversification	10.	Teach a group of students how to invest in mutual funds.
		Liquidity		
		Load		
		Mutual fund		
		Net asset value		
		Risk and reward		
7.	What Are Stock Markets?	Market	12.	Show Jasmine what determines stock prices.
		Primary market		
		Secondary market		
		Stock market		
8.	Buying Stocks on Margin	Buying on margin		No game coverage of margin buying, but good risk coverage in Gen i Mission 6 (Advise Kai on how to invest his grandmother's $10,000).
		Opportunity cost		
		Short cover		
		Short sale		

9.	Building Wealth for the Long Term	Compound interest Diversification Forms of saving and investing Reward Risk	1.	Help Angela build wealth over the long term.
10.	Financial Institutions in the U.S. Economy	Corporation Debt financing Economic investment Equity financing Financial institutions Financial investment Limited liability Partnership Primary markets Proprietorship Secondary markets Venture capitalist		No direct coverage, but several of these topics are mentioned in Missions 11 and 12.
11.	Researching Companies	Alternatives Choice Fundamental analysis Opportunity cost Scarcity	11.	Advise a Gen i donor on her $10 million investment.
12.	Credit: Your Best Friend or Your Worst Enemy?	Choice Costs and benefits Credit Debt Interest Revolving credit	5. 7.	Teach Justin about credit. Convince Paul, Fred, and Diana to reconsider their choice of financial institution.

13. Why Not Save?	Benefits Costs Goals Incentives Interest Long-term goal Medium-term goal Opportunity cost Saving Short-term goal	4. Help the O'Neils save $300 a month.
14. How Are Stock Prices Determined?	Demand Equilibrium price Shift in demand or supply Shortage Supply Surplus	12. Show Jasmine what determines stock prices.
15. The Role of Government in Financial Markets	Government failure Market failure Ponzi scheme Too Big to Fail	No direct connection, but reinforcement of Lesson 15 is available from Missions 13 (Advise Markos how to weather a crash in the scholarship fund) and 14 (Advise political leaders on their economic forecasts).
16. The Stock Market and the Economy: Can You Forecast the Future?	Business cycles Contraction Economic forecasting Expansion Gross Domestic Product Leading economic indicators Peak Recession Trough	14. Advise political leaders on their economic forecasts.

17. Lessons from History: Stock Market Crashes	Causes and effects of the stock market crash of 1929 Causes and effects of the stock market crash of 1987 Causes and effects of the stock market crash that began in 2007 Federal Reserve Monetary policy Supply and demand	13. Advise Markos how to weather a crash in the scholarship fund.
18. Managing Risk	Diversification Insurance Market price risk Risk	6. Advise Kai on how to invest his grandmother's $10,000.
19. Investing Internationally	Currency markets Diversification Exchange rate Strong and weak dollar	14. Advise political leaders on their economic forecasts.
20. The Language of Financial Markets	Bond Mutual fund Stock Stock market	Coverage throughout missions.
21. Planning Your Financial Future	Bonds Certificate of deposit Diversification Liquidity Money market account Mutual funds Principal Rate of return Risk Savings account Stocks	15. Conduct the Red Roosters Club annual financial planning workshop.

And here is a chart showing how Gen i Revolution missions can be mapped back to the content of *Learning, Earning, and Investing for a New Generation (LEIG)*:

Mission Number and Title	Key Concepts	Related Lessons
1. Help Angela build wealth over the long term.	Compound interest Saving	LEIG Lesson 9
2. Help Veronica choose a tentative career.	Investing in human capital Opportunity cost Career choice	LEIG Lesson 2
3. Help Matt decide whether to continue formal education after he graduates from high school.	Investing in human capital Opportunity cost Income	LEIG Lesson 2
4. Help the O'Neils save $300 a month for a down payment on a home.	Budgeting Financial goal setting	LEIG Lesson 1
5. Teach Justin about credit.	Credit Debt Interest	LEIG Lesson 12
6. Advise Kai on how to invest his grandmother's $10,000.	Forms of saving and investing Costs and benefits of saving Risk vs. return	LEIG Lesson 9 LEIG Lesson 13
7. Convince Paul, Fred, and Diana to reconsider their choice of financial institution.	Advantages and disadvantages of non-mainstream financial services	LEIG Lesson 12
8. Help Uncle Louie learn the basics about stocks.	Understanding stocks Dividend Saving Reading a stock table	LEIG Lesson 3 LEIG Lesson 4
9. Teach Tyrone and Felicia how to invest in bonds.	Understanding bonds Bond ratings Reading a bond table	LEIG Lesson 4 LEIG Lesson 5
10. Teach a group of students how to invest in mutual funds.	Understanding mutual funds Diversification Reading a mutual fund table	LEIG Lesson 4 LEIG Lesson 6
11. Advise a Gen i donor on her $10 million investment.	Alternatives Scarcity and choice Fundamental analysis	LEIG Lesson 1

12. Show Jasmine what determines stock prices.	Equilibrium price Shift in demand or supply	LEIG Lesson 14
13. Advise Markos on how to weather a crash in the scholarship fund.	Causes and effects of stock market crashes The Federal Reserve Monetary policy	LEIG Lesson 17
14. Advise political leaders on their economic forecasts.	Business cycles Leading economic indicators Expansion Contraction Economic forecasting	LEIG Lesson 16
15. Conduct the Red Rooster Club annual financial planning workshop.	Forms of saving and investing Diversification Risk vs. return Financial goal setting	LEIG Lesson 21

On the Web

To download the slides and activities for each lesson, find online lessons to extend the student activities, and find related material for each lesson, visit:

http://lei.councilforeconed.org

LEARNING, EARNING, AND INVESTING FOR A NEW GENERATION

Lessons correlated with Voluntary National Content Standards in Economics*

	1	2	3	4	5	6	7	8	9	10	11	12	13	14	15	16	17	18	19	20	21
Standard 1: Scarcity								x					x								x
Standard 2: Decision making			x		x	x		x	x		x	x	x					x	x		x
Standard 3: Allocation													x								
Standard 4: Incentives	x								x		x	x	x				x	x			
Standard 5: Trade							x							x							
Standard 6: Specialization																					
Standard 7: Markets and prices							x							x			x				
Standard 8: Role of prices				x										x			x				
Standard 9: Competition and market structure																					
Standard 10: Institutions						x	x		x	x	x	x					x	x		x	
Standard 11: Money and inflation																					
Standard 12: Interest rates	x				x				x												
Standard 13: Income		x																			
Standard 14: Entrepreneurship																					
Standard 15: Economic growth															x						
Standard 16: Role of government and market failure															x						
Standard 17: Government failure															x						
Standard 18: Economic fluctuations																x					
Standard 19: Unemployment and inflation																					
Standard 20: Monetary and fiscal policy																					

*Standards taken from Voluntary National Content Standards in Economics, 2nd ed., Council for Economic Education (CEE), 2010.

LEARNING, EARNING, AND INVESTING FOR A NEW GENERATION

Lessons correlated with National Standards in Personal Finance*

	1	2	3	4	5	6	7	8	9	10	11	12	13	14	15	16	17	18	19	20	21
Financial Responsibility and Decision Making																					
Standard 1: Take responsibility for personal financial decisions.	x	x																			
Standard 2: Find and evaluate financial information from a variety of sources.				x			x				x	x	x			x				x	
Standard 3: Summarize major consumer protection laws.																					
Standard 4: Make financial decisions by systematically considering alternatives and consequences.					x	x			x		x	x									x
Standard 5: Develop communication strategies for discussing financial issues.				x													x	x	x		
Standard 6: Control personal information.																					
Income and Careers																					
Standard 1: Explore career options.		x																			
Standard 2: Identify sources of personal income.		x																			
Standard 3: Describe factors affecting take-home pay.																					
Planning and Money Management																					
Standard 1: Develop a plan for spending and saving.																					
Standard 2: Develop a system for keeping and using financial records.																					

	1	2	3	4	5	6	7	8	9	10	11	12	13	14	15	16	17	18	19	20	21
Standard 3: Describe how to use different payment methods.																					
Standard 4: Apply consumer skills to purchase decisions.																					
Standard 5: Consider charitable giving.																					
Standard 6: Develop a personal financial plan.									x												x
Standard 7: Examine the purpose and importance of a will.																					
Credit and Debt																					
Standard 1: Identify the costs and benefits of various types of credit.		x										x									
Standard 2: Explain the purpose of a credit record and identify borrowers' credit report rights.																					
Standard 3: Describe ways to avoid or correct debt problems.												x									
Standard 4: Summarize major consumer credit laws.																					
Risk Management and Insurance																					
Standard 1: Identify common types of risks and basic risk-management methods.													x					x			x
Standard 2: Explain the purpose and importance of property and liability insurance protection.																		x			
Standard 3: Explain the purpose and importance of health, disability, and life insurance protection.																		x			

Saving and Investing	1	2	3	4	5	6	7	8	9	10	11	12	13	14	15	16	17	18	19	20	21
Standard 1: Discuss how saving contributes to financial well-being.	x		x			x			x	x			x								x
Standard 2: Explain how investing builds wealth and helps meet financial goals.						x			x	x			x							x	x
Standard 3: Evaluate investment alternatives.			x	x	x	x			x		x		x						x		x
Standard 4: Describe how to buy and sell investments.			x		x	x	x	x						x						x	
Standard 5: Explain how taxes affect the rate of return on investments.																					
Standard 6: Investigate how agencies that regulate financial markets protect investors.					x										x		x				

*Standards taken from National Standards in K-12 Personal Finance Education, Jump$tart Coalition for Personal Financial Literacy, 2007.

LESSON 1

WHY SAVE?

Lesson 1
Why Save?

LESSON DESCRIPTION

Following an introduction that defines *saving*, the students discuss the idea of "paying yourself first" and the reasons why people save. After reporting on their small group discussions, the students simulate the accumulation of simple interest and compound interest. They conclude the lesson by calculating both simple interest and (using the Rule of 72) the amount of time it takes to double a saved amount when interest is compounded.

INTRODUCTION

Saving is disposable income minus consumption spending. For students, disposable income may come from allowances, gifts of money, payment for jobs done at home, or paychecks from a job. A paycheck stub shows how a job contributes to disposable income. The stub shows your pay before taxes, the amount subtracted for taxes, and the income you actually receive. Only this last amount contributes to disposable income. "Paying yourself first" means saving money before spending money on consumer goods. Reasons to save vary from person to person; they might include a promise that money saved will be matched by an adult (a parent or uncle, perhaps), the satisfaction of buying a special gift for someone in the future, or the desire to buy something for one's own use in the future. Simple interest is the annual interest paid on the initial amount saved (the principal). Compound interest is interest paid on both the principal and the interest added to the principal.

CONCEPTS

Compound interest

Consumption

Disposable income

Income

Principal

Rule of 72

Saving

Simple interest

OBJECTIVES

Students will be able to:

- Define *saving*.

- Identify reasons why people save.

- Distinguish between simple and compound interest.

- Apply the formula for calculating simple interest.

- Apply the Rule of 72 to determine how much time it takes for a saved amount to double.

CONTENT STANDARDS

Voluntary National Content Standards in Economics, **2nd Edition**

- **Standard 4:** People usually respond predictably to positive and negative incentives.

- **Standard 12:** Interest rates, adjusted for inflation, rise and fall to balance the amount saved with the amount borrowed, which affects the allocation of scarce resources between present and future uses.

National Standards in K-12 Personal Finance Education, **3rd Edition**

- **Financial Responsibility and Decision Making Standard 1:** Take responsibility for personal financial decisions.

- **Saving and Investing Standard 1:** Discuss how saving contributes to financial well-being.

TIME REQUIRED

45 minutes

MATERIALS

- Slides 1.1, 1.2, 1.3, and 1.4
- One copy of Activity 1.1 for each student

PROCEDURE

1. Tell the students that this lesson focuses on saving: what it is, why people save, and how interest is calculated on money saved. Many financial experts think that Americans save too little. Data on the U.S. personal saving rate, from the Bureau of Economic Analysis (BEA), can easily be graphed using the St. Louis Federal Reserve Bank's website called Federal Reserve Economic Data (FRED). Recent data show that Americans on average save less than five percent of their disposable income.

2. **Display Slide 1.1.** Explain that disposable income equals consumption plus saving. Point out that, for students, disposable income may come from allowances, gifts of money, payment for jobs done at home, or paychecks from a job. Explain that consumption is spending on goods and services. Define *saving* by explaining that saving equals disposable income minus consumption.

3. Organize the class into groups of about five students each. Ask each group to choose a reporter to take notes and report the group's work to the class.

4. **Distribute a copy of Activity 1.1** to each student. Ask the students to read Activity 1.1 and, in their groups, discuss the two questions posed at the end of the handout. Give the students about 15 minutes to read Activity 1.1 and conduct their discussions.

5. Call on the groups' reporters to report on each group's results. Discuss the **Questions for Discussion. Ask:**

   A. What do you think is meant by this statement: "Pay yourself first"?

      ("Pay yourself first" means that a person saves before spending money on goods and services.)

   B. What are some reasons why people save?

      (Reasons vary from person to person. They might include saving money to gain the satisfaction of purchasing a special gift, to make large purchases, to meet emergencies that might arise, to qualify for matching money, and to pay for a college education.)

6. Note that all saving decisions relate to some future use of money. Point out to the students that they should have their own reasons for saving. These reasons necessarily will derive from goals the students envision. Thinking about saving, in other words, involves thinking about goals.

7. **Display Slide 1.2** and explain the Simple Interest Adds column and the Compound Interest Adds column.

8. To illustrate the information provided on Slide 1.2, conduct the following simulation in your classroom. Ask one student to write "Principal = $100" on a sheet of paper large enough for everyone to see when he or she is standing in front of the class. Ask everyone else in the class to write "$100" on a sheet of paper (once again, large enough for all to see). Ask the student with the Principal sign to stand up in front of

the class. Ask the class to define the term *principal*, making the point that it represents the amount of money that is borrowed or saved.

9. Next tell the class that they will simulate how money grows under simple interest. Review columns two (Simple Interest Adds) and three (Total Saving Using Simple Interest) of Slide 1.2. **Display Slide 1.3** and explain that simple interest is calculated in each period by multiplying the interest rate by the principal. Tell the class that for simplicity you will use a 100 percent interest rate in this exercise. Ask the students how much simple interest would be earned after year one. The answer is $100. Continue this process for five years. At this point, there should be one student in front of the class holding the Principal sign and five students holding $100 signs. Make the point that, under simple interest, the initial principal of $100 has grown to $600.

10. Next tell the class that they will simulate how money grows under compound interest. Review columns four (Compound Interest Adds) and five (Total Saving Using Compound Interest) on Slide 1.2. Make the point that under compound interest the interest is calculated on both the principal and the interest earned in the account. Once again ask the student with the Principal sign to stand up in front of the class. Once again use a 100 percent interest rate. Ask the class how much compound interest will be earned in year one. The answer, once again, is $100. Continue to year two. This time two students will need to come to the front of the class to represent the $200 in compound interest earned on the $200 ($100 of principal and $100 of interest). Continue this process for year three (four students will come forward as the $400 becomes $800), year four (eight students will come forward as

the $800 becomes $1,600), and year five (sixteen students come forward as the $1,600 becomes $3,200). *(Note: If your class is smaller than the 32 students required for this simulation, you can have each student make two signs.)*

11. Make the point that under the simple interest system, in five years the $100 in principal became $600. However, under the compound interest system, this same $100 in principal turned into $3,200. Explain that compound interest is really money that your money makes for you. One need not work longer hours or get a second job to earn this money.

12. The Rule of 72 provides an easy way to illustrate how compound interest works. **Display Slide 1.4,** "The Rule of 72." Explain that in using the Rule of 72 we divide 72 by the interest rate paid to determine how many years it will take for a saved amount to double when the interest is compounded. To apply this rule to the earlier example on Slide 1.2, divide 72 by eight percent and the result is nine years. This explains why Slide 1.2 shows the initial principal of $100 doubling in nine years when an eight percent interest rate was assumed. If the interest rate had been lower—for example, six percent— then it would have taken 12 years for the saved amount to double (72 divided by 6 = 12).

CLOSURE

13. Review the lesson. **Ask:**

   A. What is saving?

   (Saving is disposable income minus consumption. Remind the students that there are several reasons for saving, such as saving to make a large purchase, saving for emergencies, or saving to pay for a college education. Many reasons encourage many people to get an early start on saving.)

B. Pose a practice problem for use with the simple interest formula. The initial amount saved is $1,000; the interest rate is five percent. If you keep the initial $1,000 for five years, how much simple interest will be paid?

($1,000 x 5% = $50 per year x 5 years = $250)

C. Pose a practice problem for use with the Rule of 72. The initial amount saved is $500. At an interest rate of three percent, how long would it take to double that initial $500? What if the interest rate is six percent?

(72 divided by 3 = 24 years; 72 divided by 6 = 12 years)

ASSESSMENT

Multiple-Choice Questions

1. Which of the following is the best definition for *saving*?

    a. the discount received from buying something on sale
    b. *disposable income minus consumption spending*
    c. putting your money under your mattress
    d. the interest paid on a savings account

2. Which of the following is a reason to save?

    a. *Your parents place a dollar into your savings account for every dollar you save.*
    b. Your bank charges a penalty if you withdraw money from your account.
    c. The government collects high rates of taxes on interest received through saving.
    d. Having to go to the bank to make a purchase.

3. If you have $50 in a savings account for one year at an interest rate of 6 percent, how much interest will you earn at the end of the year?

    a. $5
    b. $4
    c. *$3*
    d. $2

4. If you divide the interest rate paid into 72, the result tells you how many years it will take for the amount initially saved to double if you receive compound interest. At a compound interest rate of 10 percent, how many years will it take to double your money?

    a. 2.7 years
    b. *7.2 years*
    c. 7.0 years
    d. 10.0 years

Constructed-Response Items

1. Explain, in your own words, what the statement "Pay yourself first" means.

    (Paying yourself first means making saving a priority over spending. The decision on how much to save is made before the decision on how much to spend on consumption. Paying yourself first allows a person to more easily achieve goals for saving.)

2. A friend asks you what sort of interest—simple or compound—is better. What would your answer be, and why?

    (When savings are allowed to accumulate with simple interest, the total grows more slowly than it would grow with compound interest. The rule of 72 enables you to calculate how many years it will take for a saved amount to double if you receive compound interest. Compound interest generates dramatic growth over the long term.)

Gen i Connection

Mission 1 of the Gen i Revolution game enables students to gain experience with the topics of simple and compound interest illustrated in this lesson. The premise of the mission is that a young worker, Angela, needs help making decisions on her savings plan at work. Students work interactively through a 4-1-1 tutorial session focused on the difference between simple and compound interest, including the use of an online calculator to solve for interest earned and changes in savings account balances under different scenarios. (A second tutorial session, on three rules for building wealth, reinforces material from Lesson 9 of this book, "Building Wealth over the Long Term.") The mission's conclusion calls on students to recommend investment decisions to Angela and to calculate what difference the decisions will make in her accumulation of wealth over her lifetime.

Gen i Reflection

Mission 1 showed the advantages of "buy and hold" over frequently jumping in and out of the stock market. Think about your own future investing. By your nature, would you find it easy to buy and hold, or would you be inclined to buy and sell frequently? Explain your answer.

ACTIVITY 1.1
A CONVERSATION AMONG FRIENDS

Patrick, Matthew, Elizabeth, Benjamin, and Steph are talking about money. Their teacher, Ms. Greenberg, has asked them to think about saving money. Read their conversation. Then answer the **Questions for Discussion** *that follow.*

Patrick: Last week I bought this really cool basketball jersey for $50. The week before, the price had been $57. I saved $7.

Elizabeth: But Patrick, you spent $50. I don't think this is what Ms. Greenberg means by saving.

Matthew: I think Ms. Greenberg means that saving is not spending our money now.

Benjamin: Yeah, I think Matthew is right. But it is SO hard to save. I don't really have very much money. And I want a lot of stuff.

Steph: Well, my parents want me to save some of my allowance. They said that if I have $100 saved at the end of the year, they would add $100 to it.

Elizabeth: Wow, that's pretty generous. Are you going to do it?

Steph: I'm going to try. I started a savings account at the bank.

Matthew: I don't have a savings account, but I try not to spend all the money I have because I want to buy a nice Christmas present for my dad.

Patrick: I've heard that you get interest on money you put into a savings account at a bank. Is that right, Steph?

Steph: Yeah, I think so, but I don't know much about it.

Benjamin: I really do want a new bike, and my parents said I have to save my money for it. They won't buy it for me.

Elizabeth: I want an iPad, and my parents told me the same thing.

Patrick: I just don't know how I can save any money. There are too many things to spend my money on now. I don't know if I want to give up spending.

Matthew: You're right, Patrick. It's hard to give up spending, especially when we don't have much money just now.

Benjamin: I heard some guy on TV the other day say that people should pay themselves first. I wonder what he meant by this.

Questions for Discussion

In your small groups, choose a representative to take notes and report the results of your discussion to the class. Then discuss and record your responses to the following questions:

    A. What do you think is meant by this statement: "Pay yourself first"?

    B. What are some reasons why people save?

SLIDE 1.1

Disposable Income and Saving

- Disposable income = consumption + saving
- Saving = disposable income – consumption

SLIDE 1.2

Interest Earned on an Initial $100 Saved at 8% Interest Rate

Year	Simple Interest Adds	Total Saving Using Simple Interest	Compound Interest Adds	Total Saving Using Compound Interest
1	$8.00	$108.00	$8.00	$108.00
2	$8.00	$116.00	$9.00	$117.00
3	$8.00	$124.00	$9.00	$126.00
4	$8.00	$132.00	$10.00	$136.00
5	$8.00	$140.00	$11.00	$147.00
6	$8.00	$148.00	$12.00	$159.00
7	$8.00	$156.00	$12.00	$171.00
8	$8.00	$164.00	$14.00	$185.00
9	$8.00	$172.00	$15.00	$200.00

SLIDE 1.3

Calculating Simple Interest

- Interest = Principal (amount of initial saving) x Rate (of interest being paid on savings) x Time (in years)
- Example: Simple Interest at 8% for 3 years
- Interest = ($100) x (0.08) x (3) = $24

SLIDE 1.4

The Rule of 72

- The Rule of 72 is a simple way to illustrate the magic of compound interest.
- Rule of 72
  - 72 divided by the rate of interest = the number of years it will take for a saved amount to double when interest is allowed to compound.
  - The Rule of 72 illustrates how quickly compound interest can make saved amounts grow.
- Example: Compound Interest at 8% for 9 years
  - 72 divided by 8 = nine years
  - At the end of nine years, the initial saved amount of $100 has increased to $200—double the initial amount.

LESSON 2
INVEST IN YOURSELF

Lesson 2
Invest in Yourself

LESSON DESCRIPTION

To explore the concept that people invest in themselves through education, the students work in two groups and participate in a mathematics game. Both groups are assigned mathematics problems to solve. One group is told about a special technique for solving the problems. The other group is not. The game helps the students recognize that improved human capital allows people to produce more in a given amount of time—in this example, more correct answers in the time provided, or in less time. Next, the students identify the human capital required for a variety of jobs. Finally, they learn about the connections among investment in human capital, careers, and earning potential.

INTRODUCTION

Investment takes many forms. One form is the development of human capital—the knowledge, skills, health, and values that individuals possess. People develop their human capital through formal and informal education. To obtain education, people give up something in the short run (time, effort, and money, for example) in order to gain larger returns (a good job, for example) in the future. This sort of exchange—giving up something now in order to realize gains later—is the essence of investment behavior, whether it involves putting money into a mutual fund or putting resources into education.

CONCEPTS

Human capital

Income

Investment in human capital

Opportunity cost

OBJECTIVES

Students will be able to:

- Define *human capital* and give examples of it.

- Explain how human capital is related to career choices, opportunities, and income.

- Define *opportunity cost* and give examples of it.

CONTENT STANDARDS

Voluntary National Content Standards in Economics, **2nd Edition**

- **Standard 2:** Income for most people is determined by the market value of the productive resources they sell. What workers earn primarily depends on the market value of what they produce.

National Standards in K-12 Personal Finance Education, **3rd edition**

- **Financial Responsibility and Decision Making Standard 1:** Take responsibility for personal financial decisions.

- **Income and Careers Standard 1:** Explore career options.

- **Income and Careers Standard 2:** Identify sources of personal income.

- **Credit and Debt Standard 1:** Identify the costs and benefits of various types of credit.

TIME REQUIRED

60 minutes

MATERIALS

- Slides 2.1, 2.2, 2.3, 2.4, 2.5, 2.6, and 2.7

- A copy of Activity 2.1-A for half the class

- A copy of Activity 2.1-B for half the class

- A watch, clock, or timer to count off seconds

PROCEDURE

1. Tell the students that the purpose of this lesson is to help them understand an important economic term, *human capital. Human capital* refers to the knowledge, skills, and health that individuals possess. Explain that developing human capital—through formal and informal education—is a form of investing. In devoting time, effort, and perhaps money to education, for example, students give something up now in order to gain something of value in the future.

2. Organize the class into two groups, A and B. Explain the rules for the activity to follow:

   - Each person in each group will receive some problems to solve.

   - Nobody in either group may begin to work on the problems until they are told to.

   - Everybody will have five minutes to solve the problems.

   - When a student has solved all of the problems, she or he should stand.

3. **Distribute a copy of Activity 2.1-A** *face down* to each student in group A and a copy of **Activity 2.1-B** *face down* to each student in group B.

4. Tell the students in group B that they may turn their papers over and read the instructions. They may not begin working on the problems; they may read only the instructions.

5. After several minutes, tell the members of group A to turn their papers over. Tell all the students that they may begin working to solve their problems. Keep track of time.

6. As the students finish and stand up, tell each student how much time it took him or her to solve the problems.

7. When all the students are standing, or after five minutes have elapsed, tell the students to stop working. Have them sit down.

8. **Display Slide 2.1** and have the students check their answers.

9. **Display Slide 2.2**. Ask the following questions and record the answers on Slide 2.2:

   A. How many students in group A completed the problems in less than one minute?

   (Answers will vary.)

   B. How many correct answers did you have?

   (Answers will vary.)

   C. Add the number of correct answers for those who completed the problems in less than one minute and record the total on Slide 2.2.

   D. How many students in group A took more than one minute but less than two minutes to complete the problems?

   (Answers will vary.)

   E. How many correct answers did you have?

   (Answers will vary.)

   F. Add the number of correct answers for those who completed the problems in more than one but less than two minutes and record the total on Slide 2.2.

G. How many students in group A took more than two minutes but less than three minutes to complete the problems?

(Answers will vary.)

H. How many correct answers did you have?

(Answers will vary.)

I. Add the number of correct answers for those who completed the problems in more than two but less than three minutes and record the total on Slide 2.2.

J. How many students in group A took more than three minutes but less than four minutes to complete the problems?

(Answers will vary.)

K. How many correct answers did you have?

(Answers will vary.)

L. Add the number of correct answers for those who completed the problems in more than three but less than four minutes and record the total on Slide 2.2.

M. How many students in group A took more than four minutes but less than five minutes to complete the problems?

(Answers will vary.)

N. How many correct answers did you have?

(Answers will vary.)

O. Add the number of correct answers for those who completed the problems in more than four but less than five minutes and record the total Slide on 2.2.

10. Repeat the steps in Procedure 9 for students in group B. **Ask:**

A. In general, which students had more correct answers?

(Most likely those in group B had more correct answers).

B. In general, which students were able to complete the problems faster?

(Most likely those in group B were able to complete the problems faster.)

11. Ask a student from group A and a student from group B to go to the board and show their work for the first problem. Point out that the group A and group B students used different methods to solve the problem.

12. Ask the students in group B where they learned the method they used.

(From the instructions on the handout.)

13. Ask a student from group A to read the directions on his or her handout.

14. Ask a student from group B to read the directions on his or her handout. Tell the students these were the directions provided for group B.

15. Explain that the students in group B received knowledge and skills to help them solve the problems more quickly. The knowledge and skills improved the students' human capital. Human capital is the knowledge, skills, and health that individuals possess. With improved human capital, people can produce more and better products than other people can—in the same amount of time or less. In this example, the students in group B were able to produce more correct answers than students in group A—in the same amount of time or less—because students in group B had more human capital.

16. **Display Slide 2.3**. Explain that the column on the right provides examples of human capital and the column on the left provides examples of occupations. Invite the students to speculate on what sorts of human capital people might need in order to work competently for each occupation on the list.

17. **Display Slide 2.4**. Invite the students to describe examples of how each occupation requires particular types of human capital. **Ask:**

    A. What similarities are there in the human capital required for each job listed?

    (Communication and mathematics skills.)

    B. What mathematics skills might an automotive technician/mechanic need?

    (Convert from standard to metric measures, calculate costs of labor and parts.)

    C. What are some examples of communication skills needed by a school bus driver?

    (Reading maps, street signs, schedules, a vehicle manual, a safety manual, employment information; speaking with students and co-workers; writing safety evaluations, completing the written portion of a licensure test.)

    D. Give examples of mathematics skills needed by a retail sales clerk.

    (Understanding of decimals and percents, ability to count money and make change.)

    E. For the most part, how do people obtain basic mathematics and communication skills?

    (By going to school and staying in school until graduation.)

    F. What differences are there in the human capital required for the jobs listed?

    (Some require apprenticeships and special training; some require college degrees; some require advanced degrees.)

    G. How does a carpenter acquire the education and special skills needed for the job?

    (Carpenter training programs, apprenticeship programs.)

    H. How does a mechanical engineer obtain the education and special skills needed for the job?

    (By attending college and earning a degree in mechanical engineering.)

    I. How does a medical doctor obtain the education and special skills needed for the job?

    (Graduating from college, attending medical school, completing an internship and a residency.)

    J. What are some examples of human capital that you have?

    (Answers will vary. They may include ability to read, write, work in groups, solve problems, play an instrument, use the computer, draw, sing, play a sport, and so on.)

18. **Display Slide 2.5** and explain that it shows the median yearly incomes for people holding certain jobs in 2011. Explain that *median* means that half of the workers in a particular group earn more than the median income and half earn less than the median income. Thus some people working at a given job earned more and some earned less than the amount shown.

19. Point out that, in general, high-paying occupations require more education and training than low-paying occupations. For example, doctors earn higher incomes and require more education than retail sales clerks. Tell the students that, in general, investment in human capital leads to higher pay.

20. **Display Slide 2.6** and tell the students that it shows median annual income and the unemployment rate for people by level of educational attainment. Discuss the information on Slide 2.6.

    • Associate's degrees require two years of education. These degrees are most often earned at a community college or technical college.

    • Bachelor's degrees require four years of education or more at a college or university.

    • Master's degrees require two or more years of additional education at a college or university.

    • Professional degrees require additional years of study and, often, additional training. Lawyers, medical doctors, nurses, and engineers are examples of people with professional degrees.

    • Ph. D. degrees require additional study beyond a master's degree, plus the completion of a major research project called a dissertation. College professors and research scientists usually have Ph. D. degrees.

    • Unemployment is the number of people without jobs who are actively seeking work. The unemployment rate is the number of unemployed people, expressed as a percentage of the labor force.

21. Discuss the information on Slide 2.6. **Ask:**

    A. What appears to be the relationship between educational attainment and income?

       (Higher levels of educational attainment are associated with higher levels of income.)

    B. Why might this be the case?

       (Individuals with higher levels of formal education—such as having some post-secondary education—have knowledge and skills for which employers are willing to pay more. Individuals with very low levels of formal education—such as a high school dropout—have less knowledge and fewer skills. Employers pay less to people who have a lower level of skills.)

    C. What appears to be the relationship between educational attainment and unemployment?

       (Individuals with higher levels of formal education have lower unemployment rates. Individuals with low levels of formal education have higher unemployment rates.)

    D. Why might this be the case?

       (Apparently the skills of individuals with higher levels of formal education are in greater demand by employers. Apparently the skills of individuals with lower levels of formal education are in less demand by employers.)

22. Ask the students to explore further the information provided on Slide 2.6. **Ask:** In 2010, how much more would a high school graduate expect to earn per year than an eleventh-grade dropout?

    ($31,300 – $22,200 = $9,100 more.)

23. Assuming a 40-year work life and no pay increases, how much more might a high school graduate expect to earn over a lifetime than an eleventh-grade dropout?

    ($9,100 x 40 years = $364,000 more.)

24. In 2010, how much more would a college graduate with a bachelor's degree expect to earn per year as compared to a high school graduate's annual earnings?

    ($51,900 – $31,300 = $20,600 more.)

25. Assuming a 40-year work life and no pay increases, how much more might a college graduate with a bachelor's degree expect to earn over a lifetime, as compared to a high school graduate's lifetime earnings?

    ($20,600 x 40 years = $824,000 more.)

26. **Ask:** Is education a good investment?

    (Yes. Most people with higher levels of educational attainment will earn higher incomes.)

27. Point out that there are costs associated with investment in human capital. For example, when people attend college, they must pay for tuition and fees, they must buy books, and they give up the opportunity to earn income while they are in school. (Note: Room and board costs are not included here because they are costs people pay whether they attend school or not.)

28. Explain that these costs are the opportunity cost associated with attending college. An opportunity cost is the next-best alternative a person gives up when she or he makes a choice. If people choose to attend college full-time, they give up the income that they could otherwise have earned while working. When they use money to pay for their tuition and fees and to buy books, they give up the other things they could have bought with that money (the next-best alternative use for the money).

29. **Display Slide 2.7**. Point out that there are other factors to consider when thinking about investing in your own post-secondary education. One factor is that the choice of a college major may affect the income a graduate will earn. College students who major in mathematics, chemistry, or engineering are likely to earn more income than students who major in art, history, or education. Another factor to consider is that levels of student-loan debt have been increasing. In 2011, average student-loan debt was $25,250. While taking out student loans to pay for post-secondary education often pays off, it remains wise to use debt prudently. Some students graduate with very high levels of debt—sometimes well over $100,000.

CLOSURE

30. Review the important points of the lesson by asking the following questions:

    A. What is human capital?

    (The knowledge, skills, health, and values individuals possess.)

    B. Give an example of human capital that you possess.

    (Accept a variety of answers. Some examples include the ability to read, write, compute, work in groups, play a sport, or play an instrument.)

    C. How do people invest in their human capital?

    (By going to school, finishing high school, going to college, attending training programs, practicing their skills, and living a healthy lifestyle.)

D. Why do people invest in their human capital?

(To learn new skills, to obtain a new job, to earn more income, or to improve skills and talents they already have.)

E. What is opportunity cost?

(The next-best alternative that people give up when they make a choice.)

F. What is the opportunity cost of being a full-time student after high school?

(The opportunity cost of being a full-time student is giving up the income that the individual could otherwise have earned while working. When students use money to pay for tuition and books, they give up the other things they could have bought with that money.)

G. What are the benefits associated with finishing high school and going on for additional education?

(More career options, the possibility of earning more income, and a better chance of finding a good job.)

ASSESSMENT
Multiple-Choice Questions

1. Which of the following is an example of human capital?

   a. money
   b. a factory
   c. stocks
   d. *the ability to read*

2. Each day after school, Tom practices piano for an hour. Tom could spend this hour playing video games with his friends. Playing video games with his friends is Tom's

   a. income.
   b. *opportunity cost.*
   c. favorite thing to do.
   d. investment in human capital.

3. All of the following are investments in human capital except

   a. finishing high school.
   b. attending a trade school.
   c. practicing to improve a skill.
   d. *buying a new computer.*

Constructed-Response Items

1. Your friend is a senior in high school. He has been working part-time for a local company. He enters data into the company's computer system and does other related work. He could work full-time for the company when he graduates. His starting salary would be $22,000. The idea of earning $22,000 a year is very appealing. He has also applied to a local college that offers a computer-systems degree. He would attend full-time. College is expensive; however, some financial aid is available. Based on what you've learned about investment in human capital, income, and opportunity cost, tell your friend what you think he should do, and why.

(Your friend's best choice is probably to use financial aid and go to college. The opportunity cost of this decision is the income given up over the four years and the cost of tuition, fees, and books. Over a lifetime, the additional income earned will be greater than the costs of going to college. Investment in human capital—earning a degree in computer systems—will provide skills and knowl-

edge for many different jobs, and allow for higher income in the future.)

2. The high school you attend offers students who take foreign language classes an opportunity to travel to a country in which one of the foreign languages is spoken. Students with the best ability to communicate in the second language are selected. You want to participate in the program. You studied German in middle school, but you want to make sure your written and oral communication skills in German are the very best. In terms of investment in human capital, what could you do improve your ability to write and speak in German?

(Students might suggest the following: Ask the German teacher to tutor you. Practice speaking in German with others in the class. Enroll in German class during the summer. Listen to German CDs or DVDs obtained from the library.)

Gen i Connection

The current lesson, "Invest in Yourself," connects well with Missions 2 and 3 of the Gen i Revolution game. Both game missions explore investing in human capital, careers, and opportunity cost.

In Mission 2, students take on the role of operatives advising Veronica in making a tentative career choice. Veronica is a first-year high school student who has many different interests. She is good at math and computer subjects, enjoys art and music, and loves working with people. She is starting to think about what she'd like to do to earn a living when she finishes college. The 4-1-1 tutorial shows students how to use career-choice materials and match skills with career clusters. In the conclusion, students recommend a tentative career cluster and a tentative career for Veronica, understanding that her career goals may change over time.

Mission 3 of the Gen i Revolution game involves further exploration of investment in human capital, opportunity cost, and income. In this mission students assume the role of operatives advising Matt as he decides what to do after graduating from high school. Matt has the grades to go to college, but he is tired of school work. Should he continue his formal education or go to work full-time? Students work through a 4-1-1 tutorial to calculate earnings differences across different levels of education. The mission conclusion requires students to make specific recommendations to Matt on his education after high school.

Gen i Reflection

Now that you have helped Veronica and Matt explore future careers, what are you thinking about for your own career? What can you do to better prepare yourself for a career? What sort of education after high school might be best to help you prepare for your career?

ACTIVITY 2.1-A
BUYING WITH DIMES

Directions: For each problem below, determine how many dimes you would need to buy each item. Please show your work.

1. A new DVD that sells for $17.99.

2. A top-of-the-line 52-inch TV surround-sound home-theater system that sells for $1,898.59.

3. Three candy bars that sell for $1.50.

4. Three front-row tickets to a playoff game, snacks at the game, and parking, for a total of $595.78.

5. A new pair of jeans priced at $35.99.

ACTIVITY 2.1-B
BUYING WITH DIMES

Directions: For each problem below, determine how many dimes you would need to buy each item. Use the following information:

- Write the item's price as a number without decimals. For example, $18.95 becomes 1895.

- Erase the last digit. So, 1895 becomes 189.

- Add a 1. So 189 + 1 = 190

- It would take 190 dimes to buy the item.

- There is one exception to this rule. If the number erased is 0, don't add the extra dime. For example, if the price is $18.90, simply eliminate the decimal and erase the zero. It should take 189 dimes to buy the item.

1. A new DVD that sells for $17.99.

2. A top-of-the-line 52-inch TV surround-sound home-theater system that sells for $1,898.59.

3. Three candy bars that sell for $1.50.

4. Three front-row tickets to a playoff game, snacks at the game, and parking, for a total of $595.78.

5. A new pair of jeans priced at $35.99.

SLIDE 2.1

Human Capital Production Report

Answers to the problems on Activity 2.1-A and 2.1-B

1. 180 dimes
2. 18,986 dimes
3. 15 dimes
4. 5,958 dimes
5. 360 dimes

SLIDE 2.2

Human Capital Production Report

Time	Group A		Group B	
	Number of Students	Number of Correct Answers	Number of Students	Number of Correct Answers
0 to 59 sec.				
60 to 119 sec.				
120 to 179 sec.				
180 to 239 sec.				
240 to 299 sec.				

SLIDE 2.3

LESSON 2 - INVEST IN YOURSELF

Examples of Occupations and Human Capital

Examples of Occupations

- Automotive technician/ mechanic
- Carpenter
- Family doctor
- Graphic designer
- Interpreter
- Mechanical engineer
- Retail Sales clerk

Examples of Human Capital

- Ability to use special tools or equipment
- Apprenticeship
- Communication skills
- Community college or trade school
- Four-year college degree
- Mathematics skills
- Medical school
- Special certification
- Special license

SLIDE 2.4

LESSON 2 - INVEST IN YOURSELF

Connecting Occupations and Human Capital

Examples of Occupations	Examples of Human Capital
Automotive technician/mechanic	Mathematics and communications skills plus trade school, apprenticeship, and ability to work with special tools
Carpenter	Mathematics and communications skills plus trade school, apprenticeship, and ability to work with special tools
Family doctor	Mathematics and communications skills plus medical school, internship, residency, and ability to use special tools and equipment
Graphic designer	Mathematics and communications skills plus community college or trade school and ability to work with special tools
Interpreter	Mathematics and communications skills plus college degree
Mechanical engineer	Mathematics and communications skills plus college degree and ability to work with special tools
Retail sales clerk	Mathematics and communications skills

SLIDE 2.5

Connecting Occupations and Wages

Occupations	Median Annual Wage
Automotive technician/mechanic	$ 35,110
Carpenter	$ 38,938
Family doctor	$ 153,510
Graphic designer	$ 42,400
Interpreter	$ 43,200
Mechanical engineer	$ 74,920
Retail sales clerk	$ 20,670

SLIDE 2.6

Educational Attainment: Earnings and Unemployment Rate

Educational Attainment Level	Annual Earnings	Unemployment Rate
Less than a high school diploma	$ 22, 200	14.9%
High school diploma or equivalent	$ 31,300	10.3%
Associate's degree	$ 38,350	7%
Bachelor's degree	$51,900	5.4%
Master's degree	$63,600	4.0%
Professional degree	$80,500	2.4%
Doctoral degree (Ph.D.)	$77,500	1.9%

Source: Bureau of Labor Statistics
2010 Annual averages for persons 25 and over; full-time wage and salary workers

SLIDE 2.7

LESSON 2 - INVEST IN YOURSELF

But Be Careful Out There

- The Institute for College Access & Success estimates that college gradates recently finished with an average of $25,250 in student-loan debt.

- Average student-loan debt varies by state from a high of $31,048 to a low of $20,571.

- Student-loan debt levels vary according to several factors including:

  - Differences in tuition costs and fees

  - Living expenses in the local area

  - Financial aid policies of college and universities

- While investing in human capital usually pays off, it is smart to avoid accumulating high levels of student-loan debt.

LESSON 3
WHAT IS A STOCK?

LESSON 3
WHAT IS A STOCK?

LESSON DESCRIPTION
The students work in small groups that represent households. Each household answers questions about stocks and stock markets. For each correct answer, a household earns shares of stock. At the end of the game, the groups that answered all questions correctly receive a certificate good for 150 shares of stock in The Stock Knowledge Company. They also receive dividends based on their shares. Those who answered fewer questions correctly receive fewer shares and smaller dividends. Finally, the students participate in a role playing activity to learn more about stocks.

INTRODUCTION
Stocks are sometimes called equities. *Equity* means ownership. If you own a stock, you have equity in, or own, a portion of the company that issued the stock. When a corporation decides to sell shares of its stock to the public, it hires an investment banker to sell the stock. This sale is called an initial public offering (IPO). In return for shares sold, the company receives money. After the shares are sold in the primary market, stocks are bought and sold by the public in secondary stock markets such as the New York Stock Exchange and the NASDAQ Stock Market.

CONCEPTS
Capital gain

Dividend

Income

Mutual fund

Saving

Stock

OBJECTIVES
Students will:

- Define *income, saving, stock,* and *dividend*.

- Explain why people buy stock.

- Identify advantages and disadvantages of owning stocks.

- Explain ways in which stockholders can reduce risk.

CONTENT STANDARDS
Voluntary National Content Standards in Economics, **2nd Edition**

- **Standard 2:** Effective decision making requires comparing the additional costs of alternatives with the additional benefits. Many choices involve doing a little more or a little less of something: few choices are "all or nothing" decisions.

National Standards in K-12 Personal Finance Education, **3rd Edition**

- **Saving and Investing Standard 1:** Discuss how saving contributes to financial well-being.

- **Saving and Investing Standard 3:** Evaluate investment alternatives.

- **Saving and Investing Standard 4:** Describe how to buy and sell investments.

TIME REQUIRED
45 minutes

MATERIALS
- Slides 3.1 and 3.2

- A copy of Activity 3.1 for each group

- Three copies of Activity 3.2

- A copy of Activity 3.3 for each student

- An envelope, one sheet of plain white paper, one marker, and one sheet of construction paper for each group of 3-4 students

- A roll of transparent tape for each group of 3-4 students

- A large supply of small, wrapped candies—a minimum of 30 pieces per group of 3-4 students

PROCEDURE

1. Before the class begins, write your name on the line labeled Teacher's Name on **Activity 3.1.** Make a copy of Activity 3.1 for each group of 3-4 students. Cut each copy of Activity 3.1 on the perforation lines and place the strips in an envelope. Label the envelopes Shares of Stock Group 1, Shares of Stock Group 2, Shares of Stock Group 3, and so on. There should be an envelope for each group in the classroom.

2. Introduce the lesson briefly as a lesson about stocks. Ask the students what they have heard about stocks. *(Answers will vary.)* Explain that stocks represent shares of ownership—sometimes called equity—in a corporation.

3. Tell the students that they will participate in a group activity. Each group represents a household—that is, an individual or family unit. Households earn income. Income is payments earned by households for providing resources. For example, households are in effect selling some of their time when they send an earner to work for wages or a salary. Households usually spend some of their income as consumers and save some of it. *Saving* refers to the portion of income not spent on consumption or taxes. Some households

use their savings to purchase stocks. Stocks can also be purchased on margin or with borrowed money. (Note: Purchasing stocks on margin is the subject of Lesson 8.)

4. Explain the activity to follow. Each group will have an opportunity to earn stock by correctly answering questions about stocks. Tell the students that for each correct answer, a household will receive a strip of paper worth 15 shares of stock in The Stock Knowledge Company. If the group answers all questions correctly, the strips can be taped together to create a stock certificate that represents 150 shares of The Stock Knowledge Company. Groups that answer only some of the questions correctly will own fewer shares of stock.

5. Explain that people who own shares of stock are called investors (or shareholders, or stockholders). Stockholders are partial owners of a company. The households will be partial owners of The Stock Knowledge Company.

6. Organize the class into groups of three or four students. Assign each group a number corresponding to the numbers written on the envelopes containing the strips. Distribute a piece of plain white paper and a marker to each group.

7. Tell each group to appoint a spokesperson. Tell the spokesperson to write a large "T" (using the marker) on one side of the paper and a large "F" on the other side of the paper. Explain that when a question is asked, members of the group will have a few moments to discuss the question and decide whether the answer is true or false. When told to "show the answer," the spokesperson should hold up the side of the paper displaying "T" if the group thinks the answer is true or the "F" side if the group thinks the answer is false.

8. Tell each group to appoint a stockholder. This person will hold the envelope containing the shares of stock and will take the correctly-numbered strip from the envelope when the group answers a question correctly. Each time the group answers a question correctly, it will receive a stock strip representing 15 shares of stock. These stock strips will be important when the game is over.

9. **Display Slide 3.1**, revealing only the first question. Read the question and allow the groups to decide on answers. Tell the groups to hold up their answers all together when they are told to do so. Tell the stockholders for the groups that answered the question correctly to take stock strip 1 from the envelope. Continue revealing one question at a time.

    (Answers to questions: 1. T, 2. F, 3. T, 4. F, 5. F, 6. F, 7. F, 8. T, 9. T, 10. F. Note: If a group answers question 1 incorrectly but answers question 2 correctly, the group would receive its first strip for its answer to question 2. If the group answers question 3 correctly, it would receive its second strip, and so on.)

10. When the game is over, distribute a piece of construction paper and a tape dispenser to each group. Tell the group members to tape the strips together. Point out that if they missed questions, they will not have all of the strips needed to complete the certificate.

11. Allow time for the groups to tape their strips together. **Display a slide of Activity 3.1** and explain that this is a certificate of stock ownership. If a group answered all of the questions correctly, it will have a complete certificate. **Ask**:

    A. If your group answered all of the questions correctly, how many shares of stock would the group own?

    (150)

    B. How many shares does your group own?

    (Answers will vary but could include 15, 30, 45, 60, 75, 90, 105, 120, 135, 150.)

    C. Of the 150 shares your group could have purchased, what percent does your group in fact own?

    (Answers will vary but could include: 15 shares = 10% [15/150 = 0.1; 0.1 x 100 = 10%], 30 shares = 20%, 45 shares = 30%, 60 shares = 40%, 75 shares = 50%, 90 shares = 60%, 105 shares = 70%, 120 shares = 80%, 135 shares = 90%, 150 shares = 100%.)

12. Tell the students that the groups will earn dividends based on the number of shares they own. Dividends are a part of a company's profits that may be distributed to stokeholders. For this activity, dividends will be paid in candy. Explain that the dividend paid on each share of The Stock Knowledge Company stock is one-fifth of a piece of candy. Tell each group to determine its dividends. *(15 shares = 3 pieces of candy (1/5 x 15 = 3), 30 shares = 6, 45 shares = 9, 60 shares = 12, 75 shares = 15, 90 shares = 18, 105 shares = 21, 120 shares = 24, 135 shares = 27, and 150 shares = 30.)* When the groups have calculated their dividends, distribute the candy to each group.

13. **Ask**: How do you think this game is different from occasions when dividends are distributed in real life?

    (In real life, obviously, dividends are distributed in money, not candy. More important, in real life, households don't have an opportunity to "win" stock by answering questions. Instead, they have to decide to save some of their income and use it to buy stocks. Dividends depend on the company's performance and its decisions on paying out earnings.)

14. Select three students to participate in a role playing activity about stocks. **Give each of these students a copy of Activity 3.2** and allow them a few minutes to read the play.

15. **Distribute a copy of Activity 3.3 to** each of the remaining students. Tell them that they will listen to a short play that takes place at dinnertime in the Navarro house. Tell the students to read the questions on Activity 3.3. As they watch the play, they should listen for answers to the questions.

16. Tell the three cast members to come to the front of the room and read the play. When the play is over, discuss the following:

A. What is a stock?

(Part ownership in a corporation.)

B. Why do corporations issue stock?

(To raise money to pay for equipment, buildings, and operating expenses.)

C. When the shares of stock are first issued, to whom are they sold?

(They are sold to investment banks.)

D. How does the corporation get money from the stocks?

(The investment banks pay for the stocks.)

E. Why do investment banks buy stock?

(They expect to resell the stock to the public for a higher price in the secondary market.)

F. What are stock markets?

(Places or ways in which people can buy and sell stocks.)

G. Why do people buy stocks?

(They expect to earn money.)

H. How do people earn money from stocks?

(There are two ways. They may sell the stock at a higher price than the price they paid for it, making a capital gain. They may also receive dividends.)

I. What are dividends?

(Part of the company's profits, distributed to owners.)

J. When people buy stock, is there a guarantee that they will receive dividends or that they will be able to sell the stock at a price higher than the price they paid for it?

(No.)

K. If there's no guarantee, why are people willing to buy stock?

(Because the stocks they buy might provide them with a higher return than the return they could get by putting money into other financial investments or a savings account.)

L. What determines the price of a stock?

(The value of a stock depends on whether stockholders want to keep or sell the stock and how much those who want to buy the stock are willing to pay for it.)

M. What are the main advantages of owning stock?

(Sharing in the company's profits as the company grows; having a chance to get an above-average return on a financial investment.)

N. What is the main disadvantage of owning stock?

(The chance of losing all or part of the investment.)

17. Ask the students if they know what a portfolio is and what it means to diversify. *(Answers will vary.)* Tell one student to find the meaning of *diversify* in the dictionary. Tell another student to find the meaning of *portfolio*. Have the students read the definitions. (*Diversify*: to spread out or vary investments; *portfolio*: an itemized list of investments.)

18. Explain that stockholders can reduce the chance of losing their financial investment and increase the chance of earning a solid return if they diversify their portfolios. This means they must buy various types of stock—for example, stock in an electronics company, a computer company, a company that sells prepared foods, and an entertainment company. Investors can also buy stocks of small, medium, and large firms. And stockholders can diversify by buying shares in a mutual fund. A mutual fund is a pool of money collected from different people and invested by a manager with the goal of increasing the value of each share of the fund for its investors. (Note: For additional information about mutual funds, see Lesson 6.)

CLOSURE

19. Review the lesson by asking the following questions:

A. What is income?

(Income is payments earned by households in return for providing resources, such as time worked to earn wages. More technically, income consists of all payments earned by households for selling or renting their productive resources. This would include wages for selling labor, interest for loaned money, profits for operating a family business, and rent on owned property.)

B. What is savings?

(Income not spent on consumption and taxes.)

C. What are stocks?

(Part ownership or equity in a corporation.)

D. Why do corporations issue stock?

(To raise money to pay for things needed to operate the business and earn a profit.)

E. Why do people buy stocks?

(They expect to earn a return on their investment in stocks.)

F. When stockholders sell their stock, do corporations receive the money from the sale? *(No.)* Who does? *(The stockholder.)*

G. How do stockholders earn money on their financial investment?

(By selling the stock they own at a higher price than they paid for it, and by receiving dividends.)

H. What are dividends?

(A part of a company's profits that may be distributed to shareholders.)

I. What can a corporation do with its profits besides pay dividends?

(It can put the profits back into the business.)

J. What is the main disadvantage of being a stockholder?

(The chance of losing part or all of an investment.)

K. What are the main advantages of being a stockholder?

(Sharing in the company's profits as the firm grows; having the chance to get an above-average return on a financial investment.)

L. What influences the value of a stock?

(Whether the stockholders want to keep it or sell it; how much buyers are willing to pay for it.)

M. Are stockholders guaranteed a return on their financial investment?

(No.)

N. How can stockholders reduce their chance of a loss?

(They can diversify and invest in mutual funds.)

ASSESSMENT
Multiple-Choice Questions

1. What is a stock dividend?

   a. a capital gain
   b. *part of a company's profits that is paid to owners*
   c. the price the stock is sold for
   d. the price paid when stock is sold to an investment bank

2. People buy stocks because

   a. *they expect to earn a return.*
   b. there is no chance of a loss.
   c. the government encourages them to buy stock.
   d. they are guaranteed interest payments each year.

3. One way people can earn money from stocks is by

   a. buying stock from an investment banker.
   b. selling the stock for the same price as the price they paid for the stock.
   c. selling the stock for a lower price than the price they paid for the stock.
   d. *selling the stock for a higher price than the price they paid for the stock.*

4. When people buy stock on a stock market,

   a. the corporation loses money.
   b. *the people selling the stock receive the money.*
   c. the corporation receives the money.
   d. the people buying the stock receive the money.

Constructed-Response Items

1. What can people do to reduce their chance of loss in the stock market?

   (They can diversify their portfolio—that is, they can buy many different types of stocks, or they can buy mutual funds.)

2. Explain the advantages of owning stocks.

   (Stockholders have a chance to earn money through dividends. They also may earn money by selling the stock at a higher price than they price they paid for it.)

Gen i Connection

Mission 8 of the Gen i Revolution game provides an introduction to buying and selling stocks. In this mission, students are introduced to Uncle Louie. Louie is recently retired. He is financially well off after his career in the construction industry. He wants to start investing in stocks to benefit his nephew, but he doesn't know much about buying and selling stock. In this mission's 4-1-1 tutorial, students learn about the basics of stock, why people buy stock, and what the advantages and disadvantages of owning stock are. In the mission's conclusion, students answer questions about selecting stocks for Uncle Louie.

Gen i Reflection

How would you respond if Uncle Louie asked you, "If you were in my shoes, would you be comfortable taking the risk of investing in stocks? I know my money will be safest in the bank."

ACTIVITY 3.1
THE STOCK KNOWLEDGE COMPANY

1	2	3	4	5	6	7	8	9	10

CERTIFICATE OF OWNERSHIP

THE STOCK KNOWLEDGE COMPANY

STUDENTS IN

TEACHER'S NAME:

CLASS

OWN 150 SHARES OF STOCK

IN

THE STOCK KNOWLEDGE COMPANY

15	15	15	15	15	15	15	15	15	15
Shares	Shares	Shares	Shares	Shares	Shares	Shares	Shares	Shares	Shares

ACTIVITY 3.2
STOCK TIPS FROM THE NAVARRO HOUSE

Maria, Michael, and their mom are talking about stocks and business expansion. Read their conversation as it is acted out in front of the class.

Mom: How was school today?

Maria: Okay.

Michael: Yeah, it was okay. How was work, Mom?

Mom: My corporation really needs to expand. Our new line of software is very popular and we have many orders, but we need more equipment and a larger building to keep up. We could raise some money by issuing more stock.

Michael: Mom, what is stock, and how can your company get money from stocks?

Mom: Stocks represent part ownership in a corporation. Our corporation could work with investment bankers to issue stock. We would sell that stock to the investment bank and they would give us money in return. We could use that money from the sale of the stocks to pay for equipment, buildings, and operating expenses.

Maria: Mom, why do the investment banks want stock?

Mom: The investment banks buy the stock and try to resell it at a higher price to other investors.

Michael: Some of the kids at school play a stock market game. What is a stock market, anyway?

Mom: A stock market is a way for people to buy and sell stocks. The two biggest markets are the New York Stock Exchange and the NASDAQ Stock Market. There are stock markets in other countries too. A lot of the buying and selling occurs on computer networks.

Maria: Aren't stocks just pieces of paper? Why do people want to buy stocks?

Mom: People buy stock because they expect to earn a return—that is, to make money.

Michael: How do people who buy stock make money?

Mom: They may earn money by selling the stock later for a higher price than the price they paid for it. The difference between the price paid for the stock and the higher price they receive for the stock is called a capital gain. Stockholders can also make money if the company pays dividends.

Maria: What are dividends? Sounds like something we talk about in math class.

Mom: Dividends are payments sometimes made to people who own stocks. Here is how it works. Stockholders are owners of corporations. They get to make decisions about who runs the corporation. If a company earns a profit, it may pay dividends. Dividends are a part of a company's after-tax profit that may be distributed to stockholders—the owners. Companies can also choose to put the profit back into the business.

Michael: Who decides the price for a stock? I mean, if I want to sell it at a higher price than the price I paid for it, how can I be sure the price will go up?

Mom: You can't be sure. The value of a stock depends on whether stockholders want to keep it or sell it, and on how much those who want to buy the stock are willing to pay for it. If the stock is very popular and many people want to buy it, the price would go up. Prices can go down, too. There's no guarantee.

Maria: If there's no guarantee that you can sell stock for a higher price than you paid for it, you could lose money. Wouldn't it be better to keep your money in the bank?

Mom: Well, it is always good to keep some money in the bank. It is safe there, and the bank pays interest. But people have a chance to earn an above-average return— more than they would earn in interest paid on bank deposits or through other financial investments—if they buy stocks. Usually, people who buy stock and keep it for a long period of time receive a higher return than they would with another financial investment. And there are things stockholders can do to reduce their chances of loss. They can diversify their portfolios, for example.

Michael: Mom, I have an art portfolio at school. But I don't know what any other kind of portfolio is, and I don't know what *diversify* means.

Mom: Well, I think *portfolio* and *diversify* might be a couple of good words for you to look up in the dictionary.

ACTIVITY 3.3
NOTING STOCK TIPS

Directions: Answer the questions below, using your knowledge and the content of the play, "Stock Tips from the Navarro House."

A. What is a stock?

B. Why do corporations issue stock?

C. When the shares of stock are first issued, to whom are they sold?

D. How does the corporation get money from the stocks?

E. Why do investment banks buy the stock?

F. What are stock markets?

G. Why do people buy stock?

H. How do people earn money from stocks?

I. What are dividends?

J. When people buy stock, is there a guarantee that they will receive dividends or that they will be able to sell the stock at a price higher than the price they paid for it?

K. If there is no guarantee, why are people willing to buy stock?

L. What determines the price of a stock?

M. What are the main advantages of owning stock?

N. What is the main disadvantage of owning stock?

SLIDE 3.1

Stock Questions: True or False?

1. Stocks represent ownership in a corporation.

2. People who invest in stocks cannot lose their money.

3. Mark bought 100 shares of Intel stock. Each share sold for $35.50. If no fees were involved, Mark paid $3,550 for the shares.

4. The price people pay for a stock is called a dividend.

5. The closing price for a share of Walmart stock was $37.25. This means that the price of the share was $37 and one-quarter of a dollar. One quarter of a dollar is $0.20.

6. People who own stocks are guaranteed a return on the money they have invested in stocks.

7. The only way stockholders make money is through dividend payments while they own the stock.

8. One way stockholders make money is by selling their stock for more money than they paid for it.

9. Stockholders can reduce the risk on their stock investment by diversifying their porfolios.

10. The New York Stock Exchange is the only place where people can buy and sell stocks.

SLIDE 3.2

Activity 3.1: Certificate of Ownership

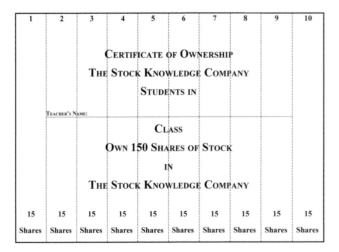

LESSON 4

FINDING FINANCIAL INFORMATION ONLINE

LESSON 4
FINDING FINANCIAL INFORMATION ONLINE

LESSON DESCRIPTION

The students learn how to read and understand information presented on financial websites. Working in pairs, they examine sample listings for stocks, mutual funds, and bonds. They participate in a scavenger hunt for financial information, using online sources. As a continuing activity, they track a stock for 10 trading days and report on news items that may have moved the stock's price during that time.

INTRODUCTION

Financial publications and websites provide extensive information about stocks, mutual funds, and bonds, including reports on stock prices, dividends, yield, and trading volume. These financial sources also carry more general articles about the world of business and finance, reporting on stock-price trends, government activities related to regulation, and the activities of companies and industries. These sources can be used to find news that affects the prices and returns of individual stocks and other financial assets.

CONCEPTS

Closing price

Dividend

Net asset value

Price/earnings ratio (P/E ratio)

Stock symbol

Trading volume

Yield

OBJECTIVES

Students will be able to:

- Read stock, mutual fund, and bond tables presented in online sources.

- Demonstrate an understanding of the data presented in the tables.

- Follow a security online.

CONTENT STANDARDS

Voluntary National Content Standards in Economics, **2nd Edition**

- **Standard 8:** Prices send signals and provide incentives to buyers and sellers. When supply or demand changes, market prices adjust, affecting incentives.

National Standards in K-12 Personal Finance Education, **3rd edition**

- **Financial Responsibility and Decision Making Standard 2:** Find and evaluate financial information from a variety of sources.

- **Financial Responsibility and Decision Making Standard 5:** Develop communication strategies for discussing financial issues.

- **Saving and Investing Standard 3:** Evaluate investment alternatives.

TIME REQUIRED

60 minutes initially; time in subsequent weeks for students to track stocks; 60 minutes at the close of the tracking period for reports.

MATERIALS

- Slides 4.1, 4.2, and 4.3

- One copy of Activities 4.1, 4.2, 4.3, 4.4, and 4.5 for each student

(Internet access required)

PROCEDURE

1. Explain that in making investment decisions, careful investors examine detailed information about stocks, mutual funds, and bonds. The most up-to-date statistical information is available online, while various websites and print publications provide broader information for context and understanding. This lesson introduces the background knowledge and skills needed for reading and understanding basic financial information.

2. **Distribute a copy of Activity 4.1** to each student. Ask the students to read the Overview of Financial Reporting. **Ask:** What sort of information is found in the financial pages?

   (The information includes changes in the financial markets and news about corporations. Online sources are especially good at instantly updating the prices of stocks, bonds, the dollar, and other currencies and commodities.)

3. Refer to the section of Activity 4.1 titled Example of Online Stock Listings. Call attention to the chosen example corporation, the Boeing Company (BA). **Display Slide 4.1**. Using the information presented in Activity 4.1, explain how to read a stock listing, column by column.

4. Organize the class into pairs. Assign the students to read the online stock listing and related explanations on Activity 4.1, and then answer the **Stock Listing Questions.** When they have finished, **display Slide 4.1** and discuss the answers:

   A. What is the 52-week high stock price for Boeing?

   ($80.65)

   B. By 10:37 a.m. on that December 19, how many shares of Boeing stock had been traded?

   (485,293)

   C. What is the 52-week low stock price for Boeing?

   ($56.01)

   D. What is the annual dividend for Boeing?

   ($1.76)

   E. What was the closing price of Boeing stock on the previous day of trading?

   ($71.01)

   F. When the website was consulted, was Boeing stock up or down for the day? How much? What percentage was that?

   (Boeing stock was up $0.29, or 0.41 percent.)

   G. What is the percentage yield for Boeing?

   (2.50 percent)

   H. What is the price/earnings ratio for Boeing?

   (14.11)

5. Ask the students to read the rest of Activity 4.1 and to answer the **Questions for Discussion** in writing. Review the answers:

   A. What is revealed about a company by the 52-week high and low?

   (These numbers show the range of the share price of the stock for the past year. The 52-week high and low numbers enable investors to see whether the stock has moved significantly in the past year, as opposed to staying in a narrow range. Some investors use this information

for hints about how well a company has been performing in the short term.)

B. Why might dividends be important to some people?

(Dividends are portions of a company's profits paid to stockholders. Some investors count on dividend payments as a source of income. Other investors see dividends as a signal of how a company's business is doing.)

C. What do investors expect to happen when the P/E ratio of a company is high for its industry?

(Investors expect the company to earn higher profits in the future.)

6. Tell the students that many investors purchase mutual funds. Explain briefly that a mutual fund is a pool of money invested by a manager on behalf of fund shareholders. The goal is to increase the value of each share of the fund for its shareholders. A mutual fund offers investors certain advantages including professional management and the reduction of risk through diversification. (Lesson 6 deals with mutual funds in more detail.)

7. Keep the students in pairs and **distribute a copy of Activity 4.2** to each student. **Display Slide 4.2.** Use the information in Activity 4.2 to explain the mutual fund listings.

8. Assign the students to read Activity 4.2 and answer the **Questions for Discussion** in writing. When they have finished, **display Slide 4.2 for the Vanguard Small-Cap Index Fund** and discuss the answers:

A. What is the Net Asset Value of the Vanguard Small-Cap Index Fund?

($32.22)

B. What is the year-to-date percentage rate of return of the Vanguard Small-Cap Index Fund?

(– 3.02 percent)

C. What is the net change in this fund's price?

(– 0.61, or negative 1.86 percent)

D. What is the current yield of this fund?

(1.07 percent, as of November 30 that year)

E. If an investor purchased 100 shares of the Vanguard Small-Cap Index Fund at the close of trading on December 18, how much would the investor pay?

(Use the Previous Close: $32.22 x 100 = $3,222)

9. **Distribute a copy of Activity 4.3** to each student. **Display Slide 4.3** and use the information in Activity 4.3 to explain the bond column headings.

10. Assign the students to read Activity 4.3 and answer the **Questions for Discussion** in writing. When they have finished, **display Slide 4.3 for the Sprint Nextel bond,** and discuss the answers:

A. What is the coupon rate of interest on the Sprint Nextel bond?

(9.250 percent)

B. What is the current price in dollars of the Sprint Nextel bond if its original price was $1,000?

($1,180 = $1,000 x 118.00 / 100)

C. What is the annual percentage return that would be received by an investor holding the Sprint Nextel bond until the maturity date?

(6.884 percent)

D. The Fitch Group rated a Raytheon 2018 bond as "A" on the same day that this Sprint Nextel listing appeared. In the opinion of the Fitch Group, which bond had a lower credit risk, Raytheon or Sprint Nextel? How can you tell?

(Raytheon had a lower credit risk with its rating of "A," compared with Sprint's "BB." In school and in the financial world, A is more desirable than B. Here the A translates to lower credit risk.)

11. For Activity 4.4, the students will track stocks online, following selected companies for 10 business days. A computer lab works best for this activity, but a small number of Internet-connected classroom computers would also work.

12. Choose a website to be used by the students for finding information about stocks. Possibilities include Yahoo! Finance (finance.yahoo.com), Google Finance (finance.google.com), and CNN Money (money.cnn.com).

13. The students will need to know the name of the company they are to follow and its stock symbol. They can find company names and symbols through online sites' lookup functions.

14. Show the students how to look up financial tables like those shown in this lesson. Yahoo! Finance, Google Finance, and CNN Money provide similar information and graphs, but there are differences in formatting and reporting.

15. **Distribute a copy of Activity 4.4** to each student. Instruct the students to enter basic information about the company they are following and to answer the questions that follow. Tell the students they will look up 10 previous days' worth of stock prices and then make daily predictions. Also tell the students that each pair of students

will be asked to present a report on the performance of the stock they followed at the end of two weeks.

16. At the end of the tracking period, ask the students to report to the class on the company they have been tracking. Allow each pair five minutes for its presentation.

*(Accept any well-documented answers. Students should describe the basics of the company [name, exchange, changes in the stock price] and comment on what trends they have been able to observe by responding to the **Questions for Discussion**.)*

CLOSURE

17. **Display Slide 4.1** and review the items reported for stocks. Ask the students to explain what they mean. Do the same with Slide 4.2 for mutual funds and with Slide 4.3 for bonds.

18. Emphasize the importance of understanding how to read the three kinds of tables introduced in this lesson. In many respects, knowing how to read the tables is demonstrating basic knowledge of the language of investment.

19. **Distribute a copy of Activity 4.5** to each student. Ask the students to answer the questions, using online financial listings. Discuss the answers.

A. Since the closing stock prices you see are from the previous trading day, the closing price you see reported today is actually from what date?

(The date is that of the previous business day. Unless you do this activity on a Monday or immediately after a holiday, the answer is "yesterday.")

B. What are the names of the two

major stock markets in the United States?

(The New York Stock Exchange [NYSE Euronext] and the NASDAQ [originally standing for National Association of Securities Dealers Automated Quotations].)

C. Complete the following table.

Company	Stock Market	Stock Symbol
Microsoft	*NASDAQ*	*MSFT*
Walmart	*NYSE*	*WMT*
eBay Inc.	*NASDAQ*	*EBAY*
Coca-Cola	*NYSE*	*KO*

D. Find the stock listing for Nike. Answer the following questions:

1. What is the stock symbol for Nike?

    (NKE)

    (Note that all the remaining answers will come from Nike's stock listing.)

2. What is the highest reported price paid for Nike during the last year?

3. What was the dividend paid by Nike during the last year?

4. How many shares of Nike stock have been traded daily, on average, over the past three months?

5. What is the current value of Nike's Price/Earnings ratio?

6. How much is Nike's market capitalization?

E. Stocks showing the highest volume of trades are referred to as "volume leaders." Look for volume leaders online and answer the following questions:

(Note that all of these answers will come from daily information on volume leaders. Internet searches of "NYSE volume leaders" and "NASDAQ volume leaders" will quickly take students to the relevant information.)

1. At the time you checked, what was the volume leader on the New York Stock Exchange? What news about that company seemed to be making the stock move?

2. At the time you checked, what was the volume leader on NASDAQ? What news about that company seemed to be making the stock move?

ASSESSMENT
Multiple-Choice Questions

1. In a stock table, "Div" stands for dividend. A dividend is

    a. a daily payment made to a stockholder.
    b. a measure of company diversification.
    c. *a share of a company's net profits paid to stockholders.*
    d. the closing stock price.

2. In a stock table, "Yield" represents

    a. the opening stock price for the trading day.
    b. *the dividend as a percentage of the price.*
    c. the percentage of stock owned by the investor.
    d. the ratio of price to earnings.

3. If you invest in a mutual fund, you become

   a.   a shareholder in the fund.
   b.   a shareholder in a stock.
   c.   a shareholder in bonds.
   d.   a shareholder of a non-stock corporation.

4. The "yield to maturity" in a bond table represents the return a bondholder would get by buying a bond at current prices and

   a.   holding it for one year.
   b.   holding it for 10 years.
   c.   holding it to collect the remaining interest but not the repayment of principal.
   d.   holding it until all interest and principal repayments had been made.

Constructed-Response Items

1. In your own words, describe what a price/earnings (P/E) ratio is.

   (The P in the ratio is for price; it refers to the price of a single share of stock. The E is for earnings per share of the stock over the last four quarters. The price divided by earnings per share yields the P/E ratio. A high P/E ratio for a given stock means investors pay a relatively high price for that stock per dollar of reported earnings. Ordinarily, investors will do this only if they expect earnings to grow.)

2. What are the differences between a stock, a mutual fund, and a bond?

   (All three are investment options. A stock represents a share of ownership in a company. A mutual fund is a pool of money used to purchase stocks, bonds, or other assets on behalf of fund shareholders. A bond is a certificate issued by a corporation or a government, promising to repay the initial amount upon maturity and also regular interest at a specified rate.)

Gen i Connection

Missions 8, 9, and 10 of the Gen i Revolution game all include sections on reading financial tables. Missions 8, 9, and 10 are sufficiently self-contained that they may be assigned before the print lessons. However, these missions may be most effective if they are assigned after their corresponding lessons for review and extension.

Here are the correspondences between the print lessons in this book and Gen i missions:

- Lesson 3 ("What Is a Stock?") is closely aligned with Gen i Mission 8, "Help Uncle Louie learn the basics about stocks."

- Lesson 5 ("What Is a Bond?) is closely aligned with Gen i Mission 9, "Teach Tyrone and Felicia how to invest in bonds."

- Lesson 6 ("What Are Mutual Funds?) is closely aligned with Gen i Mission 10, "Teach a group of students how to invest in mutual funds."

In Mission 8, the 4-1-1 tutorial presents basic information about stocks, including information about reading stock tables, as students move toward a mission conclusion. The conclusion asks students to find stocks for recently-retired Uncle Louie. In Mission 9, the 4-1-1 tutorial leads students through types of bonds, bond calculations, and bond tables to prepare for a mission conclusion. In this conclusion they will recommend bonds for Tyrone and Felicia, who are 15-year-old twins saving for college. In Mission 10, the 4-1-1 tutorial teaches mutual fund basics and reading mutual fund tables, setting up a mission conclusion on advising a student investment club.

Gen i Reflection

In this lesson and in Gen i Revolution missions, you have seen several sources of financial information. If you were asked today to find information about Ford Motor Company stock, but you could only use one source, which source would you select, and why? Which two pieces of stock information do you think would be the most important to collect?

ACTIVITY 4.1
READING A STOCK TABLE

1. Overview of Financial Reporting

A wide variety of media outlets report on the world of stocks, mutual funds, and bonds. One excellent source is *The Wall Street Journal,* in print or online at http://wsj.com (subscription required for most content). Other newspapers and their websites have up-to-date information. Broadcast and cable networks report on investments as part of their coverage. Today, however, the most current sources of information for investing are online, including Yahoo! Finance, Google Finance, and CNN Money. Like the other outlets, these sites carry articles on changes in the financial markets and news about corporations. But the online sources are especially good at instantly updating the prices of stocks, bonds, the dollar, and other currencies and commodities. With free interactive tools, you can look for financial assets meeting particular criteria or customize graphs to help you understand price movements.

2. Examples of Online Stock Listings

The table below shows a typical online finance site entry for the aerospace company Boeing, followed by descriptions of the reported data.

Boeing Company (The) Common Sto (BA) – NYSE

71.30 ↑ 0.29(0.41%) 10:37 AM EST - Real Time Price

Prev Close:	71.01	Day's Range:	71.03-71.62
Open:	71.20	52wk Range:	56.01-80.65
Bid:	71.28 x 400	Volume:	485,293
Ask:	71.31 x 900	Avg Vol (3m):	6,012,830
1y Target Est:	81.92	Market Cap:	52.99B
Beta:	1.35	P/E (ttm):	14.11
Next Earnings Date:	N/A	EPS (ttm):	5.06
		Div & Yield:	1.76 (2.50%)

Key to Stock Tables

At the top of the chart we find the stock's name and symbol along with the exchange where it is listed. The Boeing Company has the symbol BA and is traded on the New York Stock Exchange (NYSE). By typing in "BA" at websites and search engines, you can quickly get news and quotes about Boeing. "BA" uniquely identifies the stock.

Last Trade Price: This is the first and largest number you see: the price, in dollars and cents, at which the stock most recently was bought and sold. (You can refresh your browser during trading hours and see how the price changes as trades continue.)

Change: The change, positive or negative, between the most recent trade and the previous day's closing price. Positive changes are green with an up arrow. Negative changes are red with a down arrow. Changes will typically be listed as dollars and cents, and also as percentages (in parentheses).

Trade Time: The time of the reported trade. Sometimes results are almost instantaneous and are reported as "Real Time." Free services may also report trades with a 15- or 20-minute delay.

Prev Close: The price of the last trade from the previous trading session, Monday through Friday.

Open: The price of the first trade of the day.

Bid: Currently, the best price a buyer is willing to pay for a stock, followed by the multiplication symbol (x) and the number of shares that buyer would like to purchase at the bid price.

Ask: Currently, the best price at which a seller will offer a stock, followed by the multiplication symbol (x) and the number of shares that seller would like to sell.

1y Target Est: This is an estimate of the stock's "target price," the price at which the stock will be selling a year from now. The estimate comes from analysts who follow the stock. Their opinions are collected by a financial service and provided free by most financial websites. (For more detailed or personalized information, you would have to pay.)

Beta: An estimate of the stock's variability in following the overall market. For example, a stock with a beta of 1.00 has about the same variability as the overall market. A stock with a beta of 1.20 is about 20 percent more variable than the market. Traders aiming for short-term gain may seek out high-beta stocks. High-beta stocks gain more in good times (and lose more in bad times) than do low-beta stocks.

Next Earnings Date: The next date on which the company is to release earnings information.

Day's Range: The highest and lowest prices at which a stock has traded during the current session. This will be reported as "N/A" (not applicable) before the market opens.

52wk Range: The highest and lowest prices at which a stock has traded during the current 52-week period. If these numbers are very close together, it indicates a stock that has not moved very much. This may be an important and stable stock for some investors to hold. However, for players in stock market competitions and active short-term investors, a stock that moves around more may be a better choice. For those stocks that move around a lot, there will typically be reasons for the movement in the news coverage on the company.

Volume: The number of shares that have been traded during the current session.

Avg Vol (3m): The number of shares traded daily, on average. (The formula is somewhat complicated and goes back three months.) This can help you evaluate whether a given day's volume is unusually high—if it is, find out why.

Market Cap: This is the "market capitalization," or total value of the company as determined in the stock market. It equals the number of shares of stock outstanding times the current price. Diversifying a stock portfolio includes getting small-cap, mid-cap and large-cap stocks. Those seeking price movement for stock market competitions may find good bets in small-cap stocks, which are not as well known as large-cap stocks such as Apple and Coca-Cola.

P/E (ttm): This is the Price-Earnings ratio, or P/E ratio. It is calculated by dividing the stock's most recent price by its annual earnings per share. The higher the P/E ratio, the more profit growth shareholders expect from the company. A low P/E ratio means the stock's price is expected to more closely reflect the current earnings of the stock. When a company has losses for the last year, no P/E ratio will be reported. P/E ratios are useful in comparing companies in the same industry but can vary widely across industries. The "ttm" in the abbreviation stands for "trailing twelve months," meaning that earnings are calculated for the most recent 12 months.

EPS (ttm): This figure is "earnings per share," one measure of the profit attributable to each share of stock. It comes from dividing reported earnings by the number of shares of stock outstanding. Like the P/E ratio, it is commonly calculated on a "trailing twelve months" basis.

Div & Yield: These numbers show the dividend per share paid out over the last 12 months in dollars and cents, followed by the yield (that same dividend as a percentage of the most recent price per share). Dividends vary across industries, with some companies paying large dividends and others paying no dividends at all. To compare dividends across industries, use the yield figure since it is already in percentage terms. Some investors use dividends as a regular source of income and so they are interested in the dividend and yield figures. Other investors are more interested in the growth of the share price and are less concerned with dividends.

Stock Listing Questions

Directions: Use information from the online stock listings to write answers to the following questions.

A. What is the 52-week high stock price for Boeing?

B. By 10:37 a.m. on that December 19, how many shares of Boeing stock had been traded?

C. What is the 52-week low stock price for Boeing?

D. What is the annual dividend for Boeing?

E. What was the closing price of Boeing stock on the previous day of trading?

F. When the website was consulted, was Boeing stock up or down for the day? How much? What percentage was that?

G. What is the percentage yield for Boeing?

H. What is the price/earnings ratio for Boeing?

Questions for Discussion

A. What is revealed about a company by the 52-week high and low?

B. Why might dividends be important to some people?

C. What do investors expect to happen when the P/E ratio of a company is high for its industry?

Activity 4.2
Reading a Mutual Fund Table

1. What Is a Mutual Fund?

A mutual fund is a pool of money used by a company to purchase stocks, bonds, or money market assets on behalf of fund investors. Mutual funds allow the investor to diversify—to invest in many different companies and industries. Investing in a mutual fund makes you a shareholder in the fund. Each fund has a manager, whose duty is to make sound decisions on behalf of shareholders.

2. Online Mutual Fund Listings

Here is one day's listing from the Vanguard Small Cap Index Fund :

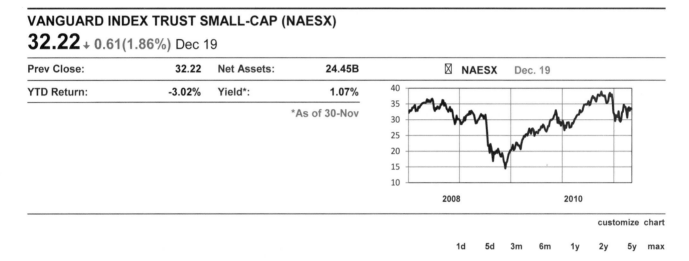

VANGUARD INDEX TRUST SMALL-CAP (NAESX)
32.22 ↓ 0.61(1.86%) Dec 19

Prev Close:	32.22	Net Assets:	24.45B
YTD Return:	-3.02%	Yield*:	1.07%
			*As of 30-Nov

⊠ NAESX   Dec. 19

customize chart

1d   5d   3m   6m   1y   2y   5y   max

Here's what the notations on the listing mean:

Net Asset Value (NAV): This is the first and largest number you see, calculated by adding up the value of the stocks, bonds, or other assets of the fund, subtracting the fund's liabilities and dividing the result by the number of fund shares available. Net Asset Value represents the value of a share of the fund. It is the price you would pay to buy a share of the fund and the price you would receive for selling a share of the fund, not counting costs of the transaction such as any fees or commissions.

Change: ↓ 0.61 shows how much the Net Asset Value changed from the previous trading day. The change is given both in dollars and cents (0.61), and in percentage form (1.86%).

Trade Time: Dec 19 is the day used to calculate Net Asset Value. Mutual funds are revalued once a day using closing prices, rather than being continuously revalued during the trading day like stocks.

Prev Close: This figure is the closing Net Asset Value from the previous day's trading.

YTD Return: This figure is the year-to-date percentage change in the fund value, including reinvestment of fund proceeds, less annual expenses paid by investors. It is recalculated monthly, so any changes since the end of last month will not be reflected in this figure.

Net Assets: This number equals the mutual fund's total assets minus total liabilities. This is the best measure of a fund's overall size. Overall size can measure popularity of a fund, but it does not reliably predict the performance of a fund.

Yield: This number represents the total dividends and interest earned by the fund's assets, net of the fund's expenses. It is stated as an annual percentage figure and, like net assets and year to date return, is calculated monthly.

Directions: Use information from the online listing examples to answer the following questions.

A. What is the Net Asset Value of the Vanguard Small-Cap Index Fund?

B. What is the year-to-date percentage rate of return of the Vanguard Small-Cap Index Fund?

C. What is the net change in this fund's price?

D. What is the current yield of this fund?

E. If an investor purchased 100 shares of the Vanguard Small-Cap Index Fund on December 18, how much would the investor pay?

ACTIVITY 4.3
READING A BOND TABLE

1. What Is a Bond?

Bonds are issued when governments or companies want to borrow large amounts of money. The buyer of a bond lends money to the bond issuers. The bond itself is simply a certificate that legally establishes the borrowing transaction and specifies what will be repaid—typically, a specified amount of interest each year up to the maturity date of the bond, at which time the original sum is also due. For example, suppose you buy a $1,000 bond in Xerox Corporation with a 10-year maturity date at 6 percent interest. This means that the corporation guarantees to pay you $60 in interest per year for 10 years. (Usually, each year's interest is divided into two payments six months apart.) Finally, when the bond matures Xerox Corporation repays you the $1,000.

Unlike stocks, corporate bonds do not represent shares of ownership in a company. Like stocks, bonds are traded in financial markets. As trading goes on, the agreed-to interest paid on a bond stays the same. But the price of a bond may change and that will change the effective interest rate earned by someone who buys the bond. Consider that $1,000 Xerox bond with a stated 6 percent interest rate. The $60 annual payment is fixed. If the price of the bond goes up to $1,200, the bondholder still receives the agreed-to $60—but that is only 5 percent of $1,200 ($60 divided by $1,200). If the price of the bond falls from $1,000 to $800, the annual interest rate increases to 7.5 percent ($60 divided by $800).

You can see that the effective interest rates received by investors change when bond prices change. When bond prices are pushed higher, interest rates fall. When bond prices fall, interest rates rise. This is referred to as the *inverse relationship between bond prices and interest rates*.

2. Online Bond Listings

Here is a sample listing for a corporate bond issued by the communications company Sprint Nextel. (Bond information is not as widespread as stock information online, nor are listings standardized. However, useful information is available through the Bond Screener tool at http://finance.yahoo.com/bonds and at http://www.morningstar.com/topics/bonds.htm.)

SPRINT NEXTEL CORP   As of 22-Dec

OVERVIEW	
Price:	118.00
Coupon (%):	9.250
Maturity Date:	15-Apr-2022
Yield to Maturity (%):	6.884
Current Yield (%):	7.839
Rating from Rating Service:	BB
Coupon Payment Frequency:	Semi-Annual
First Coupon Date:	15-Oct-1992
Type:	Corporate
Callable:	No

Price: This is the price of the bond, quoted as a percentage of the original $1,000 price. To get the current price of this bond in dollars, take the quoted price, divide by 100 and multiply by $1,000. Or, to simplify, take the quoted price, stick a dollar sign in front of it, and add a zero on the end. A bond quoted at 115, for example, is selling for ($)1,150.

Coupon (%): This is the stated interest rate when the bond was issued. The Sprint Nextel bond's coupon rate of 9.250 percent means that the bondholder gets $92.50 annually from holding the bond. (The term dates back to a time when bond investors actually clipped paper coupons to turn in to receive their interest payments.)

Maturity Date: This is the date on which the last interest payment and the return of the bondholder's original investment will take place.

Yield to Maturity (%): This number represents the annual percentage return that would be received by an investor holding the bond until the maturity date, at which time the original principal is returned and the last interest payment is made. The actual return will be different if the bondholder sells before maturity—possibly higher and possibly lower.

Current Yield (%): This is the yearly interest on a bond divided by its current selling price. It shows the return a bondholder would get by buying today and holding the bond a year, if the bond's price remains steady. The actual yield a bondholder gets will typically be higher or lower because of changes in the bond's price.

Rating from Rating Service: Here the table reports a letter rating that can be as high as AAA or as low as D, assigned to reflect the riskiness of holding the bond. Ratings come from agencies such as the Fitch Group and Standard & Poor's. Different services use the same letter grades but capitalize them differently. For example, Aaa at Moody's Investor Service is the same rating as AAA at Standard & Poor's.

Coupon Payment Frequency: This reports how frequently interest payments are made on the bond. Most bonds pay every six months (semi-annually).

First Coupon Date: This is the date when the first regular interest payment was made on the bond.

Type: This entry classifies the bond as corporate, municipal or treasury.

Callable: This entry indicates whether the borrower can redeem or "call" the bond before maturity, as specified in the bond agreement. If interest rates fall, issuers may call bonds in order to borrow at the new and lower rate. Bond investors must remember that a bond with an attractive interest rate may not actually pay that high interest if it is callable.

Questions for Discussion

Directions: Use information from the online bond listing for Sprint Nextel to answer the following questions.

A. What is the coupon rate of interest on the Sprint Nextel bond?

B. What is the current price in dollars of the Sprint Nextel bond (originally sold for $1,000)?

C. What is the annual percentage return that would be received by an investor holding the Sprint Nextel bond until the maturity date?

D. The Fitch Group rated a Raytheon 2018 bond as "A" on the same day that this Sprint Nextel listing appeared. In the opinion of the Fitch Group, which bond had a lower credit risk, the Raytheon bond or the Sprint Nextel bond? How can you tell?

ACTIVITY 4.4
TRACKING AND GRAPHING A STOCK

The Internet provides a wealth of information on financial assets, along with free interactive tools for analysis. In this activity, you will track and graph a stock, making predictions about where the price of the stock will go on the next trading day.

With a partner, select a stock you want to track. Look up the stock on a financial website (such as Yahoo! Finance, Google Finance, or CNN Money) and find out the ten most recent days' closing prices and volume. Fill in the first ten lines of the table with the information you find. Then make a prediction about whether the stock will go up or down the next day. Each day, fill in one more line of the table below and make a new prediction. After you have tracked the stock for ten days, answer the questions that follow the table.

Name of Company _____ Symbol _____ Exchange _____

	Date	Today's Close	Net Change	Volume	Prediction for Tomorrow (up or down)
1					
2					
3					
4					
5					
6					
7					
8					
9					
10					
11					
12					
13					
14					
15					
16					
17					
18					
19					
20					

1. Find the company's stock price graph on a financial website. Explore how to change the time covered by the graph and view the one-year and three-month graphs; then answer: Does the company's stock price graph show a definite upward or downward trend across the time that you tracked its stock? Explain what you see on the graph.

Answer the following questions by doing online research:

2. Where is the company located?

3. What does the company produce?

4. Who are its customers?

5. What are its plans for the future?

6. What have recent news stories reported about the company?

7. Do you think there will be a growth in demand for this company's products? Why or why not?

8. If you were interested in investing in a growth-oriented company over the long term, would you want to own this company? Why or why not?

ACTIVITY 4.5
SCAVENGER HUNT

Directions: Use online financial resources to answer each of the questions below.

A. Since the closing stock prices you see are from the previous trading day, the closing price you see reported today is actually from what date?

B. What are the names of the two major stock markets in the United States?

C. Complete the following table.

Company	Stock Market	Stock Symbol
Microsoft		
Walmart		
eBay Inc.		
Coca-Cola		

D. Find the stock listing for Nike. Answer the following questions:

1. What is the stock symbol for Nike?

2. What is the highest price paid for Nike during the last year?

3. What was the dividend paid by Nike during the last year?

4. How many shares of Nike stock have been traded daily, on average, over the past three months?

5. What is the current value of Nike's Price/Earnings ratio?

6. How much is Nike's market capitalization?

E. Stocks showing the highest volume of trades are referred to as "volume leaders." Look for volume leaders online and answer the following questions:

  1. At the time you checked, what was the volume leader on the New York Stock Exchange? What news about that company seemed to be making the stock move?

  2. At the time you checked, what was the volume leader on NASDAQ? What news about that company seemed to be making the stock move?

SLIDE 4.1

Stock listing: Boeing

Boeing Company (The) Common Sto (BA) – NYSE

71.30 ↑ 0.29(0.41%) 10:37 AM EST - Real Time Price

Prev Close:	71.01	Day's Range:	71.03-71.62	
Open:	71.20	52wk Range:	56.01-80.65	
Bid:	71.28 x 400	Volume:	485,293	
Ask:	71.31 x 900	Avg Vol (3m):	6,012,830	
1y Target Est:	81.92	Market Cap:	52.99B	
Beta:	1.35	P/E (ttm):	14.11	
Next Earnings Date:	N/A	EPS (ttm):	5.06	
		Div & Yield:	1.76 (2.50%)	

Boeing Company (The) Common Sto   Dec. 19 10:37 am EST

71.6
71.4
71.2
71

10 am   12pm   2pm   4pm

customize chart

1d   5d   3m   6m   1y   2y   5y   max

SLIDE 4.2

Mutual fund listing: Small-cap

VANGUARD INDEX TRUST SMALL-CAP (NAESX)

32.22 ↓ 0.61(1.86%) Dec 19

Prev Close:	32.22	Net Assets:	24.45B	
YTD Return:	-3.02%	Yield*:	1.07%	
			*As of 30-Nov	

☒ NAESX   Dec. 19

40
35
30
25
20
15
10

2008   2010

customize chart

1d   5d   3m   6m   1y   2y   5y   max

SLIDE 4.3

LESSON 4 - FINDING FINANCIAL INFORMATION ONLINE

Bond listing: Sprint Nextel

SPRINT NEXTEL CORP   **As of 22-Dec**

OVERVIEW	
Price:	118.00
Coupon (%):	9.250
Maturity Date:	15-Apr-2022
Yield to Maturity (%):	6.884
Current Yield (%):	7.839
Rating from Rating Service:	BB
Coupon Payment Frequency:	Semi-Annual
First Coupon Date:	15-Oct-1992
Type:	Corporate
Callable:	No

LEARNING, EARNING, AND INVESTING FOR A NEW GENERATION © COUNCIL FOR ECONOMIC EDUCATION, NEW YORK, NY

LESSON 5

WHAT IS A BOND?

LESSON 5
WHAT IS A BOND?

LESSON DESCRIPTION

In this lesson the students learn what bonds are and how bonds work. They learn basic terminology related to bonds. They participate in a simulation activity aimed at showing that bonds are certificates of indebtedness, similar to an IOU note. Finally, they explore credit ratings in order to determine the relationship between ratings and bond coupons.

INTRODUCTION

Corporations and local, state, and federal governments often want to raise money in order buy new equipment, pay off debts, or finance general operations. They sometimes borrow this money from the public by selling bonds. A bond is an "I owe you" certificate given to a lender (the holder of the bond) by a borrower (the bond seller). The bond states the terms of this special kind of loan: that the borrower will pay back the entire amount borrowed (called the principal) and will pay the lender something additional (an interest payment) for the use of his or her money. The borrower promises to pay back the loan on a particular day (the bond's maturity date), at a predetermined rate of interest (the bond's coupon rate).

Buying a bond is like buying stock, since each such purchase is an investment. But stocks differ from bonds in an important way: stocks make no promises about paying the stockholder dividends or returns. For example, Company X may generate enough profit to permit a dividend for all stockholders in the company, but Company X is under no obligation to pay out such a dividend. It may decline to do so. Also, it is possible that the price of Company X stock might fall over time. If Company X issues a bond, however, the company promises to pay back the principal (the face value of the bond) plus interest. If you purchase a bond from Company X and hold it to maturity, you can calculate how much you're supposed to be paid back by the company. Government-issued bonds (particularly those issued by the U.S. government) carry very little risk; bonds issued by corporations carry more risk. Part of this risk is measured by the credit rating of the bond's issuer. Such ratings are indicators of the ability of a corporation or a government to repay its debts. In general, bond-rating agencies rate bonds on a scale from Aaa (highest quality) to C (no interest paid, bankruptcy filed, or in default). These ratings help investors make decisions about which bonds to buy.

CONCEPTS

Bond

Bond rating

Coupon

Coupon bond

Coupon rate

Face value

Maturity date

Par value

Risk

Zero-coupon bond

OBJECTIVES

Students will:

- Explain what a bond is and how bonds are used by governments and corporations.

- Define *face value, coupon,* and *maturity date.*

- Distinguish between coupon bonds and zero-coupon bonds.

- Identify the relationship between a bond's rating, risk, and rate of return.

CONTENT STANDARDS

Voluntary National Content Standards in Economics, **2nd Edition**

- **Standard 2:** Effective decision making requires comparing the additional costs of alternatives with the additional benefits. Many choices involve doing a little more or a little less of something: few choices are "all or nothing" decisions.

- **Standard 12:** Interest rates, adjusted for inflation, rise and fall to balance the amount saved with the amount borrowed, which affects the allocation of scarce resources between present and future uses.

National Standards in K-12 Personal Finance Education, **3rd Edition**

- **Financial Responsibility and Decision Making Standard 4:** Make financial decisions by systematically considering alternatives and consequences.

- **Saving and Investing Standard 3:** Evaluate investment alternatives.

- **Saving and Investing Standard 4:** Describe how to buy and sell investments.

- **Saving and Investing Standard 6:** Investigate how agencies that regulate financial markets protect investors.

TIME REQUIRED

90 minutes

MATERIALS

- Slides 5.1, 5.2, 5.3, and 5.4

- Activity 5.1: Investor Dollars. Photocopy and cut out enough $100 slips so that, on average, each lender (one-half of the students) has $200. That is, if

there are 13 lenders, cut out no more than 26 $100 slips.

- Activity 5.2: Role Cards and IOU slips. Photocopy and cut out enough role cards and IOU slips for one-half of the students.

- One copy of Activity 5.3, 5.4, and 5.5 for each student

PROCEDURE

1. Briefly introduce the topic of borrowing. Mention that some people disapprove of borrowing. Ask the students to describe situations in which they have borrowed something—some money, perhaps, or a bicycle or an article of clothing. Discuss these instances briefly. Raise a question, "If borrowing is a bad thing, as some people say, why do people borrow so often?" Ask the students to list several reasons why people might choose to borrow.

   (To buy a car, buy a house, pay for college, and so on.)

2. Continue the discussion by asking the students if they have ever lent something to someone. If they have, what did they lend and why did they lend it? Guide the discussion to another question: "Would you be more likely to lend to people who promised to pay you back with more than you lent them?" Discuss responses briefly. Explain that, to follow up on these discussions, the students will play a game that involves the concepts of lending and borrowing.

3. Organize the class in two groups of equal size. Assign one group (half of the students) to be lenders. **Distribute $100 slips (from Activity 5.1)** to the lenders so that, on average, each lender has $200. Do not give all the lenders $200; give some lenders $100 and some $300. Tell the lenders that they will do some lending and that their goal

in making loans is to get the greatest return they can on their money. They should seek out the borrowers who offer the best terms.

4. Assign the other half of the class to be borrowers. **Distribute one role card and three IOU slips (from Activity 5.2)** to each borrower. Tell the borrowers that their goal is to sell all their IOU slips to the lenders.

5. Tell the students that they will have five to ten minutes to move about the classroom to sell and buy IOU slips.

6. When time has elapsed, have the students return to their seats. Ask the following questions:

   A. How many lenders lent all their money?

   (All should have.)

   B. How many borrowers sold all their IOU slips?

   (There should be several students who were not able to sell all, or any, of their slips.)

   C. Why were the lenders willing to buy some IOUs and not others?

   (Answers will vary. Some lenders are likely to state that some borrowers probably would be unable to pay back their loans—for example, the borrower who wanted to open the ice cream stand at the skating rink.)

7. Tell the lenders to assume that a year has passed; now it is time to collect on their IOUs. **Display Slides 5.1 and 5.2.** Ask the lenders to write down the payments they received from their borrowers. Ask for a show of hands of lenders who received at least the amount they lent; and from those who received a payment in excess of the amount they lent; and from those who received

a payment less than the amount they lent. Ask why some lenders made a return while others did not. Discuss the responses.

8. Tell the students that, like individuals, governments and corporations often need to raise money for equipment, expansion, or operations. For these purposes, governments and corporations often borrow money, using something called a *bond*. Explain that a bond is a certificate of indebtedness—that is, an IOU certificate given to a lender (the purchaser of the bond) by a borrower (the corporation or government issuing the bond).

9. **Distribute a copy of Activity 5.3** to each student. Tell the students to read the first three sections of this activity. **Ask:** What are the main differences between government bonds and corporate bonds?

   (U.S. government bonds are backed by the U.S. government and thus are less risky than corporate bonds.)

10. Have the students read the section of Activity 5.3 titled How Bonds Work. At the same time, **display Slides 5.3 and 5.4.** Point out the difference between a coupon and a zero-coupon bond. Explain that a coupon bond pays out interest at set intervals, with a final payment that includes the original principal (or par value) at the maturity date. A zero-coupon bond, on the other hand, pays all the interest and the principal of the bond at the maturity date. **Ask:** Why would a person purchase a coupon bond rather than a zero-coupon bond?

    (Someone who wants a steady income stream, such as a retiree, might prefer a coupon bond.)

11. Have the students complete their reading of Activity 5.3. Ask them to list

several reasons why investors would buy bonds, particularly in light of the fact that, over time, stocks have outperformed bonds.

(Less risk and the certainty of fixed income over time may make bonds attractive to retired people and others who want the income that bonds generate; also, some bonds generate lower tax liability than stocks.)

12. Ask the students to quickly review the terms at the end of Activity 5.3. **Distribute a copy of Activity 5.4** to each student and have the students complete the Bond Quiz. Discuss their answers: *Answers: 1. c, 2. a, 3. c, 4. b, 5. b.*

13. Ask the students to recall the IOU activity. How many lenders received less than their promised payment? Would they have made different decisions if they had known more in advance about the borrowers? *(Probably so.)* Explain that, for the same reason, people who buy bonds also would like to know about bond issuers. That is why bonds are often rated; the ratings are intended to provide information to investors about the level of risk associated with particular bonds. Make the point that these ratings, provided by bond-rating services, are only estimates. Estimates are sometimes incorrect, particularly during a financial crisis. (Note: If time permits, discussion could touch on the role of the rating agencies in the financial crisis of 2007-2008. See Lawrence J. White, "Markets: The Credit Rating Agencies," *Journal of Economic Perspectives* 24 (2), Spring 2010, pp. 211-226.)

14. **Distribute a copy of Activity 5.5** to each student. Have the students read the introduction and examine the Moody's Investor Service bond-rating categories. Explain that Moody's, as

well as two other rating agencies (Fitch and Standard and Poors), provide valuable information about the likelihood that governments and corporations will be able to pay off their bond obligations. The lower the rating, the more likely a firm or government will default on the bonds and not be able to pay the interest and principal back to investors.

15. Ask the students to examine the table with selected coupon rates across various Moody's ratings. Explain that these are real data drawn from actual bonds that had a one-year maturity date. Ask them to complete the table by calculating the average coupon rates for the selected Moody's ratings categories.

(Average coupons: Aaa: 4.50, Aa: 6.60, Baa: 8.42, Caa: 9.79, C: 12.08.)

16. Once the students have calculated these rates, have them plot the average coupon rate for each rating on the figure titled Average Coupon Rates for Sample Bonds by Selected Moody's Ratings. Upon completion, have the students answer the **Questions for Discussion.**

(A. An inverse relationship: as bond ratings fall, coupon rates rise; B. Corporations with poor ratings must offer higher rates in order to overcome investor concern about the risk of default; C. Investors who buy C-rated bonds do so because, for these investors, the hope of high returns outweighs the potential risks involved.)

CLOSURE

17. Review the main points of the lesson, using these questions:

A. What is a bond?

(A bond is a certificate acknowledging a loan from the lender to a government or corporation.)

B. Why would someone buy a bond?

(To earn income. The bond's issuer promises to pay a specified rate of interest during the life of the bond and to repay the original loan. There is also the possibility of reselling the bond for a capital gain rather than holding it to maturity.)

C. Which type of bond is the least risky for investors? Why?

(U.S. government bonds are the least risky because they are backed by the U.S. government.)

D. What is a U.S. savings bond?

(U.S. savings bonds are issued by the U.S. government and are available in smaller denominations than other U.S. bonds. They are issued at half the face value and mature at face value at a date in the future.)

E. What is a municipal bond?

(A bond issued by a state or local government.)

F. What is a major tax benefit of holding municipal bonds?

(The bondholder does not have to pay federal tax on the interest.)

G. If corporate bonds are riskier than U.S. government bonds, why do people buy corporate bonds?

(Corporate bonds generally pay a higher interest rate.)

H. What is the difference between a coupon bond and a zero-coupon bond?

(A coupon bond pays interest at fixed intervals; a zero-coupon bond pays all of its interest and principal at the bond's maturity date.)

ASSESSMENT
Multiple-Choice Questions

1. What is a bond?

   a. a certificate of ownership in a corporation, with the right to a share of the earnings
   b. *a certificate representing a loan from an investor to a corporation or government entity*
   c. a payment from an investor to a corporation for the rights to future profits
   d. a group of stocks sold together for a set price

2. A bond that pays all of its interest and principal at the bond's maturity date is called a

   a. *zero-coupon bond.*
   b. bond fund.
   c. coupon bond.
   d. par-value bond.

3. Generally speaking, which of the following best describes the relationship between a bond's coupon rate and its credit rating?

   a. The relationship cannot be determined.
   b. As the bond's rating improves, the coupon rate increases.
   c. As the bond's rating declines, the coupon rate decreases.
   d. *As the bond's rating improves, the coupon rate decreases.*

4. All of the following are reasons to buy bonds except

    a. bonds may outperform the stock market during certain periods of time.
    b. *bonds generally have outperformed the stock market over the last 100 years.*
    c. bonds pay out interest at set intervals, allowing people to live off the income.
    d. investing in bonds may generate less tax liability than investing in stocks.

Constructed-Response Items

1. Explain why bond ratings, such as those provided by Moody's Investors Service, are important for investors.

    (Bond ratings address the risk of default and the relationship between credit rating and the coupon rate. These services save investors time and resources that they might otherwise have to spend researching bonds on their own.)

2. Describe the difference between a coupon bond and a zero-coupon bond.

    (Coupon bond: coupon [interest] payments set at fixed intervals; final payment at maturity includes the principal plus the final coupon value. Zero-coupon bond: purchased at a price below the par [face] value, no interest payments made until maturity when the principal and accumulated interest are paid.)

Gen i Connection

Mission 9 of the Gen i Revolution game introduces students to Tyrone and Felicia, 15-year-old twins. They plan to go to college, but they will need to help their parents pay for the tuition. They plan to save money from their summer jobs. A family friend suggests that they should invest their money in bonds rather than putting the money into a savings account. The students teach Tyrone and Felicia how to invest in bonds. In the mission's 4-1-1, students complete exercises that help them understand what bonds are, how they are used by companies and governments, and what the advantages and disadvantages of owning bonds are. For the mission conclusion, students solve bond problems and make recommendations to Tyrone and Felicia about appropriate bonds.

Gen i Reflection

Now that you have helped Tyrone and Felicia learn about bonds, think about your own personal attitude toward risk and return. Would you rather own an Aaa-rated bond that paid 4 percent interest or a Baa-rated bond that paid 8 percent interest? Explain your choice.

ACTIVITY 5.1
INVESTOR DOLLARS

$100	$100	$100
$100	$100	$100
$100	$100	$100
$100	$100	$100
$100	$100	$100
$100	$100	$100
$100	$100	$100

ACTIVITY 5.2
ROLE CARDS AND IOUS

You are trying to raise $300 to buy a new bike in order to expand your already successful paper route. **Role Card 1**	**IOU:** For lending me **$100**, I agree to pay you **$110** at the end of the year. Signed, *Paper route mogul*
IOU: For lending me **$100**, I agree to pay you **$110** at the end of the year. Signed, *Paper route mogul*	**IOU:** For lending me **$100**, I agree to pay you **$110** at the end of the year. Signed, *Paper route mogul*
You are trying to raise $300 to buy a new bicycle in order to hang out with your friends in a bike club. **Role Card 2**	**IOU:** For lending me **$100**, I agree to pay you **$120** at the end of the year. Signed, *Future bike club member*
IOU: For lending me **$100**, I agree to pay you **$120** at the end of the year. Signed, *Future bike club member*	**IOU:** For lending me **$100**, I agree to pay you **$120** at the end of the year. Signed, *Future bike club member*

You are trying to raise $300 for tuition payments to the local art school. Once you finish school, you plan to put your talents to work for Disney Studios as an animator.

Role Card 3

IOU:

For lending me **$100**, I agree to pay you **$110** at the end of the year.

Signed,
Future Disney animator

IOU:

For lending me **$100**, I agree to pay you **$110** at the end of the year.

Signed,
Future Disney animator

IOU:

For lending me **$100**, I agree to pay you **$110** at the end of the year.

Signed,
Future Disney animator

You are trying to raise $300 for tuition payments to the local art school. Once you finish school, you plan to put your talents to work as a graffiti artist, "tagging" buildings at night.

Role Card 4

IOU:

For lending me **$100**, I agree to pay you **$120** at the end of the year.

Signed,
Future graffiti vandal

IOU:

For lending me **$100**, I agree to pay you **$120** at the end of the year.

Signed,
Future graffiti vandal

IOU:

For lending me **$100**, I agree to pay you **$120** at the end of the year.

Signed,
Future graffiti vandal

You are trying to raise $300 to buy a new lawn mower for your landscaping business. Business has been so good that you need another mower to meet the demand.

Role Card 5

IOU:

For lending me **$100**, I agree to pay you **$110** at the end of the year.

Signed,
Lawn maintenance mogul

IOU:

For lending me **$100**, I agree to pay you **$110** at the end of the year.

Signed,
Lawn maintenance mogul

IOU:

For lending me **$100**, I agree to pay you **$110** at the end of the year.

Signed,
Lawn maintenance mogul

You are trying to raise $300 to start a hot chocolate stand you want to open this summer in front of the local pool. You are convinced that, even in the heat of summer, people want the "heartwarming feeling that a good cup of hot cocoa brings."

Role Card 6

IOU:

For lending me **$100**, I agree to pay you **$110** at the end of the year.

Signed,
Hot cocoa entrepreneur

IOU:

For lending me **$100**, I agree to pay you **$110** at the end of the year.

Signed,
Hot cocoa entrepreneur

IOU:

For lending me **$100**, I agree to pay you **$110** at the end of the year.

Signed,
Hot cocoa entrepreneur

You are trying to raise $300 to start an ice cream stand this winter in front of the local outdoor ice skating rink. You are convinced that, even in the cold of winter, people want the "feeling of summer that an ice cream cone covered with sprinkles brings."

Role Card 7

IOU:

For lending me **$100**, I agree to pay you **$120** at the end of the year.

Signed,
Ice cream entrepreneur

IOU:

For lending me **$100**, I agree to pay you **$120** at the end of the year.

Signed,
Ice cream entrepreneur

IOU:

For lending me **$100**, I agree to pay you **$120** at the end of the year.

Signed,
Ice cream entrepreneur

You are trying to raise $300 to start a t-shirt printing business at your school. You have conducted a survey of your classmates and are convinced that students will eagerly buy your custom designed t-shirts.

Role Card 8

IOU:

For lending me **$100**, I agree to pay you **$110** at the end of the year.

Signed,
Future t-shirt mogul

IOU:

For lending me **$100**, I agree to pay you **$110** at the end of the year.

Signed,
Future t-shirt mogul

IOU:

For lending me **$100**, I agree to pay you **$110** at the end of the year.

Signed,
Future t-shirt mogul

ACTIVITY 5.3
THE ABCS OF BONDS

What Are Bonds?

Imagine that you are in the ice cream store with a friend on a Thursday evening and want to get a hot fudge sundae, but you realize you don't have any cash. You know you'll be getting your paycheck the next day, so you ask your friend to lend you a few dollars so you can have the sundae now. In return for the loan, you agree to pay your friend back tomorrow and buy lunch on Saturday as well. You may even write out the amount owed on a slip of paper, an "I.O.U." Your friend, finding these terms to his liking, lends you the money, and you enjoy a delicious sundae.

Governments and corporations often find themselves short of cash, just as you were on Thursday. One way to generate these needed resources is to issue *bonds*. A bond is similar to an I.O.U. When you purchase a bond, you are lending money to a government, a corporation, or some other entity, known as the bond *issuer*. In exchange for this loan, the issuer promises to pay you a specified rate of interest during the life of the bond and to repay the original loan (referred to as the *face value* or *par value* of the bond) when it comes due at its *maturity date*.

U.S. Government Bonds

When the U.S. government spends more than it collects in taxes, it borrows money by issuing bonds to cover the difference. The bonds issued by the U.S. government are called Treasury bonds. A special type of Treasury bond is a U.S. savings bond. U.S. savings bonds are issued in smaller amounts than other Treasury bonds. They are issued at half the face value and mature at face value at a date determined by the interest rate. For example, a $1,000 face value U.S. savings bond might sell for $500 today and, at the date of maturity, be redeemable for $1,000 (the face value). Treasury bonds and U.S. savings bonds are widely regarded as the safest bond investments, even in times of financial crisis. U.S. bonds are considered safest because they are backed by "the full faith and credit" of the U.S. government; an investor is therefore nearly certain to get paid back. In addition, the interest paid on U.S. government bonds cannot be taxed by state or local governments.

Municipal bonds are issued by states, counties, cities, towns, villages, and other units of local government. These bonds are considered fairly safe, but they are riskier than U.S. government bonds. The risk level for a municipal bond depends on the financial condition of the state or local government that issued it. The interest paid on most municipal bonds is not taxed by the federal government.

Corporate Bonds

As corporations grow, they often don't generate enough money to pay for the supplies necessary to keep growing. Many corporations issue bonds to pay for new capital equipment or to cover operating expenses. When a company issues bonds, it borrows money from investors in exchange for agreeing to pay them interest on their money at a set date in the future. Corporate bonds are generally riskier than government bonds because even large, stable companies are much more likely to go out of business than the U.S. government. Corporate bonds can also be the most lucrative bonds to invest in, as the investor is generally rewarded for the extra risk undertaken.

How Bonds Work

The most basic bond is called a *coupon bond*. Coupon bonds pay out an interest payment (called the *coupon*) to the investor every six months. The *principal* (also called the *face value* or *par value* of the bond) is paid to the investor at a specified *maturity date*, which can range from a few months to 30 years. These bonds are said to be *fixed-income* securities because the amount the investor receives is set, or fixed, by the coupon rate. Figure 1 presents a timetable showing how coupon payments work.

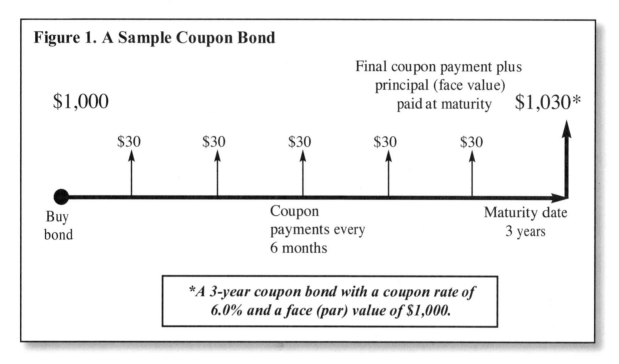

Figure 1. A Sample Coupon Bond

Final coupon payment plus
principal (face value)
paid at maturity

$1,000

$1,030*

$30 $30 $30 $30 $30

Buy
bond

Coupon
payments every
6 months

Maturity date
3 years

**A 3-year coupon bond with a coupon rate of
6.0% and a face (par) value of $1,000.*

The other common bond is called a *zero-coupon bond*. Unlike coupon bonds, zero-coupon bonds do not make periodic interest payments to the investor. Rather, investors buy the bond at a reduced face value; then, at the maturity date, investors receive one payment. The payment is equal to the principal of the bond plus the interest that has accumulated during the time the bond has been held by the investor. Someone saving for a small child's future college expenses might use zero coupon bonds, set to pay off at the beginning of the college years. A U.S. savings bond is an example of a zero-coupon bond. Figure 2 presents a time-table graph showing how zero-coupon bonds work.

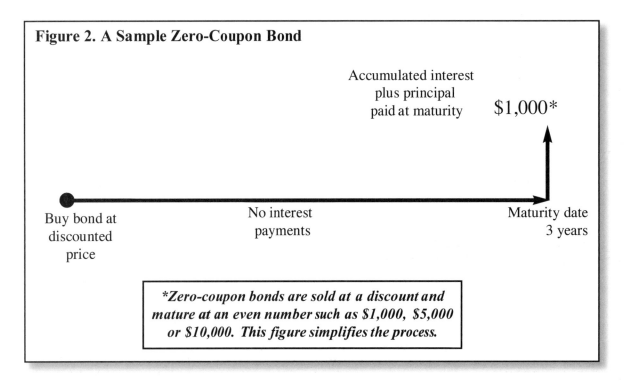

Figure 2. A Sample Zero-Coupon Bond

Accumulated interest plus principal paid at maturity

$1,000*

Buy bond at discounted price

No interest payments

Maturity date 3 years

*Zero-coupon bonds are sold at a discount and mature at an even number such as $1,000, $5,000 or $10,000. This figure simplifies the process.

Why Buy a Bond?

Over the last 100 years, the stock market has provided, on average, higher returns than other forms of investment. So why not just invest in stocks? Although bonds do not provide the same rate of return as stocks in the long run, they have several characteristics that investors value.

First, safety. Many bonds provide investors with relatively safe investments. Treasury bondholders can be almost certain that they will receive the amount they originally invested, plus interest, and corporate bondholders can have nearly the same certainty. By contrast, investors can lose their entire investment in individual stocks; in fact, that outcome occurs frequently—as it did, for some investors, in the recession of 2007-2009.

Second, regular income. Coupon bonds pay interest to investors at set intervals, and this arrangement can provide valuable income for those who need a regular cash flow—retirees, for example. If someone owned $100,000 worth of coupon bonds that paid 8 per cent interest annually (that would be $8,000 per year), one-half of that interest would be sent to the bondholder every six months, providing income to invest elsewhere.

Third, capital gains. Some people buy bonds to earn capital gains. Bond prices tend to change with interest rates. When interest rates fall, bond prices rise. When interest rates rise, existing bond prices fall. Some people buy bonds to make capital gains when interest rates fall. To do this, you must sell a bond at a new, higher price before the maturity date.

Fourth, taxes. Bonds can also provide a tax advantage. When a government issues bonds to raise money to build bridges or roads, the interest investors earn can be tax-exempt. Earnings on U.S. Treasury bonds are exempt from state and local taxes. Earnings on municipal bonds are exempt from federal taxes. Tax exemption can be an important factor for those who are eager to reduce the amount they pay in taxes.

A Review of Bond Terminology

Bond	Bonds are similar to an I.O.U. When you buy a bond, you make a loan to a government or a corporation in return for promised repayment at a specified rate of interest.
Coupon bond	A bond that pays out interest at fixed intervals (usually every six months) over the time the bond is held by the investor.
Coupon	The interest payment on a coupon bond.
Face value	The price an investor pays for a bond (also called par value or principal).
Fixed-income security	An investment in which the amount of income an investor receives is set, or fixed, by the issuer.
Issuer	The entity (government or corporation) that writes the bond purchased by investors.
Maturity date	The date at which the bond matures and the final payment is made to the investor.
Municipal bond	A bond issued by state or local governments.
Par value	The price an investor pays for a bond (also called face value or principal).
Principal	The initial cost of the bond (also known as the par value or face value of the bond).
Zero-coupon bond	A bond whose purchase price is below face value. One payment is made at maturity that includes the principal plus accumulated interest.

ACTIVITY 5.4
A BOND QUIZ

1. What is a bond's coupon rate?

    a. the value of a bond at its issue date
    b. the value of a bond at its maturity date
    c. the percentage interest to be paid by the bond issuer
    d. the purchase price of a bond

2. A bond's face value may also be called the

    a. par value.
    b. coupon.
    c. maturity.
    d. final payment.

3. Which of the following is the least risky investment?

    a. corporate bonds
    b. stocks
    c. U.S. Treasury bonds
    d. mutual funds

4. A bond's interest rate is called its

    a. par value.
    b. coupon rate.
    c. face value.
    d. principal.

5. A zero-coupon bond pays interest

    a. periodically.
    b. at the maturity date.
    c. at the time of purchase.
    d. never.

ACTIVITY 5.5
BOND RATINGS

Bonds are generally less risky than stocks. U.S. Treasury bonds carry very little risk for the investor because the U.S. government is unlikely to go bankrupt and default on its bonds. Defaulting means the issuer is unable to make further interest and principal payments to the bond holder. Because corporations can and sometimes do go into bankruptcy, the default risk for corporate bonds is higher than the risk for government bonds.

In order to help individual investors make better decisions about their investments, many corporate bonds are rated by a third-party source such as Moody's Investor Service. These ratings describe the creditworthiness of the issuer. The higher the rating, the less likely the corporation will go into default. Moody's ratings for bonds are as follows:

Moody's Investor Service Bond-Rating Codes

Aaa	Highest quality
Aa	High quality
A	Upper-medium quality
Baa	Medium grade
Ba	Somewhat speculative
B	Low grade, speculative
Caa	Low grade, default possible
Ca	Low grade, partial recovery possible
C	Default, recovery unlikely

These ratings are quite sensitive to perceived risk. Even a small change in perceived risk can make the bond rating change. U.S. Treasury bonds were rated Aaa by all of the major rating services until 2011, when one service downgraded them to Aa. Budget difficulties in Washington had slightly increased the still-tiny probability of a default on Treasury bonds.

Using Bond Ratings: An Exercise

A strong relationship exists between the credit rating of a bond and its coupon rate. This relationship can be determined by examining a few sample cases. The following table reports the coupon rate for three corporate bonds in several of Moody's rating codes. Each of these bonds has a one-year maturity date.

Directions: In the bond rating table that follows, calculate the average coupon rate for each Moody's category. Then enter the average in the third column ("Average").

Moody's Bond Credit Ratings	Coupon Rate		Average	
Category 1: Aaa	Bond 1:	4.125		
Aaa	Bond 2:	5.125		Average coupon for **Aaa** rated bonds
Aaa	Bond 3:	4.250		
Category 2: Aa	Bond 1:	6.625		
Aa	Bond 2:	6.250		Average coupon for **Aa** rated bonds
Aa	Bond 3:	6.923		
Category 3: Baa	Bond 1:	8.250		
Baa	Bond 2:	8.875		Average coupon for **Baa** rated bonds
Baa	Bond 3:	8.125		
Category 4: Caa	Bond 1:	10.125		
Caa	Bond 2:	9.750		Average coupon for **Caa** rated bonds
Caa	Bond 3:	9.500		
Category 5: C	Bond 1:	11.500		
C	Bond 2:	12.875		Average coupon for **C** rated bonds
C	Bond 3:	11.875		

Source: Bond coupon rates for coupon bonds with one-year maturity dates issued by corporations; obtained using a search at http://www.bondpage.com/.

Now plot these results on the diagram below.

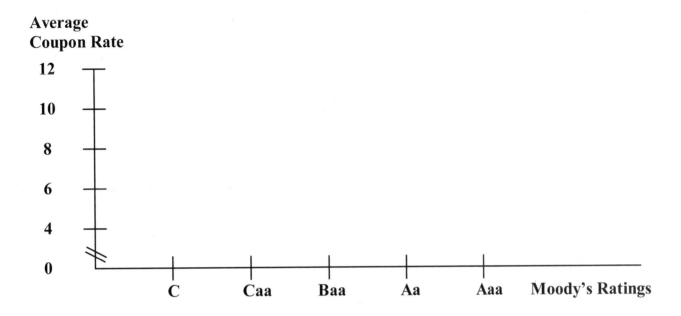

Then answer the following questions.

Questions for Discussion

A.   What is the relationship between bond rating and coupon rate?

B.   Why do corporations with lower credit ratings offer higher coupons or interest rates on their bonds?

C.   Why would investors buy a bond rated Caa or C?

SLIDE 5.1

ONE YEAR LATER

BORROWER	AFTER ONE YEAR...
You are trying to raise $300 to buy a new bike in order to expand your already successful paper route.	The bike helped double the size of the paper route. Pay each bearer of this bond $110.
You are trying to raise $300 to buy a new bicycle in order to hang out with your friends in a bike club.	The bike club detracted from your school-work, forcing you to quit your after-school job. Pay each bearer of this bond $100.
You are trying to raise $300 for tuition payments to the local art school. Once you finish school, you plan to put your talents to work for Disney Studios as an animator.	You finished art school and took a job at MGM Studios. Pay each bearer of this bond $110.
You are trying to raise $300 for tuition payments to the local art school. Once you finish school, you plan to put your talents to works as a graffiti artist, "tagging" buildings at night.	You are arrested and spend six months in juvenile hall. Pay each bearer of this bond $0.00.
You are trying to raise $300 to buy a new lawnmower for your landscaping business. Business has been so good that you need another mower to meet the demand.	Business improves after the addition of the new mower. Pay each bearer of this bond $110.

SLIDE 5.2

ONE YEAR LATER

BORROWER	AFTER ONE YEAR...
You are trying to raise $300 to start a hot chocolate stand you want to open this summer in front of the local pool. You are convinced that, even in the heat of summer, people want the "heart-warming feeling that a good cup of hot cocoa brings."	Bad idea! No one wants hot cocoa in 100° heat! Pay each bearer of this bond $50.
You are trying to raise $300 to start an ice cream stand this winter in front of the local outdoor ice skating rink. You are convince that, even in the cold of winter, people want the "feeling of summer that an ice cream cone covered with sprinkles brings."	Bad idea! No one wants ice cream in the middle of winter! Pay each bearer of this bond $50.
You are trying to raise $300 to start a t-shirt printing business at your school. You have conducted a survey of your classmates and are convinced that students will eagerly buy your custom designed t-shirts.	Great idea! The t-shirt business is a hit with your classmates! Pay each bearer of this bond $100.

SLIDE 5.3

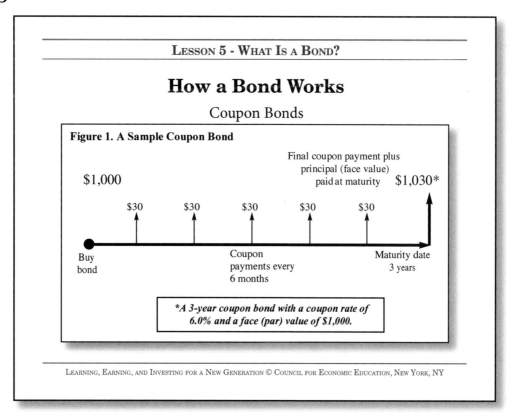

SLIDE 5.4

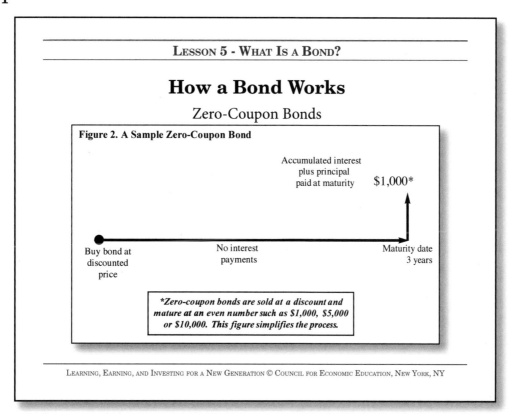

LESSON 6

WHAT ARE MUTUAL FUNDS?

LESSON 6
WHAT ARE MUTUAL FUNDS?

LESSON DESCRIPTION

The students form class investment clubs that work much in the way mutual funds do. They invest $3,000 (300 shares at $10 a share) in up to six stocks. One year later they revalue their shares and determine whether shares in their class investment clubs have increased or decreased in value. Finally, they read about mutual funds and learn that the concept behind mutual funds is similar to the concept behind their class investment clubs.

INTRODUCTION

A mutual fund is a pool of money invested by a manager with the goal of increasing the value of each share of the fund for its investors. A mutual fund provides diversification, spreads risk, and provides the convenience of buying and selling shares in the fund on any business day. These are the reasons why more Americans invest through mutual funds than directly in the stock, bond, or money markets.

CONCEPTS

Diversification

Liquidity

Load

Mutual fund

Net asset value

Risk and reward

OBJECTIVES

Students will be able to:

- Explain how mutual funds work.

- Identify the advantages and disadvantages of investing in mutual funds.

- Use the terminology of mutual funds.

- Calculate the value of an investment on a per-share basis.

CONTENT STANDARDS
Voluntary National Content Standards in Economics, 2nd Edition

- **Standard 2:** Effective decision making requires comparing the additional costs of alternatives with the additional benefits. Many choices involve doing a little more or a little less of something: few choices are "all-or-nothing" decisions.

- **Standard 10:** Institutions evolve and are created to help individuals and groups accomplish their goals. Banks, labor unions, markets, corporations, legal systems, and not-for-profit organizations are examples of important institutions. A different kind of institution, clearly defined and enforced property rights, is essential to a market economy.

National Standards in K-12 Personal Finance Education, 3rd edition

- **Financial Responsibility and Decision Making Standard 4:** Make financial decisions by systematically considering alternatives and consequences.

- **Saving and Investing Standard 1:** Discuss how saving contributes to financial well-being.

- **Saving and Investing Standard 2:** Explain how investing builds wealth and helps meet financial goals.

- **Saving and Investing Standard 3:** Evaluate investment alternatives.

- **Saving and Investing Standard 4:** Describe how to buy and sell investments.

TIME REQUIRED
60 minutes

MATERIALS
- Slides 6.1, 6.2, and 6.3
- One copy of Activity 6.1, 6.2, 6.3, and 6.4 for each student.

PROCEDURE
1. Explain to the students that they are going to learn about mutual funds. More Americans invest in stocks and bonds through mutual funds than in any other way.

2. Tell the students that a mutual fund is like an investment club with thousands of members. An investment club is any group of people who pool their money, invest, and share the profits or losses. The class is now going to form investment clubs with just a few members.

3. Organize the class into groups of no more than five members each. Tell the students that each group is an investment club. Investment club members will have to make some decisions about where to invest their money.

4. **Distribute a copy of Activity 6.1** to each student. Discuss Activity 6.1 and make sure the students understand these major points:

   - Each club has $3,000 to invest.

   - The club sold 300 shares at $10 each to members to raise the money that they will invest.

   - They may buy any of six stocks. They must buy at least three stocks, but they may divide their money among all six stocks if they wish to do so.

   - They must invest the entire $3,000.

   - They must fill out the chart at the

end of Activity 6.1. The investment value must be $3,000 (total of the last column). The price per share will be $10 ($3,000 / 300).

5. Give the groups about 15 minutes to make their investment decisions and complete the charts. Be sure to check their math because the rest of the activity will not work unless their math is correct.

6. **Distribute a copy of Activity 6.2** to each student. Explain that it is now one year later. The value of the shares of stock they could have bought has changed. Column 2 of Activity 6.2 shows the new per-share price of the stocks. How well did their selected stocks perform?

7. **Display Slide 6.1** as an example of how the chart should be completed. Make sure the students understand that this is an example; their charts will differ depending on which stocks they purchased and how many shares they purchased.

8. Ask the groups to complete their charts and check the math. The amount invested will still be $3,000, and the number of shares of stock owned will be the same as in Activity 6.1. The price of the stocks and the investment value of the fund will have changed.

9. Ask the following questions about what happened to the clubs' investments:

   A. Did the price per share of the investment club increase or decrease?

   (Answers will vary.)

   B. What determined whether the price per share of the investment club increased or decreased?

   (The investment value one year later, which is determined by the price of the stocks purchased.)

C. If you had a real investment club and bought stocks, what would increase the value of the investments one year later?

(Choosing stocks that increase in price or pay high dividends.)

D. Assume that more students want to join your investment club and purchase shares. What price would you charge them? Why?

(The price per share one year later or the price per share on the day they want to buy shares. At that price, they buy shares equal to what the shares are worth on that day.)

10. **Display Slide 6.2**. Explain that mutual funds work like the students' investment clubs, but with more investors. Stress the key features of mutual funds including price per share, role of the fund manager, and fees.

11. **Distribute a copy of Activity 6.3** to each student. The students should read it and answer the questions at the end.

12. **Display Slide 6.3.** Make the point that mutual funds are not all the same. They have different investment objectives. Some mutual funds concentrate on reducing risk and have relatively low returns. Some offer greater potential rewards along with greater risk.

13. Discuss the answers to the **Questions for Discussion** at the end of Activity 6.3:

A. What is a mutual fund?

(A pool of money used by an investment company to buy a variety of stocks and bonds.)

B. A friend tells you, "All mutual funds are the same." How do you reply to your friend?

(Your friend is wrong. Mutual funds have different investment objectives and buy different stocks and bonds.

Different funds have different managers and different styles.)

C. What is an advantage of buying a load fund? What is a disadvantage?

(Advantage: A salesperson or investment advisor provides help in choosing a fund. Disadvantage: A load fund costs more because the investor must pay a sales commission.)

D. What is an advantage of buying a no-load fund? What is a disadvantage?

(Advantage: There is no sales commission, and therefore the cost is less. Disadvantage: The investor must select the fund without advice from a fund representative. The investor must do his or her own research.)

E. What should you consider when deciding which mutual fund to buy?

(Performance, cost, convenience, and your tolerance for risk. Have the students elaborate on these considerations.)

F. More Americans own mutual funds than individual stocks and bonds. Why do you think this is so?

(Mutual funds provide diversification, professional management, and ease of buying and selling. It is safer to have money invested in 200 stocks or bonds than in only a few; mutual fund investors spread the risk.)

G. If your class participates in a stock market simulation that allows you to buy mutual funds, what type of fund should you buy? Why?

(Because stock market simulations are for a short time period, you

would probably buy a high-risk, high-reward fund. You might win big or lose big, but if instead you buy safer funds, you have little chance of winning a short-term game.)

H. What are the advantages and disadvantages of buying index mutual funds rather than actively managed funds?

(Index funds provide more diversification and lower management fees. Index funds are designed to provide returns similar to returns from an unmanaged market index. Actively managed funds can provide higher returns, although studies show most actively managed funds have under-performed index funds.)

I. If you want to buy a mutual fund so that you will have money to buy a house 10 years from now, what type of fund should you buy? Why?

(You would buy a fund that you think would increase the most in value over the 10 years; you would look for funds with consistently good long-term records.)

CLOSURE

14. Tell the students that every mutual fund must provide potential investors with a prospectus. Tell them that they will now apply their knowledge by reading some statements from a prospectus.

15. **Distribute a copy of Activity 6.4** to each student. Have the students read the activity and answer the questions.

16. Discuss the answers:

A. You worry a lot about the stock market and you want to limit the risk of losing your money. Would you buy this fund?

(No. It is an aggressive growth fund specializing in small companies.)

B. Does this fund charge a sales commission?

(No.)

C. Is it good or bad for investors that this fund charges no 12b-1 fees?

(It is good for investors. Some funds charge up to an additional 1 percent, which is used to advertise the fund.)

D. How much does this fund charge in fees?

(.91 percent)

E. In your opinion, how does the fund's past performance look?

(It did well last year, losing less money than most indexes, which are averages of groups of stocks or funds. During the 10-year period, it beat all averages. A fund should compare its performance not only to the general market but to indexes that track stocks it buys and other similar stocks. The Russell 2000 is a small-company index, and the Lipper index is for funds specializing in small stocks.)

F. Does this mean the fund will perform well in the future?

(Not necessarily. Past performance does not guarantee future performance. Nevertheless, the fund's track record is good. A prospective investor should check to see if the fund's investment manager has changed.)

ASSESSMENT
Multiple-Choice Questions

1. A mutual fund without a sales charge is called

   a. a load fund.
   b. *a no-load fund.*
   c. a 12b-1 fund.
   d. an aggressive growth fund.

2. Which of the following statements about mutual funds is true?

   a. All mutual funds are the same.
   b. *Mutual funds allow investors to spread risk among several stocks and bonds.*
   c. Load funds do not charge a sales commission but invest in lower-quality stocks.
   d. Many mutual funds do not charge management fees.

3. A 12b-1 fee is a

   a. sales commission.
   b. management fee.
   c. *fee to pay for fund advertising.*
   d. fee to pay the fund's brokerage commissions.

4. In a mutual fund, the price per share that investors pay is called the

   a. *net asset value.*
   b. management fee.
   c. load.
   d. 12b-1 charge.

Constructed-Response Items

1. Which factors should an investor consider before purchasing a mutual fund?

   (Students should discuss performance, cost, goals, and convenience.)

2. Your grandparents gave you $1,000 to help pay for your college education. You will graduate from high school in four years. What type of mutual fund should you buy?

(Although answers will vary, students should evaluate risk and reward. Since four years is a short time in which to invest the $1,000, students might argue that lower-risk mutual funds such as bond funds or income funds might be appropriate, but much will depend on each student's tolerance for risk and other circumstances.)

Gen i Connection

Mission 10 of the Gen i Revolution game is all about mutual funds—what they are, as well as the advantages and disadvantages of investing in them. In this mission, students take on the role of operatives advising a student investment club on how to invest in mutual funds. Along the way, students learn that a mutual fund is a pool of money invested by a manager. They learn how to read a mutual fund table. Importantly, they recognize that mutual funds provide diversification. The 4-1-1 tutorial session is similar to Activity 6.1. The print version allows students to choose the amounts of shares they buy. In the 4-1-1, the shares are already chosen, but it has the advantage of being more interactive. For the mission conclusion, students solve mutual fund questions and make recommendations about appropriate mutual funds to the investment club.

Gen i Reflection

Gen i Revolution Mission 10 introduces the idea of a student investment club. Some college and university business programs offer this sort of investment experience to their students. If your school began offering such a club, would you want to join it? Discuss the factors that would influence your decision.

ACTIVITY 6.1
CLASS INVESTMENT CLUBS

The members of your class have decided to form investment clubs. Class members may buy as many shares in a club as they like, for $10 per share. Each club sold 300 shares and collected $3,000. Now it's time to invest the money.

Your club held its first meeting and decided to invest in stocks. The club members proposed different stocks to buy. Here is a rundown on the stocks proposed.

1. American Cellular, $5 per share

This is a new cellular company that features high-tech services such as advanced video. So far, the company has not made a profit, but it expects to do very well soon.

2. Big Box Stores, $20 per share

Big Box Stores is one of the leading discount retailers in the country. Same-store sales have increased steadily in each of the last five years.

3. Biotech Industries, $10 per share

Biotech Industries is a pharmaceutical company that specializes in developing cutting-edge drugs. It has some profitable products, but so far its profits are small.

4. General Grocery, $20 per share

This is a leading grocery store chain. Sales are generally steady and do not change much with the economy's ups and downs. However, some experts predict that the growing trend toward eating out in restaurants will hurt future sales.

5. Giant Auto, $10 per share

Giant Auto is one of the three leading automobile manufacturers in the world. The company's profits depend on economic conditions. Profits are high in times of strong economic growth and poor in bad times or recessions.

6. Gold Mining Group, $5 per share

GMG is a gold-mining company. The price of gold often rises in bad times or recessions and falls in good times.

Your club decided to invest all 300 shares or $3,000 in at least three of these companies. Decide how to invest the money, and record your investments in Table 1.

Table 1: Making Investment Choices

Company	Price per Share	No. of Shares Owned	Amount Invested
American Cellular			
Big Box Stores			
Biotech Industries			
General Grocery			
Giant Auto			
Gold Mining Group			
Total Investment Value (add last column)			

Number of shares <u>300</u>   *Price per share <u>$10</u>

The price per share is the amount invested divided by the number of shares.

ACTIVITY 6.2
A CLASS INVESTMENT CLUB ONE YEAR LATER

One year later, the prices of your investments have changed. The price per share of each investment is listed in Table 1 below.

Complete the chart to determine how well your investment club did. The value of your investment depends on the companies in which you invested.

Table 1: One Year Later

Company	Price per Share	No. of Shares Owned	Amount Invested	Investment Value 1 Year Later
American Cellular	$8			
Big Box Stores	$23			
Biotech Industries	$8			
General Grocery	$22			
Giant Auto	$11			
Gold Mining Group	$4			
Total Investment Value (add last column)				

Number of shares <u>300</u>   *Price per share ____

The price per share is the total investment value (one year later) divided by the number of shares.

ACTIVITY 6.3
MUTUAL FUND FACTS

A mutual fund is a pool of money similar to the money collected by a class investment club. A fund manager decides how to invest the money, with the goal of increasing the value of each share of the fund for the investors. That will happen only if the value of the investments chosen by the fund manager increases.

Investors may buy shares of open-end mutual funds each business day for the net asset value (NAV, in the fund listing), the investment value of each share. The net asset value is calculated each day by dividing the total value of the investments by the number of shares. This is how you calculated the value of the shares of your investment club. You may also sell your shares in an open-end mutual fund on any business day and receive the NAV.

More Americans invest through mutual funds than by any other investment method. There are thousands of mutual funds. There are stock mutual funds, bond mutual funds, stock and bond mutual funds, and money-market funds. There are mutual funds that specialize in almost any type of stock or bond. Some mutual funds, called index funds, buy the stocks that allow investors' returns to match a particular index—for example, the Standard & Poors Index of 500 large stocks. Index funds can provide more diversification than actively managed funds. In addition, the management fee of an index fund (discussed later) should be lower because the fund manager does not have to research which stocks to buy and sell. For this reason, many experts advise buying a fund that tracks a broad market index if only one fund is bought.

Some mutual funds buy high-risk investments and some buy low-risk investments. How can you choose the right mutual fund? Here are some factors to consider.

1. **Performance.** Buy mutual funds that you believe will perform well. Performance is the most important factor to consider. However, your consideration of performance must be tempered by how much risk you are willing to take. A mutual fund prospectus lists the stocks or bonds a fund owns and provides information on the fund's performance. But past performance does not guarantee that the fund will do as well in the future. The fund manager is a key to a fund's performance. It is a good thing if the fund manager has had favorable results and has worked for the fund for a significant period of time.

2. **Cost.** A mutual fund company makes money by charging investors various fees. These fees are a cost to investors. The lower the costs, the better it is for investors—as long as performance is strong. Here are some typical costs of mutual funds:

    - Some funds charge a *load*. A load is a sales commission. It is usually a percentage of the price, and it can be as high as 8 percent. A front-end load is paid when you buy shares, and a back-end load is paid when you sell shares. A no-load fund does not charge a sales commission. If you need help in choosing a fund, you might consider paying an investment advisor a load or commission for advice. If you do not need help, choose a no-load fund.

    - All funds charge a *management fee* and have *expenses*. The lower the management fee and the expenses, the better it is for investors.

- Some mutual funds charge a *12b-1 fee*. This fee, which can be as high as 1 percent of the fund's value, is used by the company to advertise the fund to the public. Unless the fund has great performance, it is better to avoid funds with 12b-1 fees.

3. **Convenience.** A fund that provides good service is very helpful to investors. Are the statements easy to read? Are the fund's service representatives knowledgeable and helpful? Is it easy to make additional investments in the fund? Can you buy small amounts of the fund? Can you exchange shares in the fund for shares in another of the company's funds? Some fund families have dozens of different funds for different investment objectives.

Advantages of Investing in Mutual Funds

Why buy a mutual fund? After all, you can buy stocks and bonds directly. Many investors find that buying mutual funds provides several advantages over buying individual stocks and bonds. These advantages can make the extra costs worthwhile.

1. **Professional management.** When you buy a mutual fund, a professional money manager chooses your stocks. The performance of your investment club depended on which stocks you bought. A professional manager might be able to make these choices better than you can. If you don't think this is true, you can buy an index fund. An index fund follows a stock average, attempting to match the performance of the average. For example, a Standard & Poors 500 Index fund can simply buy all 500 stocks that are in the index, in that way seeking to match the index's performance. The investor gets average performance. Over the years, a majority of actively managed funds have failed to beat average performance.

2. **Diversification.** *Diversification* means you spend your money on several stocks and bonds rather than just a few. If one or two stocks or bonds in your mutual fund decrease sharply in value, your loss will be less than if you own only a few stocks or bonds. If a class investment club bought only one stock, it could have a greater loss or greater gain than if the club bought several stocks. Your risk is greater the fewer stocks you buy. A mutual fund may own 500 or more different stocks.

3. **Liquidity.** *Liquidity* refers to the ease with which an asset may be exchanged for cash. A home is usually a valuable asset, but it is not a highly liquid asset because it cannot be exchanged for cash until the owner succeeds in selling it, which may take some time and effort. A mutual fund, by contrast, is a highly liquid asset. If you own shares in a mutual fund, you can sell your shares at the net asset value (NAV) on any business day. Of course, you may need to sell the fund for less per share than what you paid for it, and lose money.

4. **Investment objective.** There is a mutual fund for almost any objective or goal. When you determine your goals and the risks you are willing to take, you can probably find a mutual fund that matches them.

Questions for Discussion

A. What is a mutual fund?

B. A friend tells you, "All mutual funds are the same." How do you reply to your friend?

C. What is an advantage of buying a load fund? What is a disadvantage?

D. What is an advantage of buying a no-load fund? What is a disadvantage?

E. What should you consider when deciding which mutual fund to buy?

F. More Americans own mutual funds than individual stocks and bonds. Why do you think this is so?

G. If your class participates in a stock market simulation that allows you to buy mutual funds, what type of fund should you buy? Why?

H. What are the advantages and disadvantages of buying index mutual funds rather than actively managed funds?

I. If you want to buy a mutual fund so that you will have money to buy a house 10 years from now, what type of fund should you buy? Why?

ACTIVITY 6.4
A MUTUAL FUND PROSPECTUS

1. All mutual funds must supply potential investors with a prospectus. A prospectus is a document that provides information about the fund's investment objectives, investment strategy, past performance, costs, and other charges. The bullet points below present excerpts from one fund's prospectus. Read the excerpts, including the table showing **Average Annual Total Returns.**

    • The fund is an aggressive stock fund seeking long-term capital growth primarily through investments in small, rapidly growing companies.

    • Investing in smaller companies generally involves greater risk than investing in larger companies. Stocks of small companies are subject to more abrupt or erratic price movements than the stocks of larger companies.

    • The fund is 100 percent no-load. There are no 12b-1 fees.

    • The fund's annual management fee and other expenses are .91 percent. These expenses are deducted from the fund's assets.

    • The table below summarizes the fund's average annual returns for one year, five years, and 10 years.

Average Annual Total Returns

Fund Intervals	1 year	5 years	10 years
Returns before taxes	-2.84%	8.07%	13.75%
Returns after taxes on distributions	-3.33	6.37	11.03
Returns after taxes on distributions and sale of fund shares	-1.30	6.27	10.56
Russell 2000 Growth Index	-9.23	2.87	7.19
Russell 2000 Index	2.49	7.52	11.51
S&P 500 Stock Index	-11.89	10.70	12.94
Lipper Small-Cap Fund Index	-9.32	6.45	10.29

2. Then use your understanding of the prospectus to answer the following **Questions for Discussion:**

    A. You worry a lot about the stock market and want to limit the risk of losing your money. Would you buy this fund?

B. Does this fund charge a sales commission?

C. Is it good or bad for investors that this fund charges no 12b-1 fees?

D. How much does this fund charge in fees?

E. In your opinion, how does the fund's past performance look?

F. Does this mean the fund will perform well in the future?

SLIDE 6.1

One Year Later: An example

This is an example of what might have happened to a class investment club's shares of stock.

Company	Price per Share	Number of Shares Owned	Amount Invested	Investment Value One Year Later
American Cellular	$8	100	$500	$800
Big Box Retail	$23	50	$1,000	$1,150
Biotech Industries	$8	0	0	$0
General Grocery	$22	0	0	$0
Giant Auto	$11	100	$1,000	$1,100
Gold Mining Group	$4	100	$500	$400
Total Investment Value (add last column)			$3,000	$3,450

Number of shares <u>300</u>   *Price per share <u>$11.50</u>

*The price per share is the total investment value (one year later) divided by the number of shares.

SLIDE 6.2

How Mutual Funds Work

- The price per share changes every day and depends on the value of the investments.

- The value of the investments depends on the performance of the assets chosen by the fund manager. Unlike members of an investment club, mutual fund investors do not decide which stocks or bonds the fund will buy or sell. The fund manager does that.

- A mutual fund charges investors for the financial management it provides. The investor may also pay brokers' fees and other costs. These costs are deducted from the value of the investments. The lower these costs, the higher the investors' returns from a set of holdings.

- Some mutual funds charge a sales commission called a load. The higher the load, the less the actual investment made on behalf of the investor. Lower loads are better for investors, other things being equal.

SLIDE 6.3

Types of Mutual Funds

Low Risk and
Low Potential Reward

High Risk and
High Potential Reward

Money market funds (short-term securities)	Bond funds (corporate or longer-term government bonds)	Income funds (high-yield stocks and bond funds)	Growth funds (larger company stocks; long-term capital gains)	Aggressive growth funds (smaller company stocks; short- and long-term capital gains).

LESSON 7
WHAT ARE STOCK MARKETS?

LESSON 7
WHAT ARE STOCK MARKETS?

LESSON DESCRIPTION

The lesson introduces conditions necessary for market economies to operate. Against this background, students learn concepts and background knowledge—including primary and secondary markets, the role of investment banks, and initial public offerings (IPOs)—needed to understand the stock market. The students also learn about different characteristics of major stock markets in the United States and overseas. In a closure activity, students match stocks with the market in which each is most likely to be traded.

INTRODUCTION

For many people, the word *market* may be closely associated with an image of a place—perhaps a local farmer's market. For economists, however, *market* need not refer to a physical place. Instead, a market may be any organization that allows buyers and sellers to communicate about and arrange for the exchange of goods, resources, or services. Stock markets provide a mechanism whereby people who want to own shares of stock can buy them from people who want to sell shares of stock.

The three largest stock markets in the world are the New York Stock Exchange (NYSE), the NASDAQ Stock Market, and the Tokyo Stock Exchange. Although these markets differ from one another, especially in the kinds of stock traded and the mechanisms used for trading, all three are known as secondary markets. They are different from a primary market in which a company sells shares and receives money in an initial public offering (IPO).

CONCEPTS

Initial public offering (IPO)

Market

Primary market

Secondary market

Stock market

OBJECTIVES

Students will:

*   Identify conditions needed for a market economy to operate.

*   Describe the stock market as a special case of markets more generally.

*   Differentiate three major world stock markets and predict which market might list certain stocks.

CONTENT STANDARDS
Voluntary National Content Standards in Economics, **2nd Edition**

*   **Standard 5:** Voluntary exchange occurs only when all participating parties expect to gain. This is true for trade among individuals or organizations within a nation, and among individuals or organizations in different nations.

*   **Standard 7:** A market exists when buyers and sellers interact. This interaction determines market prices and thereby allocates scarce goods and services.

*   **Standard 10:** Institutions evolve and are created to help individuals and groups accomplish their goals. Banks, labor unions, markets, corporations, legal systems, and not-for-profit organizations are examples of important institutions. A different kind of institution, clearly defined and enforced property rights, is essential to a market economy.

National Standards in K-12 Personal Finance Education, 3rd Edition

- **Financial Responsibility and Decision Making Standard 2:** Find and evaluate financial information from a variety of sources.

- **Saving and Investing Standard 4:** Describe how to buy and sell investments.

TIME REQUIRED

60 minutes

MATERIALS

- Slide 7.1

- A copy of Activity 7.1 for each student

(Internet access required)

PROCEDURE

1. Tell the students that this lesson focuses on markets in general and on the stock market in particular. **Ask:** What is a market? What is a stock market?

2. To begin discussing markets, ask the students to list several markets they have participated in over the last few weeks. *(Examples might include a farmers' market, a supermarket, a retail store, a gasoline station.)*

3. Ask the students to think about what it would take to establish and maintain markets of the sort they have mentioned. What sort of legal and economic environment would be necessary? The question is somewhat abstract. To help the students get at it, you might use the following prompt: **We couldn't have markets unless we had** _____. Challenge the students to complete the statement. Provide help as necessary. Make a list of the necessary conditions on the board. The list should include the following:

- **Private property.** Markets depend on an individual's ability to own and sell property. In market transactions, people can choose to sell property to others and transfer the right of ownership with the sale.

- **Competition.** Markets foster competition because they allow the entry of many producers striving to meet the demands of consumers. Competition pressures these producers to satisfy consumer demand or be forced from the market by others who can.

- **The profit motive.** Profits act as incentives for individuals and firms. In market transactions, individuals and firms that satisfy consumer desires and produce efficiently are rewarded with profits.

- **Voluntary exchange.** Because consumers have choices in a market, market exchanges are voluntary. This allows consumers and producers to focus on what they do best and to trade with others who specialize in different areas. Markets encourage trade and thus create wealth.

4. Introduce the lesson's focus on stock markets by reference to the previous discussion. Just as there is a market for music downloads (iTunes), blue jeans (department store), or books (bookstore), there is a market for stocks. Somebody who wants to buy stocks can buy them at a stock market.

5. Explain that stock markets operate in the same sort of legal and economic environment needed by other markets. Stock markets are places where *private property* (shares of ownership) is bought and sold. Stock markets are *competitive* markets, with thousands of

buyers and sellers striving to make the best trades they can. The *profit motive* prompts traders to obtain and keep any gains they can make from stock trading. And stock markets depend on *voluntary exchange*. Stock trades are not coerced; rather, buyers and sellers choose to participate in their efforts to invest money wisely.

6. As necessary, pause here to establish clearly what a stock is (or review Lesson 4). Explain that a stock is a share of ownership in a company. If you buy 100 shares of Acme Electronics, you become a part-owner (100 shares' worth) of Acme Electronics. And why would people want to buy stock in a given company? Identify two main reasons: (a.) they expect to share in a company's profits (called dividends) paid out to shareholders; (b.) they believe the price of the company's stock will rise above the price they paid for it—in other words, that their asset will grow in value.

7. Ask the students if they have ever seen a stock store at the mall. If not at the mall, where can you go to buy stocks? Explain that almost all stock sales and purchases—often called stock trades— are handled by a specialized salesperson called a broker. In addition, almost all stocks are sold by these brokers in secondary markets.

8. To distinguish between primary and secondary markets, **Display Slide 7.1.** Explain that companies such as Company X often seek additional resources to expand or run their business. One way to generate these resources is to offer all, or a portion, of the company for sale to the public-at-large ("take a company public"). This is done in the primary market through an initial public offering (IPO) in which stocks are sold to large investment banks. Investment banks then sell the shares

to brokerage houses, and brokers offer the shares for sale to individuals and institutional buyers on the secondary market through one of the major stock exchanges like the New York Stock Exchange (NYSE), the NASDAQ Stock Market in the United States, or a stock market in another country, such as the London Stock Exchange or the Tokyo Stock Exchange.

9. **Distribute a copy of Activity 7.1** to each student. Have the students read the introduction. Briefly review the overview of market mechanics, using **Slide 7.1** as needed.

10. Have the students read the descriptions of the three major stock markets. Call on students to identify the distinctive characteristics of each of the three markets. Record their responses on the board. Sample responses:

New York Stock Exchange (NYSE)	NASDAQ Stock Market	Tokyo Stock Exchange
Founded in 1792.	*Founded in 1971.*	*Founded in 1878.*
About 3,500 companies listed.	*About 2,800 companies listed.*	*About 2,300 companies listed.*
Home of large and well-established companies.	*Considered the home of tech stocks.*	*Home of the Nikkei 226 index.*
Listed companies must have at least $100,000,000 in outstanding stock and trade an average of at least 100,000 shares per day.	*No physical location; trades done via computer network.*	*Companies separated into three categories: large, mid-sized, and growth/startup.*
1,336 member seats.	*Largest market in terms of stocks traded.*	*104 members.*
	No fixed number of members.	

11. Have the students complete the **Place the Stock** activity. Answers:

Market	Stocks		
New York Stock Exchange (NYSE)	*Con Ed*	*DuPont*	*McDonald's*
NASDAQ Stock Market	*Atari*	*Intel*	*Telecom Austria*
Tokyo Stock Exchange	*Toyota*	*POSCO*	*YTL Corporation*

CLOSURE

12. Briefly review major points of the lesson. The students have studied concepts and background information about stock markets, including the general legal and economic conditions that support markets generally. They have learned that the stock market is a specialized market in which shares of stock are bought and sold. Also review the three stock markets discussed in this lesson.

13. Organize the class into groups of four students each. Working in their groups, the students should look at the clothing and shoes they are wearing, their backpacks or book bags, and any other items they may have brought with them to class. Can they identify the companies that made these items? If so, have them list several of the companies on a piece of paper. Then ask the students to make some well-informed guesses about which stock markets the companies that made their products might be listed on. For example, if a student has an AT&T cell phone, she might guess that AT&T is a high-tech firm listed on the NASDAQ (although this guess would be wrong). If a student is wearing Nike shoes, he might guess that the stock of this company, given the company's size, would be traded on the NYSE (and he would be

correct). If a student has a calculator, it might be made by Casio or Sony. Both of these firms are traded on the Tokyo Stock Exchange. Once the students have made their guesses, ask them to use the internet in class to determine which ones are correct and which are incorrect (or you might assign this as homework or a library project).

ASSESSMENT
Multiple-Choice Questions

1. All of the following conditions are essential to a market economy except

    a. the private property of individuals is well defined and protected.
    b. *the government controls decisions about production and consumption.*
    c. competition puts pressure on businesses to satisfy consumer desires.
    d. profits are an incentive for producers to respond to consumer choices.

2. In the case of stock trades, the secondary market consists of

    a. *the trading of a company's stock in a stock market.*
    b. the purchase of a company's stock by an investment bank.
    c. the first offering of a company's stock to the public.
    d. all trading that occurs in the initial public offering of the stock.

3. All of the following are true of the New York Stock Exchange except that

    a. it has a fixed number of memberships called "seats."
    b. it operates a physical trading floor rather than being all electronic.
    c. it contains a smaller proportion of young technology companies than the NASDAQ Stock Market.
    d. *it is the largest stock market in terms of trade volume.*

4. Which of these is an accurate state-ment about the NASDAQ and NYSE?

    a. The NASDAQ Stock Market is a secondary market; the NYSE is a primary market.
    b. *Membership on the NYSE is limit-ed; the NASDAQ has an open mem-bership.*
    c. Trading on both the NASDAQ Stock Market and the NYSE is lim-ited to one physical location.
    d. The NASDAQ Stock Market was founded before the NYSE.

Constructed-Response Items

1. Identify and briefly explain four condi-tions that enable market economies to operate.

    *(**Private property.** Markets depend on an individual's ability to own and sell property. In market transactions, people can choose to sell property to others and transfer the right of ownership with the sale. **Competition.** Markets foster com-petition because they allow the entry of many producers striving to meet the de-mands of consumers. Competition pres-sures these producers to satisfy consum-er demand or be forced from the market by other producers who can. **The profit motive.** Profits act as incentives for individuals and firms. Individuals and firms that satisfy consumer desires and produce efficiently are rewarded with profits. **Voluntary exchange.** Because consumers have choices in a market, all exchanges are voluntary. This allows consumers and producers to focus on what they do best and to trade surplus production or wealth. Markets encour-age trade and thus create wealth.)*

2. Describe the difference between pri-mary and secondary stock markets.

    (In the primary market, the firm sells stock to an investment bank. This is

often referred to as an initial public offering [IPO]) or "going public." In the secondary market, shares of stock are bought and sold by individuals and brokers in a stock market.)

Gen i Connection

Among the print lessons in this book, Lesson 7 ("What Are Stock Markets?") and Lesson 14 ("How Are Stock Prices Determined?") have close ties to Mission 12 of the Gen i Revolution game, "Show Jasmine what determines stock prices." In this mission, Jasmine needs help in understanding the stock market so that she can help her clients make trades. The 4-1-1 tutorial guides students to equilibrium at the intersection of demand and supply curves, and it shows them how events could change equilibrium stock prices. As students complete this mission, they find themselves on the floor of a fictional stock exchange as they are asked to react to the news of the day and help Jasmine predict changes in stock prices.

Gen i Reflection

Jasmine learned in Gen i Revolution Mission 12 that she would have to react quickly to incoming news in order to be a successful stock trader. Some jobs are like that, requiring constant attention and fast action. Other jobs, such as accounting, call for patience and discipline but not as much fast action. Thinking about your own skills and abilities, which type of job would you find more satisfying? Explain your answer.

ACTIVITY 7.1
MEET THE STOCK MARKETS

The stock market is an institution enabling people who want to buy shares of stock to buy them from others who want to sell shares of stock. This market matches buyers and sellers and provides a means for reaching mutual agreement on price. That is, the price of a share of stock is set at the moment when a buyer and seller agree to make a trade, and not before. The stock market is more than a physical location (and need not be a physical location at all); it is a set of arrangements, advertisements, online transactions, computer listings and personal relationships that make it possible for stocks to be traded.

Although often referred to as if it were a single entity, "the stock market" is actually a number of different markets. The three largest stock markets in the world are the New York Stock Exchange (NYSE), NASDAQ Stock Market, and the Tokyo Stock Exchange in Japan.

The New York Stock Exchange (NYSE)

The oldest stock exchange in the United States, the NYSE was founded in 1792 when 24 brokers agreed to form the exchange. Today about 3,500 public companies are traded on the NYSE, and these companies have a combined value of about $13.5 trillion. Generally, small corporations' stocks are not listed on the NYSE. In order to be listed on the NYSE, the company must have outstanding share value (the value of all the shares of stock not owned by the company itself) of at least $100 million and must trade at a volume of at least 100,000 shares per day.

The NYSE operates a trading floor in New York City. Members of the NYSE—1,336 brokers and specialists—carry out all trades. Members are said to have a "seat" on the NYSE, although they never actually sit down, and such seats have sold for as much $4 million in recent years. Investors purchase stocks by placing orders with brokers from around the United States and the world. These brokers then place floor orders at the NYSE, and those orders are filled by the members. In recent years, nearly 80 percent of the order volume has been delivered electronically.

NASDAQ Stock Market

The NASDAQ Stock Market began trading in 1971, and in 1999 it surpassed the NYSE as the largest stock market (as measured by volume of stock trades) in the United States. The NASDAQ Stock Market is unique because it does not reside any single location. Rather, trades are executed using the NASDAQ's sophisticated computer and telecommunication network. As the world's first electronic stock market, it is made up of the NASDAQ National Market and the NASDAQ Small Cap Market. The NASDAQ allows multiple market participants to trade through its electronic communications network structure, thus increasing competition.

The NASDAQ Stock Market currently lists the stocks of more than 2,800 companies, with a combined value of $3.2 trillion. The NASDAQ is widely known as the home of many of the world's largest technology-based companies, particularly those involved with computers, software, and the internet. More shares are traded on the NASDAQ than any other stock market in the world, largely because membership is not limited to a fixed number of seats. Any firm or individual that meets certain requirements may join the NASDAQ. This policy allows more than 300 "market makers" (also known as dealers, to their customers) to operate like retail store owners, buying inventory of stock shares to sell to their customers.

Stock Indexes

Several important stock indexes are tracked on U.S. markets. A stock index is a composite of the value of a number of stocks used to measure the ups and downs of the overall market. The most famous stock index is the Dow Jones Industrial Average (DJIA), or "the Dow," which consists of 30 of the biggest companies in the United States including firms such as Walt Disney, Coca Cola, and Walmart. Today, the Dow is the most widely followed measurement of the stock market. A second important index of stocks is the Standard and Poor's (S&P) 500. This index uses the stock prices of 500 companies including Boeing, Microsoft, and 3M.

Tokyo Stock Exchange

The Tokyo Stock Exchange (TSE) was established in 1878 in Tokyo, Japan. It has almost 2,300 listed companies with a combined value of $3.8 trillion, making it the third-largest stock exchange in the world. Stocks listed on the TSE are separated into the First Section for large companies, the Second Section for mid-sized companies, and the Mothers Section for high-growth startup companies.

The best known TSE stock index is the Nikkei 225. Formerly called the Nikkei Dow Jones Stock Average, it consists of 225 of the biggest companies in Japan including firms such as Mitsubishi, Sony, and Sharp. Many major Japanese companies are also listed on the NYSE via American Depositary Receipts (ADR), which represent shares of foreign-based corporations so American investors can buy shares in the United States.

Place the Stock

Listed below are brief descriptions of nine stocks that are listed on one of the three major world stock markets described above. After reading these descriptions, and using what you know about each market, place each stock in the appropriate place on the grid that follows. Pay close attention to the information provided. For example, newer high-tech companies are more likely to be listed on the NASDAQ Stock Market (which opened in 1971).

1. POSCO
    A multinational steel-making company headquartered in Pohang, South Korea. It had an output of 35.4 million metric tons of crude steel in 2010, making it the world's third-largest steelmaker. POSCO currently operates two integrated steel mills in South Korea, in Pohang and Gwangyang. In addition, POSCO operates a joint venture with U.S. Steel, USS-POSCO, which is located in Pittsburg, California.

2. ATARI
    Atari's principal activities are to develop, publish, and distribute interactive entertainment software for leisure entertainment, gaming enthusiasts, and children's markets for a variety of platforms. This stock was first listed in 1998, and shares traded often average more than 100,000 per day.

3. DUPONT
    Founded in 1802, this firm offers a wide range of innovative products and services for markets including agriculture, nutrition, electronics, communications, safety and protection, home and construction, transportation, and apparel. Operating in approximately 90 countries, this company's stock is part of both the Dow Jones and the S&P 500 stock indexes.

4. INTEL

Intel's principal activities are to design, develop, manufacture, and market computers, networking, and communication products. Listed since 1998, this stock regularly averages over 10 million shares traded per day.

5. MCDONALD's

McDonald's Corporation operates in the food-service industry, franchising quick-service restaurant businesses under the McDonald's brand. This stock was first listed in 1966; it is part of the Dow Jones Industrial Average. Shares traded often average near 10 million per day.

6. TOYOTA

Toyota Motor Corporation is one of the world's largest automobile manufacturers. Founded in 1937, Toyota manufactures, sells, leases, and repairs passenger cars, trucks, buses, and their related parts worldwide. Shares traded often average near 10 million per day.

7. TELEKOM AUSTRIA

This group's principal activities are to provide fixed-line and wireless communication services in Austria and throughout Europe. Listed since 1998, this stock averages 1,000 shares traded per day.

8. CONSOLIDATED EDISON (CONED)

Con Edison of New York provides electric power in all of New York City (except Queens) and most of Westchester County. This stock was first listed in 1824. Shares traded per day often exceed one million.

9. YTL CORPORATION

YTL Corporation is Malaysia's leading integrated infrastructure conglomerate. The company is involved with utilities, high-speed rail projects, and construction. The stock was first listed in 1985; shares traded per day average about 10,000.

Match the Stocks to the Markets

Market	Stocks		
New York Stock Exchange (NYSE)			
NASDAQ Stock Market			
Tokyo Stock Exchange			

SLIDE 7.1

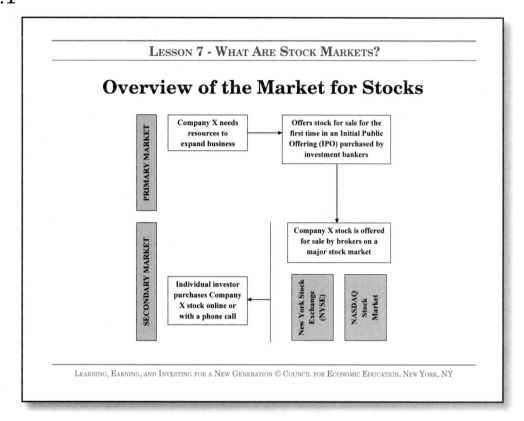

LESSON 8

BUYING ON MARGIN
AND SELLING SHORT

Lesson 8
Buying on Margin and Selling Short

LESSON DESCRIPTION

The students learn about buying on margin and selling short. They learn that buying on margin and selling short can increase potential gains for investors, but at the risk of greater potential losses. They read two short plays to help them understand buying on margin and short selling; then they work in groups to solve problems that illustrate the potential risks and rewards of these two investment techniques.

INTRODUCTION

In stock market simulations and games, students can practice selling short and buying on margin. The simulations and games available for use reflect conditions in real-world markets.

Buying on margin and selling short may help students do well as they compete in stock market games and simulations. Students should understand, however, that using these techniques in real markets involves high levels of risk.

One important rule from economics is that everything has a cost. When this rule is applied to buying stocks, it means the higher the expected return on a given purchase, the riskier that purchase will be. Buyers of stock must be compensated for risk. Buying on margin and selling short are methods that can increase returns, but only by increasing risk.

CONCEPTS

Buying on margin

Opportunity cost

Short cover

Short sale

OBJECTIVES
Students will be able to:

- Explain the difference between a bull market and a bear market.

- Explain and illustrate the technique of buying on margin.

- Explain and illustrate the technique of selling short.

- Analyze the rewards and risks of selling short and buying on margin.

CONTENT STANDARDS
Voluntary National Content Standards in Economics, **2nd Edition**

- **Standard 1:** Productive resources are limited. Therefore, people cannot have all the goods and services they want; as a result, they must choose some things and give up others.

- **Standard 2:** Effective decision making requires comparing the additional costs of alternatives with the additional benefits. Many choices involve doing a little more or a little less of something: few choices are "all or nothing" decisions.

National Standards in K-12 Personal Finance Education, **3rd Edition**

- **Saving and Investing Standard 4:** Describe how to buy and sell investments.

TIME REQUIRED

90 minutes

MATERIALS

Slides 8.1 and 8.2

Desk and three chairs for the play (Activity 8.1)

Four copies of Activity 8.1 and 8.3, one for each student in the play

One copy of Activities 8.2 and 8.4 for each student

PROCEDURE

1. Introduce the lesson by explaining briefly that it focuses on two investment techniques that can be very risky. Explain that people take risks only if the reward is great enough. Tell the students to think about a team scoring a touchdown in a close football game. Now the coach has to decide whether to send the kicker in for an extra point attempt—or go for two. **Ask:** Since it's safer to kick, why don't coaches always go for the one extra point? *(Because the reward is greater if the team completes a two-point conversion.)* In a similar way, investors may take on additional risk, but only if the reward is great enough.

2. Now tell the students they will learn about two risky investment techniques that also may have higher rewards: buying on margin and selling short. **Display Slide 8.1**. By reference to the slide, tell the students about bull markets and bear markets. In bull markets, stock prices keep going up. In bear markets, stock prices keep going down. Bull markets and bear markets can influence the decisions investors make about taking a risk—by changing the rewards. The lesson that follows develops that point.

3. Explain that the first step is to learn about buying on margin. **Distribute copies of Activity 8.1**. Tell the students that they will serve as an attentive audience while four of their classmates perform a play about buying stocks on margin. Set up the props (a desk and three chairs) and assign students to play the roles of Katie, Stock-broker Luke, Jeremy, and the Moderator. Call for the play to proceed.

4. Discuss the play, using the following questions:

   A. What is "buying on margin"?

   (Buying stock on credit or with borrowed money.)

   B. When you buy on margin, how much of the purchase price must you put up in cash?

   (50 percent.)

   C. Who determines this percentage?

   (The Federal Reserve Board.)

   D. Why do you think there is a limit on the amount of money brokers can lend?

   (If brokers lend too much money, investors buying on margin could suffer big losses. Big losses on margin accounts were part of the problem during the stock market crash in 1929. Stock owners received margin calls that they couldn't meet.)

   E. What are the advantages of buying stock on margin?

   (An investor who uses borrowed money to buy stock can buy more stock than he otherwise could have—and perhaps make higher returns.)

   F. What are the disadvantages of buying stock on margin?

   (Investors buying on margin must pay interest on their loans. Also, if the price for stock bought on margin goes down, the investor will suffer losses.)

5. Develop the point that buying on margin entails risk as well as reward. **Display Slide 8.2**. Explain that the examples presented on the slide demonstrate

potential advantages and risks associated with buying stocks on margin. The risk may be acceptable, but only if the investor thinks that taking the chance will be worthwhile—just as a football coach may take the risk of going for two points if the running back is playing well that day. Also tell the students that *leverage* is another word for debt. An investor who buys stocks on margin is "leveraging," or buying stocks with borrowed money. (The same stockbroker usually handles the loan and the stock transactions).

6. Focus on the first row of the chart on Slide 8.2. It shows that the investor purchases stock using his or her own $100 of capital without borrowing any more money. In this example, the investor buys one share of stock at a P1 of $100. Assume that the price rises to a P2 of $110 (a rise of 10 percent). The investor has now made a 10 percent return and now has $110 of capital.

7. Focus on the second row of the chart. It shows that the investor uses $100 of his or her own money, but also borrows $900 from the broker and purchases the same stock for P1 of $100. In this case the investor has also purchased one share (as in the first row), but in addition has bought nine shares with borrowed money ("on margin"). This technique enables the investor to buy a total of 10 shares. If we assume again that the price rises to $110, the investor now owns $1,100 of stock (10 shares x $110 per share). The investor could pay back the borrowed $900 and still have $200 left ($1,100 – $900 = $200). This represents a doubling of the original $100 of capital, or a 100 percent increase.

8. Focus on the third row of the chart. Again, it shows an investor buying $100 worth of stock and borrowing

$900 to buy more; however, this time the stock price falls by $10 (or 10 percent) to $90. Now the investor owns $900 in stock (10 shares x $90) but also owes the broker $900. In other words, the investor has lost 100 percent of his or her original capital.

9. Overall, Slide 8.2 makes the point that an investor who buys on margin increases the potential rewards from buying stock. However, the investor also faces increased risk, as the third example shows. In that case, when the stock went down by only 10 percent, all of the investor's capital was wiped out. (For simplicity, this example assumes that the investor pays no interest on the borrowed money. Interest is required in real-world investment markets, making the loss even worse if stocks bought on margin go down.)

10. To provide more examples of what can happen when investors buy on margin, **distribute copies of Activity 8.2** to all the students. Have the students read down to "Margin Worksheet." Help by explaining the examples given in the reading, as necessary. Then ask the students to work in small groups to answer the questions in three worksheet situations. Discuss the students' work and the answers for each situation.

Situation 1

Mrs. Smith buys on margin 100 shares of Coca-Cola stock at $30 per share.

a. *The total market value of the stock Mrs. Smith buys is $3,000.*

b. *The amount of money that Mrs. Smith must pay for this purchase (her initial margin requirement) is $1,500.*

c. *The maximum amount of money that a brokerage firm could lend Mrs. Smith (her debt) is $1,500.*

d. *Mrs. Smith's equity is $1,500.*

Situation 2

The value of Mrs. Smith's shares of Coca-Cola rises to $40 per share.

a. *The market value of Coca-Cola shares in Mrs. Smith's account is now $4,000.*

b. *The amount of money she owes the brokerage firm (her debt) is $1,500.*

c. *Mrs. Smith's equity is $2,500*

Situation 3

The value of Mrs. Smith's shares of Coca-Cola falls to $20 per share.

a. *The market value of Coca-Cola shares in Mrs. Smith's account is now $2,000.*

b. *The amount of money she owes the brokerage firm (her debt) is $1,500.*

c. *Mrs. Smith's equity is $500*

11. Ask the students to look back at the three situations summarized in the worksheet on Activity 8.2. What do these situations suggest about when it might, or might not, make sense for an investor to take a risk by buying on margin?

(During a bull market, it might make sense for an investor to buy on margin. Stock bought on margin will yield higher equity when the stock price goes up. The reverse holds for a bear market. Stock bought on margin will produce big losses when the stock price goes down.)

12. Turn next to the investment strategy called short selling. Tell the students that short selling is a technique some investors use to increase their profits in a bear market.

13. Ask the students how they would feel if someone borrowed their skateboard and then sold it, promising to pay them back with a new skateboard. *(Most students would feel cheated or betrayed.)* Although it is not socially acceptable to sell a borrowed item, tell students that something similar happens when an investor sells stocks short. Challenge the students to imagine how the selling of a borrowed skateboard could possibly pay off for both the lender and the borrower. If the students can't think of such a possibility, give them a hint. Suppose the borrower could sell the borrowed skateboard for more money than it would take to buy a new one. What difference might that make?

(The borrower in this case could buy a brand new skateboard, return the new board to the lender, and keep the profits from the sale.)

14. Explain that the selling of a borrowed skateboard illustrates how people can make money when they sell short a stock that is going down. They borrow the stock and sell the stock right away at its current high market price. Later they repay the stock loan by purchasing shares and giving them back to the lender. But because they have bought the shares for repayment at a lower price, they have made a profit. Further, the repaid shares are just like the shares that were borrowed, making the transaction socially acceptable—in a way that selling someone's unique skateboard might not be acceptable, even if the loan was repaid with a new skateboard.

15. Now consider how the selling of a borrowed skateboard might cause a loss. The borrower sells the borrowed skateboard but now finds the money from the sale is not enough to buy a new skateboard. In this case, the borrower has to buy the lender a new skateboard, using his own money, since the sale didn't cover the costs of returning the borrowed board. Again, this is similar to what happens with stocks in a short sale. Suppose someone sells borrowed stock, planning to repay the loan with stock bought at a lower price—but now the price of the stock goes up. Now the borrower must buy the stock to repay the loan at a higher price, losing money on the deal.

16. Explain that once again the students will provide an attentive audience while four of their classmates perform a short play, this time a play about selling short. **Distribute copies of Activity 8.3** to each student. Assign students to play the roles of Moderator, Stockbroker Luke, Jeremy, and Katie. Call for the play to proceed.

17. Discuss the play, using the following questions:

    A. How would you describe a short sale?

       (A short sale involves a sale of stock borrowed from a broker; the borrower will be obliged to buy the stock later and to return it to the lender.)

    B. Why is a short sale the opposite of the usual stock trade?

       (In a normal trade, you buy the stock first and sell it later. In a short sale, you sell borrowed stock first and buy it back later.)

    C. What is a short cover?

       (Buying back stock originally borrowed from the broker in a short sale.)

    D. Why do people sell stock short?

       (They hope to sell the borrowed shares at a high price and buy the shares back later at a lower price. Then they can return the stock to the broker, satisfying the loan, and make a gain.)

    E. Why might the price of a stock fall?

       (Demand for the stock might fall. That might happen because the broader economy has taken a downturn, or because the company in question is having financial trouble, or because of widespread negative news about the company or the industry.)

    F. Why is selling short risky?

       (If the price of the stock goes up, the short seller still has to buy the stock back—at a higher price. There is no limit to how high the stock price can rise.)

    G. What costs are involved in selling short?

       (Short sellers must pay a broker's fee when they sell short and when they short cover.)

    H. Why must an investor open a margin account with at least 50 percent of the value of the short sale in the account?

       (To protect the broker who is lending the stock. If the price of the stock rises too much, the short seller might not be able to buy back the stock and return it.)

18. Provide more examples showing the potential for gains and losses arising from short sales. **Distribute a copy of Activity 8.4** to each student. Show them how to solve Situation 1.

Situation 1

A stock owner sells short 200 shares of a stock at $50 per share. He buys them back for replacement (short covers) at $40 per share. Did he make a gain or loss? *Gain.* How much? *$1,640.*

Short sale (200 x $50)	$10,000
Broker's fee	– $200
Proceeds	$9,800
Short cover (200 x $40)	$8,000
Broker's fee	+ $160
Cost	$8,160

Proceeds from the short sale ($9,800) – Cost of short cover ($8,160) = Gain ($1,640)

19. Provide time for the students to continue their work on Activity 8.4. They should work on the next two situations in small groups. When they have finished, discuss their work and the correct answers for Situations 2 and 3.

Situation 2

A stock owner sells short 100 shares of XYZ Corporation at $20 per share and has to short cover them at $40. Did he make a gain or loss? *Loss.* How much? *$2,120.*

Short sale (100 x $20)	$2,000
Broker's fee	– $40
Proceeds	$1,960
Short cover (100 x $40)	$4,000
Broker's fee	+ $80
Cost	$4,080

Proceeds from the short sale ($1,960) – Cost of short cover ($4,080) = Loss ($2,120)

Situation 3

A stock owner sells short 100 shares of Apple Pie Corporation at $50 per share. The initial margin requirement is 50 percent. How much money must be deposited in the margin account?

($2,500, calculated as $5,000 x 0.5)

CLOSURE

20. **Display Slide 8.1. Ask:**

A. How can bullish stock buyers increase their gains or returns?

(By buying stock on margin.)

B. How can bearish stock buyers increase their gains or returns?

(By selling short.)

C. Why do most stock buyers avoid buying on margin or selling short?

(These techniques are risky and can result in large losses.)

ASSESSMENT
Multiple-Choice Questions

1. What does it mean to "sell short"?

   a. Selling short means selling stock soon after you buy it.
   b. Selling short means buying stock on credit.
   c. Selling short means selling your own stock when you think it will go down in price.
   d. *Selling short means selling stock you don't own.*

2. If a stock buyer buys on margin, what does she think will happen to the price of the stock?

   a. *It will increase quickly.*
   b. It will increase slowly.
   c. It will decrease quickly.
   d. It will stay the same.

3. If a stock buyer sells a stock short, what does he think will happen to the price of the stock?

    a. *It will decrease quickly.*
    b. It will increase slowly.
    c. It will increase quickly.
    d. It will stay the same.

4. What is a short cover?

    a. *A stock buyer buys back and returns stock she borrowed from a broker.*
    b. A stock buyer keeps her stock for no longer than one month.
    c. A stock buyer sends out a margin call.
    d. A stock buyer is short on the money he needs to pay back a margin purchase.

Constructed-Response Items

1. You sell 100 shares of Intel stock short at $50 per share. Four months later, you short cover it for $10. The brokerage firm receives a 2 percent commission on the short sale and short cover. How much gain will you earn on this transaction? Show your work.

Proceeds from sale	*$5,000*
– 2% commission	*– $100*
– cost of short cover	*– $1,000*
– 2% commission	*– $20*
Net Gain	*$3,880*

2. You buy $10,000 of Nike stock on 50 percent margin. The price falls 10 percent. How much equity do you have in the stock? By what percentage has your equity increased or decreased? Show your work.

Current value of stock	*$9,000*
Debt owed to broker	*$5,000*
Equity	*$4,000*

    Percentage decrease in equity = $5,000 – $4,000 = $1,000 / $5,000 = 20 percent loss

Gen i Connection

Although there is no Gen i Revolution mission on margin buying and short selling of stocks, there is a good 4-1-1 tutorial on risk and return in Mission 6, "Advise Kai on how to invest his grandmother's $10,000." The tutorial explains how achieving a greater return generally requires taking more risk. The current print lesson, "Buying on Margin and Selling Short," shows how this strategy amplifies the potential for gains and the risk of loss. Mission 6 is largely self-contained and may be assigned at any time. Its premise is that Kai has received $10,000 as a gift, to be saved for college, and Kai is looking for a good place to put the money. Students consider investment alternatives and, in the mission conclusion, get top points for recommending a bond mutual fund over individual stocks. Also note that the teachers' guides that accompany both the national Stock Market Game (http://www.smgww.org/) and Stock Market Simulation (http://www.nationalsms.com/) provide lessons and resources that illustrate the concepts of short selling and buying stocks on margin.

Gen i Reflection

Several different Gen i Revolution missions make the point that to receive a higher return, it is necessary to assume more risk. Among people graduating from high school today, do you think financial risk-takers will be more or less successful than their more cautious classmates? Explain your answer.

ACTIVITY 8.1
A MARGINAL PLAY

Stockbroker Luke, Katie, and Jeremy are sitting around a desk near a sign labeled "Brokerage Office." The Moderator is standing in front of the classroom.

Jeremy: Last year the Dow Jones Average was up 30 percent. I think this year looks just as good. The bull market is roaring. How can I make the most of this?

Stockbroker Luke: First, you need to buy quality companies. Second, don't forget that stock prices can go down.

Katie: Jeremy, don't be too greedy. You know the stock market can be risky.

Jeremy: I just want to take full advantage of a bull market.

Moderator: Jeremy and Katie are about to learn how buying on margin can increase their returns on their stock purchases, as well as their risks.

Katie: What exactly is "buying on margin"?

Stockbroker Luke: Buying on margin is buying stock on credit (or leverage). It's similar to borrowing money to buy a car or a house. Only instead of borrowing to buy goods and services, you borrow to buy more stock.

Jeremy: Could you give me an example of buying on margin?

Stockbroker Luke: Suppose a person wants to buy 100 shares of stock at $100 per share, for a total cost of $100,000. Unfortunately, the person has only $5,000. She could still buy these 100 shares by borrowing money from a brokerage company. Borrowing money from a brokerage company in order to buy stocks is called buying stocks on margin.

Katie: Can you borrow as much as you want?

Stockbroker Luke: No. You can only borrow 50 percent or one half of the money needed to buy stock. This is true for all brokerage firms. The limit is set by the Federal Reserve Board, which has the authority to determine this margin requirement.

Moderator: The Federal Reserve is the central bank that regulates all banks and many other financial institutions in the United States. Many people call it "the Fed."

Jeremy: How do we buy on margin?

Stockbroker Luke: For an investor to buy stocks on margin, the stock broker must set up a margin account for that investor in a brokerage office. A margin account is an account that allows a buyer to buy stock on credit.

Katie: Don't brokerage firms worry that stock buyers won't pay back the money they have borrowed?

Stockbroker Luke: Brokerage firms limit their risk by requiring collateral. Collateral consists of shares of stock or cash that can be used to repay the loan.

Moderator:	Whenever an individual borrows large sums of money in the real world, the lender often asks for collateral. Collateral is something of value that a borrower uses to back up his promise to repay the loan. The borrower signs a legal agreement allowing the lender to take the collateral if the loan isn't repaid. A house is often signed over as collateral for a mortgage loan. A car is often signed over as collateral for a car loan. In a margin account, cash and stocks already owned are held as collateral by the brokerage firm for loans made to buy stock.
Jeremy:	Do brokerage firms charge anything for this service?
Stockbroker Luke:	Yes. In addition to the fee for buying or selling the stock, the brokerage firm charges interest on the loan. The interest is deducted from the buyer's account.
Katie:	What happens if you buy on margin and the value of the stock you bought goes down?
Stockbroker Luke:	Then the value of your account goes down. If it goes down enough, you may have to put up more collateral. This is called a margin call. If you can't meet this margin call, your stock will be sold.
Moderator:	We have seen that by borrowing the money to buy stock, stock buyers can increase their gains if the stock price rises. However, if the stock price falls, stock buyers can lose a greater proportion of their money than they would have lost if they paid cash for the stock.

ACTIVITY 8.2
MARGIN PROBLEMS

Names _____

The amount of collateral that the investor must deposit to open a margin account for buying stock is called the *initial margin requirement*. The initial margin requirement must be 50 percent (one half) of the total value of the stocks being purchased or sold short. For example: to make a $10,000 stock purchase on margin, the investor must put $5,000 worth of collateral into the margin account.

The investor's actual ownership in the account is called the *equity*. It is determined by subtracting the investor's debt (what is owed to the brokerage firm) from the value of the investor's stock (what is owned). Here is a sample margin account:

Current value of stock purchased	$10,000
Debt (money owed to broker)	– $5,000
Equity (amount owned by investor)	$5,000

Suppose the price of the stock increases. The market value of the stock will rise, and so will the investor's equity.

Current value of stock purchased	$11,000
Debt (money owed to broker)	– $5,000
Equity (amount owned by investor)	$6,000

Suppose the price of the stock falls. The market value of the stock will fall, and so will the investor's equity.

Current value of stock purchased	$9,000
Debt (money owed to broker)	– $5,000
Equity (amount owned by investor)	$4,000

Many stock market games and simulations allow students to buy stocks on margin. In these cases, the internet site will act as your broker and lend you a portion of the money you need to buy more stock. Since the initial margin requirement in most games is 50 percent, you can typically borrow up to one-half of the value of the stocks being purchased or sold short.

In many games this means that you can buy approximately $200,000 worth of stock (less the broker's fees). $100,000 will come from your beginning account balance, and the game or simulation will lend you $100,000. In this case, you have borrowed the greatest amount possible because of the 50 percent margin requirement ($200,000 worth of stock x 50 percent = $100,000 loan). The game or simulation will typically hold your $200,000 worth of stock as collateral for the loan.

Now see if you understand all of this by solving the following problems.

Margin Worksheet

Directions: Read each situation below and fill in the blanks.

Situation 1

Mrs. Smith buys 100 shares of Coca-Cola stock on margin at $30 per share.

a. The total market value of the stock Mrs. Smith buys is $_____

b. The amount of money that Mrs. Smith must pay for this purchase (her initial margin requirement) is $_____

c. The maximum amount of money that the brokerage firm could lend Mrs. Smith (her debt) is $_____

d. Mrs. Smith's equity is $_____

Situation 2

The value of Mrs. Smith's 100 shares of Coca-Cola rises to $40 per share. Calculate the following:

a. The market value of Coca-Cola shares in Mrs. Smith's account is now $_____

b. The amount of money she owes the brokerage firm (her debt) $_____

c. Mrs. Smith's equity is $_____

Situation 3

The value of Mrs. Smith's 100 shares of Coca-Cola falls to $20 per share. Calculate the following:

a. The market value of Coca-Cola shares in Mrs. Smith's account is now $_____

b. The amount of money she owes the brokerage firm (her debt) is $_____

c. Mrs. Smith's equity is $_____

ACTIVITY 8.3
GET SHORTY: A STOCK MARKET PLAY

Katie, Jeremy, and Stockbroker Luke are sitting around a desk near a sign labeled "Brokerage Office." The Moderator is standing in front of the classroom.

Katie:	Hi, Luke. That stock you helped me buy last year has really done well. This is my brother, Jeremy. He's also interested in buying stock. [*Jeremy shakes hands with Stockbroker Luke.*]
Jeremy:	We've heard there is a way to make money when the price of a stock goes down. Is this really possible? I think we're going into a bear market.
Stockbroker Luke:	Yes, definitely. It's a strategy called "selling short." It is very risky. Are you sure you're interested?
Jeremy:	I'm game. Give us the information on this short stuff.
Stockbroker Luke:	Selling short reverses the regular way you buy and sell stock. In a normal trade, you buy stock first and sell later, just as Katie did when she bought some shares with me last year. Selling short, however, means that you sell stock first and buy it back later.
Katie:	That sounds really weird. How can you sell stock that you don't own?
Moderator:	Katie, like many other buyers of stocks, is confused. Perhaps Stockbroker Luke can make this process clearer.
Stockbroker Luke:	Let me continue. As you said, Katie, selling short means selling stock you don't already own. Investors can do this simply by borrowing stock from a broker. Brokerage companies have a large number of stocks that they are holding for customers or that they own themselves. They are willing to lend these shares of stock to buyers of stock who are interested in selling short.
Jeremy:	Do the short sellers get to keep the money from the short sale?
Stockbroker Luke:	No. We stockbrokers aren't crazy. Investors who sell short must later buy back the stock and return it to the broker. The broker is only *lending* the stock to be sold. The broker holds the money collected from the sale of the stock for security on the loan of the stock shares.
Moderator:	When the stock buyer buys back the stock to return it to the broker, that action is called a "short cover."
Katie:	Well, if they don't get to keep the money, why would the stock buyers want to sell borrowed stock?
Stockbroker Luke:	That's an easy one to answer. Stockholders sell short only when they think the price of the stock will fall. Short sellers must later buy back the stock and return it to the brokerage company, which is the short cover. Eventually, they must cover their shorts. They hope they can buy it back at a lower price.

Jeremy:	So if I decided to short sell 100 shares of Coca-Cola, your firm would lend me the stock. You would sell it for me tomorrow at, say, $40 per share. You would hold the $4,000 in my account until I decide to buy back the Coca-Cola stock.
Katie:	And if the price of the Coca-Cola stock falls to $30, then Jeremy could replace the borrowed stock at the lower price of $3,000 and make a gain of $1,000.
Moderator:	The broker would use the $4,000 Jeremy received for the original short sale to buy back the stock (or the short cover). Since only $3,000 is needed to buy back the stock, Jeremy would make a gain of $1,000.
Jeremy:	What happens if the price of the stock goes up?
Stockbroker Luke:	In that case, you're in trouble if you are the short seller. Of course, if the price goes up, you must replace the shares at the higher price. This would cost you money. That's why selling short is so risky. There is no limit on how high the price can go.
Moderator:	If the price of Coca-Cola goes up to $50 per share, Jeremy would have to buy it back (or short cover) for $5,000. Since Jeremy already had $4,000 in his account from the short sale, he would have to come up with an additional $1,000 to buy back the stock. In this case, Jeremy would lose money.
Katie:	Obviously, you would only want to sell stock short if you thought the price was going to go down.
Jeremy:	I have heard of several companies that are not doing so well lately. I think their stock prices might go down. Would you be willing to help me choose stocks to short sell? I know I need a broker to complete the trades involved.
Stockbroker Luke:	Of course. However, I must tell you about the costs involved. Our company charges a fee for all short sales and short covers. The fees are determined by how much the stock sold for, or how much the short cover is worth.
Moderator:	The broker's fee is called a commission. It is charged on all transactions: buys, sales, short sales, and short covers.
Katie:	You mean that Jeremy would pay you a commission on the short sale and again on the short cover. That's what I did last month when I bought Walt Disney stock for the first time and then sold a few weeks later.
Stockbroker Luke:	Since you two seem to understand this so well, I'd like to explain one more thing about selling short. A short seller must open a margin account and deposit at least 50 percent of the value of the short sale in the account. You may use cash to open this account, but the broker won't pay you interest on your deposit.

Moderator:	The margin account is required by the Federal Reserve. It is a way of protecting brokerage firms. If the price of the stock sold short goes up too much, too fast, the short seller may not be able to buy it back to return it to the brokerage company.
Jeremy:	Thank you so much for your time. I'll go home and do some research and call you next week.
Katie:	Yes, thanks. I learned a lot, too. But I don't think short selling is for me. I'll stick to the regular way we've been buying and selling stock.

Activity 8.4
Margin Problems

Name _____

Directions: Read each situation below and fill in the blanks. Be sure to include the cost of the broker's fee in your calculations. The broker's fee is 2 percent for the short sale and 2 percent for the short cover. Show your work in the space provided.

Situation 1

A stock owner sells short 200 shares of stock at $50 per share. He buys them back for replacement (short cover) at $40 per share.

Did he make a gain or loss?_____

How much?_____

Situation 2

A stock owner sells short 100 shares of XYZ Corporation at $20 per share and has to short cover them at $40.

Did he make a gain or loss?_____

How much?_____

Situation 3

A stock owner sells short 100 shares of Apple Pie Corporation at $50 per share. The initial margin requirement is 50 percent.

How much money must be deposited in the margin account?_____

SLIDE 8.1

Bull Markets and Bear Markets

- A bull market is a stock market with rising prices over an extended time. Buying on margin can increase gains in a bull market.

- A bear market is a stock market with falling prices over an extended period of time. Selling short can increase gains in a bear market.

SLIDE 8.2

Margin Buying: The Good and the Ugly

Own Capital	Borrowed Capital	P1	Shares	P2	Position	Profit	Return	Own Capital
No Leverage Price Increases 10%								
$100	$0	$100	1	$110	$110	$10	10%	$110
Leverage 10-1 Asset Price Increases 10%								
$100	$900	$100	10	$110	$1,100	$100	100%	$200
Leverage 10-1 Asset Price Decreases 10%								
$100	$900	$100	10	$90	$900	–$100	–100%	$0

LESSON 9

BUILDING WEALTH OVER THE LONG TERM

LESSON 9
BUILDING WEALTH OVER THE LONG TERM

LESSON DESCRIPTION

The students are introduced to the case of Charlayne, a woman who becomes, accidentally, a millionaire. Charlayne's success, the students learn, was unexpected, but not a miracle. It can be explained by three widely understood rules for building wealth over the long term: saving early, buying and holding, and diversifying. The lesson uses Charlayne's decisions to illustrate each of these rules. It also addresses the risks and rewards associated with different forms of saving and investing.

INTRODUCTION

Making use of compound interest, holding for the long term, and diversification are widely regarded as successful strategies for building wealth. Albert Einstein once called compounding "the greatest mathematical discovery of all time." Time is critical: starting to save early allows savings to earn interest on the interest earned previously. Allowing savings to grow over many years is also an important strategy for success. This means that to build wealth over time, you have to hold on to your long-term savings. You can't be dipping into them frequently, or they won't compound over time in the same way. Finally, don't put all your eggs in one basket. To diversify means to hold a variety of financial assets rather than just one. To diversify is to take on many small risks rather than one large risk.

CONCEPTS

Compound interest

Diversification

Forms of saving and investing

Reward

Risk

OBJECTIVES

Students will be able to:

- Explain why an early start in saving and investing increases a household's capacity to build wealth.

- Compare the strategy of buying and holding financial assets as opposed to trading assets frequently.

- Explain the benefits of diversification.

- Identify different forms of saving and investing; discuss the costs and benefits of each.

CONTENT STANDARDS
Voluntary National Content Standards in Economics, 2nd Edition

- **Standard 2:** Effective decision making requires comparing the additional costs of alternatives with the additional benefits. Many choices involve doing a little more or a little less of something: few choices are "all or nothing" decisions.

- **Standard 10:** Institutions evolve and are created to help individuals and groups accomplish their goals. Banks, labor unions, markets, corporations, legal systems, and not-for-profit organizations are examples of important institutions. A different kind of institution, clearly defined and enforced property rights, is essential to a market economy.

- **Standard 12:** Interest rates, adjusted for inflation, rise and fall to balance the amount saved with the amount borrowed, which affects the allocation of scarce resources between present and future uses.

National Standards in K-12 Personal Finance Education, 3rd edition

- **Financial Responsibility and Decision Making Standard 1:** Take responsibility for personal financial decisions.

- **Financial Responsibility and Decision Making Standard 4:** Make financial decisions by systematically considering alternatives and consequences.

- **Planning and Money Management Standard 6:** Develop a personal financial plan.

- **Saving and Investing Standard 1:** Discuss how saving contributes to financial well-being.

- **Saving and Investing Standard 2:** Explain how investing builds wealth and helps meet financial goals.

- **Saving and Investing Standard 3:** Evaluate investment alternatives.

TIME REQUIRED

90 minutes

MATERIALS

- Slides 9.1 to 9.17

- One copy of Activities 9.1, 9.2, and 9.3 for each student

- Duplicated copies of Floor Markers 1 through 5 listing alternative assets: Savings Accounts, Certificates of Deposit, Bonds, Stocks, Real Estate

PROCEDURE

1. Tell the students that the purpose of this lesson is to explain how individuals can build wealth over the long term. **Display Slide 9.1**; introduce, briefly, the three rules of saving and investing to be emphasized in the lesson:

   1. Start early

   2. Buy and hold

   3. Diversify

2. Explain that it is possible to become a millionaire by saving regularly. The lesson will show how an ordinary wage earner named Charlayne did just that. **Display the first line of Slide 9.2**. Mask the other lines on the slide. Explain that savings of $25 per week, matched by an employer's contribution of $25 per week, comes to $2,600 per year. Show how that sum of money can grow to $2,704 at the end of the year. **Then reveal the next line of Slide 9.2** and indicate that the second-year total would be $5,624.32. Note that because all her earnings stay in her account, Charlayne is now receiving earnings on earnings.

3. Move down to year 9 of Slide 9.2 and show that Charlayne's account at that point was worth $39,171.66. Point out that in this year, Charlayne continued to save. And because she had started early and kept at it, she did amazingly well. **Display Slides 9.3 through 9.5** to show that by the time Charlayne reached retirement age, the value of her account had grown to more than $1 million.

4. **Display Slide 9.6.** Explain that when you leave money in an account to earn a return for a long time, it's not just your original money that's working for you. Instead, you earn interest on interest, or earnings on earnings.

5. **Display Slide 9.7.** Explain that Charlayne's co-worker Marcus had the same opportunity that Charlayne had. But Marcus didn't get an early start. He tried to make up for his later start by saving diligently for 36 years. **Display Slides 9.8 through 9.10.** Note that while Marcus accumulated an impressive $500,000 plus, he never caught up with Charlayne.

6. **Display Slide 9.11.** Explain that in addition to starting early, individuals also can help themselves to be financially successful if they buy and hold for the long run. To buy and hold for the long run, people should do the following:

    - Spend less than they receive.

    - Become connected to financial institutions.

    - Manage credit responsibly.

7. Develop the idea of buying and holding stocks, bonds, and mutual funds for the long run. **Display Slide 9.12.** Explain that Charlayne held on to her investments over the years as financial markets went up and down. Emphasize these points:

    - It's easy to get pessimistic when financial assets go down, but that's a bad time to sell.

    - It's easy to get optimistic when financial assets go up, but that's a bad time to buy.

    - Historically, the stock-market roller coaster ends up higher than it started out. Over long periods of time, people have done well by leaving their money in the stock market.

8. Introduce the topic of diversification. **Display Slide 9.13.** Explain that people have long known it is unwise to concentrate risk. For investors, reducing risk involves holding various assets instead of concentrating wealth on a single asset. Diversifying is taking on many small risks rather than one large risk.

9. **Distribute a copy of Activity 9.1** to each student. Explain that Activity 9.1 reviews the saving experiences of Charlayne and Marcus and explains the other two rules for building wealth over the long term. Ask the students to read Activity 9.1 and complete the **Questions for Discussion. Ask:**

    A. What are the three rules of wealth building?

    (Start early, buy and hold, and diversify.)

    B. Explain how Charlayne, the accidental millionaire, followed all three rules.

    (Charlayne began saving regularly when she started her first job. She left her savings alone even when she encountered financial difficulties. Her savings therefore grew, enhanced by compound interest. Her savings plan provided for diversification; she was able to own many different financial assets at the same time.)

10. **Distribute a copy of Activity 9.2** to each student; ask the students to read the Activity and then follow along as you explain several of its key points. **Display Slide 9.14** and discuss the advantages and disadvantages of different forms of saving and investing.

11. Place Floor Markers 1 through 5 on the floor at the edges of the room. Tell the students that each of them has $5,000 to invest. Ask them to show where they would put their money. For example, those who prefer stocks will walk over to the floor marker that says **Stocks**.

12. When all the students have chosen a position, ask them to explain their decisions. Then have them sit down again. In their explanations, the students usually mention both risk and return. Some will insist they need more information to make a decision.

13. **Display Slide 9.15.** Explain that the students may be able to make better decisions if they learn more about the

situation. The first item on Slide 9.15 is the $5,000 decision the students just made in procedure 11. Read the second item and ask the students to stand up and show where they would put their money. Some students will return to the same floor marker as before, but some will make different decisions. Go through the other items on Slide 9.15, showing how the students' movements correspond to "movements" by investors —making different decisions, depending on the circumstances.

14. **Display Slide 9.16**. Explain that the preceding activity has illustrated something about the trade-off between risk and return. If you want a safe investment, you have to settle for a low return (at the bottom of the pyramid). If you want the prospect of higher returns, you have to take risk (move toward the top of the pyramid).

15. **Display Slide 9.17**. Explain that a mutual fund pools investors' money and puts it into the markets on their behalf. Tell the students that mutual funds allow people in effect to own small amounts of many different assets. Thus mutual funds provide one means by which investors can easily diversify.

16. Ask the students to respond to the **Questions for Discussion** on Activity 9.2.

    Ask: What are the advantages and disadvantages of alternative forms of saving and investing?

    - Savings accounts: They provide a small but steady return, and they involve virtually no risk.

    - Certificates of deposit (CDs): They are safe, too, but they pay little more in interest than regular savings accounts.

- Bonds: Buying bonds is in effect lending money to a corporation or government. The return on bonds is higher than the return on savings accounts and CDs, but bonds also involve more risk.

- Stocks: When investors buy stock, they acquire ownership shares in a company. Stocks are a higher-risk investment option than bonds and savings accounts; stocks also offer the potential of higher returns.

- Real estate: People who invest in real estate face the risks and potential benefits of being a landlord. (Note that here we're talking about owning real estate as an investment—not owning our own homes.)

CLOSURE

17. Summarize the lesson briefly by stating that, over time, it is possible for ordinary people to become well off.

    Ask: What are the three rules for building wealth?

    (Start early, buy and hold, diversify.)

18. Stress the importance of diversification. Explain that it is very difficult to know in advance how stocks, bonds, or mutual funds are likely to perform in the future. **Distribute a copy of Activity 9.3** to each student (or download and print a more recent version from http://www.callan.com/research/periodic/). Explain that the Callan Periodic Table of Investment Returns illustrates how investment returns change from year to year by sector. Point out that the top row is always the top performer for each year. For example, the top performer in 2008 was U.S. bonds (abbreviated BC Agg in the table) at 5.24 percent. However, show students how badly those same bonds performed in the next two years, achieving the very

bottom return on the table both in 2009 and in 2010. Or, show students why it would have been a bad idea to dump emerging markets stocks (MSCI Emerging Markets on the table) after their devastating 53.18 percent loss in 2008. They had the worst return on the table that year, but rebounded to the best return of all in 2009 with a striking 79.02 percent gain. Explain to students that the table shows how no one can predict which asset class will be next year's winner. It pays to diversify!

ASSESSMENT
Multiple-Choice Questions

1. What are the three rules for building wealth over the long term?

   a. *Start early, buy and hold, and diversify.*
   b. Seek liquidity, loans, and limits.
   c. Trade early, trade often, trade confidently.
   d. Short buy, short cover, and buy on margin.

2. Trying to "time the market" by frequent buying and selling violates which rule of long-term savings?

   a. Start early
   b. *Buy and hold*
   c. Seize and desist
   d. Diversify

3. Which of the following would be considered the savings alternative with the highest risk and the highest reward?

   a. Bonds
   b. *Individual stocks*
   c. Certificate of deposit
   d. Stock mutual funds

4. Which of the following would be considered the savings alternative with the lowest risk and the lowest reward?

   a. Bonds
   b. Real estate
   c. *Certificate of deposit*
   d. Stocks

Constructed-Response Items

1. Roosevelt is 25 years old and has just started his job as an elementary-school teacher. He had never thought much about becoming financially independent until he attended a seminar called Three Rules to Help Teachers Become Millionaires. Based on Charlayne's experience, explain the three rules that Roosevelt learned to consider.

   (Roosevelt learned about the importance of starting to save at a young age. He also learned that it is important to buy and hold. This would allow his savings to grow from compound interest. Finally, he learned that the savings plan he chooses should provide for diversification. By investing in a mutual fund, for example, he would be able to own many different financial assets at the same time.)

2. Will has saved $3,000. He intends to use it to make a down payment on a car. But he wants to buy the car in six months, not right now. He is thinking about using the $3,000 in the meantime to buy stock in a company he has been studying. Use the concepts of risk and reward to explain why this may not be his best alternative. Suggest a better alternative for him to consider.

   (All investment decisions involve at least an implicit decision about risk and reward. Buying stock usually involves more risk than putting money into a savings account or a certificate of deposit. Investing over time and spreading the risk over several alternatives

[that is, diversifying] helps to reduce the risks associated with holding stocks. Will is planning to use his $3,000 relatively soon. If he buys stock now in one company, he gets none of the benefits that come with diversification. A better idea would be to place the $3,000 in a savings account or a certificate of deposit. The rewards would be less, but the risks would be near zero. Will could count on having his $3,000, plus a bit more, in six months.)

Note to Teachers: Is 8 Percent Reasonable?

The examples in this lesson assume a long-run return to holding stocks of 8 percent. In view of recent financial market turmoil, is that reasonable? We believe that it is, considering the following evidence:

- The longest data series on stocks reflect returns above 8 percent. One conservative calculation puts the average return at 9.23 percent (See Aswath Damodaran, "Annual Returns on Stock, T.Bonds and T.Bills: 1928 - Current," available online: http://w4.stern.nyu.edu/~adamodar/New_Home_Page/datafile/histret.html)

- As for mutual funds that people can buy, conservatively managed funds have averaged more than 8 percent for long periods of time. The Vanguard Wellington Fund, originated in 1929, currently reports a return since inception of 8.16 percent. (See The Vanguard Group, "Vanguard Wellington Fund Investor Shares," available online: https://personal.vanguard.com/us/FundsSnapshot?FundId=0021&FundIntExt=INT)

- Passively managed index funds, which do not seek to beat the market but only mirror its returns, have returns since inception of greater than 8 percent. Two widely cited examples include the Vanguard Total Stock Market Index at 8.31 percent. See The Vanguard Group, "Vanguard Total Stock Market Index Fund Investor Shares," available online: https://personal.vanguard.com/us/FundsSnapshot?FundId=0085&FundIntExt=INT) and the Vanguard 500 Index at 10.47 percent (see The Vanguard Group, "Vanguard 500 Index Fund Investor Shares," available online: https://personal.vanguard.com/us/FundsSnapshot?FundId=0040&FundIntExt=INT).

These past returns do not guarantee that future stock returns will equal or exceed 8 percent. That's part of the risk: you simply don't know how stocks will do. Almost certainly, there will be some years with hair-raising losses. However, if stocks remained below the return of other investments across the long-term future, it would amount to a reversal of long-standing patterns in the U.S. economy.

Gen i Connection

Mission 1 of the Gen i Revolution game provides an interactive introduction to the principles of wealth building: start early, buy and hold, and diversify. The principles are specifically taught and reinforced in a 4-1-1 tutorial titled, "Three Rules for Building Wealth." In the mission, students take on the role of operatives advising Angela Morrison, who has just started a new job. Angela has been told she has the opportunity to put aside money through a company plan known as a 401(k), but she doesn't know where to start. After working through the tutorials and answering question from operatives, students conclude the mission by making specific recommendations on Angela's 401(k).

In classroom experience, Mission 1 is relatively demanding and it calls for a number of computations by the students. Students do not have to do these computations by hand, however, because an interactive calculator is available within the mission.

Gen i Reflection

You have just started work on your first job, like Angela in Mission 1. Your employer has automatically enrolled you in a program to set aside $80 a month toward your retirement–but, if you wish, you may fill out paperwork to cancel your enrollment. If you do that, you'll get $80 more per month (before taxes) to spend but you won't be saving automatically for your future. Will you stay in the program or get out? Explain your answer.

ACTIVITY 9.1
STRATEGIES FOR WEALTH BUILDING

For many people who are struggling from month to month financially, even the term "wealth building" seems alien. Yet when people spend less than they receive and make good decisions, they can, slowly over time, build up the value of what they own.

Wealth building is good for individuals, families, and society because it improves people's quality of life. Whatever goods and services you would like for yourself, your family, or nation—better housing, higher-quality medical care, or anything else—they can be more nearly within reach if you engage effectively in wealth building.

The Three Rules

Many people act as if wealth building were very complex. In fact, an effective approach to wealth building can be summarized in three rules:

1. Start early.

2. Buy and hold.

3. Diversify.

Case Study: Charlayne, the Accidental Millionaire

When Charlayne was getting started in her first job, she didn't use any of her pay to play the lottery or head for the casino along with all her friends. "Come on," they said. "It's the only way you'll ever be a millionaire." She took note of the "Who Wants to Be a Millionaire?" show on television. But she was pretty sure she would never become a millionaire by hitting the lottery or answering game-show questions. Yet Charlayne became a millionaire. How?

Charlayne made an important decision when she began to work. With advice from the company's benefits manager, she decided to have $25 withheld from each weekly paycheck and put into a mutual fund account. That wasn't easy to do. Charlayne had many possible uses for an extra $25 each week. But the benefits manager persuaded her that putting $25 aside each week would be the best thing to do for her future.

Charlayne's company matched the $25 deposit she made each week. This meant an immediate doubling of Charlayne's weekly savings.

Over time, Charlayne didn't exactly forget about her account, but she didn't always monitor it closely. As printed statements arrived in the mail, generally showing that the value of her account was increasing, Charlayne became increasingly comfortable about her retirement plan.

There were times when Charlayne really would have liked to have the money she was saving. But she never considered trying to take her money out of the retirement account. Somehow she found a way to scrape through when there was a financial crisis.

When Charlayne retired, it became clear that her sustained program of investment had served her well. She had become a millionaire. Her retirement account was worth more than a million dollars. Steady payments from that account enabled Charlayne to travel and visit her grandchildren, go to movies or concerts when she wanted to, and live in comfort. She was even able to help with college expenses for next-generation members of her family.

Most people are skeptical when they're told that matched weekly contributions of $25 could make them millionaires — but the math works. The next chart shows how the money kept growing, in this case, until Charlayne became a millionaire.

The chart assumes an average return of 8 percent each year, calculated on the average yearly balance and compounded once per year.

Charlayne Becomes a Millionaire — Accidentally

Year	Beginning Balance	Addition to Principal	Return	Ending Balance
0	$0.00	$2,600.00	$104.00	$2,704.00
1	$2,704.00	$2,600.00	$320.32	$5,624.32
2	$5,624.32	$2,600.00	$553.95	$8,778.27
3	$8,778.27	$2,600.00	$806.26	$12,184.53
4	$12,184.53	$2,600.00	$1,078.76	$15,863.29
5	$15,863.29	$2,600.00	$1,373.06	$19,836.35
6	$19,836.35	$2,600.00	$1,690.91	$24,127.26
7	$24,127.26	$2,600.00	$2,034.18	$28,761.44
8	$28,761.44	$2,600.00	$2,404.92	$33,766.36
9	$33,766.36	$2,600.00	$2,805.31	$39,171.66
10	$39,171.66	$2,600.00	$3,237.73	$45,009.40
11	$45,009.40	$2,600.00	$3,704.75	$51,314.15
12	$51,314.15	$2,600.00	$4,209.13	$58,123.28
13	$58,123.28	$2,600.00	$4,753.86	$65,477.14
14	$65,477.14	$2,600.00	$5,342.17	$73,419.32
15	$73,419.32	$2,600.00	$5,977.55	$81,996.86
16	$81,996.86	$2,600.00	$6,663.75	$91,260.61
17	$91,260.61	$2,600.00	$7,404.85	$101,265.46
18	$101,265.46	$2,600.00	$8,205.24	$112,070.70
19	$112,070.70	$2,600.00	$9,069.66	$123,740.35
20	$123,740.35	$2,600.00	$10,003.23	$136,343.58
21	$136,343.58	$2,600.00	$11,011.49	$149,955.07
22	$149,955.07	$2,600.00	$12,100.41	$164,655.47
23	$164,655.47	$2,600.00	$13,276.44	$180,531.91
24	$180,531.91	$2,600.00	$14,546.55	$197,678.46
25	$197,678.46	$2,600.00	$15,918.28	$216,196.74
26	$216,196.74	$2,600.00	$17,399.74	$236,196.48
27	$236,196.48	$2,600.00	$18,999.72	$257,796.20
28	$257,796.20	$2,600.00	$20,727.70	$281,123.89
29	$281,123.89	$2,600.00	$22,593.91	$306,317.80

30	$306,317.80	$2,600.00	$24,609.42	$333,527.23
31	$333,527.23	$2,600.00	$26,786.18	$362,913.41
32	$362,913.41	$2,600.00	$29,137.07	$394,650.48
33	$394,650.48	$2,600.00	$31,676.04	$428,926.52
34	$428,926.52	$2,600.00	$34,418.12	$465,944.64
35	$465,944.64	$2,600.00	$37,379.57	$505,924.21
36	$505,924.21	$2,600.00	$40,577.94	$549,102.14
37	$549,102.14	$2,600.00	$44,032.17	$595,734.32
38	$595,734.32	$2,600.00	$47,762.75	$646,097.06
39	$646,097.06	$2,600.00	$51,791.76	$700,488.83
40	$700,488.83	$2,600.00	$56,143.11	$759,231.93
41	$759,231.93	$2,600.00	$60,842.55	$822,674.49
42	$822,674.49	$2,600.00	$65,917.96	$891,192.45
43	$891,192.45	$2,600.00	$71,399.40	$965,191.84
44	$965,191.84	$2,600.00	$77,319.35	$1,045,111.19
45	$1,045,111.19	$2,600.00	$83,712.90	$1,131,424.08

Call Charlayne lucky if you want to, but most people could do what she did. In getting her lifetime net wealth to $1 million by age 65, she followed the three rules:

1. Start early. Charlayne began saving when she turned 20, so she had 45 years in which her savings could grow.

2. Buy and hold. Charlayne bought a tiny bit more in financial assets each payday with the small amount withheld from her pay. She never touched that account as it grew over the years. Most importantly, she did not withdraw her money and spend it even when times were tough.

3. Diversify. Charlayne's retirement account was invested in a broad variety of financial assets. It wasn't put into any one asset.

And that is how Charlayne became a millionaire. Let's look at the three rules she followed in more detail.

Rule 1: The Importance of an Early Start

Rule 1 says "Start early." Money that's saved early so that it can work for a long time has a great deal of importance in overall wealth building.

An early start works well because of the magic of compounding. When you save money, you receive a return. In the case of bank accounts, that return is called interest. If you leave the interest in the account, that money also earns interest. In other words, you earn interest on interest. The longer this process goes on, the more it works for you.

Next is a different example that also shows the importance of an early start: Charlayne had a co-worker who didn't start early. Instead of starting to save at the beginning of her career, Marcus held off for 10 years. Then, like Charlayne, he saved $25 per week, and his company matched these deposits for the next 35 years. Marcus accumulated more than $500,000 by saving as he did. (See the chart.) That's a lot of money. But because Charlayne started early, she became a millionaire and Marcus did not. This example shows how you need to get an early start in order to build significant wealth in a lifetime.

But even if you don't get an early start, then (like Marcus) you can still take big steps toward wealth building. You just have to save more (or settle for less) than if you had gotten off to an early start.

Marcus's Mistake: Waiting to Start Saving

Year	Beginning Balance	Addition to Principal	Return	Ending Balance
0	$0		$0	$0
1	$0		$0	$0
2	$0		$0	$0
3	$0		$0	$0
4	$0		$0	$0
5	$0		$0	$0
6	$0		$0	$0
7	$0		$0	$0
8	$0		$0	$0
9	$0		$0	$0
10	$0.00	$2,600.00	$104.00	$2,704.00
11	$2,704.00	$2,600.00	$320.32	$5,624.32
12	$5,624.32	$2,600.00	$553.95	$8,778.27
13	$8,778.27	$2,600.00	$806.26	$12,184.53
14	$12,184.53	$2,600.00	$1,078.76	$15,863.29
15	$15,863.29	$2,600.00	$1,373.06	$19,836.35
16	$19,836.35	$2,600.00	$1,690.91	$24,127.26
17	$24,127.26	$2,600.00	$2,034.18	$28,761.44
18	$28,761.44	$2,600.00	$2,404.92	$33,766.36
19	$33,766.36	$2,600.00	$2,805.31	$39,171.66
20	$39,171.66	$2,600.00	$3,237.73	$45,009.40
21	$45,009.40	$2,600.00	$3,704.75	$51,314.15
22	$51,314.15	$2,600.00	$4,209.13	$58,123.28
23	$58,123.28	$2,600.00	$4,753.86	$65,477.14
24	$65,477.14	$2,600.00	$5,342.17	$73,419.32
25	$73,419.32	$2,600.00	$5,977.55	$81,996.86
26	$81,996.86	$2,600.00	$6,663.75	$91,260.61
27	$91,260.61	$2,600.00	$7,404.85	$101,265.46
28	$101,265.46	$2,600.00	$8,205.24	$112,070.70
29	$112,070.70	$2,600.00	$9,069.66	$123,740.35

30	$123,740.35	$2,600.00	$10,003.23	$136,343.58
31	$136,343.58	$2,600.00	$11,011.49	$149,955.07
32	$149,955.07	$2,600.00	$12,100.41	$164,655.47
33	$164,655.47	$2,600.00	$13,276.44	$180,531.91
34	$180,531.91	$2,600.00	$14,546.55	$197,678.46
35	$197,678.46	$2,600.00	$15,918.28	$216,196.74
36	$216,196.74	$2,600.00	$17,399.74	$236,196.48
37	$236,196.48	$2,600.00	$18,999.72	$257,796.20
38	$257,796.20	$2,600.00	$20,727.70	$281,123.89
39	$281,123.89	$2,600.00	$22,593.91	$306,317.80
40	$306,317.80	$2,600.00	$24,609.42	$333,527.23
41	$333,527.23	$2,600.00	$26,786.18	$362,913.41
42	$362,913.41	$2,600.00	$29,137.07	$394,650.48
43	$394,650.48	$2,600.00	$31,676.04	$428,926.52
44	$428,926.52	$2,600.00	$34,418.12	$465,944.64
45	$465,944.64	$2,600.00	$37,379.57	$505,924.21

Rule 2: Buy and Hold

The second rule is "Buy and hold." This means that to build wealth over time, you have to hold on to your long-term savings. You can't be dipping into them frequently, or they won't compound over time in the same way.

To buy and hold, you have to have your finances in order. Here are three steps to consider:

- Spend less than you receive. You do this either by earning more or spending less. You can help yourself to spend less by keeping track of where your money is going; then you cut back in places where you can save small amounts. You take the small amounts you're saving and get them out of sight so you won't be tempted to spend what's there.

- Make intelligent choices about financial institutions. Here the goal is to open and maintain accounts at mainstream financial institutions such as banks, credit unions, and brokerages. Then you can accomplish savings and budgeting goals that simply wouldn't be possible if you were still operating on a cash basis.

- Manage your credit properly. When you're managing your credit properly, you're limiting the number of credit cards you have. You're limiting your purchases to what you can pay off each month, without leaving a balance to accumulate interest that you'll also have to pay. As time goes by, your credit score goes up, making it possible for you to borrow when you have a good reason to borrow.

If you're doing all this, you can buy and hold with confidence. Remember the case of Charlayne, the accidental millionaire? Surprisingly, one of the smartest things she did with her retirement account was to neglect it. She just kept having money taken out of her paycheck and put into financial assets, no matter what.

That meant that when her financial assets declined in value because of the normal ups and downs of the market, she didn't change her strategy. Even when the market crashed and the news was full of doom and gloom, she kept her money invested. Financial assets were then, at down-market times, relatively cheap, and her regular contributions bought more than they bought when financial assets were more expensive.

When financial markets went up, those inexpensively-bought financial assets became worth a whole lot more. Charlayne saw televised accounts of people who became rich overnight playing the stock market because the values of their financial assets had become so high. But she didn't think she could play that game, so she just left her retirement fund alone. She held onto it and kept most of the gains, though she was aware that markets were always going up and down.

Over time, Charlayne came out better than many people who worked much harder trying to make more. They tried to jump in and out of the markets with their retirement money. They tried to "buy low" and "sell high," but in the end didn't do as well as people like Charlayne who stuck with the unexciting rule, "buy and hold."

Rule 3: Diversify

Somebody probably once told you, "Don't put all your eggs in one basket." This saying hearkens back to the time when knocking over a single basket might wipe out a week's supply of eggs from the henhouse—if you had put all the eggs in one basket.

To diversify is to take on many small risks rather than one large risk. If you put all of your savings into a new start-up toy company, you could get rich if the company succeeded. Or you could lose all your money if the company failed. That's like having all your eggs in one basket. The same point would apply if you were approached by someone proposing that you invest in a business opportunity. If you put all your savings there, you would again be putting your money at risk.

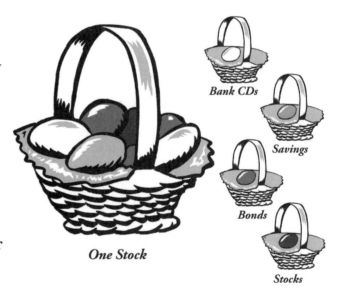

Bank CDs

Savings

Bonds

One Stock

Stocks

Any time you take one large risk with your money, you're not diversifying. That's dangerous. It's far safer to spread risks out. This means holding a variety of financial assets rather than just one.

Questions for Discussion

A. What are the three rules of wealth building?

B. Explain how Charlayne, the accidental millionaire, followed all three rules.

ACTIVITY 9.2
FORMS OF SAVING AND INVESTING

Below are some of the assets you can choose when you're thinking about where to put your money. We'll start with the safest kinds and then proceed down the list to some riskier ones.

- Savings Accounts. These accounts are kept at banks. They are insured by the federal government, and no one has ever lost even a penny of federally-insured individual savings deposits. Your money will be safe in a savings account. There are two other things to know about savings accounts, however. The first is that the money won't be as easy to spend as cash or money in a checking account. You'll have to make a separate transaction to withdraw the money from a savings account before you can spend it. The second is that the money will not earn a high return. The interest paid on savings is small but steady.

- Certificates of Deposit. Just like savings accounts, certificates of deposit (often called CDs) are made available by banks and are federally insured. When you buy a certificate of deposit, you're tying your money up for a specified period—from one month to a number of years. That means it's harder to spend than money from a checking or savings account. Before spending it, you have to wait until the term is up—or be assessed interest penalties for an early withdrawal. In return for giving the bank greater use of your money, you earn interest at rates somewhat higher than the rates paid on a savings account.

- Bonds. When you buy a bond, in effect you're making a loan. You're lending your money to the organization that issued the bond. The bond will specify under what terms you get your money repaid and what the interest will be. Some bonds are very safe, such as those issued by the federal government.

  Some bonds have medium safety, such as those issued by major corporations. Almost certainly, you'll get your money back with interest, but there's a chance that a major corporation could fail. Some bonds are known as "junk bonds." Junk bonds are high-risk investments. There is a real probability that the companies issuing them may not be able to pay investors back.

- Stocks. When you buy a stock, you're actually becoming a part-owner of a corporation. Ownership is easy to see when four people contribute equally to a new corporation and each owns a fourth of the venture. All four would share in the profits of the business and all four would have a fourth of the decision-making authority. Ownership is harder to see in today's corporations. But while modern corporations issue millions of shares, the principle is the same. If a corporation issues 200 million shares of stock, then buying a share makes you a 1 200-millionth owner of the corporation. You have a claim on 1 200-millionth of the worth of the corporation, and you have 1 200-millionth of the decision-making authority in the corporation. More importantly for investors, some corporations make payments to shareholders, called dividends. You can earn money with stocks by getting dividends, and also by the increase in the value of the stock over time, if the company does well. Of all the assets mentioned so far, stocks carry the highest risk. Some stocks are considered safe or conservative—such as stocks of well-established companies in stable markets. Other stocks are more speculative, such as those of new and growing companies. But there is always risk in holding stocks, along with the possibility of a high return.

- Real Estate. When you own your own home for a long time, it's a relatively safe investment. You pay on the home and you get a place to live. Over time, its value will likely go up and you'll pay down the amount of the loan. But it's also possible to invest in real estate as a landlord. You might buy half of a duplex and rent it out, for example. Being a landlord can be rewarding, but you should know that there are risks that come with investing in real estate (other than your own home). You are responsible for the upkeep on a rental property you own, and also for finding renters who will pay their rent on time. If something breaks, you have to fix it or hire someone to fix it. If a renter is late with a monthly payment, that doesn't excuse you from making payments to the bank on any loans you used to buy the property.

Risk and Return

You may have noticed a relationship in reading about different forms of investing. Safe investments don't offer a big return. If you choose the safety of a bank account for your money, you won't earn a lot of money on your account.

The other side of the coin is that riskier investments offer the possibility of a larger return. If they didn't, nobody would invest in them. As we move from bank assets to bonds to stocks and real estate, we're moving toward assets with many possibilities for things to go wrong—and for things to go right. A company whose stock you buy may succeed wildly or go bankrupt, or anything in between. You take that risk when you own a single company's stock.

Look at the pyramid in the accompanying figure. Toward the bottom of the pyramid there are safe places to keep money. They offer lower returns than the riskier investments noted toward the top. In investing, you should build the bottom of the pyramid with safe investments like bank accounts and certificates of deposit first. Later you can venture into riskier choices, closer to the top of the pyramid.

The Risk-Return Pyramid

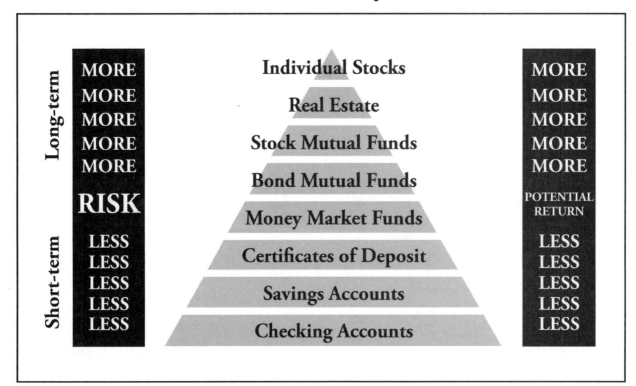

Mutual Funds

How do we get a high return while managing the risk? The answer lies in diversifying. When we diversify, we take a lot of small risks rather than a single large risk. The small risks don't add up to much, and they get smaller and smaller over time for an investor who buys and holds onto a variety of financial assets.

We might think of diversifying as a matter of buying small amounts of a lot of different stocks or bonds. But because it costs something to buy each asset, that approach would quickly get to be expensive. Fortunately, there are mutual funds that buy financial assets on behalf of individual investors.

A mutual fund gets a pool of money by accepting payments from thousands of individual investors. It invests its pool of money in a collection of assets. As that collection generates income, the mutual fund sends that income back to its investors in proportion to how much money they have put in. Because of its large size, a mutual fund can efficiently buy large numbers of different stocks and bonds. In the pyramid diagram we saw, mutual funds have lower risks than the individual stocks and bonds that make them up. For example, a single speculative stock has high risk near the top of the pyramid—but a mutual fund made up of speculative stocks has somewhat lower risks because it pools a variety of those stocks. A mutual fund made up entirely of government bonds has very low risks.

Charlayne, the accidental millionaire, owes much of her success to mutual funds. The money in her retirement fund—as is true for most retirement funds—was invested in diversified mutual funds. Charlayne indirectly owned stock in a wide variety of companies. Thus when technology stocks boomed, some of her money was in technology stocks. Also, when automotive company stocks lost value, she didn't lose nearly as much as she would have if she had owned only auto stocks.

Mutual funds are nowhere near as safe as bank deposits. When markets go down, mutual funds follow them down, depending on which stocks and bonds the funds are holding. Over time, however, mutual funds have been an excellent investment, far surpassing bank accounts and bonds in their long-term returns. Many ordinary people have become millionaires by starting early, buying and holding, and using mutual funds to diversify.

Questions for Discussion

What are the advantages and disadvantages of alternative forms of saving and investing?

- Saving Accounts
- Certificates of Deposit
- Bonds
- Stocks
- Real Estate

ACTIVITY 9.3
DIVERSIFICATION

The Callan Periodic Table of Investment Returns

Annual Returns for Key Indices (1992–2011) Ranked in Order of Performance

Rank	1992	1993	1994	1995	1996	1997	1998	1999	2000	2001	2002	2003	2004	2005	2006	2007	2008	2009	2010	2011
1	Russell 2000 Value 29.14%	MSCI Emerging Markets 74.84%	MSCI EAFE 7.78%	S&P/Citi 500 Growth 38.13%	S&P/Citi 500 Growth 23.97%	S&P/Citi 500 Growth 36.52%	S&P/Citi 500 Growth 42.16%	MSCI Emerging Markets 66.42%	Russell 2000 Value 22.83%	Russell 2000 Value 14.02%	BC Agg 10.26%	MSCI Emerging Markets 56.28%	MSCI Emerging Markets 25.95%	MSCI Emerging Markets 34.54%	MSCI Emerging Markets 32.59%	MSCI Emerging Markets 39.78%	BC Agg 5.24%	MSCI Emerging Markets 79.02%	Russell 2000 Growth 29.09%	BC Agg 7.84%
2	Russell 2000 18.41%	MSCI EAFE 32.57%	S&P/Citi 500 Growth 3.13%	S&P 500 37.58%	S&P 500 22.96%	S&P 500 33.36%	S&P 500 28.58%	Russell 2000 Growth 43.09%	BC Agg 11.63%	BC Agg 8.43%	MSCI Emerging Markets -6.00%	Russell 2000 Growth 48.54%	Russell 2000 Value 22.25%	MSCI EAFE 13.54%	MSCI EAFE 26.34%	MSCI EAFE 11.17%	Russell 2000 Value -28.92%	Russell 2000 Growth 34.47%	Russell 2000 26.85%	S&P/Citi 500 Growth 4.65%
3	MSCI Emerging Markets 11.40%	Russell 2000 Value 23.77%	S&P 500 1.32%	S&P/Citi 500 Value 36.99%	S&P/Citi 500 Value 22.00%	Russell 2000 Value 31.78%	MSCI EAFE 20.00%	S&P/Citi 500 Growth 28.24%	S&P/Citi 500 Value 6.08%	Russell 2000 2.49%	Russell 2000 Value -11.43%	Russell 2000 Value 47.25%	MSCI EAFE 20.25%	S&P/Citi 500 Value 5.82%	Russell 2000 Value 23.48%	S&P/Citi 500 Growth 9.13%	Russell 2000 -33.79%	MSCI EAFE 31.78%	Russell 2000 Value 24.50%	S&P 500 2.11%
4	S&P/Citi 500 Value 10.52%	Russell 2000 18.88%	S&P/Citi 500 Value -0.64%	Russell 2000 Growth 31.04%	Russell 2000 21.37%	S&P/Citi 500 Value 29.98%	S&P/Citi 500 Value 14.69%	MSCI EAFE 26.96%	Russell 2000 -3.02%	MSCI Emerging Markets -2.37%	MSCI EAFE -15.94%	Russell 2000 46.03%	Russell 2000 18.33%	S&P 500 4.91%	S&P/Citi 500 Value 20.81%	Russell 2000 Growth 7.05%	S&P/Citi 500 Value -34.92%	S&P/Citi 500 Growth 31.57%	MSCI Emerging Markets 19.20%	S&P/Citi 500 Value -0.48%
5	Russell 2000 Growth 7.77%	S&P/Citi 500 Value 18.61%	Russell 2000 -1.54%	Russell 2000 28.45%	Russell 2000 16.49%	Russell 2000 22.36%	BC Agg 8.70%	Russell 2000 21.26%	S&P 500 -9.11%	Russell 2000 Growth -9.23%	Russell 2000 -20.48%	MSCI EAFE 38.59%	S&P/Citi 500 Value 15.71%	Russell 2000 Value 4.71%	Russell 2000 18.37%	BC Agg 6.97%	S&P 500 -37.00%	Russell 2000 27.17%	S&P/Citi 500 Value 15.10%	Russell 2000 Growth -2.91%
6	S&P 500 7.62%	S&P 500 13.37%	Russell 2000 Value -1.82%	Russell 2000 Value 25.75%	Russell 2000 Growth 11.26%	Russell 2000 Growth 12.95%	Russell 2000 Growth 1.23%	S&P 500 21.04%	MSCI EAFE -14.17%	S&P/Citi 500 Value -11.71%	S&P/Citi 500 Value -20.85%	S&P/Citi 500 Value 31.79%	Russell 2000 Growth 14.31%	Russell 2000 4.55%	S&P 500 15.79%	S&P 500 5.49%	Russell 2000 Growth -38.54%	S&P 500 26.47%	S&P 500 15.06%	Russell 2000 -4.18%
7	BC Agg 7.40%	S&P/Citi 500 Growth 10.08%	Russell 2000 Growth -2.43%	BC Agg 18.46%	MSCI EAFE 6.05%	BC Agg 9.64%	Russell 2000 -2.55%	S&P/Citi 500 Value 12.73%	S&P/Citi 500 Growth -22.08%	S&P 500 -11.89%	S&P 500 -22.10%	S&P 500 28.68%	S&P 500 10.88%	Russell 2000 Growth 4.15%	Russell 2000 Growth 13.35%	S&P/Citi 500 Value 1.99%	S&P/Citi 500 Growth -39.22%	S&P/Citi 500 Value 21.17%	S&P/Citi 500 Growth 15.05%	Russell 2000 Value -5.50%
8	S&P/Citi 500 Growth 5.06%	BC Agg 9.75%	BC Agg -2.92%	MSCI EAFE 11.21%	MSCI Emerging Markets 6.03%	MSCI EAFE 1.78%	Russell 2000 Value -6.45%	BC Agg -0.82%	Russell 2000 Growth -22.43%	S&P/Citi 500 Growth -12.73%	S&P/Citi 500 Growth -23.59%	S&P/Citi 500 Growth 25.66%	S&P/Citi 500 Growth 6.13%	S&P/Citi 500 Growth 4.00%	S&P/Citi 500 Growth 11.01%	Russell 2000 -1.57%	MSCI EAFE -43.38%	Russell 2000 Value 20.58%	MSCI EAFE 7.75%	MSCI EAFE -12.14%
9	MSCI EAFE -12.18%	Russell 2000 Growth 1.68%	MSCI Emerging Markets -7.32%	MSCI Emerging Markets -5.21%	BC Agg 3.64%	MSCI Emerging Markets -11.59%	MSCI Emerging Markets -25.34%	Russell 2000 Value -1.49%	MSCI Emerging Markets -30.61%	MSCI EAFE -21.44%	Russell 2000 Growth -30.26%	BC Agg 4.10%	BC Agg 4.34%	BC Agg 2.43%	BC Agg 4.33%	Russell 2000 Value -9.78%	MSCI Emerging Markets -53.18%	BC Agg 5.93%	BC Agg 6.54%	MSCI Emerging Markets -18.17%

© 2012 Callan Associates Inc.

- **S&P 500** measures the performance of large capitalization U.S. stocks. The S&P 500 is a market-value-weighted index of 500 stocks that are traded on the NYSE, AMEX and NASDAQ. The weightings make each company's influence on the Index performance directly proportional to that company's market value.

- **S&P/Citigroup 500 Growth** and **S&P/Citigroup 500 Value** measure the performance of the growth and value styles of investing in large cap U.S. stocks. The indices are constructed by dividing the market capitalization of the S&P 500 Index into Growth and Value indices, using style "factors" to make the assignment. The Value Index contains those S&P 500 securities with a greater-than-average value orientation, while the Growth Index contains those securities with a greater-than-average growth orientation. The indices are market-capitalization-weighted. The constituent securities are not mutually exclusive.

- **Russell 2000** measures the performance of small capitalization U.S. stocks. The Russell 2000 is a market-value-weighted index of the 2,000 smallest stocks in the broad-market Russell 3000 Index. These securities are traded on the NYSE, AMEX and NASDAQ.

- **Russell 2000 Value** and **Russell 2000 Growth** measure the performance of the growth and value styles of investing in small cap U.S. stocks. The indices are constructed by dividing the market capitalization of the Russell 2000 Index into Growth and Value indices, using style "factors" to make the assignment. The Value Index contains those Russell 2000 securities with a greater-than-average value orientation, while the Growth Index contains those securities with a greater-than-average growth orientation. Securities in the Value Index generally have lower price-to-book and price-earnings ratios than those in the Growth Index. The indices are market-capitalization-weighted. The constituent securities are not mutually exclusive.

- **MSCI EAFE** is a Morgan Stanley Capital International Index that is designed to measure the performance of the developed stock markets of Europe, Australasia and the Far East.

- **MSCI Emerging Markets** is a Morgan Stanley Capital International Index that is designed to measure the performance of equity markets in 21 emerging countries around the world.

- **BC Agg** is the Barclays Capital Aggregate Bond Index (formerly the Lehman Brothers Aggregate Bond Index). This index includes U.S. government, corporate and mortgage-backed securities with maturities of at least one year.

Callan   Knowledge. Experience. Integrity.

SLIDE 9.1

Three Rules for Building Wealth

1. Start early.
   - Give money time to grow.

2. Buy and hold.
   - Keep your money invested.

3. Diversify.
   - Don't put all your eggs in one basket.

SLIDE 9.2

Charlayne Becomes a Millionaire – Accidentally

Year	Beginning Balance	Addition to Principal	Return	Ending Balance
0	$0.00	$2,600.00	$104.00	$2,704.00
1	$2,704.00	$2,600.00	$320.32	$5,624.32
2	$5,624.32	$2,600.00	$553.95	$8,778.27
3	$8,778.27	$2,600.00	$806.26	$12,184.53
4	$12,184.53	$2,600.00	$1,078.76	$15,863.29
5	$15,863.29	$2,600.00	$1,373.06	$19,836.35
6	$19,836.35	$2,600.00	$1,690.91	$24,127.26
7	$24,127.26	$2,600.00	$2,034.18	$28,761.44
8	$28,761.44	$2,600.00	$2,404.92	$33,766.36
9	$33,766.36	$2,600.00	$2,805.31	$39,171.66
10	$39,171.66	$2,600.00	$3,237.73	$45,009.40

SLIDE 9.3

Charlayne Becomes a Millionaire – Accidentally (Cont.)

11	$45,009.40	$2,600.00	$3,704.75	$51,314.15
12	$51,314.15	$2,600.00	$4,209.13	$58,123.28
13	$58,123.28	$2,600.00	$4,753.86	$65,477.14
14	$65,477.14	$2,600.00	$5,342.17	$73,419.32
15	$73,419.32	$2,600.00	$5,977.55	$81,996.86
16	$81,996.86	$2,600.00	$6,663.75	$91,260.61
17	$91,260.61	$2,600.00	$7,404.85	$101,265.46
18	$101,265.46	$2,600.00	$8,205.24	$112,070.70
19	$112,070.70	$2,600.00	$9,069.66	$123,740.35
20	$123,740.35	$2,600.00	$10,003.23	$136,343.58
21	$136,343.58	$2,600.00	$11,011.49	$149,955.07
22	$149,955.07	$2,600.00	$12,100.41	$164,655.47
23	$164,655.47	$2,600.00	$13,276.44	$180,531.91

SLIDE 9.4

Charlayne Becomes a Millionaire – Accidentally (Cont.)

24	$180,531.91	$2,600.00	$14,546.55	$197,678.46
25	$197,678.46	$2,600.00	$15,918.28	$216,196.74
26	$216,196.74	$2,600.00	$17,399.74	$236,196.48
27	$236,196.48	$2,600.00	$18,999.72	$257,796.20
28	$257,796.20	$2,600.00	$20,727.70	$281,123.89
29	$281,123.89	$2,600.00	$22,593.91	$306,317.80
30	$306,317.80	$2,600.00	$24,609.42	$333,527.23
31	$333,527.23	$2,600.00	$26,786.18	$362,913.41
32	$362,913.41	$2,600.00	$29,137.07	$394,650.48
33	$394,650.48	$2,600.00	$31,676.04	$428,926.52
34	$428,926.52	$2,600.00	$34,418.12	$465,944.64
35	$465,944.64	$2,600.00	$37,379.57	$505,924.21
36	$505,924.21	$2,600.00	$40,577.94	$549,102.14

SLIDE 9.5

Charlayne Becomes a Millionaire – Accidentally (Cont.)

37	$549,102.14	$2,600.00	$44,032.17	$595,734.32
38	$595,734.32	$2,600.00	$47,762.75	$646,097.06
39	$646,097.06	$2,600.00	$51,791.76	$700,488.83
40	$700,488.83	$2,600.00	$56,143.11	$759,231.93
41	$759,231.93	$2,600.00	$60,842.55	$822,674.49
42	$822,674.49	$2,600.00	$65,917.96	$891,192.45
43	$891,192.45	$2,600.00	$71,399.40	$965,191.84
44	$965,191.84	$2,600.00	$77,319.35	$1,045,111.19
45	$1,045,111.19	$2,600.00	$83,712.90	$1,131,424.08

SLIDE 9.6

The Magic of Compounding

- When you save, you earn interest.

- When you take the interest out and spend it, it stops growing.

- But if you leave the interest in your account so it can grow, you start to earn interest on the interest you earned previously.

- Interest on interest is money you didn't work for. It is money your money makes for you!

- Over time, interest on interest can increase your total savings greatly.

SLIDE 9.7

LESSON 9 - BUILDING WEALTH OVER THE LONG TERM

Marcus's Mistake

Year	Beginning Balance	Addition to Principal	Return	Ending Balance
0	$0		$0	$0
1	$0		$0	$0
2	$0		$0	$0
3	$0		$0	$0
4	$0		$0	$0
5	$0		$0	$0
6	$0		$0	$0
7	$0		$0	$0
8	$0		$0	$0
9	$0		$0	$0
10	$0.00	$2,600.00	$104.00	$2,704.00

LEARNING, EARNING, AND INVESTING FOR A NEW GENERATION © COUNCIL FOR ECONOMIC EDUCATION, NEW YORK, NY

SLIDE 9.8

LESSON 9 - BUILDING WEALTH OVER THE LONG TERM

Marcus's Mistake (Cont.)

11	$2,704.00	$2,600.00	$320.32	$5,624.32
12	$5,624.32	$2,600.00	$553.95	$8,778.27
13	$8,778.27	$2,600.00	$806.26	$12,184.53
14	$12,184.53	$2,600.00	$1,078.76	$15,863.29
15	$15,863.29	$2,600.00	$1,373.06	$19,836.35
16	$19,836.35	$2,600.00	$1,690.91	$24,127.26
17	$24,127.26	$2,600.00	$2,034.18	$28,761.44
18	$28,761.44	$2,600.00	$2,404.92	$33,766.36
19	$33,766.36	$2,600.00	$2,805.31	$39,171.66
20	$39,171.66	$2,600.00	$3,237.73	$45,009.40
21	$45,009.40	$2,600.00	$3,704.75	$51,314.15
22	$51,314.15	$2,600.00	$4,209.13	$58,123.28
23	$58,123.28	$2,600.00	$4,753.86	$65,477.14

LEARNING, EARNING, AND INVESTING FOR A NEW GENERATION © COUNCIL FOR ECONOMIC EDUCATION, NEW YORK, NY

SLIDE 9.9

LESSON 9 - BUILDING WEALTH OVER THE LONG TERM

Marcus's Mistake (Cont.)

24	$65,477.14	$2,600.00	$5,342.17	$73,419.32
25	$73,419.32	$2,600.00	$5,977.55	$81,996.86
26	$81,996.86	$2,600.00	$6,663.75	$91,260.61
27	$91,260.61	$2,600.00	$7,404.85	$101,265.46
28	$101,265.46	$2,600.00	$8,205.24	$112,070.70
29	$112,070.70	$2,600.00	$9,069.66	$123,740.35
30	$123,740.35	$2,600.00	$10,003.23	$136,343.58
31	$136,343.58	$2,600.00	$11,011.49	$149,955.07
32	$149,955.07	$2,600.00	$12,100.41	$164,655.47
33	$164,655.47	$2,600.00	$13,276.44	$180,531.91
34	$180,531.91	$2,600.00	$14,546.55	$197,678.46
35	$197,678.46	$2,600.00	$15,918.28	$216,196.74
36	$216,196.74	$2,600.00	$17,399.74	$236,196.48

SLIDE 9.10

LESSON 9 - BUILDING WEALTH OVER THE LONG TERM

Marcus's Mistake (Cont.)

37	$236,196.48	$2,600.00	$18,999.72	$257,796.20
38	$257,796.20	$2,600.00	$20,727.70	$281,123.89
39	$281,123.89	$2,600.00	$22,593.91	$306,317.80
40	$306,317.80	$2,600.00	$24,609.42	$333,527.23
41	$333,527.23	$2,600.00	$26,786.18	$362,913.41
42	$362,913.41	$2,600.00	$29,137.07	$394,650.48
43	$394,650.48	$2,600.00	$31,676.04	$428,926.52
44	$428,926.52	$2,600.00	$34,418.12	$465,944.64
45	$465,944.64	$2,600.00	$37,379.57	$505,924.21

SLIDE 9.11

Buy and Hold

In order to leave money in savings or investments, you have to do these things:

- Spend less than you receive. How?
  Perhaps you could…
  Earn more by improving your formal education or job skills.
  Spend less by using a budget to keep track of where your money is going.

- Become connected to financial institutions. How?
  Open and maintain accounts at mainstream financial institutions —
  banks, credit unions, and brokerages.

- Manage your credit responsibly. How?
  Limit the number of credit cards you have.
  Limit your purchases to amounts you can pay off each month.
  Apply for loans when you are confident that your current income (in the
  case of college loans, future income) will allow you to repay the loan.

SLIDE 9.12

The Stock Market Roller Coaster

If you buy and sell on the ups and downs, you may lose money.

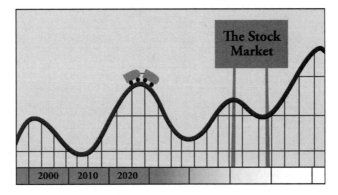

Those who have held stocks for the long term have found the ups
are greater than the downs.

SLIDE 9.13

LESSON 9 - BUILDING WEALTH OVER THE LONG TERM

Don't Put All Your Eggs in One Basket

One Stock

Bank CDs

Savings

Bonds

Stocks

With your money spread out across a variety of assets (stocks, bonds, and cash, for example), you're not hurt badly when any one asset does poorly.

SLIDE 9.14

LESSON 9 - BUILDING WEALTH OVER THE LONG TERM

Forms of Saving and Investing: Some Benefits and Costs

- Savings accounts: provide a small but steady return.

- Certificates of deposit: very safe, but instant access carries a penalty.

- Bonds: lending money to a corporation or government, with a promise of higher returns than those offered by bank savings accounts and CDs.

- Stocks: part ownership in a company, offering higher risks and, potentially, higher returns than some other investments.

- Real estate: the risks and benefits of being a landlord.

SLIDE 9.15

Investment Situations

1. You have $5,000 to invest. No other information is available.

2. You have $4,000 that you'll need six months from now.

3. You inherited $10,000 from your great-aunt; she has suggested that you save it for use in your old age.

4. You are just starting a career and can save $50 per month for retirement.

5. A new baby arrives, and Mom and Dad plan to save $100 a month for the child's college education.

SLIDE 9.16

The Pyramid of Risk and Return

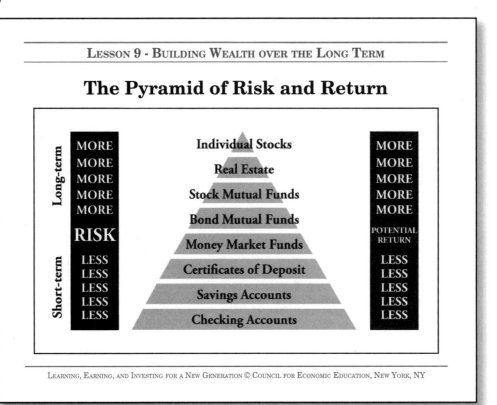

SLIDE 9.17

Mutual Funds

- A mutual fund pools investors' money.

- The fund puts its investors' money into the markets on their behalf.

- In effect, investors own small amounts of many different assets.

- Mutual funds enable investors to avoid the risk that comes from owning any one asset. In other words, mutual funds make it easy to diversify.

Floor Marker 1

Savings Account

Floor Marker 2

Certificate of Deposit

Floor Marker 3

Bonds

LESSON 9 - BUILDING WEALTH OVER THE LONG TERM

Floor Marker 4

Stocks

LEARNING, EARNING, AND INVESTING FOR A NEW GENERATION © COUNCIL FOR ECONOMIC EDUCATION, NEW YORK, NY

LESSON 9 - BUILDING WEALTH OVER THE LONG TERM

Floor Marker 5

Real Estate

LEARNING, EARNING, AND INVESTING FOR A NEW GENERATION © COUNCIL FOR ECONOMIC EDUCATION, NEW YORK, NY

LESSON 10

FINANCIAL INSTITUTIONS IN THE U.S. ECONOMY

LESSON 10
FINANCIAL INSTITUTIONS IN THE U.S. ECONOMY

LESSON DESCRIPTION

The students participate in a brief trading activity that shows how financial institutions bring savers and borrowers together, thus channeling saving into investment. The students then learn how a growing business gains access to funds, often starting as a proprietorship but at some point "going public" to issue securities that are then traded in secondary markets. Students see that although popular attention is focused on these secondary markets, it is in primary markets that firms actually gain access to capital. These points are reinforced through a case study of Apple's "missing billionaire," a co-founder of the famed technology company who left after only two weeks.

INTRODUCTION

Saving occurs when people consume less than their income, making growth of their personal wealth possible. However, that saving cannot help the economy achieve its full potential unless it is channeled into investment. Financial institutions provide the means for this channeling. Banks provide checking and savings accounts for depositors and make loans to qualified borrowers. These loans can go to individuals for use in making big-ticket purchases, but they also can help businesses grow. Businesses get access to funds through a variety of institutions—as small as the corner bank or as large as international stock exchanges.

CONCEPTS

Corporation

Debt financing

Economic investment

Equity financing

Financial institutions

Financial investment

Limited liability

Partnership

Primary markets

Proprietorship

Secondary markets

Venture capitalist

OBJECTIVES

Students will be able to:

- Identify the role of financial institutions in channeling saving to investment.

- Explain the difference between primary and secondary markets.

- Explain the difference between debt and equity financing.

- Explain how a small business can grow if it has a good business plan and access to funds.

- Describe the characteristics of proprietorships, partnerships, and corporations.

CONTENT STANDARDS
Voluntary National Content Standards in Economics, 2nd Edition

- **Standard 10:** Institutions evolve and are created to help individuals and groups accomplish their goals. Banks, labor unions, markets, corporations, legal systems, and not-for-profit organizations are examples of important institutions. A different kind of institution, clearly defined and enforced property rights, is essential to a market economy.

National Standards in K-12 Personal Finance Education, **3rd edition**

- **Saving and Investing Standard 1:** Discuss how saving contributes to financial well-being.

- **Saving and Investing Standard 2:** Explain how investing builds wealth and helps meet financial goals.

TIME REQUIRED

90 minutes

MATERIALS

- Slides 10.1, 10.2, 10.3, 10.4, and 10.5

- Activity 10.1, duplicated and cut apart to provide a card for each student

- A copy of Activity 10.2 and 10.3 for each student

PROCEDURE

1. Tell the students that this lesson will help them understand the importance of financial institutions such as banks and financial markets in the economy. Explain that smoothly functioning financial markets are critical to our nation's economy. People who have a lot of saved money—for example, older people who have saved all of their lives—often do not have highly productive uses for that money. At the same time, others (for example, young entrepreneurs with ideas for new enterprises) could productively employ that money and provide a return to the saver. The financial system helps both sets of parties by channeling funds from saving into investment. The results include access to capital, healthy returns to savers, and the overall creation of wealth and jobs in the process.

2. Tell the students they are going to participate in a brief trading activity. **Distribute a card from Activity 10.1** to each student. Tell the students that

they should try to find someone who wants *exactly* what they have and has *exactly* what they want.

3. Allow about two minutes for the students to trade. Discuss the following:

    A. How many of you were able to find someone who had what you wanted?

    (No one.)

    B. How many of you were willing to lend money if you could earn interest?

    (Five. There may be more than five if additional copies of Activity 10.1 were used.)

    C. How many of you wanted to borrow money and pay interest on the loan?

    (Five.)

    D. Why didn't you borrow from and lend to one another?

    (No one wanted to borrow the amount I had to lend. No one wanted to lend the amount I wanted to borrow.)

    E. How many of you wanted to buy stock?

    (Four.)

    F. How many of you wanted to sell stock?

    (Four.)

    G. Why didn't you buy from and sell to one another?

    (Each wanted to buy a stock other than the stock available for sale.)

    H. How many of you wanted to buy bonds?

    (Two.)

I. How many of you wanted to sell bonds?

(Two.)

J. Why didn't you buy from and sell to one another?

(Each wanted to buy a bond other than the bonds available for sale.)

4. Point out that the students have just experienced how hard it may be to find partners for making exchanges. Without intermediaries, you have to find someone whose financial goals match up just right with yours. **Display Slide 10.1.** Tell the students that in market economies, people develop financial institutions, such as banks and credit unions, to make it easier for these interactions to occur. Financial institutions are intermediaries that channel savings into economic investment. There are many examples of financial institutions, including life insurance companies, investment companies, finance companies, and pension funds. Financial institutions also provide a way for individuals and companies to invest.

5. Tell the students that financial markets work better if they can bring together large numbers of savers and investors. You may want to use the analogy of a neighborhood rummage sale, compared with eBay. If you want to buy or sell a particular baseball card, it is unlikely that you could make a good transaction among only the people who have come to the rummage sale. On eBay, in contrast, the market consists of baseball card buyers and sellers around the world.

Explain that financial markets can bring together savers and investors from around the world.

6. **Distribute a copy of Activity 10.2** to each student and explain that students will learn about Apple's missing billionaire—someone who might have made billions of dollars from his early involvement in the technology company Apple, but ended up making only $1,500. Tell the students they will read the story and then study a chart with numbered statements about different forms of business organization. Tell them to be prepared to say which numbered statement applies to the listed statements about Apple's financial history. Allow 15 minutes for students to read and prepare, individually or in groups.

7. **Display Slides 10.2 and 10.3** and remind students that they contain the numbered statements from Activity 10.2 that they will be using.

8. **Display Slide 10.4** and ask the students for their responses to the questions on the slide (A through C on the first slide). Remind them that you are looking for a numbered statement about advantages and disadvantages of different forms of business organization.

A. In the early years when Steve Jobs worked by himself, he knew he was good at marketing, but he missed the technical skills of his friend Steve Wozniak.

8. (Sole proprietorship-disadvantage: Management's human resources limited to one person.)

B. Worried about his responsibility for Apple's debts, Ronald Wayne left the young company after only two weeks.

16. (Partnership-disadvantage: Personal responsibility for the business's debts; unlimited liability.)

C. The death of Steve Jobs in 2011 was difficult for Apple, but the corporation continued operations without interruption.

18. (Corporation-advantage: Unlimited life, even after death of founders.)

9. **Display Slide 10.5** and continue with student responses to the questions on the slide (D through F on this slide).

D. Apple shareholders have worried about executives' determination to spend whatever money it takes to defeat the rival smartphone operating system, Android, fearing the impact on profits and the value of their investment.

22. (Corporation-disadvantage: Separation of ownership [shareholders] from control [executives].)

E. When Steve Jobs and Steve Wozniak were running Apple in the early days, they had disputes about required components for new designs.

14. (Partnership-disadvantage: Conflicts between partners possible.)

F. It was easy for Steve Wozniak to start operating as a free-lancer for occasional technology jobs in California in the 1970s.

1. (Sole proprietorship-advantage: Easy to start up and shut down.)

CLOSURE

10. **Distribute a copy of Activity 10.3** on "going public" to each student. (This activity reinforces basic points first made in Lesson 7.) Explain that "going public" is a term that applies to an Initial Public Offering of stock. It is often the concluding phase of a successful startup that might have begun as a proprietorship or partnership. Give the students 15 minutes to read the activity and tell them that you will be asking for some classifications when they have finished reading.

11. Review the point that IPOs are arranged in the primary market, and that firms face additional regulations and reporting requirements when they go public. Remind them of the two most important points about the secondary market, in which existing shares change hands:

• Almost all daily stock market news is about the secondary market.

• Companies do not receive any funding when their stock trades on the secondary markets.

12. With students, go over Activity 10.3's **Questions for Discussion:**

Classify each of the following situations as being part of the primary market or the secondary market:

A. A college endowment fund buys 40,000 shares of IBM stock on the New York Stock Exchange. *(secondary)*

B. An excited reporter says, "Intel Corp. shares skyrocketed in trading today, with investors pushing the share price sharply higher." *(secondary)*

C. Facebook, formerly a secretive and closely held enterprise, found that it would have to disclose financial data it had kept hidden before its widely celebrated Initial Public Offering. *(primary)*

D. A teacher leading a class in a stock market competition says, "Participants may choose any stock traded on the major exchanges." *(secondary)*

E. The evening business news report says, "Venture capitalists found that a big gamble paid off today, walking away with a small fortune when the long-shot technology company GACC went public." *(primary)*

ASSESSMENT
Multiple-Choice Questions

1. What is the primary function of the economy's financial institutions?

    a. *Bringing borrowers and lenders together*
    b. Manufacturing real goods and services
    c. Regulating the supply of money and the U.S. government budget
    d. Making sure people have enough money to meet their monthly expenses

2. Which of the following is considered a financial institution?

    a. A manufacturer of farm equipment
    b. *A life insurance company*
    c. A small business seeking an operating loan
    d. A saver interested in getting a good return at a low risk

3. Which of the following is considered a major disadvantage of organizing a business enterprise as a partnership?

    a. The partnership has an unlimited life.
    b. The partnership is the costliest form of business organization to start up and shut down.
    c. The partnership is required to register as a public corporation with the government.
    d. *The partnership makes all of the partners liable for the obligations of the partnership.*

4. What does it mean for a corporation to "go public"?

    a. It advertises and sells its products publicly for the first time.
    b. It uses publicly funded facilities such as airports and highways for the first time.
    c. *It makes an Initial Public Offering (IPO) of its stock.*
    d. It becomes regulated by a state or federal Public Utilities Commission.

Constructed-Response Items

1. Imagine a world in which a used car buyer would arrange to obtain an auto loan directly with someone seeking to lend money. Describe what it would take to arrange a $12,000 loan with monthly payments in such a world. In the real world, do banks need to find someone willing to lend $12,000 in order to make the loan? Explain your answer.

    (In such a world, someone seeking to borrow $12,000 to buy a used car would need to find a lender willing to give up the $12,000 in return for monthly payments over a period of years. As in the simulation game played in this lesson, differences in amounts desired to borrow or lend would prevent a transaction. In real-world banking, the bank pools the deposits of customers and lends money on their behalf to qualified loan applicants. In this way it earns the money necessary to pay interest on deposits. Because the bank pools many customers' deposits, no single customer needs to have a spare $12,000 in order for the bank to make the loan.)

2. History records that, in its early days, Apple Computer had difficulty coming up with the money it needed to operate. Banks and venture capitalists were unsure that Apple's business would succeed well enough to guarantee repayment. Were the banks and venture capitalists being overly cautious, or should they have foreseen Apple's success? Explain your answer.

(Accept any well-supported answer. Some students will say that Apple's success should have been so obvious that the banks and venture capitalists were in fact being overly cautious. Others will point out that small technology companies frequently go out of business, and that Apple's success was not obvious before the fact.)

Gen i and EconEdLink Connection

There is no mission in the Gen i Revolution game that directly addresses the subject matter of this lesson. Two missions, however, are indirectly related to the content. In Mission 11, "Advise a Gen i donor on her $10 million investment," students learn about the investment alternatives that have been created by financial institutions. In Mission 12, "Show Jasmine what determines stock prices," students learn about the role of the stock market in bringing together buyers and sellers of securities.

On EconEdLink, "Business Ownership: How Sweet It Can Be!" is an interactive lesson based on real-life entrepreneurs who started businesses producing chocolate candy and cookies. It explores alternative forms of business organization and reinforces concepts from this lesson (http://www.econedlink.org/lessons/index.php?lid=533&type=educator). Another lesson, "It's a Not So Wonderful Life," explains the role of banks as financial intermediaries and also goes into detail about how banks create money (http://www.econedlink.org/lessons/index.php?lid=698&type=educator).

Gen i Reflection

The stocks in the Gen i Revolution game are issued by corporations. Smaller enterprises are often organized as partnerships or proprietorships. Would you rather work for a corporation, or as a partner in a small business with your best friend, or as a sole proprietor? Explain your choice.

ACTIVITY 10.1
SAVE, LEND, BUY, SELL CARDS

Directions to the teacher: Duplicate this sheet as necessary and cut cards from it in sufficient quantity to provide each student with one card.

You have saved $10,000. You are willing to lend the money if the borrower will pay interest.	You want to borrow $17,000 to buy a new car. You are willing to pay interest on the loan.
You have saved $3,000. You are willing to lend the money if the borrower will pay interest.	You want to sell MSTrans Incorporated stock to expand your business.
You have saved $20,000. You want to buy stock in Aerostar Corporation.	You need money to send your daughter to college. You are willing to sell your Burger Barn stock.
You have saved $14,000. You are willing to lend the money if the borrower will pay interest.	You want to borrow $5,000 to go on vacation. You are willing to pay interest on the loan.
You have saved $6,000 and want to buy StarPics stock.	You want to build a factory. You want to sell DelMouse corporate bonds to raise the money to build the factory.
You have saved $15,000. You want to buy Automotors corporate bonds.	You are the state government. You want to borrow $500,000 to repair roads. You want to sell bonds to do this.
You have saved $50,000. You want to buy NewsAmerica stock.	You want to borrow $10,000 to put an addition on your home. You are willing to pay interest on the loan.
You have saved $7,000. You are willing to lend the money if the borrower will pay interest.	You want to borrow $800 to buy a new refrigerator. You are willing to pay interest on the loan.
You want to sell your Electroworks stock and use the money to make a down payment on a house.	You want to buy 500 shares of Medicine Makers stock.
You have saved $20,000 and you want to buy LV Power and Light corporate bonds.	You want to sell your shares of Invest Up stock.
You have saved $2,000. You are willing to lend the money if the borrower will pay interest.	You want to borrow $15,000 to buy parts for your small computer company. You are willing to pay interest on the loan.

ACTIVITY 10.2
APPLE'S MISSING BILLIONAIRE

Many people know the story of how Steve Jobs and Steve Wozniak started Apple Computer in a California garage and later transformed it into the world's largest technology company. But few people know about Apple's missing billionaire, Ronald Wayne. Understanding the story requires knowing something about the three basic forms of business organization: *sole proprietorship, partnership,* and *corporation.*

If you have ever been paid to cut a lawn or look after children for a neighbor, you have been a sole proprietor: the only owner of a business, who receives all the profits and bears all the losses. When Steve Jobs did electronics work on the side as a young free-lancer, he was a sole proprietor.

In the early years, however, Jobs did little without his friend Wozniak, who actually invented the Apple I computer. Jobs got a local computer store to agree to buy 50 of the computers at $500 each—but neither he nor Wozniak had enough money to buy necessary parts for assembly. With the computer store's 50-computer order in hand, Jobs persuaded a supplier to provide the parts on 30 days' credit. Jobs and Wozniak built and delivered the computers, collected payment from the computer store, and turned around to pay the parts supplier on time. To continue financing their company, they sold personal possessions such as a prized Volkswagen bus.

Jobs and Wozniak soon learned that makeshift financing would not be sufficient to fuel Apple's growth. That's where the missing billionaire came in. Jobs and Wozniak called on their older friend, Ronald Wayne, for help. Wayne drew up a contract that officially made Apple a partnership, a business owned and managed by two or more individuals. (In a partnership the owners receive all the profits and bear all the losses.) The original contract gave Jobs 45 percent, Wozniak 45 percent, and Wayne 10 percent of the new company.

In a partnership, typically, all partners are responsible for the partnership's debts. Only two weeks after joining the partnership, Wayne got nervous because Jobs had borrowed $15,000 for materials on a new computer contract. (Jobs's borrowing inspired the card in Activity 10.1 that says "You want to borrow $15,000 to buy parts for your small computer company.") Wayne feared that he had more to lose because he had invested more personal money than the youthful Jobs and Wozniak. "I was getting too old, and those two were whirlwinds," Wayne later told an interviewer. (Source: Nick Allen, "U.S. Pensioner Gave Up £15bn Slice of Apple," *The Telegraph*, April 23, 2010, available online: http://www.telegraph.co.uk/technology/apple/7624539/US-pensioner-Ronald-Wayne-gave-up-15bn-slice-of-Apple.html.)

That is why Ronald Wayne gave up 10 percent of Apple Computer. He received payment in full for $1,500 later, when a check arrived in the mail.

Apple periodically struggled with finding enough funding. Keep in mind that in the early years, no one knew Apple would later succeed as it did. Some of its funding came from *venture capitalists,* investors who make money available for innovative projects. Venture capitalists face high probabilities of losses but also the possibility of large returns.

In 1980, Apple made an initial public offering of stock, offering its shares for general sale for the first time. The IPO set Apple's total value at $1.8 billion. After expenses, the proceeds of the IPO went to fund Apple's expansion. At this point it became a fully public corporation. Today anyone can buy Apple stock.

When Apple issues new stock as it did in 1980, it is engaging in *equity financing*. People who buy the stock get ownership shares or equity in the corporation. When Apple borrows money instead of issuing stock, it is engaged in *debt financing*. Debt and equity create different risks for the firm. Firms that use debt financing have to pay back the money on time or face severe consequences. Equity financing requires no fixed repayment—the firm can return large sums to stockholders if it is doing well, or it can return little or nothing if it is not doing well. But in using equity financing, a firm is selling off pieces of itself, whereas debt financing leaves ownership intact. Firms use a mix of debt and equity financing to get the funds used for their operations and growth.

In Figure 1 you will see numbered statements that apply to partnerships, proprietorships, and corporations. Be prepared to say which numbered statement applies to the listed statements (A. through F.) about Apple's financial history.

Figure 1: Advantages and Drawbacks of Different Organizational Forms

Sole proprietorship advantages	1. Easy to start up and shut down
	2. Proprietor has control over profits and operations
	3. Pride of being the only owner
	4. Lower taxes (no corporate income taxes)
Sole proprietorship disadvantages	5. Personal responsibility for the business's debts (unlimited liability)
	6. Difficulty in raising funds
	7. Responsibility for all losses
	8. Management's human resources limited to one person
Partnership advantages	9. Easier to raise funds than fund raising in a sole proprietorship
	10. Management's human resources go beyond one person
	11. Pride of being (with partners) the owners
	12. Lower taxes (no corporate income taxes)
Partnership disadvantages	13. Profits are split among partners, rather than going solely to proprietor
	14. Conflicts between partners possible
	15. Possible instability when a partner leaves
	16. Personal responsibility for the business's debts (unlimited liability)
Corporation advantages	17. Transferability of shares to anyone who wants to own stock
	18. Unlimited life, even after death of founders
	19. Liability of shareholders is limited to their investment
Corporation disadvantages	20. Costly to start up and shut down
	21. Higher taxes (subject to corporate income taxes)
	22. Separation of ownership (shareholders) from control (executives)

A. In the early years when Steve Jobs worked by himself, he knew he was good at marketing, but he missed the technical skills of his friend Steve Wozniak.

B. Worried about his responsibility for Apple's debts, Ronald Wayne left the young company after only two weeks.

C. The death of Steve Jobs in 2011 was difficult for Apple, but the corporation continued operations without interruption.

D. Apple shareholders have worried about executives' determination to spend whatever money it takes to defeat the rival smartphone operating system, Android, fearing the impact on profits and the value of their investment.

E. When Steve Jobs and Steve Wozniak were running Apple in the early days, they had disputes about required components for new designs.

F. It was easy for Steve Wozniak to get paid as a free-lancer for occasional technology jobs in California in the 1970s.

ACTIVITY 10.3
WHAT IT MEANS TO "GO PUBLIC"

It is a big day in the life of an enterprise when it "goes public"—that is, it has an Initial Public Offering (IPO) of its stock. Until it is big enough to go public, it typically has to patch together whatever financing it can. Even if it has good products and a bright future, it may be limited in its ability to raise money to support its growth.

The simplest form of business organization, the sole proprietorship, is often quite limited in the funds it can raise. Bank loans and the owner's savings are possibilities. As soon as a proprietorship gives someone a piece of the enterprise in return for financing, it has turned into something different, typically a partnership. Funding for partnerships is limited to the partners' resources and what they can borrow. A growing enterprise may also attract the attention of investors called *venture capitalists* who specialize in identifying promising startups and providing funding in return for a share of the new enterprise. Because venture capitalists are working with risky startups, they require a high rate of return on successful projects to offset the losses that naturally occur some of the time. For venture capitalists, an IPO often represents a payday—a time when they can cash in their share of a new enterprise by selling their shares on the now-available open market.

When the enterprise goes public, it issues shares of stock that give each shareholder a piece of the company. The shareholders in turn provide funding that goes to the enterprise. Going public gives an enterprise access to the global markets. The amount of funds potentially available will be limited only by the quality of the firm's products and plans.

In our economy, IPOs are arranged by the set of institutions called the *primary market*. The primary market consists of those offering stock, those buying it, and the brokerages that bring buyers and sellers together. In the primary market, firms give up some control and they receive funding. They also take on substantial new requirements to report on their activities and finances to regulatory agencies. Reporting requirements are much stricter for public enterprises.

Once stock has been issued, the new shareholders may trade or sell their shares. For example, an investor who initially bought Apple shares in an IPO might convert those shares to cash by selling them on a stock exchange. This transaction is part of the *secondary market,* in which existing shares of stock are bought and sold. There are two important things to know about the secondary market:

1. Almost all of the stock market news you hear daily is about the secondary market. This includes all of the reporting about stock prices that went up and down on major stock exchanges. It also includes all of the reporting on stock market indicators.

2. Companies do not receive any funding when their stock trades on the secondary markets. Think about it: If Pat one day buys 100 shares of Apple stock from Terry, the money goes to Terry—not Apple. Years ago, when the shares were first issued, the money did go to Apple. But every time the shares have been traded on a stock exchange since then, money and shares changed hands without the money going to Apple.

Questions for Discussion

Classify each of the following situations as being part of the primary market or the secondary market:

A. A college endowment fund buys 40,000 shares of IBM stock on the New York Stock Exchange.

B. An excited reporter says, "Intel Corp. shares skyrocketed in trading today, with investors pushing the share price sharply higher."

C. Facebook, formerly a secretive and closely held enterprise, found that it would have to disclose financial data it had kept hidden before its widely celebrated Initial Public Offering.

D. A teacher leading a class in a stock market competition says, "Participants may choose any stock traded on the major exchanges."

E. The evening business news report says, "Venture capitalists found that a big gamble paid off today, walking away with a small fortune when the long-shot technology company GACC went public."

SLIDE 10.1

Matching Savers and Borrowers

1. It is hard to match up savers' goals and borrowers' requests directly.

2. Financial institutions do this job; for example:
   - Banks pool savers' money together and lend from the pool.
   - Life insurance companies use policyholders' funds to build up a pool from which survivors can be paid.
   - Pension funds use workers' saved money to lend and invest, using the returns to finance the workers' retirements.

3. Financial institutions provide ways for people to save and invest.

SLIDE 10.2

Advantages and Drawbacks

Sole proprietorship advantages	1.	Easy to start up and shut down
	2.	Proprietor has control over profits and operations
	3.	Pride of being the only owner
	4.	Lower taxes (no corporate income taxes)
Sole proprietorship disadvantages	5.	Personal responsibility for the business's debts (unlimited liability)
	6.	Difficulty in raising funds
	7.	Responsibility for all losses
	8.	Management's human resources limited to one person
Partnership advantages	9.	Easier to raise funds than fund raising in a sole proprietorship
	10.	Management's human resources go beyond one person
	11.	Pride of being (with partners) the owners
	12.	Lower taxes (no corporate income taxes)

SLIDE 10.3

Advantages and Drawbacks (Cont.)

Partnership disadvantages	13. Profits are split among partners, rather than going solely to proprietor 14. Conflicts between partners possible 15. Possible instability when a partner leaves 16. Personal responsibility for the business's debts (unlimited liability)
Corporation advantages	17. Transferability of shares to anyone who wants to own stock 18. Unlimited life, even after death of founders 19. Liability of shareholders is limited to their investment
Corporation disadvantages	20. Costly to start up and shut down 21. Higher taxes (subject to corporate income taxes) 22. Separation of ownership (shareholders) from control (executives)

SLIDE 10.4

Apple's Financial History-1

A. In the early years when Steve Jobs worked by himself, he knew he was good at marketing but missed the technical skills of his friend Steve Wozniak.

B. Worried about his responsibility for Apple's debts, Ronald Wayne left the young company after only two weeks.

C. The death of Steve Jobs in 2011 was difficult for Apple, but the corporation continued operations without interruption.

SLIDE 10.5

Apple's Financial History-2

D. Apple shareholders have worried about executives' determination to spend whatever money it takes to defeat the rival smartphone operating system, Android, fearing the impact on profits and the value of their investment.

E. When Steve Jobs and Steve Wozniak were running Apple in the early days, they had disputes about required components for new designs.

F. It was easy for Steve Wozniak to get paid as a free-lancer for occasional technology jobs in California in the 1970s.

LESSON 11
RESEARCHING COMPANIES

LESSON 11
RESEARCHING COMPANIES

LESSON DESCRIPTION

Applying economic reasoning, the students gather information about investment possibilities. They learn that the cost of acquiring information must be compared to the anticipated benefit the information will provide. The students recognize that among specialists there is intense competition to find information about companies. They select companies for their research by participating in a classroom drawing and by listing companies they know.

INTRODUCTION

In the search for information about investment possibilities, individual investors are not alone. Banks, brokerage firms, and mutual funds employ analysts to find and interpret information, competing with one another as they try to win customers. Because these specialists produce detailed information for all sectors of the economy, the field is heavily tracked over. It is therefore difficult for individuals to find surprises—to find companies likely to produce *unexpected* high returns. Acknowledging these difficulties, this lesson surveys certain practices often used to research investment possibilities, focusing especially on the fundamental analysis of company performance.

CONCEPTS

Alternatives

Choice

Fundamental analysis

Opportunity cost

Scarcity

OBJECTIVES

Students will be able to:

- Develop criteria to use in choosing stocks.

- Use criteria to choose among stock investment possibilities.

- Identify the cost of seeking more information.

- Recognize and apply basic techniques of fundamental analysis.

CONTENT STANDARDS

Voluntary National Content Standards in Economics, **2nd Edition**

- **Standard 2:** Effective decision making requires comparing the additional costs of alternatives with the additional benefits. Many choices involve doing a little more or a little less of something: few choices are "all-or-nothing" decisions.

- **Standard 10:** Institutions evolve and are created to help individuals and groups accomplish their goals. Banks, labor unions, markets, corporations, legal systems, and not-for-profit organizations are examples of important institutions. A different kind of institution, clearly defined and enforced property rights, is essential to a market economy.

National Standards in K-12 Personal Finance Education, **3rd edition**

- **Financial Responsibility and Decision Making Standard 1:** Take responsibility for personal financial decisions.

- **Financial Responsibility and Decision Making Standard 2:** Find and evaluate financial information from a variety of sources.

- **Financial Responsibility and Decision Making Standard 4:** Make financial decisions by systematically considering alternatives and consequences.

- **Saving and Investing Standard 3:** Evaluate investment alternatives.

TIME REQUIRED

75 minutes

MATERIALS

- Slides 11.1, 11.2, 11.3, and 11.4

- One copy of Activity 11.1 for each student

- Cards cut from Activity 11.2 to use for a classroom drawing

PROCEDURE

1. Tell the students that this lesson focuses on research investors might carry out in order to increase chances for success in making investments. Show the students some stock pages from a newspaper or the home page of a financial website. Go through the listings slowly and note the many stocks, bonds, and mutual funds that are available for investors to buy.

2. Explain that about 8,000 firms are listed on the New York Stock Exchange, the oldest stock market in the United States. Thousands more are listed on the NASDAQ Stock Market, and still more are listed on stock exchanges based in other countries. Out of all these companies, how does one pick the stocks most likely to increase in price?

3. **Display Slide 11.1** and discuss the guidelines it presents for applying economic reasoning to researching stocks. Stress the point that there is a great deal of information available about possible investments. The important thing at the outset is to not get overwhelmed. Investors engaged in research face a classic scarcity problem: an investor's time is limited, while the available information is vast.

4. **Display Slide 11.2** Note that there is intense competition among financial institutions to find information about companies. Analysts doing research for these institutions are not looking merely for good companies. It is easy to identify good companies, and good companies don't necessarily provide high returns on investments. That is because good companies typically attract many investors, and high demand pushes stock prices up for those companies, decreasing investors' chances to make big gains. Instead of searching merely for good companies, institutional researchers look for companies that might generate *surprises:* unexpected high returns. Paradoxically, surprises are hard to find precisely because so many people are trying to find them. In a field that gets examined so carefully, it is difficult for individuals to get in early, ahead of others, on the purchase of stocks that are underpriced and likely to produce (unexpected) high returns.

5. **Distribute a copy of Activity 11.1** to each student. Explain that this handout provides a useful tool for summarizing important characteristics of various companies. We will explain the sections of the handout shortly, but first we need to decide which companies to study.

6. Explain that many economists believe it is not possible to predict which stocks will outperform others. Stocks picked at random sometimes perform as well as stocks picked by experts. Conduct a brief demonstration to illustrate picking stocks by random—a low-cost ap-

proach. Place the cards you have cut out from Activity 11.2 in a container in front of the room for a drawing. Explain that the names of 30 well-known companies and their stock symbols are marked on cards in the container. Walk around the room to each student's desk; ask each student to draw the name of one company from the container. Tell the students to enter the names of their companies into the chart labeled **Company Selected in the Classroom Drawing** in Activity 11.1. Now that each student has one company to study, let's examine some other approaches.

7. Explain that another easy method for selecting stocks is by focusing on companies one knows. If you have noticed a company that seems popular—its stores are crowded, or your friends make favorable comments about its products or services—perhaps you should look further into that company. Ask the students to identify companies whose products they buy, stores they shop in, or games they play. Tell the students to add the names of three of these companies in the remaining charts in Activity 11.1.

8. A more time-consuming method of choosing stocks involves researching a company's financial information. **Display Slide 11.3**. This slide introduces an approach for analyzing stocks called *fundamental analysis*. Fundamental analysis involves the use of basic information about a company—information about its size, sales, earnings, and stock prices—to make decisions.

9. Now that the students have identified companies to study, they need to obtain some information about these companies. Explain that information is abundant and may be obtained from many different sources. Activity 11.1 suggests that students visit the websites http://finance.yahoo.com or www.morningstar.

com. *Value Line* publications are also good sources, providing information in print and electronically on stocks, mutual funds, and other products. *Value Line Ratings & Reports,* for example, supplies one-page reports on approximately 1,700 companies and more than 90 industries. *Value Line Ratings & Reports* is often available in libraries or from brokerage firms.

10. To elaborate on the fundamental analysis approach, **display Slide 11. 4.** Explain the terms introduced on the slide that correspond with the terms in Activity 11.1. Also refer to the completed chart on Microsoft in Activity 11.1 to help illustrate the following points:

- **Symbol:** A stock symbol or ticker symbol is an abbreviation of the company name to be used for purposes of trading. Ask the students to note, for example, that the symbol for Microsoft is MSFT.

- **Stock exchange:** The two largest stock markets in the United States are the New York Stock Exchange (NYSE) and the NASDAQ Stock Market. "NASDAQ" originally stood for National Association of Securities Dealers Automated Quotations. Ask the students to note that Microsoft is traded on the NASDAQ.

- **Market capitalization ("Cap"):** This is a measure of the size of a company, based on the dollar value of the company. It is calculated by multiplying the outstanding shares by the current stock price. Typically, companies are placed in one of three categories: large-cap, mid-cap, or small-cap. Definitions and implications of these classifications can vary. Larger companies may be less vulnerable to ups and downs in the economy. With more resources, they might be able to handle a temporary decline in demand for their products. Smaller companies may have greater potential for growth but might be threatened if demand for their products would sharply decline. Note that Microsoft is a very large-cap company.

- **Share price:** This is the price of the stock. Most investors hope to select a stock whose share price will increase after they purchase it. Most sources display charts reflecting the changes in the share price over the past month, one year, two years, and so forth. Note the share price of Microsoft.

- **Price/earnings ratio:** The price/earnings or P/E ratio is the recent stock price divided by 12 months of earnings per share. It is a measure of how much the investor will pay for a dollar of earnings or profits. A high P/E within an industry could indicate a young, fast-growing company. A low P/E within an industry indicates a less risky, more stable company. Companies with low P/E ratios are more likely to pay dividends. A start-up company may have no earnings yet, and thus no P/E ratio. When compared to others in the same industry, Microsoft has a relatively low P/E ratio.

- **Annual revenue or sales:** Sales over the past three-to-five years point to how well a company is doing in its industry. Rising sales suggests that a company is producing goods or services that are popular with its customers. Microsoft's sales have been rising nearly every year over the past decade. Revenues fell 3 percent in 2009 during the recession, and then returned to their usual pattern: 7 percent

growth in 2010 and 12 percent growth in 2011.

- **Earnings per share:** Companies that are profitable over the long term tend to have rising share prices. Earnings per share (EPS) is a measure of how a company's profits compare to the number of shares. Rising earnings per share suggest that a company is well managed. Microsoft's EPS increased from $2.13 in 2010 to $2.75 in 2011.

11. **Ask:** What sort of investor might wish to buy Microsoft?

    (Accept a variety of answers. Students might suggest that an investor who is searching for a safe investment in a large, well-managed company might consider buying shares in Microsoft. Investors looking for strong growth in the short term might look elsewhere.)

12. Explain that a final method for selecting stocks is to let other people do research for you so that you can follow the recommendations of experts in the field. This method is called following expert advice. Stock analysts are professionals who study stocks for a living. Their recommendations to buy, sell, or hold stocks can be found at many different websites, such as http://finance.yahoo.com.

13. Ask the students to complete Activity 11.1 by using the suggested websites or other sources of information. They should analyze this information with their classmates and decide which companies they think they would like to invest in for the long term. They may wish to add new companies to study during the semester.

CLOSURE

14. Summarize the key generalizations emphasized in this lesson:

   A. The number of stocks listed on stock exchanges is great. Investors could never master all relevant information about all these stocks; therefore investors will always make choices based on less-than-complete information.

   B. Many economists believe that it is impossible to predict stocks that will be surprises, yielding unexpected high returns.

   C. People can make investment decisions by random selection or by personal preferences. Neither of these approaches involves much cost of acquiring information.

   D. Fundamental analysis is another research method. This approach establishes criteria which may indicate future increases in stock prices. Fundamental analysts stress the importance of basic information about companies, such as size, sales, and profits.

   E. It is costly in time and effort to acquire information about individual stocks. Investors should seek to acquire such information if the anticipated benefits of the research outweigh the anticipated costs.

   F. No matter how carefully one makes financial choices, the choices may turn out to involve surprising results. No one can foresee the future with certainty.

ASSESSMENT
Multiple-Choice Questions

1. Which of the following is used by fundamental analysts to research a stock?

   a. The P/E ratio
   b. Resistance level
   c. Support level
   d. The S/E ratio

2. There are thousands of stocks, but investors have limited time and resources to use in researching stocks. The economic concept that refers to this problem is

   a. inflation.
   b. multiple propensity to consume.
   c. scarcity.
   d. density.

3. Random selection of stocks is the easiest and least costly method of selecting stocks for investment. Why don't people use this method more often?

   a. It is too easy to make money this way. People would feel guilty.
   b. Companies do not allow investors to choose stocks in this manner.
   c. Governmental regulation does not permit investors to select stocks in this manner.
   d. Investors think the benefits of doing more research outweigh the costs of the research.

Constructed-Response Items

1. Respond to the following statement, commenting on potential advantages and disadvantages of selecting stocks at random:

   "People waste their time researching stocks. Just pick one! If the market goes up, the stock will go up."

   (Advantage: Competition to acquire information about stocks is intense. It is almost impossible to know in ad-

vance whether a stock will yield an unexpectedly high return. It might be wiser to simply select stocks at random. Disadvantage: Not all stocks move as the market average moves. The market could move up while one particular stock does not. Also, the cost of researching stocks may be worth paying if the research helps the investor find stocks that become more valuable than stocks picked at random.)

2. Respond to the following statement.

    "Investing in individual stocks is a good way to gain wealth, but only if you are willing to do the work. Investors must learn everything about the stocks they own. They should read extensively in financial articles, a wide range of annual reports, background news from at least two newspapers, as well as *Value Line Reports.* If you can't do this homework, you should not invest in individual stocks."

    (No one can read everything about all the stocks on the market. Investors should focus on the information that is most important to them and become familiar with that information. Even if one could read everything about a stock, the effort still would not guarantee big gains. No information predicts the future perfectly.)

Gen i Connection

Mission 11 of the Gen i Revolution ("Advise a Gen i donor on her $10 million investment") focuses on how fundamental analysts try to select promising stocks using share price, P/E ratio, annual revenue, and earnings per share. The mission setting is that Gen i has been operating on limited funds for as long as anyone can remember. Now, a philanthropist has stepped forward who wishes to donate $10 million to the cause. Students work interactively through 4-1-1 tutorial sessions which present various strategies for investing, stressing the idea that it is difficult to earn unusual gains in the stock market. Students conclude the mission by advising the donor on how to invest $10 million, currently in gold, so as to maximize returns over 20 years. Top points go to those choosing broadly diversified stocks (through mutual funds).

Gen i Reflection

The mysterious donor in Gen i Revolution Mission 11 currently has $10 million in gold. If you had a large amount of money, would you be comfortable keeping it in gold? What benefits might be involved? What costs?

ACTIVITY 11.1
RESEARCHING YOUR STOCK PICKS

Directions: Read the definitions in Part 1. Then choose the companies that you wish to study. List their names in the charts in Part 3. Visit websites that have good financial information such as http://finance.yahoo.com or www.morningstar.com to find and record the information requested in each section of the chart. Write the information in the spaces provided.

Part 1: Definitions and Numbers to Help You Understand a Company

Symbol: A stock symbol or ticker symbol is an abbreviation of the company name to be used for purposes of trading.

Stock exchange: The two largest stock markets in the United States are the New York Stock Exchange (now owned by NYSE Euronext) and the NASDAQ.

Market capitalization: This is a measure of the size of a company, based on the dollar value of the company. It is calculated by multiplying the outstanding shares by the current stock price. Typically, companies are placed in one of three categories (but the definitions can vary):

- Large-cap: Value of $10 billion or more

- Mid-cap: Value of $2 to $10 billion

- Small-cap: Value of $1 billion or less

Share price: This is the price of the stock.

Price/earnings ratio: The price/earnings or P/E ratio is the recent stock price divided by 12 months of earnings per share. It is a measure of how much the investor will pay for a dollar of earnings or profits. A high P/E within an industry could indicate a young, fast-growing company. A low P/E within an industry indicates a less risky, more stable company. Companies with low P/E ratios are more likely to pay dividends. A start-up company may have no earnings yet, and thus no P/E ratio. To learn whether a P/E ratio is high or low, compare the P/E ratio of one company to others in the same industry.

Annual revenue or sales: Sales over the past three-to-five years point to how well a company is doing in its industry. Rising sales suggests that a company is producing goods or services that are popular with its customers.

Earnings per share: Companies that are profitable over the long term tend to have rising share prices. Earnings per share is a measure of how a company's profits compare to the number of shares.

Part 2: Microsoft: A Completed Example

Here is a completed example of a chart using the definitions explained above. The company being studied is Microsoft. The data were obtained from http://finance.yahoo.com.

Company Name	Symbol	Exchange	Today's Date	Market Capital-ization
Microsoft	MSFT	NASDAQ	Dec. 29, 2011	$218.55 billion
	Share Price	P/E Ratio	Annual Revenue or Sales	Earnings per Share
	$25.98	$9.46	$71.12 billion	$2.75

Part 3: Your Turn

Complete the following chart for the companies you selected in the classroom drawing.

Company Name	Symbol	Exchange	Today's Date	Market Capital-ization
	Share Price	P/E Ratio	Annual Revenue or Sales	Earnings per Share

Now complete the following three charts for the companies you choose.

Company 1

Company Name	Symbol	Exchange	Today's Date	Market Capital-ization
	Share Price	P/E Ratio	Annual Revenue or Sales	Earnings per Share

Company 2

Company Name	Symbol	Exchange	Today's Date	Market Capital-ization
	Share Price	P/E Ratio	Annual Revenue or Sales	Earnings per Share

Company 3

Company Name	Symbol	Exchange	Today's Date	Market Capital-ization
	Share Price	P/E Ratio	Annual Revenue or Sales	Earnings per Share

ACTIVITY 11.2
COMPANY NAMES FOR CLASS DRAWING

Allstate Insurance ALL	American Eagle Outfitters AEO	American Express Company AXP	Apple Computer Inc. AAPL	Apache Corp. APA
Auto-Zone Inc. AZO	Best Buy Company BBY	Boeing Company BA	Campbell Soup CPB	Cisco Systems CSCO
Coca-Cola Co. KO	Dell Computer DELL	DineEquity, Inc. DIN	Disney Company DIS	ExxonMobile Corp. XOM
FedEx Corp. FDX	Ford Motor Company F	Garmin Ltd. GRMN	Google Inc. GOOG	Harley Davidson HDI
Home Depot Inc. HD	Johnson & Johnson JNJ	Macy's Inc. M	McDonalds Corp. MCD	Nokia Corp. NOK
Proctor & Gamble Co. PG	Southwest Airlines Co. LUV	Starbucks Corp. SBUX	Target Corp. TGT	Verizon Communications VZ

SLIDE 11.1

Thinking Economically About Researching Stocks

- Investors face scarcity: Investors' time is limited while the information available regarding stocks is vast.

- Here are some recommendations to consider
  - Recognize that you cannot know it all.
  - Select a few companies to research. Then follow their progress closely.
  - Find a few good sources of information about stocks. Many online sources have great data and are easy and fast to use.
  - Stop looking for new information when you think the benefits received from more information are less than the costs of additional research.

SLIDE 11.2

Surprises Are Rare

- Many individuals spend a great deal of time and effort trying to find companies whose stock prices might increase faster than average for the market.

- Many financial institutions—brokerage companies, banks, life insurance companies—spend even more time and effort trying to identify companies whose stock prices might increase faster than average for the market.

- It is very difficult to earn unusual gains in the stock market because most of the information about most companies is already known.

- People who earn above-average returns from their stocks are usually surprised. But it is hard even for experienced investors to find surprises in the market.

SLIDE 11.3

Fundamental Analysis

• Fundamental stock analysts examine the basic performance of a company and use results to make investment decisions.

• They pay special attention to these factors:

  ▪ Size of the company

  ▪ Changes in sales

  ▪ Changes in earnings

  ▪ Demand for the company's goods and services

SLIDE 11.4

Stock-Selection Data Used by Fundamental Stock Analysts

• Symbol

• Stock exchange

• Share price

• Market capitalization

• Price/earnings ratio

• Annual revenue or sales

• Earnings per share

LESSON 12

CREDIT: YOUR BEST FRIEND OR YOUR WORST ENEMY?

LESSON 12
CREDIT: YOUR BEST FRIEND OR YOUR WORST ENEMY?

LESSON DESCRIPTION

The students complete an exercise that shows how credit can be their worst enemy. They learn how quickly credit-card balances can grow and how long it can take to pay off a credit-card debt. They also learn that credit can be their best friend. Working in small groups, they consider seven scenarios and decide in each case whether it would be wise for the people involved to use credit. They discuss their conclusions and develop a list of criteria suitable for use in making decisions about credit.

INTRODUCTION

Unwise use of credit can lead people to spend more money than they can afford to pay back, reducing their ability to make purchases or save money in the future. Many borrowers fall behind in their credit payments, jeopardizing their capacity to borrow in the future, and some wind up facing foreclosures or declaring bankruptcy. When it is well used, however, credit can provide substantial benefits. People can use credit to deal with emergency situations or to purchase valuable assets, such as an automobile or a home, or to pay for an education. It is in the students' interest, therefore, to learn to analyze the costs and benefits of using credit.

CONCEPTS

Choice

Costs and benefits

Credit

Debt

Interest

Revolving credit

OBJECTIVES

Students will be able to:

- Calculate interest payments, minimum balances, and the cost of credit.

- Develop and apply criteria for determining when the use of credit is appropriate.

CONTENT STANDARDS

Voluntary National Content Standards in Economics, **2nd Edition**

- **Standard 2:** Effective decision making requires comparing the additional costs of alternatives with the additional benefits. Many choices involve doing a little more or a little less of something: few choices are "all-or-nothing" decisions.

- **Standard 10:** Institutions evolve and are created to help individuals and groups accomplish their goals. Banks, labor unions, markets, corporations, legal systems, and not-for-profit organizations are examples of important institutions. A different kind of institution, clearly defined and enforced property rights, is essential to a market economy.

National Standards in K-12 Personal Finance Education, **3rd edition**

- **Financial Responsibility and Decision Making Standard 1:** Take responsibility for personal financial decisions.

- **Financial Responsibility and Decision Making Standard 4:** Make financial decisions by systematically considering alternatives and consequences.

- **Credit and Debt Standard 1:** Identify the costs and benefits of various types of credit.

- **Credit and Debt Standard 3:** Describe ways to avoid or correct debt problems.

TIME REQUIRED
45 minutes

MATERIALS
- Slides 12.1, 12.2, and 12.3

- One copy of Activity 12.1, 12.2, and 12.3 for each student

PROCEDURE
1. Tell the students that in this lesson they will examine the good and the bad sides of using credit. They will learn how to decide when it is and is not a good idea to use credit. Remind the students that problems with credit have been much in the news. There are many reports of families and even college students having large amounts of credit-card or student-loan debt. After the recession of 2007-2009 and the collapse of the housing market that came with it, many homeowners could no longer afford to pay their home mortgages and faced foreclosures.

2. To get started, explain that some definitions might help. **Display Slide 12.1** and discuss the definitions of *credit* and *revolving credit*.

3. **Distribute a copy of Activity 12.1** to each student. Tell the students to read Part 1, which tells how Justin used his credit card, and to fill in the blanks as they go. Then they should complete the worksheet in Part 2 of Activity 12.1. (Note: Many credit-card issuers now charge considerably less than 18 percent interest; but as Justin is quite young and this is his first credit card,

18 percent is not an unrealistic figure in his case).

4. **Display Slides 12.2 and 12.3.** Review the answers to Activity 12.1. All the answers are provided except for the answer to the Bonus Question at the end. It is provided in procedure 6.

5. Explain that it is now time to address the Bonus Question posed at the end of Activity 12.1: If Justin held to his resolution and made payments of $55 each month, how long do you think it would take him to pay what he owes? Write the following terms on the board in spaced intervals: *6 months, 12 months, 18 months, 24 months, 30 months.* Read off each time period and ask the students to raise their hands to indicate their estimates of the time it would take Justin to pay off his credit-card balance if he did not make any more charges and paid the minimum balance each month.

6. Tell the students that you did that math for Justin this time and that it would take 23 months—nearly two years—for Justin to pay off his credit-card balance if he paid $55 each month. Remind them that interest is charged each month on the unpaid balance—even if no further purchases are made using the card. Tell the students that the total amount Justin will have to pay back is $1,226.88. Justin made total purchases of $1,051.67. The remaining $175.21 is the cost of credit in his case.

7. Explain that credit can cause problems. People with high monthly payments often find that they cannot afford to buy things that they want to buy now, and cannot afford to save money for the future, because so much of their income is going to pay for past purchases. Sometimes people fall behind and fail to make monthly payments on their

unpaid balances; this leads to financial penalties that add to their debt. Some people accumulate so much debt that they must face foreclosures or declare bankruptcy. These outcomes severely limit their capacity to borrow in the future. Still, when it is used appropriately, credit can be a good friend.

8. Ask the students to consider this situation: "It is midnight and your car breaks down on [some local highway]. You are far from home. You use your cell phone to call an emergency auto-repair service. The service representative tells you that a service visit will cost $50, plus the cost of any parts and labor that are needed to get you driving again. You have $7.57 in your pocket. Should you use a credit card?"

(Accept a variety of answers. Most students will probably agree that this would be an appropriate time to use a credit card.)

9. Organize the class into groups of three or four students and **distribute a copy of Activity 12.2** to each student. Give the groups 15 minutes to discuss the scenarios and decide whether the use of credit is a good idea in each case.

(Ana should take out the student loan. The additional training will increase her income and allow her to repay the loan. However, she should still be careful. Some students wind up with large student-loan debts. She should borrow only as much money as she actually needs and for any loan she considers she should learn exactly what her monthly repayment requirements would be before she signs the loan papers.)

(For Dave Larson, using credit to buy the stamp now may be a good idea, since the stamp may become more valuable in the future. On the other hand, Dave can't be certain how much the stamp will gain in value. The decision here could go either way.)

(Caroline Potter should use credit to buy a more dependable car. She might lose her income completely if she cannot get to work regularly and on time. Her current repair bills are large.)

(Jake Purdy might increase his income by buying the new car—if it actually is true that the new car would impress his customers. That is uncertain. But it is certain that payments on the new car would be high, and Jake's salary is not high. Jake should keep his old car and explore other, less costly ways to please his customers—by providing better service, for example.)

(Felicia Washington should buy the cheaper dress and pay cash rather than borrow.)

(Mike Chiang is paying only the minimum balance on each of his credit-card accounts, and he has to work a part-time job to make those payments. How will he be able to make the higher payments that will result from his trip? This is an easy call: don't do it, Mike!)

(John and Jackie should wait. While the mortgage terms are tempting, the interest rate on the loan will increase after 12 months, adding to their mortgage payment. Most importantly, they have no savings. If they were to encounter any unexpected home repairs—which is very likely—the new expenses could force them into debt, perhaps causing them to default on the loan and face a foreclosure. They should remain in the apartment for the time being and try to build up some savings before considering home ownership.)

CLOSURE

10. Ask the class to develop criteria for determining when it is appropriate to use credit. Remind them to use ex-

amples presented in Activity 12.2 and elsewhere in this lesson as sources of ideas for formulating criteria. List their criteria on the board.

(Possible answers include using credit to make an investment in your future, as Ana Rodriguez and Caroline Potter did; to meet an emergency situation, such as the car problem described in Procedure 8; to buy something that will cost more later, as long as the cost of credit does not exceed the savings on the item you purchase; or to acquire something of great value that you may not be able to obtain at a later date.)

ASSESSMENT
Multiple-Choice Questions

1. A disadvantage of a revolving credit account is that

   a. it is illegal.
   b. it is very difficult for borrowers to qualify for such an account.
   c. the balance must be paid off every month.
   d. *balances can rise quickly if only the minimum payment is made each month.*

2. Making purchases on credit

   a. is never a good idea.
   b. *is a good idea if the benefits to the purchaser are greater than the costs.*
   c. decreases the cost of the purchase to the borrower.
   d. is a good idea if the purchaser has so many credit payments that he or she is unable to live comfortably.

3. If you have a credit card charging 12 percent annual interest, the total amount you owe each month is

   a. *the unpaid balance on your credit card plus 1 percent interest on the previous balance.*
   b. the unpaid balance on your credit card plus 12 percent interest on the previous balance.
   c. 1 percent interest on the unpaid balance.
   d. 12 percent interest on the unpaid balance.

4. Which of the following is the best use of credit?

   a. You can't buy everything you want on your current income.
   b. *You can take advantage of a sale price that is lower than the normal cost of the item plus your cost of credit.*
   c. You have a credit card with a low interest rate.
   d. You want to purchase something now instead of having to wait until later to use it.

Constructed-Response Items

1. What are the advantages and disadvantages of using credit?

   *(**Advantages:** Credit is useful in an emergency; it can be used to acquire valuable assets; it allows consumers to take advantage of opportunities such as sales.)*

   *(**Disadvantages:** Credit increases the cost of purchases; it reduces the capacity of borrowers to make future purchases; and it may cause individuals to borrow more than they can afford to pay back—perhaps leading to personal bankruptcy.)*

2. Define *revolving credit* and discuss its advantages and disadvantages.

(Revolving credit is credit that is available up to a limit and automatically renewed as debts are paid off or paid down by partial payments. Revolving credit enables consumers to pay for their purchases over a period of time rather than immediately. But interest continues to accrue on unpaid balances; and, since many people make only the minimum payment each month, revolving credit may come at a high cost.)

Gen i Connection

In Mission 5 of the Gen i Revolution, Justin (from Activity 12.1) is again learning about credit. Once again, Justin charges purchases but pays only the minimum on his account, and soon he gets into credit trouble. Students work interactively through a 4-1-1 tutorial that shows how to calculate payments, how to read a credit statement, and when to use credit. The mission includes additional questions and exercises on credit to build useful knowledge. Students conclude by answering questions about getting Justin out of credit-card trouble and keeping him out of credit trouble in the future.

Although not related directly to investment, Mission 7 of the Gen i Revolution game provides useful background on alternative financial institutions such as check-cashing stores, rent-to-own stores, and payday lenders. Paul, Fred, and Diana are using alternative financial institutions. They are "unbanked" in that they have no relationships with mainstream financial institutions. The 4-1-1 tutorial discusses advantages and disadvantages of alternative institutions, providing the background that helps to convince Paul, Fred, and Diana to reconsider their decision to use alternative financial institutions. Students conclude by recommending better choices to Paul, Fred, and Diana.

Gen i Reflection

People sometimes go to alternative financial institutions such as payday lenders to avoid awkward personal situations. If you needed money to get a car fixed and your only choices were a payday loan or asking a relative for a loan, which would you prefer? What would the advantages and disadvantages be of each alternative?

ACTIVITY 12.1
JUSTIN JABOWSKI AND HIS MAGICAL MONEY MACHINE

Directions: The following paragraphs in Part 1 explain how Justin Jabowski used his credit card over a four-month period. Read the information and fill in the blanks (this will call for doing some simple math). When you have finished your work on Part 1, transfer the numbers you have entered to the **Do the Math for Justin** worksheet in Part 2.

Part 1: Justin and his Credit Card

Justin Jabowski is a high school junior with a part-time job. In January he acquired his first credit card. His credit-card account charges an annual interest rate of 18 percent. This means that every month Justin pays a finance charge of 1.5 percent (that's 18 percent divided by 12 months) on his unpaid balance. And every month Justin must make a minimum payment of 5 percent of the unpaid balance.

In January Justin used his credit card to buy two shirts and a pair of pants, at a total price of $160. He also charged a new pair of shoes on his card, at a price of $75. When his first credit-card bill arrived in February, Justin owed _____. Since his account provides for a 30-day grace period, Justin did not owe any finance charges immediately. Justin has heard that it is a good idea to pay the entire bill each month and thus avoid finance charges; but he was a little short of cash in February, so he mailed in only the minimum payment of _____. His unpaid balance on the card was _____.

In February Justin treated himself and his girlfriend to an evening out at a rock concert. He charged two concert tickets for $50 each, plus a handling fee of $3 per ticket. He enjoyed the performing group's music so much that he bought three of the group's CDs at $17 each, using his credit card. When his bill for March arrived, Justin owed _____ for the new charges, his previous balance, and the finance charge on the previous balance. He was a little short of cash at the time, so he made only the minimum payment of _____.

In March, Justin had a great opportunity to go skiing with his friend Travis. Travis's parents had rented a ski condo. They planned to make the trip by driving; by joining them, Justin was able to get free lodging, transportation, and breakfasts. But lunches and dinners for the three-day outing cost him $150 (he treated Travis and his parents to lunch one day), and ski-lift tickets for three days came to $120. Justin's total credit-card bill at the beginning of April was _____ for the new charges, the previous balance, and the finance charge on the previous balance. By then Justin had become alarmed at the size of his credit-card bill; but he was still a little short on cash, so he made only the minimum payment of _____.

After he mailed off his April payment, Justin resolved firmly to stop charging things on his card until he could get his entire balance paid off. Unfortunately, his car broke down the next day, and the repair bill came to $490. He needed the car to get to work and school, so he charged the repairs. His total credit-card balance in May was _____.

Taken aback by his growing balance, Justin swore not charge another dime until he paid the balance off entirely. He decided to pay $55 a month for as long as it would take to pay it off.

Part 2: Do the Math for Justin

January   Purchases   _____

                   Minus minimum payment   _____

                   Unpaid balance   _____

February   Purchases   _____

                   Previous balance   _____

                   Plus finance charge   _____

                   Total owed   _____

                   Minus minimum payment   _____

                   Unpaid balance   _____

March   Purchases   _____

                   Previous balance   _____

                   Plus finance charge   _____

                   Total owed   _____

                   Minus minimum payment   _____

                   Unpaid balance   _____

April   Purchases   _____

                   Previous balance   _____

                   Plus finance charge   _____

                   Total owed   _____

                   Minus minimum payment   _____

                   Unpaid balance   _____

Bonus Question

If Justin held to his resolution and made payments of $55 each month, how long do you think it would take him to pay what he owes?

ACTIVITY 12.2
SHOULD YOU BORROW?

Ana Rodriguez graduated from high school last year with a good grade-point average. She works as a receptionist at a physical-therapy clinic, making $8.50 an hour. She would like to become a physical therapist. The work appeals to her, and salaries for physical therapists are excellent. Within a few years of finishing her training, she could earn more than $50,000 a year. But Ana's parents cannot afford to pay for the training Ana will need. Ana has investigated student loans, but she knows she would have to pay back anything she might borrow over a 10-year period. Should Ana take out a student loan?

Dave Larson is an avid stamp collector. For a long time he has wanted to own a Bolivian Double Eagle stamp. This stamp is very hard to find, and Dave believes it will gain value in the future. Dave learns that his favorite stamp store has a Bolivian Double Eagle for sale, priced at $200. Dave doesn't have that much money in savings, but he is afraid that if he doesn't buy the stamp now, someone else will. Should he use his credit card to buy the stamp?

Caroline Potter is a single mother with two small children. She commutes 15 miles to work five days a week, driving an old car that has developed several problems. Caroline has been late to work twice in the last month because of car problems, and each of the problems has saddled her with a large repair bill. Should Caroline buy a better used car, even though she will have to borrow money and take on monthly car payments?

Jake Purdy just got a great job working as a salesman. His salary isn't high, but he can earn excellent commissions if he makes a lot of sales. Jake has a reliable car, but he has his eye on an expensive new model that would make a better impression on his customers (and also on his dates), he thinks. Car payments for the new model would be high, but Jake feels that he can make enough in sales commissions to cover the cost. Should he take out a loan and buy the new car?

Felicia Washington is the homecoming queen at her high school. She is going to the homecoming dance with the best-looking guy in the senior class. She goes shopping for a new dress to wear to the dance. She finds a nice dress for $119—an amount she could pay in cash. However, she also finds a spectacular dress priced at $229. She could buy this dress with her credit card. Sure, it's a lot of money, Felicia thinks, but she owes it to her public and her date to look dazzling for the big event. Should Felicia put the spectacular dress on her credit card?

Mike Chiang is a community-college student. He has three credit cards, all charged close to the limit. Mike manages to make the minimum payments each month, thanks to his part-time job at Pizzas-R-Us. Mike really, really wants to go with his friends on a spring-break trip to Padre Island, Texas, but he doesn't see how he can afford to do it. Then he receives a friendly letter from one of his credit-card companies. "Dear Mr. Chiang," it begins, "Since you are one of our most-valued customers and always make your payments on time, we are raising your credit limit by $2,000." Mike is thrilled! Now he can go to Padre Island with his friends. Should he do it, charging his expenses to his card?

John and Jackie are a young, newly married couple who soon will have their first child. They are just getting started in their jobs and they have not begun to save money. They live from paycheck to paycheck. Currently they are living in small, two-bedroom, one-bath apartment. They are interested in buying a home, and they have found a modest, three-bedroom, two-bath home that they like. They have spoken to a mortgage broker, and she explained that John and Jackie would qualify for a 30-year home mortgage. While this mortgage comes with a relatively high interest rate and upfront fees, the interest rate for the first twelve months has been reduced. And the loan does not require a down payment—which would cost several thousand dollars John and Jackie do not have. This mortgage would allow John and Jackie to move into the "starter" home they are interested in much sooner than they had imagined. Should they take out the mortgage?

SLIDE 12.1

Credit Definitions

Credit
- The ability to obtain goods and services before paying for them, based on a promise to pay later.
- Individuals who use credit are borrowing money.

Revolving credit
- Credit that is available up to a limit and automatically renewed as debts are paid off or paid down.
- People who use revolving credit often make partial payments on their unpaid balances at regular intervals.
- Credit-card accounts offer revolving credit to credit-card users.

SLIDE 12.2

Answers to Worksheet for Justin Jabowski

January	Purchases	$235.00
	Minus minimum payment	11.75
	Unpaid balance	223.25
February	Purchases	157.00
	Previous balance	223.25
	Plus finance charge	3.35
	Total owed	383.60
	Minus minimum payment	19.18
	Unpaid balance	364. 42

SLIDE 12.3

Answers to Worksheet for Justin Jabowski

March	Purchases	270.00
	Previous balance	364.42
	Plus finance charge	5.47
	Total owed	639.89
	Minus minimum payment	31.99
	Unpaid balance	607.90
April	Purchases	490.00
	Previous balance	607.90
	Plus finance charge	9.12
	Total owed	1,107.02
	Minus minimum payment	55.35
	Unpaid balance	1,051.97

LESSON 13

WHY NOT SAVE?

LESSON 13
WHY NOT SAVE?

LESSON DESCRIPTION

The students examine risk-oriented behavior, considering why people often engage in behavior that is dangerous or unhealthy. They are introduced to the concept of *cost/benefit analysis* and asked to apply what they learn to questions about saving. They generate lists of savings goals and categorize those goals as short-term, medium-term, and long-term. They learn why long-term goals are more difficult to achieve than short-term goals.

INTRODUCTION

It is a basic principle of economics that people strive to make decisions that will serve their interests. Saving money early and often would serve most people well, helping them to achieve their goals. Yet many people are poor savers, saving too little or not at all. Why? The explanation has to do with a particular complication involved in the weighing of costs and benefits. The costs of some decisions are immediate and certain, while the benefits sought may occur only in the future and may therefore seem uncertain to the people involved.

CONCEPTS

Benefits

Costs

Goals

Incentives

Interest

Long-term goal

Medium-term goal

Opportunity cost

Saving

Short-term goal

OBJECTIVES

Students will be able to:

- Define *costs, benefits, incentives, interest, saving,* and *opportunity cost.*

- Analyze the costs and benefits of saving.

- Give examples of opportunity cost.

- Identify short-, medium-, and long-term savings goals.

- Explain why a savings goal might be short-term for one person and medium- or long-term for another.

CONTENT STANDARDS
Voluntary National Content Standards in Economics, **2nd Edition**

- **Standard 1:** Productive resources are limited. Therefore, people cannot have all the goods and services they want; as a result, they must choose some things and give up others.

- **Standard 2:** Effective decision making requires comparing the additional costs of alternatives with the additional benefits. Many choices involve doing a little more or a little less of something: few choices are "all or nothing" decisions.

- **Standard 3:** Different methods can be used to allocate goods and services. People, acting individually or collectively through government, must choose which methods to use to allocate different kinds of goods and services.

- **Standard 4:** People usually respond predictably to positive and negative incentives.

National Standards in K-12 Personal Finance Education, 3rd edition

- **Financial Responsibility and Decision Making Standard 1:** Take responsibility for personal financial decisions.

- **Risk Management and Insurance Standard 1:** Identify common types of risks and basic risk-management methods.

- **Saving and Investing Standard 1:** Discuss how saving contributes to financial well-being.

- **Saving and Investing Standard 2:** Explain how investing builds wealth and helps meet financial goals.

- **Saving and Investing Standard 3:** Evaluate investment alternatives.

TIME REQUIRED

45 minutes

MATERIALS

- Slides 13.1 to 13.7

- Sticky notes for each group of 3-4 students

- One copy of Activities 13.1, 13.2, and 13.3 for each student

PROCEDURE

1. Tell the students that the purpose of this lesson is to examine risk-oriented behavior. People usually know what is good for them, but they often act as if they don't know. Some people drive too fast on icy roads, or they fail to take medications prescribed by a doctor, or they never get around to checking tire pressure on their cars. Such behavior seems odd. Why would people do things that don't seem to be in their interest? Why would they put themselves at risk of loss or harm? Invite the students to suggest explanations; discuss their ideas briefly. Then tell them that in this lesson they will use principles of economic reasoning to analyze one particular form of puzzling behavior: the failure of many people to save money.

2. **Display Slide 13.1.** Pose each question from the slide, one at a time, and have the students raise their hands if they think the answer is "yes." Next to each question, record the number of students who respond positively. That should include most everyone.

3. Explain that it might help to understand these puzzling events if we approach them with certain principles of economics in mind. **Display Slide 13.2.** Explain that economic analysis involves comparing the costs and the benefits of the alternatives in any situation that requires a decision. Costs are all the things that have to be given up when a choice is made. Benefits are any gains or favorable outcomes that make people more satisfied when a choice is made. Costs are negative; benefits are positive. However, people don't get benefits unless they pay some costs.

4. **Display Slide 13.3.** Pursue the analysis by reference to diet and exercise. Most people know that eating a healthful diet and participating in regular exercise are important. Discuss the following:

   - What are the benefits of eating a healthful diet and exercising regularly?

     (Feel better, look better, reduce your risk of heart disease, reduce your risk of cancer, and boost your life expectancy.)

   - Do these benefits of diet and exercise occur now or in the future?

     (Although people may start to feel better right away, most of the benefits occur in the future.)

- If people choose a healthful diet and exercise regularly, are they guaranteed these benefits? Can they count on them for sure?

  (No. Some people may still get heart disease or cancer, no matter what they eat or how well they exercise. Also, a person engaged in a diet-and-exercise program could die prematurely from any number of causes other than heart disease or cancer.)

- What are the costs of choosing a healthful diet and exercising regularly?

  (Possibilities include giving up food that tastes really good, paying dues for membership at a fitness club, spending time on exercise that you could spend in other ways—napping, reading, gardening, watching television, playing video games.)

5. Emphasize the point that the costs of choosing a healthful diet and exercising regularly occur right now, and they are certain. However, most of the benefits of choosing a healthful diet and exercising regularly occur in the future, and they are uncertain. Many people attach a very high value to the present; they may choose to avoid immediate, certain costs if the alternative choice offers only remote, uncertain benefits. A similar analysis applies in the case of decisions about saving.

6. **Display Slide 13.4.** Explain that the term *saving* refers to setting aside income not spent on consumption or taxes. Most people know that starting to save money at an early age and saving regularly are good habits that lead to financial well-being. Yet many people in the United States fail to begin saving early and fail to continue saving regularly. Discuss the following:

- What are the benefits of saving?

  (Saving money helps people to attain their goals for the future; it also helps to create a feeling of security and satisfaction.)

- What are the costs of saving?

  (People who save money give up the chance to use that money in the present. That may mean giving up things they could obtain in the present if they weren't saving.)

- When do the benefits of saving occur?

  (In the future.)

- When do the costs of saving occur?

  (In the present.)

7. Emphasize the point that the costs of saving are immediate and certain. If people choose to save part of their income, they give up the things they could buy with their income in the present. The benefits of saving occur in the future, and they are uncertain. Events can conspire to prevent people from reaping the benefits of saving; somebody might save money to build a comfortable retirement home, for example, and then get killed in an automobile crash prior to retirement.

8. Explain that when we use cost-benefit analysis, it is important to consider the broad idea of opportunity cost, not merely dollars spent. An opportunity cost is the next-best alternative a person gives up in making a choice. For example, the choice to exercise for an hour each day means giving up the next-best alternative use of that hour—perhaps watching television or reading or spending time with a friend. In the case of budgeting, saving money for the future means giving up the opportunity to spend money in the present.

9. Economists have also learned from other research that people are sometimes inconsistent in their behavior over time. **Display Slide 13.5.** Explain that people may promise themselves to eat less; but then when the time comes to have a snack, they eat it. They may promise themselves to exercise; but when the time comes to go running or biking or head to the gym, they choose to do something else. Spending often provides instant gratification; it enables people to have what they want now. Saving is like passing up a snack or going to the gym. It requires a sacrifice in the present for a reward in the future.

10. Explain that setting goals is an important factor related to saving money. Goals are aims or desired results that act as incentives. Incentives are rewards or advantages that encourage people to do something. People usually save money with goals in mind—perhaps vacations, gifts, video games, a down payment on a home or car, college education, retirement. Such goals act as incentives—as targets to shoot for—thus motivating people to develop the habit of saving.

11. **Display Slide 13.6** and discuss the information it presents.

    • People who save usually have savings goals. These are aims or desired results that people hope to achieve.

    • Short-term savings goals are those that can be achieved in one year or less. For example, the goal of saving to buy a cool video game may be a short-term goal.

    • Medium-term savings goals are those that can be achieved in one-to-five years. For example, the goal of saving to pay for a vacation might be a medium-term goal.

    • Long-term savings goals require more than five years to achieve. For example, the goal of saving enough money to pay for a college education would be a long-term goal for most people.

12. Tell the students that they are going to classify some typical savings goals. Organize the class into groups of three or four students. **Distribute Activity 13.1.** Explain that each group will have 10 minutes to decide whether the savings goal in each situation is a short-term, medium-term, or long-term savings goal.

13. Discuss the students' answers to Activity 13.1.

    (A. It will take Tia 50 months or a little more than four years to save enough money for a guitar and guitar lessons. This is a medium-term savings goal.)

    (B. It will take Harry about eight months to save enough money for a mountain bike. This is a short-term savings goal.)

    (C. It will take Taylor nearly 17 months to save enough money for the TV and sound system. This is a medium-term savings goal.)

    (D. It will take the Newton family about 50 months to save enough money for the family vacation. This is a medium-term savings goal.)

    (E. It will take Jessie and Janice [with help from their relatives] about 125 months [nearly 11 years] to save enough money for Julia's college education. This is a long-term savings goal.)

14. Now that the students have considered the situations identified on Activity 13.1, ask them to list some of their own savings goals and to estimate whether they are short-term, medium-term, or long-term goals. **Display Slide 13.7**

and discuss the students' goals. Enter their goals into the appropriate place in the slide.

15. Explain that the amounts people can save in any time period vary depending on their incomes, earnings, and expenses. Long-term goals are usually more difficult to meet than short-term goals. When people strive to save for more than five years, there is ample time for emergencies or attractive opportunities to present themselves before the long-term savings goal is met. If an emergency or an opportunity that seems more compelling than the long-term savings goal does arise, the saver may give up on the savings goal in order to obtain something that looks important in the present. As economists would put it, the opportunity cost of saving may seem greater than the opportunity cost of the emergency or the new, attractive opportunity.

CLOSURE

16. Review the lesson. **Ask:**

A. What does it mean to save?

(To save is to set money aside for future use. Money saved is money not spent to buy things now, or to pay taxes.)

B. Suppose that you wanted to convince your parents to purchase a cool new smartphone. What are some benefits of owning the smartphone that you could use to make your argument?

(Possibilities include using the phone to keep in contact with friends and relatives, fast communication in time of an emergency, access to school communications such as online homework assignments, and the value of playing educational games.)

C. Your parents will probably point out that there are costs associated with buying a new smartphone. What are some of these costs?

(The amount paid for the smartphone and service; time spent playing games or texting that could be spent doing other things; individuals absorbed in texting friends and using various smartphone apps may spend less time in communication with family members.)

D. What is the opportunity cost of buying the smartphone?

(Answers will vary. The opportunity cost is next-best alternative given up when a choice is made. Someone who bought the phone instead of a new tablet computer that she really wanted might say that her opportunity cost was the tablet computer she didn't get.)

E. What is the opportunity cost of buying things today?

(Things you could buy in the future, or future savings.)

F. What is a short-term savings goal? What might be an example?

(One that can be achieved in one year or less. A Mother's Day gift might be an example.)

G. What is a medium-term savings goal? What might be an example?

(One that can be achieved in one-to five-years. A home theater system might be an example.)

H. What is a long-term savings goal? What might be an example?

(One that takes more than five years to achieve. Having ample savings for retirement might be an example.)

I. Why might a long-term goal for one person be a medium-term goal for another?

(Because one person may be able to save more each week or month, thus reaching the goal sooner than a person who saves less.)

J. Why are long-term savings goals more difficult to achieve than short-term goals?

(For long-term goals there is more time in which emergencies or new consumer-purchase opportunities may arise—possibly displacing long-term goals. Often an emergency or a new consumer-purchase opportunity will seem more important or more desirable than the long-term goal. The saver then gives up saving for the long-term goal in favor of spending for the emergency or the new consumer purchase.)

ASSESSMENT
Multiple-Choice Questions

1. A short-term goal is one that

   a. is easy to achieve.
   b. *can be achieved in less than one year.*
   c. can be achieved in one-to-five years.
   d. can be achieved in more than five years.

2. A long-term goal is one that

   a. few people manage to achieve.
   b. can be achieved in less than one year.
   c. *can be achieved in more than five years.*
   d. can be achieved in one-to-five years.

3. Matt has decided to stop paying for Tae Kwon Do lessons after school in order to save money so that he will have plenty of spending money for a family trip that is coming up before long. Instead of doing Tae Kwon Do, he will use the fitness room the school offers community members, at no cost, during after-school hours. For Matt, giving up Tae Kwon Do is an example of

   a. goals that Matt wants to achieve.
   b. incentives that encourage Matt to save.
   c. *an opportunity cost related to Matt's decision to save.*
   d. an opportunity benefit related to Matt's decision to save.

Constructed-Response Items

1. You want your parents to buy you a new mountain bike. They ask you to prepare an argument that will convince them they should buy the bike. Write a paragraph in which you describe the costs and benefits associated with buying the bike.

   (Although answers will vary, students should identify costs that include the amount to be paid for the bike, expenses to maintain the bike, any related expenses for safety equipment, and the cost of time spent riding the bike. Students should also identify benefits such as exercise, ability to be with friends, efficient transportation, and fresh air.)

2. Your friend Alex is trying to save money to buy a leather jacket. This is a long-term goal for Alex, and he is having a lot of trouble saving toward the goal. Explain to Alex why long-term goals are more difficult to achieve than short-term goals.

   (With a long-term goal, there is more time in which emergencies or other occasions for spending might arise, interfering with saving. If the brakes fail on Alex's car, for example, spending money on new brakes might seem more important than saving for the long-term goal.)

Gen i Connection

The material in this lesson is nicely reinforced by Mission 4 of the Gen i Revolution ("Help the O'Neils save $300 a month for a down payment on a home"). In the mission, students take on the role of operatives advising the O'Neils. The O'Neils have two children, and they wish to buy their first home soon. Students work interactively through a 4-1-1 tutorial that covers goal-setting and budgeting. They learn about spending categories and setting priorities to order to foster saving. At the end of the mission, students must recommend spending cuts in the O'Neils' budget that will allow them to save $300 per month toward their goal of buying a home.

Gen i Reflection

In Mission 4 of the Gen i Revolution, Clayton discovers he is spending way too much on his racing hobby—but only after a detailed examination of where the money is going. If you were Clayton, do you think you would have realized sooner that you were spending too much on your race hobby? Or would you know without even looking at receipts and online records? Explain your answer.

ACTIVITY 13.1
SETTING GOALS: INCENTIVES TO SAVE

Part 1: Classifying Savings Goals

Directions: Read the sections below on savings goals and situations. Calculate the number of months required to achieve each goal. Draw a circle for each goal to indicate whether it is a short-term, medium-term, or long-term savings goal.

Types of Savings Goals

- Short-term savings goals: Can be achieved in one year or less.

- Medium-term savings goals: Can be achieved in one-to-five years.

- Long-term savings goals: Can be achieved in five years or longer.

Saving Situations

1. Tia wants to buy a guitar and have a year's worth of guitar lessons. She estimates the cost at $1,750. Tia can save $35 a month. What sort of savings goal is this?

   Circle One:

   - Short-term goal

   - Medium-term goal

   - Long-term goal

2. Harry wants to buy a mountain bike. He estimates the cost at $650. Given that he works after school at a part-time job, Harry figures that he can save $20 a week. What sort of savings goal is this?

   Circle One:

   - Short-term goal

   - Medium-term goal

   - Long-term goal

3. Taylor has a new job. He wants to save money for a large-screen TV and sound system. The cost will be $2,500. Taylor figures he can save $150 a month. What sort of savings goal is this?

   Circle One:

   - Short-term goal

   - Medium-term goal

   - Long-term goal

4. The Newton family wants to save money for a family vacation to Orlando, Florida. The cost will be $5,000. The parents figure they can save $100 a month for the trip. What sort of savings goal is this?

Circle One:

- Short-term goal

- Medium-term goal

- Long-term goal

5. Jessie and Janice Weber are a young married couple who recently had their first child, Julia. Knowing that college will be expensive, they have already started a fund to save money for Julia's college education. Each year, they (along with other family members including grandparents, aunts, and uncles) contribute a total of $1,200 to Julia's college fund. They figure they will need to save a total of about $150,000. What sort of savings goal is this?

Circle One:

- Short-term goal

- Medium-term goal

- Long-term goal

SLIDE 13.1

LESSON 13 - WHY NOT SAVE?

Why Don't People Save When They Know They Should?

Question	Number of Yes Responses
How many of you know that smoking is unhealthy?	
How many of you know people who smoke?	
How many of you know that eating foods that are high in fat content, such as fast foods and packaged snacks, isn't healthy?	
How many of you know people who eat foods that are high in fat content?	
How many of you know that regular exercise provides many health benefits?	
How many of you know people who don't exercise regularly?	

SLIDE 13.2

LESSON 13 - WHY NOT SAVE?

Costs and Benefits

- Costs are all the things that have to be given up when a choice is made.

- Costs are negative.

- Benefits are any gains or favorable outcomes that make people more satisfied when a choice is made.

- Benefits are positive.

SLIDE 13.3

LESSON 13 - WHY NOT SAVE?

The Costs and Benefits of Diet and Exercise

- What are the benefits of eating a healthful diet and exercising regularly?

- Do these benefits of diet and exercise occur now or in the future?

- If people choose a healthful diet and exercise regularly, are they guaranteed these benefits? Can they count on them for sure?

- What are the costs of choosing a healthful diet and exercising regularly?

SLIDE 13.4

LESSON 13 - WHY NOT SAVE?

The Costs and Benefits of Saving

- Saving means setting money aside instead of spending it or using it to pay taxes.

- What are the benefits of saving?

- What are the costs of saving?

- When do the benefits of saving occur?

- When do the costs of saving occur?

SLIDE 13.5

LESSON 13 - WHY NOT SAVE?

People Are Inconsistent Over Time

- People are sometimes inconsistent in their plans and their actions.
  - They promise themselves to eat less; but when the time comes to have a snack, they eat it.
  - They promise themselves to exercise; but when the time comes to go running or biking or head to the gym, they choose to do something else.

- Spending may provide instant gratification; it often enables people to have what they want now.

- Saving is like passing up a snack or going to the gym. It requires a sacrifice in the present for a reward in the future.

LEARNING, EARNING, AND INVESTING FOR A NEW GENERATION © COUNCIL FOR ECONOMIC EDUCATION, NEW YORK, NY

SLIDE 13.6

LESSON 13 - WHY NOT SAVE?

Goals for Saving

- People who save usually have savings goals. These are aims or desired results that people hope to achieve.

- Short-term savings goals are those that can be achieved in one year or less.

- Medium-term savings goals are those that can be achieved in one-to-five years.

- Long-term savings goals require more than five years to achieve.

LEARNING, EARNING, AND INVESTING FOR A NEW GENERATION © COUNCIL FOR ECONOMIC EDUCATION, NEW YORK, NY

SLIDE 13.7

LESSON 13 - WHY NOT SAVE?

Types of Savings Goals?

Short-Term Savings Goals	Medium-Term Savings Goals	Long-Term Savings Goals

HOW ARE STOCK PRICES DETERMINED?

LESSON 14
HOW ARE STOCK PRICES DETERMINED?

LESSON DESCRIPTION
The students participate in a simulated stock market activity that shows how the price of a share of stock is determined in a competitive market. They analyze the simulation to learn that stock prices are established through the interaction of supply and demand.

INTRODUCTION
The laws of supply and demand apply to all markets, including financial markets. *Demand* refers to the different quantities of a stock that people will purchase at various prices during a specific period of time. *Supply* refers to the different quantities of a stock that will be offered for sale at various prices during a specific period of time. The equilibrium price is the price at which buyers want to buy the same amount of a stock that sellers want to sell. Shifts in demand and supply generate new prices.

CONCEPTS
Demand

Equilibrium price

Shift in demand or supply

Shortage

Supply

Surplus

OBJECTIVES
Students will:

- Make decisions about buying and selling shares of stock, based on their expectations of the profitability of a fictional corporation.

- Graph demand and supply curves.

- Graph shifts in demand and supply curves.

- Identify equilibrium prices.

CONTENT STANDARDS
Voluntary National Content Standards in Economics, **2nd Edition**

- **Standard 5:** Voluntary exchange occurs only when all participating parties expect to gain. This is true for trade among individuals or organizations within a nation, and among individuals or organizations in different nations.

- **Standard 7:** A market exists when buyers and sellers interact. This interaction determines market prices and thereby allocates scarce goods and services.

- **Standard 8:** Prices send signals and provide incentives to buyers and sellers. When supply or demand changes, market prices adjust, affecting incentives.

National Standards in K-12 Personal Finance Education, **3rd edition**

- **Saving and Investing Standard 4:** Describe how to buy and sell investments.

TIME REQUIRED
75 minutes

MATERIALS
- Slides 14.1, 14.2, 14.3, 14.4, 14.5, 14.6, 14.7, 14.8, and 14.9

- Activity 14.1 (enough copies for half of the students)

- Activity 14.2 (enough copies for half of the students)

- A copy of Activity 14.3 and 14.4 for each student

- Cards cut from Activity 14.5 and 14.6,

used to establish a deck of Seller Cards and a deck of Buyer Cards

- A copy of Activity 14.7 for each student

PROCEDURE

1. Introduce the lesson's focus on stock prices. These prices are important for an obvious reason. When they go up, some people make money; when they go down, some people lose money. The gains and losses may be large. But why does all this happen? Why do stock prices change?

2. Explain that there is widespread speculation among investors and media commentators about why prices change in the stock market. Some observers emphasize the influence of political developments. Others hint at dark conspiracies among insiders in the financial world. Economists emphasize basic economic principles. Whatever politicians and financial wheeler-dealers might be doing, they say, prices in the stock market are determined by supply and demand. This lesson focuses on that explanation, beginning with a simulation activity.

3. Organize the class into two groups of equal size: buyers and sellers. **Distribute one copy of Activity 14.1** to the buyers. **Distribute one copy of Activity 14.2** to the sellers. Ask the buyers to follow along as you read the text on Activity 14.1 to the class. Ask the buyers to complete the table on Activity 14.1. Ask the sellers to follow along as you read the text on Activity 14.2 to the sellers. Ask the sellers to complete the table on Activity 14.2.

4. **Display Slide 14.1.** Ask for a volunteer from the buyers' group to read the number of cups of coffee he or she would be willing to buy at each price. Write these numbers in column 1. Ask the same question of three more vol-

unteers from the buyers' group and write the numbers of cups in columns 2, 3, and 4. Then total the numbers and enter them in column 5. **Display Slide 14.2** and repeat the same procedure for the sellers.

5. **Display Slide 14.1** again. Ask the students whether they can see any pattern in the totals in column 5. *(The totals show that people will buy more cups of coffee at lower prices and fewer at higher prices.)* Inform the students that they have discovered a basic principle of economics—the law of demand. This is a key principle for describing the behavior of consumers. **Display Slide 14.3** to stress this point.

6. **Display Slide 14.2** again. Ask the students to look for another pattern in the totals in column 5. *(The totals show that people will produce more at higher prices and less at lower prices.)* Inform the students that they have discovered another basic principle of economics—the law of supply. This is a key principle for describing the behavior of producers. **Display Slide 14.3** again to stress this point.

7. Tell the students they will now use their knowledge of supply and demand to participate as buyers and sellers in a stock market. Keep the class grouped as buyers and sellers. **Distribute a copy of Activity 14.3** and read it aloud with the students.

8. **Distribute a copy of Activity 14.4** to all the students and explain that they should use it to record every transaction they make. Review the details of the score sheet.

9. Clear a large area in the classroom and designate it as the trading floor.

10. Have the Sell Cards and Buy Cards from Activities 14.5 and 14.6 ready; the cards should be kept in separate decks

and shuffled between each round of play. Assign one student to be keeper of the cards and another to record the transactions on Slide 14.4.

11. **Distribute the first Buy and Sell Cards—one to each student.** Each student should examine his or her card and record the number on the card on the score sheet. Then open the market for trading.

12. After five minutes, stop the first round of trade. **Display Slide 14.4** (which the recorder has completed for the first round, to show the students a summary of their exchanges). Tell the students that information on the summary shows a wide range of prices, with more prices clustering near $15 because there is neither a shortage nor a surplus at $15. This price of $15, where the market is balanced, is called the *equilibrium price.* Students will discover that their total gain will probably be greatest if they conclude more exchanges at $15, even though each of those exchanges provides a smaller gain than they originally wanted. As the students obtain more information about the equilibrium price, exchange prices will concentrate more closely around it.

13. Have the students play the second and third rounds of trading. After the last round, **use Slide 14.4** to display a summary of their exchanges. Ask the students what, if anything, that information tells them.

(The information should indicate that as trading progressed through each round, competition among players helped concentrate exchange prices more closely around the price of $15.)

14. **Distribute Activity 14.7.** Ask the students to read Part 1 and Part 2. Allow them time to draw the demand and supply curves on Figure 2 and respond to the **Questions for Discussion. Display Slide 14.5** and discuss the answers.

A. What is the law of demand?

(Buyers want to buy fewer stocks at higher prices than at lower prices.)

B. What is the law of supply?

(Sellers are willing to offer more stocks for sale at higher prices than at lower prices.)

C. What is the equilibrium price of Mighty Wings stock in Figure 2?

($15)

D. What would happen if the price of Mighty Wings were above $15?

(When the price is above the equilibrium price, buyers will buy less. There is a surplus.)

E. What would happen if the price of Mighty Wings were below $15?

(When the price is below the equilibrium price, sellers will offer less. There is a shortage.)

15. Ask the students to read Parts 3 and 4 of Activity 14.7. Ask them to complete the new demand schedule in Figure 3, graph the new demand curve on Figure 2, and respond to the **Questions for Discussion. Display Slide 14.6. Ask:**

A. What happened to demand? *(There was an increase in demand.)*

B. What happened to the equilibrium price? *(The equilibrium price increased to about $16.70.)*

Figure 3

Supply and Demand Schedules for Mighty Wings, Inc. Stock

Price per Share	Number of Shares Sellers Want to Sell	Number of Shares Buyers Want to Buy
$25		6
$20		
$15		
$10	2	
$5	0	

16. Ask the students to read Part 5 of Activity 14.7. Ask them to complete the new supply schedule in Figure 3, graph the new supply curve on Figure 2, and respond to the **Questions for Discussion.**

17. **Display Slide 14.7. Ask:**

    A. What happened to supply?

       (There was a decrease in supply.)

    B. What happened to the equilibrium price?

       (The equilibrium price increased to about $18.30. This is the intersection of S2 and D2.)

18. Explain that in the stock market, the laws of supply and demand are influenced by the expectations of buyers and sellers. For example, sometimes buyers buy stocks even as the price is rising. This seems to violate the law of demand. **Display Slide 14.8** and explain how the expectations of buyers and sellers can influence their decisions.

CLOSURE

19. **Display Slide 14.9** and review the main points of the lesson:

    • The law of demand states (with respect to stocks) that buyers choose to purchase more shares at lower prices than at higher prices.

    • The law of supply states (with respect to stocks) that sellers choose to sell more shares at higher prices than at lower prices.

    • An equilibrium price for stocks exists when the quantity of shares demanded at that price equals the quantity of shares being supplied.

    • For a given stock, prices change as a result of changes in the supply of and demand for that stock.

ASSESSMENT

Multiple-Choice Questions

1. Prices will probably rise for the shares of a particular corporation when

   a. the government allows stock prices to rise.
   b. sellers expect the company's profits to decrease.
   c. *buyers expect the company's profits to increase.*
   d. the New York Stock Exchange allows stock prices to rise.

2. The demand curve for shares of stock shows

   a. how many shares will be offered for sale at each price.
   b. how many shares will be demanded at the equilibrium price.
   c. how many shares will be demanded at the lowest possible price.
   d. *how many shares will be demanded at each price.*

3. If demand for the shares of a particular corporation decreases, what will happen to the price at which those shares can be sold?

    a. *The price will probably fall.*
    b. The price will probably rise.
    c. The price may either rise or fall.
    d. The price will probably remain the same.

4. Stockholders will be most willing to sell their shares if

    a. *they believe that the price they can get for their shares is higher than the potential value of the shares.*
    b. they believe that the company will become more profitable in the future.
    c. they believe that the price they can get for their shares is lower than the potential value of the shares.
    d. they believe that demand for the shares will rise in the future.

Constructed-Response Items

1. Consider the following comment made in a television news program editorial:

    > *Stock prices are too high! The average person cannot afford to buy stocks as an investment anymore. This situation is a threat to our economy. If people cannot afford to buy stocks, they will lose faith in the American Dream. Government regulators should require all sellers to make stocks available at $30 or less so everyone can afford them. If stock in good companies were available at a low price, everyone would have a chance to be rich.*

    Use the concepts of *supply, demand,* and *equilibrium price* to evaluate this statement.

    (Setting the price of stocks at $30 or less would prevent the price from respond-ing to changing conditions of supply and demand. If the price is set below the equilibrium price, many people wishing to buy stocks will not be able to purchase them because sellers will not make enough stock available at that low price to satisfy every buyer. Moreover, if you can buy a stock at a low price but the price cannot rise in the future, you will not make money or grow wealthier.)

2. Explain how investors' beliefs about the future profitability of a corporation affect the supply of and demand for its shares, and the equilibrium price of its shares.

    (When investors believe that a corporation will become more profitable in the future, demand for the stock will rise and the price will rise. Supply of the stock will probably decrease because shareholders will want to hold onto their shares unless they can get very high prices for them. When investors believe that the profits of the corporation will fall, demand for the corporation's shares will fall, as will the price of the shares. Supply will probably increase because shareholders will be more eager to sell.)

Gen i Connection

Mission 12 of the Gen i Revolution helps students understand the fundamentals of stock markets. Although the mission may be used with Lesson 7 ("What Are Stock Markets?"), it fits especially well with the current lesson, "How Are Stock Prices Determined?" The mission setting is that Jasmine needs to understand the stock market so that she can help her clients make trades. In this mission's 4-1-1 tutorial, students complete an interactive supply and demand schedule, are introduced to the concepts of surplus and shortage, and complete activities on the laws of supply and demand. Students can successfully conclude the mission by predicting stock prices and changes in stock prices based on supply and demand information.

(Note: Activity 14.3 is designed to be played in person by a group of interacting students; students therefore may find it more engaging than the interactive graphs in Mission 12. We recommend using both as complementary activities. Your students may find it interesting to answer a summary debriefing question: What are the differences between playing the stock trading game in person and clicking through the same graphs in an interactive game?)

Gen i Reflection

In Mission 12 of the Gen i Revolution, you learn what determines stock prices. Often on news broadcasts you will hear that a particular news event—such as a favorable report on the economy—sent stock prices higher. But if you ask floor traders why prices went up on a particular day, they might say, "Because I had more buy orders than sell orders." Are these explanations different? Explain.

ACTIVITY 14.1
STOMPING GROUNDS: BUYERS

Coffee is your favorite drink. For you and everyone in your family, a good day begins with a nice fresh cup.

Stomping Grounds, Inc. is a new coffee shop. You stopped there recently and loved the coffee. Amy Donald, the owner, is trying to decide how many cups of Stomping Grounds coffee customers like you are willing to buy at different prices. How many cups of Stomping Grounds coffee would you buy each week?

Your answer would probably depend on the price per cup. Read the table below. For each of the prices listed, estimate the maximum number of cups you would buy per week. Begin at the bottom of the table. Suppose Amy is giving away coupons for free cups of coffee. In the bottom blank, opposite $0, enter the maximum number of cups you would want to have per week if the coffee was free. Then go to the next price, $1. Write the maximum number of cups per week you might buy if you had to pay $1 for each cup. Then make similar estimates for each of the other prices. If you would not buy any cups at a particular price, write a zero in the blank next to that price.

Prices for One Cup of Stomping Grounds Coffee	Number of Cups of Stomping Grounds Coffee You Would Buy Each Week
$10	
$5	
$4	
$3	
$2	
$1	
$0 (Amy is giving away coupons for free coffee.)	

Activity 14.2
Stomping Grounds: Sellers

You are desperate for cash. You have begged your friends for money. "No deal," they said. You asked your parents for an increase in your allowance. The answer was a big "No." You called old Uncle Bart on your cell phone. Another "No"—but worse. He didn't even remember your name.

You decide to take matters into your own hands and search for a job. You notice that Stomping Grounds, Inc., a trendy new coffee shop, is looking for employees. It looks like a nice place to work.

Amy, the owner of Stomping Grounds, has a plan for you to consider. If you worked for Stomping Grounds, you could choose the number of hours you would work each week, and you could arrange the hours to fit your schedule. How many hours per week do you think you would be willing to work at Stomping Grounds to earn money? The answer might depend on the pay you would earn. Examine the table below. Then estimate the maximum number of hours you would be willing to work at each wage level.

For example, suppose Amy offered you a job as a volunteer, at no wage. Write in the number of hours you would be willing to work each week at the wage of $0 in the table below. Then consider another wage, $10 per hour. How many hours would you work at that wage? Write in that number, too. Complete all the blanks in the same manner. If you would not work at a particular wage, write a zero in the blank next to the wage.

Wages You Would Earn for One Hour of Work	Hours per Week You Would Work at This Wage
$30	
$25	
$20	
$15	
$10	
$0 (You are a volunteer.)	

ACTIVITY 14.3
MIGHTY WINGS GAME

Overview

In the following game, you will buy or sell stocks in an imaginary business called Mighty Wings, Inc. Half of you will be buyers and half will be sellers. In addition, a Card Keeper will give you a card with important instructions about each exchange. A Recorder will keep track of the exchanges you make.

You will play the game in three five-minute rounds. Your goal is to make as much money as you can by the end of the game. If you are a seller, however, you must deal with the law of demand when you try to get a high price for your shares. If you are a buyer, you must deal with the law of supply when you try to pay a low price for the shares you want.

Directions

1. Buyers will start the game with one Buy Card and one score sheet. The Buy Card will say "You are authorized to BUY one share of Mighty Wings, paying as little as possible. If you spend more than _____, you will lose money." The exact price is written on the Buy Card.

   • Record the price shown on your Buy Card on your score sheet.

   • When the round starts, try to buy at the lowest price the seller will agree to. If you pay exactly the price written on your card, you will break even for that transaction. If you pay less than the price on your card, the difference is a gain. If you pay more than the price on your card, the difference is a loss.

   • You may buy shares of stock at any price, as long as you can find a willing seller. But that price must always be in multiples of 5. That is, the price for one share may be $5, $10, $15, $20, and so on.

   • As soon as you have bought a stock, record the transaction on your score sheet.

   • Report the price you have negotiated to the Recorder; the Recorder will keep a tally on the Classroom Tally Sheet.

   • Turn in your card. Receive a new card and begin the negotiation process anew.

2. Sellers start the game with one Sell Card and one score sheet. The Sell Card will say "You are authorized to SELL one share of Mighty Wings, for as much as possible. If you sell for less than ____, you will lose money." The exact price is written on the Sell Card.

   • Record the price shown your sell order on your score sheet.

   • When the round starts, try to sell at the highest price you can get. If you get exactly the price written on your card, you will break even for that transaction. If you get more than the price on your card, the difference is a gain. If you get less than the price on your card, the difference is a loss.

   • You may sell shares of stock at any price, as long as you can find a willing buyer. But that price must always be in multiples of 5. That is, the price for one share may be $5, $10, $15, $20, and so on.

- As soon as you have sold a stock, record the transaction on your score sheet.

- Turn in your card. Receive a new card and begin the negotiation process anew.

3. When the teacher says, "The market is open," buyers and sellers should meet in the designated area and try to agree on a price for one share of stock.

4. The goal of buyers and sellers is to earn as much money as they can. Buyers will do this by purchasing stock for a price lower than the prices shown on their cards. Sellers make money by selling for higher prices than the prices shown on their cards.

5. Every time a price is agreed on and a sale is made, the buyer must report the price to the Recorder, who will enter it on the Classroom Tally Sheet.

6. As soon as buyers and sellers receive new cards, they should return to the market and try to make another deal.

7. All students are free to make as many transactions in a round as time permits. Once the teacher says, "The market is closed," no further transactions will count.

ACTIVITY 14.4
SCORE SHEET FOR THE MIGHTY WINGS GAME

Name _____ Date _____

Circle one: I Am a Buyer   I Am a Seller

Number of Exchanges	Price on Your Card	Transaction Price	Gain	Loss
1				
2				
3				
4				
5				
6				
7				
8				
9				
10				
11				
12				
13				
14				
15				
Total				

Net Gain or Loss (Circle one) _____

ACTIVITY 14.5
SELL CARDS

Sell one share of Mighty Wings, Inc. for as much as you can get. But if you accept less than $10 you will lose money.	Sell one share of Mighty Wings, Inc. for as much as you can get. But if you accept less than $10 you will lose money.	Sell one share of Mighty Wings, Inc. for as much as you can get. But if you accept less than $10 you will lose money.	Sell one share of Mighty Wings, Inc. for as much as you can get. But if you accept less than $10 you will lose money.
Sell one share of Mighty Wings, Inc. for as much as you can get. But if you accept less than $10 you will lose money.	Sell one share of Mighty Wings, Inc. for as much as you can get. But if you accept less than $10 you will lose money.	Sell one share of Mighty Wings, Inc. for as much as you can get. But if you accept less than $15 you will lose money.	Sell one share of Mighty Wings, Inc. for as much as you can get. But if you accept less than $15 you will lose money.
Sell one share of Mighty Wings, Inc. for as much as you can get. But if you accept less than $15 you will lose money.	Sell one share of Mighty Wings, Inc. for as much as you can get. But if you accept less than $15 you will lose money.	Sell one share of Mighty Wings, Inc. for as much as you can get. But if you accept less than $15 you will lose money.	Sell one share of Mighty Wings, Inc. for as much as you can get. But if you accept less than $15 you will lose money.
Sell one share of Mighty Wings, Inc. for as much as you can get. But if you accept less than $15 you will lose money.	Sell one share of Mighty Wings, Inc. for as much as you can get. But if you accept less than $15 you will lose money.	Sell one share of Mighty Wings, Inc. for as much as you can get. But if you accept less than $20 you will lose money.	Sell one share of Mighty Wings, Inc. for as much as you can get. But if you accept less than $20 you will lose money.
Sell one share of Mighty Wings, Inc. for as much as you can get. But if you accept less than $20 you will lose money.	Sell one share of Mighty Wings, Inc. for as much as you can get. But if you accept less than $20 you will lose money.	Sell one share of Mighty Wings, Inc. for as much as you can get. But if you accept less than $20 you will lose money.	Sell one share of Mighty Wings, Inc. for as much as you can get. But if you accept less than $20 you will lose money.
Sell one share of Mighty Wings, Inc. for as much as you can get. But if you accept less than $20 you will lose money.	Sell one share of Mighty Wings, Inc. for as much as you can get. But if you accept less than $20 you will lose money.	Sell one share of Mighty Wings, Inc. for as much as you can get. But if you accept less than $25 you will lose money.	Sell one share of Mighty Wings, Inc. for as much as you can get. But if you accept less than $25 you will lose money.
Sell one share of Mighty Wings, Inc. for as much as you can get. But if you accept less than $25 you will lose money.	Sell one share of Mighty Wings, Inc. for as much as you can get. But if you accept less than $25 you will lose money.		

ACTIVITY 14.6
BUY CARDS

Buy one share of Mighty Wings, Inc. for as little as you can. But if you pay more than $5 you will lose money.	Buy one share of Mighty Wings, Inc. for as little as you can. But if you pay more than $5 you will lose money.	Buy one share of Mighty Wings, Inc. for as little as you can. But if you pay more than $5 you will lose money.	Buy one share of Mighty Wings, Inc. for as little as you can. But if you pay more than $5 you will lose money.
Buy one share of Mighty Wings, Inc. for as little as you can. But if you pay more than $10 you will lose money.	Buy one share of Mighty Wings, Inc. for as little as you can. But if you pay more than $10 you will lose money.	Buy one share of Mighty Wings, Inc. for as little as you can. But if you pay more than $10 you will lose money.	Buy one share of Mighty Wings, Inc. for as little as you can. But if you pay more than $10 you will lose money.
Buy one share of Mighty Wings, Inc. for as little as you can. But if you pay more than $10 you will lose money.	Buy one share of Mighty Wings, Inc. for as little as you can. But if you pay more than $10 you will lose money.	Buy one share of Mighty Wings, Inc. for as little as you can. But if you pay more than $10 you will lose money.	Buy one share of Mighty Wings, Inc. for as little as you can. But if you pay more than $10 you will lose money.
Buy one share of Mighty Wings, Inc. for as little as you can. But if you pay more than $15 you will lose money.	Buy one share of Mighty Wings, Inc. for as little as you can. But if you pay more than $15 you will lose money.	Buy one share of Mighty Wings, Inc. for as little as you can. But if you pay more than $15 you will lose money.	Buy one share of Mighty Wings, Inc. for as little as you can. But if you pay more than $15 you will lose money.
Buy one share of Mighty Wings, Inc. for as little as you can. But if you pay more than $15 you will lose money.	Buy one share of Mighty Wings, Inc. for as little as you can. But if you pay more than $15 you will lose money.	Buy one share of Mighty Wings, Inc. for as little as you can. But if you pay more than $15 you will lose money.	Buy one share of Mighty Wings, Inc. for as little as you can. But if you pay more than $15 you will lose money.
Buy one share of Mighty Wings, Inc. for as little as you can. But if you pay more than $20 you will lose money.	Buy one share of Mighty Wings, Inc. for as little as you can. But if you pay more than $20 you will lose money.	Buy one share of Mighty Wings, Inc. for as little as you can. But if you pay more than $20 you will lose money.	Buy one share of Mighty Wings, Inc. for as little as you can. But if you pay more than $20 you will lose money.
Buy one share of Mighty Wings, Inc. for as little as you can. But if you pay more than $20 you will lose money.	Buy one share of Mighty Wings, Inc. for as little as you can. But if you pay more than $20 you will lose money.		

Activity 14.7
Understanding Supply, Demand, and Equilibrium Price

Part 1: Equilibrium Price

Why did exchange prices of Mighty Wings stock concentrate around $15 per share? The answer is that this price is the only one at which there was neither a shortage nor surplus in the market. Here's why.

A market exists whenever buyers and sellers exchange with one another. But the amount sellers want to sell can be very different from the amount buyers want to buy. In the game you played, only a price of $15 per share balanced these two amounts.

Figure 1 below shows what was happening in the market for Mighty Wings stocks. The table shows what all the buyers' cards were telling them to do. And it shows what all the sellers' cards were telling them to do.

Figure 1

Price Per Share	Number of Shares Sellers Want to Sell	Number of Shares Buyers Want to Buy
$25	26	0
$20	22	6
$15	14	14
$10	6	22
$5	4	26

Note that the equilibrium price is the only one at which buyers want to buy the same number of shares that sellers want to sell. Here, a price of $15 is the equilibrium price because it balances these two quantities at 14 shares.

Part 2: How to Balance a Market

The numbers in Figure 1 illustrate the laws of supply and demand. Sellers offer more stocks for sale at higher prices than at lower prices. In contrast, buyers want to buy fewer stocks at higher prices than at lower prices.

For example, look at Figure 1 to see what happens when the price is $25. At this price, sellers want to sell 26 shares. But buyers do not want to buy any shares at that price. So the market is unbalanced. A surplus of 26 shares exists. This means sellers want to sell 26 more shares than buyers want to buy at that price. Because of the surplus, sellers reduce their prices. Only by decreasing their prices to $15 per share can they sell all the shares they want to sell.

On the other hand, the price can also be too low. Look what happens when the price is $10 per share. Here, too, the market is unbalanced. A shortage of 16 shares exists. This means that buyers want to buy 16 more shares than sellers want to sell at that price. Because of the shortage, buyers increase their prices. Only by increasing their prices to $15 per share can they buy all the shares they want.

A price of $15 per share turns out to be a special price. It is special because of what it does: It balances the number of shares that buyers and sellers want to trade. Because of its special role in balancing the shares demanded and supplied, this price is called the equilibrium price. It is the only price at which the shares demanded and supplied are in equilibrium.

We can use a graph to show what happens in a market. This may not seem important now, but it is useful when the supply and demand curves change. Draw a graph in Figure 2 to illustrate the information contained in Figure 1. Label the demand curve with "D" and the supply curve with "S."

Figure 2

Supply and Demand Curves for Mighty Wings, Inc. Stock

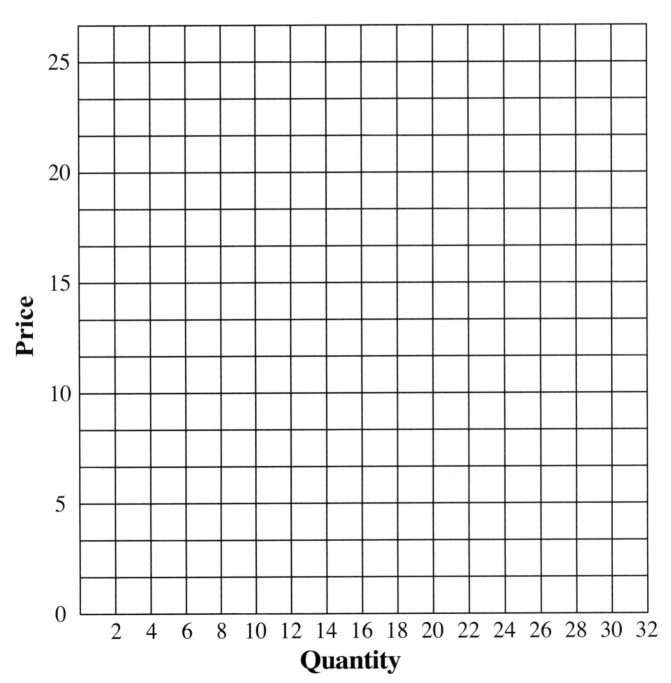

Questions for Discussion

A. What is the law of demand?

B. What is the law of supply?

C. What is the equilibrium price of Mighty Wings in Figure 2?

D. What would happen if the price of Mighty Wings rose above $15?

E. What would happen if the price of Mighty Wings fell below $15?

Part 3: The Ups and Downs of Stock Prices

The game you played shows how buyers and sellers adjust their prices to reach a balance, or equilibrium. But these balances seldom stay the same. Demand and supply are continually changing, and buyers might want to buy more at each possible price. If so, they bid the price up to a new equilibrium level. Or sellers might want to sell more at each possible price. If so, they push the price down to a new equilibrium level.

So there is no mystery behind the ups and downs of prices for stocks—or for other goods and services. Prices change because buyers and sellers become more or less willing to buy or sell something. Then they work out new equilibrium prices to balance the market—just as your class did for Mighty Wings, Inc. stocks.

Part 4: A Change in Demand

Let's see how an equilibrium price can change when the demand for Mighty Wings, Inc. stock is greater at every price. Suppose that Mighty Wings, Inc. makes high-quality roller skates. This year, however, roller skates are the latest fad. Profits for Mighty Wings, Inc. have increased greatly, and people want to buy six more shares of its stock at every price. Fill in the new demand schedule in Figure 3. Next, label the original demand curve in Figure 2 as D1. Then graph this year's change by drawing a demand curve on Figure 2. Label the new demand curve D2.

Figure 3

Supply and Demand Schedules for Mighty Wings, Inc. Stock

Price per Share	Number of Shares Sellers Want to Sell	Number of Shares Buyers Want to Buy
$25		6
$20		
$15		
$10	2	
$5	0	

Questions for Discussion

A. What happened to demand?

B. What happened to the equilibrium price?

Part 5: Change in Supply

Sellers now expect the price of a share of Mighty Wings, Inc. stock to rise in the future. Sellers offer four fewer shares at each price. Write the number of shares sellers are now willing and able to sell in Figure 3. First, label the original supply curve S1; then draw a new supply curve on Figure 2. Label the new supply curve S2.

Questions for Discussion

A.   What happened to supply?

B.   What happened to the equilibrium price (compare the prices on D2 and S2)?

The completed Figures 2 and 3 show an increase in demand and a decrease in supply. Demand increased and supply decreased because the stock is now more attractive. Current owners want to hold on to more shares. And other investors are more eager to buy shares for themselves.

SLIDE 14.1

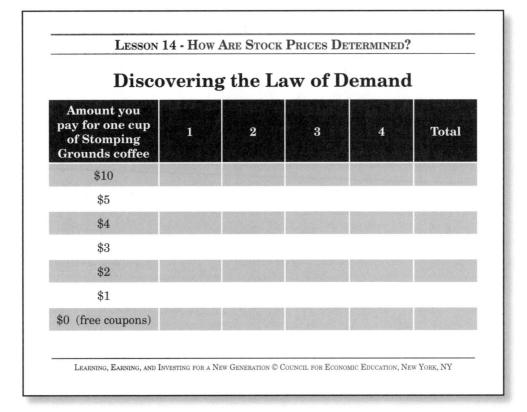

Discovering the Law of Demand

Amount you pay for one cup of Stomping Grounds coffee	1	2	3	4	Total
$10					
$5					
$4					
$3					
$2					
$1					
$0 (free coupons)					

SLIDE 14.2

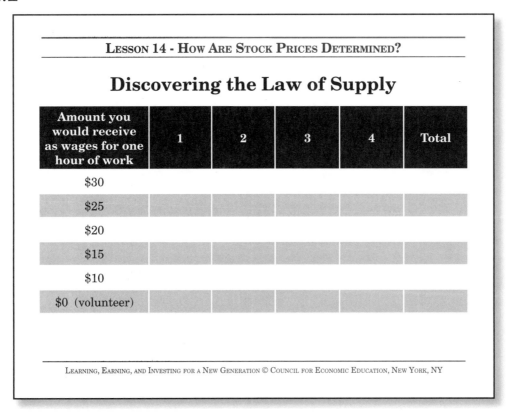

Discovering the Law of Supply

Amount you would receive as wages for one hour of work	1	2	3	4	Total
$30					
$25					
$20					
$15					
$10					
$0 (volunteer)					

Slide 14.3

The Laws of Demand and Supply

- **Law of Demand:** At lower prices, people choose to buy more. At higher prices, people choose to buy less.

- **Law of Supply:** At higher prices, people choose to produce more. At lower prices, people choose to produce less.

Slide 14.4

Classroom Tally Sheet

Price	Round 1	Round 2	Round 3
$50			
45			
40			
35			
30			
25			
20			
15			
10			
$5			

SLIDE 14.5

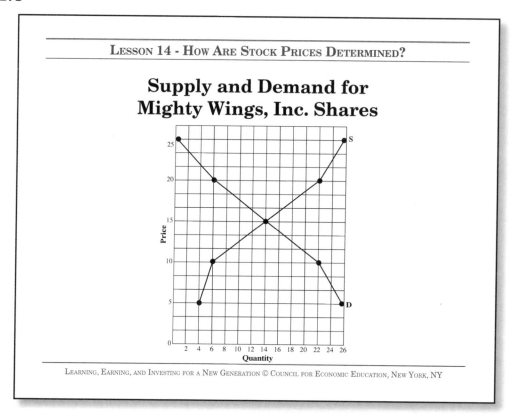

SLIDE 14.6

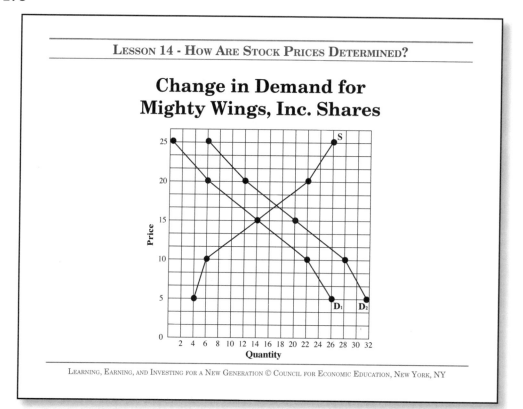

Slide 14.7

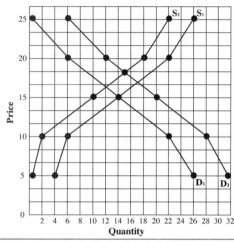

Slide 14.8

The Role of Expectations

Demand in Stock Markets

People are more likely to buy stock in a given company if they have positive expectations regarding the success of that company.

They might expect:

- The share price to increase.
- An improved dividend payment.

Supply in Stock Markets

People are more likely to sell stock in a given company if they have negative expectations regarding the success of that company.

They might expect:

- The stock price to decrease in response to changes in the industry, world events, or other uncertainties.
- The dividend to decrease.
- Better opportunities to purchase other stocks, bonds, or other types of investments.

SLIDE 14.9

LESSON 14 - HOW ARE STOCK PRICES DETERMINED?

Review of Supply and Demand

- The law of demand states (regarding stocks) that buyers choose to purchase more shares at lower prices and fewer shares at higher prices, all else constant.

- The law of supply states (regarding stocks) that sellers choose to sell more shares at higher prices and fewer shares at lower prices, all else constant.

- An equilibrium price exists when the quantity of shares demanded at that price equals the quantity of shares supplied.

- Stock prices change as a result of changes in the supply of and demand for shares of the stock in question.

THE ROLE OF GOVERNMENT IN FINANCIAL MARKETS

LESSON 15
THE ROLE OF GOVERNMENT IN FINANCIAL MARKETS

LESSON DESCRIPTION

The students learn how government regulation of financial markets is intended to protect investors from fraud and prevent market failure. They also learn how regulatory efforts may be weakened or negated by government failure. In addition to the possibilities of market failures and government failures, students are shown that businesses sometimes lose money because of inherent risk and not because of any wrongdoing. Students consolidate their learning by playing a "blame game," applying distinctions between government failure, market failure, and no failure.

INTRODUCTION

When there is a market failure, participants and the economy in general may suffer. In the markets for ordinary products and services, market failure is characterized by inefficiency and under- or over-production. In financial markets, market failure takes the form of information problems that may lead to fraud, unexpected risks, and other problems. However, correcting market failure is not straightforward because regulatory policies often have unintended effects. Also, for investors, there is risk in holding all financial assets. Although assuming risk can lead to higher payoffs, it also can lead to losses, even in the absence of government or market failures. Sensible policy choices balance the risks of market failure with the risks of government failure.

CONCEPTS

Government failure

Market failure

Ponzi scheme

OBJECTIVES

Students will be able to:

- Explain that securities markets are subject to market failure.

- Explain that the regulation of securities markets is subject to government failure.

- Explain what a Ponzi scheme is and why it must eventually fail.

CONTENT STANDARDS

Voluntary National Content Standards in Economics, **2nd Edition**

- **Standard 16:** There is an economic role for government in a market economy whenever the benefits of a government policy outweigh its costs. Governments often provide for national defense, address environmental concerns, define and protect property rights, and attempt to make markets more competitive. Most government policies also have direct or indirect effects on people's incomes.

- **Standard 17:** Costs of government policies sometimes exceed benefits. This may occur because of incentives facing voters, government officials, and government employees, because of actions by special interest groups that can impose costs on the general public, or because social goals other than economic efficiency are being pursued.

National Standards in K-12 Personal Finance Education, **3rd edition**

- **Financial Responsibility and Decision Making Standard 1:** Take responsibility for personal financial decisions.

- **Saving and Investing Standard 6:** Investigate how agencies that regulate financial markets protect investors.

TIME REQUIRED

60 minutes

MATERIALS

- Slides 15.1 to 15.15

- One copy of Activity 15.1 for each student

PROCEDURE

1. Tell the students that this lesson is about government regulation of financial markets. **Display Slide 15.1.** Explain that financial markets may fail when dishonest participants engage in deception or fraud. Certain government regulations are intended to prevent such failures. It is possible, however, that a regulation itself may fail. That is, regulation is vulnerable to government failure, when policy and budget choices by government officials result in inefficiency. Finally, some bad outcomes for investors are simply the product of business decisions that did not work out—cases in which there is no market failure and no government failure.

2. **Display Slide 15.2** and introduce the Securities and Exchange Commission (SEC). It is a federal agency responsible for enforcing federal securities laws and regulating the securities industry. By reference to Slide 15.2, explain that SEC regulation occurs in three main areas: (1) to prevent companies offering stocks from making dishonest statements, it enforces reporting and disclosure requirements; (2) to discourage unfair treatment of investors, it enforces rules and monitors trading; (3) to deal with outright fraud and theft of investors' funds, it undertakes enforcement action, including lawsuits.

3. **Display Slide 15.3.** Remind the students that in addition to market failure, there can also be government failure. For example, the Federal Reserve System's policies did not stem the tide of bank failures in the 1930s. As recently as 2008, the SEC discovered that it had failed to detect a totally fraudulent scheme, with investor losses estimated at $65 billion.

4. **Display Slide 15.4.** Tell the students that a Ponzi scheme is a fraudulent enterprise that attracts investors even though it has no real profits or assets. Instead, it recruits investors with promises of high gains. Early investors are paid using money the scheme managers collect from later investors. Eventually it must collapse because it has no real profits or assets to draw on.

5. **Display Slide 15.5.** Tell students that the largest Ponzi scheme in history was operated by financier Bernard Madoff from the early 1990s until 2008. It was undetected by the SEC for several years even though its operations fell clearly within the SEC's territory. An internal SEC report said that the agency was repeatedly tipped off about Madoff, but no thorough and competent review was performed.

6. **Display Slide 15.6.** Remind the students that not all losses are caused by fraud. Some adverse outcomes for investors are simply a result of ordinary business risk. Neither the SEC nor any other agency can remove this risk. When fully informed investors lose money because of business results, there is neither market failure nor government failure.

7. **Distribute Activity 15.1** and tell students they are about to play a game called "The Blame Game." Give them about 15 minutes to read the activity.

8. Now **Display Slide 15.7** and tell the students you will be outlining investment situations to them. They will classify each situation by moving in the classroom to indicate their choice: moving to one side for "market failure," moving to the other side for "government failure," and standing in place at their seats for "no market or government failure." (Slide 15.7 shows these directions with large arrows.)

9. **Display Slide 15.8** and read the description ("Pay package snag: Investment fund managers take on excessive risk because their pay packages reward them for high returns, but provide no penalty for losing shareholders' money. The fund's disclosures meet the letter of the law, but they understate the risk."). **Ask:** "Is this market failure, government failure, or neither? Move around to indicate your choice."

(The best answer is "market failure"; the managers are not respecting shareholders' wishes. Some students may choose "government failure" because the fund's disclosures met the letter of the law but they were not adequate to protect shareholders.)

10. **Display Slide 15.9** and read the description ("Grocery startup: Webvan. com pioneers the online grocery business, grows too fast, and fails. Although there is no fraud, because of the business risk investors lose all the money they put into it."). **Ask:** "Is this market failure, government failure, or neither? Move around to indicate your choice."

(The correct answer is "no market or government failure," indicated by students standing in place. Webvan presented ordinary business risk with no guarantee of success. There was no indication of fraud, no indication of market failure, and no indication of government failure.)

11. **Display Slide 15.10** and read the description ("Home-loan mess: Government housing policy requires risky loans to less qualified customers, and many of the new homeowners are then unable to make their payments. Securities based on the loans fail and the housing market crashes.") **Ask:** "Is this market failure, government failure, or neither? Move around to indicate your choice."

(The best answer is "government failure." Government failure [defined as a situation in which "policy and budget choices by officials result in inefficiency"] is at the heart of the problem as described. "Market failure" has some merit, but is not as good an answer because the market crash was initiated by government decisions.)

12. **Display Slide 15.11** and read the description ("AOL-Time Warner: After full disclosures and despite high hopes, a merger of media giant Time Warner with internet startup AOL loses billions of dollars of investor money."). **Ask:** "Is this market failure, government failure, or neither? Move around to indicate your choice."

(The best answer is "No market or government failure," indicated by students standing in place. The phrase "full disclosures" suggests the absence of fraud and deception; this was just a merger that did not work out.)

13. **Display Slide 15.12** and read the description ("Senior sales push: A high-pressure phone bank sells stocks over the phone to uninformed residents of nursing homes. Although investigators can find no violations of law, it is clear that the buyers did not understand the risks."). **Ask:** "Is this market failure, government failure, or neither? Move around to indicate your choice."

(The best answer is "market failure"

because of the high pressure sales pitch and uninformed buyers. Some students may choose "government failure" because the law was not violated, reasoning that what was done should have been illegal. Some students may say there was no failure, but even the strongest defenders of markets would find the described practices questionable.)

14. **Display Slide 15.13** and read the description ("Your results may vary: After becoming fully informed about the risks and returns of holding stocks for the long term, an individual investor finds that stocks have gone down overall for a ten-year period."). **Ask:** "Is this market failure, government failure or neither? Move around to indicate your choice."

(The correct answer is "No market or government failure," indicated by students standing in place. Stock market returns are not guaranteed; there is no indication of dishonesty, fraud or government regulatory mistakes in this case.)

15. **Display Slide 15.14** and explain that there are two kinds of risk in financial markets. First, there is *security-specific risk*, the risk that any one stock or bond might fail. Traditionally, government regulation has been focused on security-specific risk. (Point out that the investment risks monitored today by the SEC generally are considered to be well controlled.) Second, as the events of 2007-2009 illustrate, there is a possibility of *systemic risk*, the risk that the entire system could fail. For example, a brokerage house with billions owed throughout the financial system might create a systemic risk. In the years 2007-2009, traditional regulation did not deal well with systemic risk. The main practical question in dealing with systemic risk is when to bail out troubled firms.

CLOSURE

16. **Display Slide 15.15.** Summarize by pointing out that the Securities and Exchange Commission can require disclosure and enforce laws against fraud, but it does not attempt to guarantee any gains.

    Ask: Can government regulators assure you that investing in the stock market will enable you to make long-term gains? Explain your answer.

    (No. Regulators can only set and enforce rules of the game. It is quite possible to lose money even when there has been no wrongdoing.)

17. Remind the students that as future investors, they will be responsible for researching the risks and returns of investments they are considering.

    Ask: If an investment sounds too good to be true, can you assume that the investment is legitimate because of government regulation of securities markets? Explain your answer.

    (No. Even with regulations in place, individuals need to check out investments for themselves. Although most investments are legitimate, it is impossible to detect and eliminate all fraud—even in the case of Ponzi schemes).

ASSESSMENT
Multiple-Choice Questions

1. Which of the following is a recognized function of the Securities and Exchange Commission?

    a. Guaranteeing that investors will receive a fair return if they invest carefully
    b. *Requiring accurate disclosures of companies' financial information*
    c. Controlling the total quantity of money in the economy
    d. Ensuring the safety of individuals' bank deposits

2. In a Ponzi scheme, where does the money to pay off early investors come from?

    a. From the proceeds of stock issued by a fake company
    b. From fraudulent stock options
    c. *From money paid in by later investors*
    d. From subprime real estate loans

3. Which of the following would be clear evidence of a market failure?

    a. Investors losing money after buying the stock of a high-tech startup company
    b. Investors losing money after buying a widely diversified set of stocks
    c. An individual shareholder selling a stock just before it unexpectedly doubled in price
    d. *A group of investors discovering that relevant risks were not disclosed to them*

4. Because of government regulation of securities markets, investors can assume

    a. *a high probability, but not certainty, that reporting and disclosure requirements are being met.*
    b. certainty that securities offered for sale are not fraudulent.
    c. certainty that stocks will outperform bonds over the long term.
    d. no insurance coverage for saved or invested funds, not even those held in individual bank accounts.

Constructed-Response Items

1. Terry is a young investor who opened a 401(k) account at work and has money regularly put into it from his paychecks. Terry has also followed the standard advice of buying and holding diverse stocks in the 401(k). There have been up years and down years for Terry, but—following a recent crash in stock values—the amount in the account is equal only to the sum of all the contributions he has made. That is, his return so far is zero. Has investment regulation failed Terry? That is, did his zero return result from a failure that government policy is designed to fight? Explain your answer.

    (Regulation is aimed at preventing fraud and unfair dealing. In this case, there is no indication that Terry is the victim of either fraud or unfair dealing—it's just that stock returns have been low. Therefore there is no government cause or cure for Terry's low return. Historically, stock returns are not guaranteed, and there are sometimes long flat periods in which returns are low overall. However, it is also true that, in the historical pattern, the highest returns went to investors like Terry who stayed invested. When the stock market improved, their holdings were already invested and ready to grow.)

2. Your aunt and uncle are thinking about investing money with a new financial adviser. The financial adviser has no local office and no other local customers, but he claims to have achieved extremely high returns over the past four years. Your aunt and uncle are a little suspicious, but they believe all financial advisers are regulated by the government and therefore they don't have to worry about fraud. What is your advice to your aunt and uncle?

    (A variety of answers can be accepted, but the best answers will point out [1] that even with government regulation investors are responsible for protecting themselves against fraud; [2] that Ponzi schemes still operate today; and [3] that extremely high returns are unlikely in a legitimate investment vehicle over a four-year period, unless it is an unusually prosperous time in financial markets overall.)

Gen i Connection

There is no Gen i Revolution mission directly related to government regulation of financial markets. The Gen i Revolution game is directed toward individual decision making and financial planning rather than public policy—which is the focus of this lesson. However, there are two somewhat related missions that may be useful to assign at this point, if students have not already played these missions:

1. Mission 13, in which students advise Markos on how to weather a crash in the scholarship fund, points out the nature of financial crashes.

2. Mission 14, in which students advise political leaders on their economic forecasts, relates the stock market to the broader economy.

EconEdLink Connection

"Guess Who's Coming to Dinner?" on EconEdLink (www.econedlink.org/e522) provides a general introduction to government regulation. The specific topic is food safety, but much of the content applies equally to financial regulation. In the first activity, students use the 1906 Pure Food and Drugs Act in a case study to explore why the government intervened to regulate safety and quality. In a second activity, students examine ways in which government regulation has improved consumer access to food and nutrition information. Students use this information to make a choice between two food products.

Gen i Reflection

In Mission 13 of the Gen i Revolution, a segment of the market has crashed. When such a crash happens, are you more likely to believe that the market has failed or that the government has failed? Or are you more likely to think the crash was not anyone's fault? Explain your answer.

ACTIVITY 15.1
MARKET FAILURE VS. GOVERNMENT FAILURE VS. NO FAILURE

What Is Market Failure?

The market for apples generally does a good job of allocating apples. Participants buy and sell, and they all feel the benefits exceed the costs. But what if an unethical apple producer used illegal and unsafe pesticides? Then apple buyers would inadvertently be buying a product with costs greater than benefits. When a market does not allocate resources properly, there is a *market failure*. Markets for tangible goods and services fail when participants do not have to bear the full costs of their transactions—like an apple grower secretly using that illegal pesticide. The same principle applies in financial markets. When a dishonest market participant engages in deception or fraud, costs are shifted and the market fails. Consider what would happen if a financial advisor deliberately denied the presence of risk while getting clients to invest in speculative stocks. The clients would end up with riskier investments than they intended—an instance of market failure.

Federal Regulation: The Securities and Exchange Commission

Congress established the Securities and Exchange Commission in 1934, following widespread financial problems that ushered in the Great Depression. Here are three major problems that can make financial markets fail, along with SEC measures aimed at preventing those problems:

1. **Dishonest statements from companies offering stocks.** The SEC combats this problem with reporting and disclosure requirements.

2. **Unfair treatment of investors.** The SEC combats this problem with rules and monitoring of trading.

3. **Outright fraud and theft of investors' funds.** The SEC combats this problem with enforcement actions, including lawsuits.

What Is Government Failure?

In financial markets, government regulation is aimed at providing information and enforcement to prevent dishonest and unfair dealing. But regulation does not always work as intended. Just as there is market failure, so too there can be *government failure*, defined as "policy and budget choices by government officials that result in inefficiency." For example, the Federal Reserve System was set up in 1914 to guard against financial instability in the banking system, but the Federal Reserve failed its first big test in the banking crises of the early 1930s.

The possibility of government failure means we cannot always be sure that regulation will solve a market problem. Below is a recent example.

Bernard Madoff's Ponzi Scheme

The investment scam called a "Ponzi scheme" was named after Charles Ponzi, who was born in Italy but became a swindler in North America. The scheme involves a mythical investment fund that has no real profits or assets. Instead, it recruits investors with promises of high gains. As recruiting continues, early investors are paid with money collected from later investors—but the scheme must eventually collapse because of the lack of actual profits or assets to generate a return over the long term.

The largest Ponzi scheme in history operated right under the SEC's nose for years. It was run by New Yorker Bernard Madoff from the early 1990s until 2008. Investors' losses were estimated at $65 billion.

The Madoff fund operated as a classic Ponzi scheme. It had no real assets or investments, and was able to pay off early investors only from funds invested by new investors. Madoff's Ponzi scheme went undetected by the SEC even though its operations fell clearly under SEC jurisdiction. After the Ponzi scheme fell apart and Madoff went to jail, an internal SEC report laid out the agency's multiple failures in the case of Madoff:

- The agency was repeatedly tipped off about Madoff.

- There were "detailed and substantive complaints."

- There were three examinations and two investigations by SEC staff, but the internal report said no thorough and competent review was performed.

(Source: U.S. Securities and Exchange Commission, "Investigation of Failure of the SEC to Uncover Bernard Madoff's Ponzi Scheme," August 31, 2009, available online: http://www.sec.gov/news/studies/2009/oig-509.pdf)

This was a case of government failure.

When Markets Work but Investors Lose Money

Historically, stocks have yielded high returns, on average, but any one stock is always subject to substantial risk. A company might misjudge markets or fail to control costs or engage in unwise expansion—causing stockholders to lose part, or even all, of the value of their investments. Investors cannot strive for a high return by investing in stocks without bearing risk.

This risk-bearing by stockholders means that good-faith investments may result in substantial losses. Losses may occur even when there is no market failure and no government failure. Regulation by authorities such as the SEC can work to guarantee the integrity of the process of buying and selling stocks. However, it is not designed to guarantee investment outcomes.

Snapple iced tea products provide a good illustration of this point. The shareholders of Quaker Oats expected high returns when Quaker bought Snapple in 1994. Quaker had enjoyed success in managing its sports drink Gatorade, making it a widely recognized and profitable brand. Quaker's success in dealing with grocery store chains and retailers promised similar success for Snapple. Yet Quaker stumbled badly and never made a success of Snapple. After paying $1.7 billion for Snapple in 1994, it sold Snapple for $300 million in 1997. Quaker's shareholders lost more than a million dollars a day on the deal.

As bad as the deal was, it complied fully with securities laws. Investors were warned of the risk. It was simply a business deal that did not work out. Thus there was no government failure and no market failure to blame.

The Blame Game: Market, Government, or Neither?

In this classification game you will be shown several investments that have gone bad. You will be asked to assign blame, indicating your answer by:

- ← Moving to that side of the classroom for "market failure"

- Moving to the other side of the classroom for "government failure" →

- Standing in place if there is no market failure and no government failure.

If more than one answer seems to apply, pick the one you believe is most relevant.

The investment situations you are to consider are listed below. Think about each one and prepare to classify each as a market failure, a government failure or no failure:

- **Pay package snag:** Investment fund managers take on excessive risk because their pay packages reward them for high returns, but provide no penalty for losing shareholders' money. The fund's disclosures meet the letter of the law, but they understate the risk.

- **Grocery startup:** Webvan.com pioneers the online grocery business, grows too fast, and fails. Although there is no fraud, because of the business risk investors lose all the money they put into it.

- **Home-loan mess:** Government housing policy requires risky loans to less qualified customers, and many of the new homeowners are then unable to make their payments. Financial distress spreads and the housing market crashes.

- **AOL-Time Warner:** After full disclosures and despite high hopes, a merger of media giant Time-Warner with Internet startup AOL loses billions of dollars of investor money.

- **Senior sales push:** A high-pressure phone bank sells stocks over the phone to uninformed residents of nursing homes. Although investigators can find no violations of law, it is clear that the buyers did not understand the risks.

- **Your results may vary:** After becoming fully informed about the risks and returns of holding stocks for the long term, an individual investor finds that stocks have gone down overall for a ten-year period.

SLIDE 15.1

LESSON 15 - THE ROLE OF GOVERNMENT IN FINANCIAL MARKETS

Financial Market Problems

1. Financial markets may fail.

2. Government regulation is aimed at preventing market failure.

3. Regulation is itself subject to government failure.

4. Some investors' losses result from business decisions that did not work out (no market failure and no government failure).

SLIDE 15.2

LESSON 15 - THE ROLE OF GOVERNMENT IN FINANCIAL MARKETS

The SEC and Market Failure

The Securities and Exchange Commission (SEC) is a federal agency authorized to enforce securities laws and issue regulations aimed at three problems:

1. Dishonest statements from companies offering stocks.

   SEC role: reporting and disclosure requirements.

2. Unfair treatment of investors.

   SEC role: rules and monitoring of trading.

3. Outright fraud and theft of investors' funds.

   SEC role: enforcement actions, lawsuits.

SLIDE 15.3

LESSON 15 - THE ROLE OF GOVERNMENT IN FINANCIAL MARKETS

Government Failure

1. Like markets, government policies and programs may fail.

2. The Federal Reserve System failed to prevent bank failures in the 1930s.

3. In 2008, the SEC failed to identify and take action against a totally fraudulent investment scheme run by Bernard Madoff, in which investors lost billions of dollars.

SLIDE 15.4

LESSON 15 - THE ROLE OF GOVERNMENT IN FINANCIAL MARKETS

What Is a Ponzi Scheme?

- Named after Charles Ponzi, who was born in Italy but became a swindler in North America

- Ponzi schemes operate with no real profits or assets

- Investors are recruited with promises of high gains

Charles Ponzi

- Early investors are paid with money collected from later investors

- Eventually such a scheme collapses since no real profits or assets exist to sustain it

SLIDE 15.5

LESSON 15 - THE ROLE OF GOVERNMENT IN FINANCIAL MARKETS

History's Largest Ponzi Scheme

- Operated by New Yorker Bernard Madoff, 1991- 2008
- Investor losses estimated at $65 billion
- The scheme was based on no real assets or investments; it paid early investors with money from later investors
- The scheme, clearly within SEC jurisdiction, went undetected by the SEC:
  - SEC was repeatedly tipped off
  - Multiple examinations and investigations
  - Yet fraud went undetected

Bernard Madoff

SLIDE 15.6

LESSON 15 - THE ROLE OF GOVERNMENT IN FINANCIAL MARKETS

Pay Your Money, Take Your Chances

1. Investing in stocks: potential for high returns, but with risk
2. Some investors' losses arise from ordinary business risk
3. No government agency can remove this risk
4. When fully informed investors lose money because of business results:
   - there is no market failure
   - there is no government failure

SLIDE 15.7

LESSON 15 - THE ROLE OF GOVERNMENT IN FINANCIAL MARKETS

A Classification Game

Indicate your answer:

Move to that side of the classroom for "market failure."

Move to that side of the classroom for "government failure."

Stand in place if there is no market failure and no government failure.

SLIDE 15.8

LESSON 15 - THE ROLE OF GOVERNMENT IN FINANCIAL MARKETS

Pay Package Snag

Investment fund managers take on excessive risk because their pay packages reward them for high returns, but provide no penalty for losing shareholders' money. The fund's disclosures meet the letter of the law but they understate the risk.

← Market failure   No failure, stand in place   Government failure →

SLIDE 15.9

LESSON 15 - THE ROLE OF GOVERNMENT IN FINANCIAL MARKETS

Grocery Startup

Webvan.com pioneers the online grocery business, grows too fast, and fails. Although there is no fraud, because of the business risk investors lose all the money they put into it.

← Market failure   No failure, stand in place   Government failure →

SLIDE 15.10

LESSON 15 - THE ROLE OF GOVERNMENT IN FINANCIAL MARKETS

Home-loan Mess

Government housing policy requires risky loans to less qualified customers, and many of the new homeowners are then unable to make their payments. Financial distress spreads and the housing market crashes.

← Market failure   No failure, stand in place   Government failure →

SLIDE 15.11

AOL-Time Warner

After full disclosures and despite high hopes, a merger of media giant Time Warner with Internet startup AOL loses billions of dollars of investor money.

← Market failure   No failure, stand in place   Government failure →

SLIDE 15.12

Senior Sales Push

A high-pressure phone bank sells stocks over the phone to uninformed residents of nursing homes. Although investigators can find no violations of law, it is clear that the buyers did not understand the risks.

← Market failure   No failure, stand in place   Government failure →

SLIDE 15.13

Your Results May Vary

After becoming fully informed about the risks and returns of holding stocks for the long term, an individual investor finds that stocks have gone down overall for a ten-year period.

← Market failure   No failure, stand in place   Government failure →

LEARNING, EARNING, AND INVESTING FOR A NEW GENERATION © COUNCIL FOR ECONOMIC EDUCATION, NEW YORK, NY

SLIDE 15.14

Two Kinds of Risk

- **Security-specific risk:** the risk that any one stock or bond might fail

- **Systemic risk:** the risk that the entire system could fail because of interconnections among banks, brokerages, and other financial institutions.

LEARNING, EARNING, AND INVESTING FOR A NEW GENERATION © COUNCIL FOR ECONOMIC EDUCATION, NEW YORK, NY

SLIDE 15.15

LESSON 15 - THE ROLE OF GOVERNMENT IN FINANCIAL MARKETS

Why You're Responsible

- Government regulation aims mainly at disclosure and fair dealing, but it cannot guarantee a return on investments.

- Criminals operating fraudulent investment schemes will claim to be safe, registered, and licensed.

- Even when regulation is adequate to handle security-specific risk, systemic risk may occur.

LEARNING, EARNING, AND INVESTING FOR A NEW GENERATION © COUNCIL FOR ECONOMIC EDUCATION, NEW YORK, NY

THE STOCK MARKET AND THE ECONOMY: CAN YOU FORECAST THE FUTURE?

LESSON 16
THE STOCK MARKET AND THE ECONOMY: CAN YOU FORECAST THE FUTURE?

LESSON DESCRIPTION

The students study a graph that illustrates the phases of a typical business cycle. They examine ways in which stock prices may affect overall consumption and investment in the economy. After studying The Conference Board's 10 leading economic indicators, they try their hand at economic forecasting and compare their forecasts to a record of what actually happened.

INTRODUCTION

The economy never stands still—it has ups and downs. Economists call this up-and-down activity a *business cycle*. A business cycle starts with a period of expansion, when the economy is growing. At some point it reaches a *peak*, the high point of the expansion phase. After the peak there is a period of *contraction* in which the economy is declining. Eventually it reaches a *trough*, the low point of a contraction phase. The stock market, like the economy, also has ups and downs over time. To describe these phases and to make predictions about where the economy is headed in a business cycle, economists use leading economic indicators such as average weekly hours worked in manufacturing and average weekly claims for unemployment. Forecasting is complex, and forecasts are not always accurate.

CONCEPTS

Business cycles

Contraction

Economic forecasting

Expansion

Gross Domestic Product

Leading economic indicators

Peak

Recession

Trough

OBJECTIVES

Students will:

- Describe the phases of a typical business cycle.

- Explain how changes in the stock market may affect the overall economy.

- Use stock prices and leading economic indicators to forecast Gross Domestic Product (GDP).

CONTENT STANDARDS

Voluntary National Content Standards in Economics, **2nd Edition**

- **Standard 18:** Fluctuations in a nation's overall levels of income, employment, and prices are determined by the interaction of spending and production decisions made by all households, firms, government agencies, and others in the economy. Recessions occur when overall levels of income and employment decline.

National Standards in K-12 Personal Finance Education, **3rd edition**

- **Financial Responsibility and Decision Making Standard 2:** Find and evaluate financial information from a variety of sources.

TIME REQUIRED

60 minutes

MATERIALS

- Slides 16.1, 16.2, 16.3, and 16.4

- A copy of Activity 16.1 for each student

- A copy of Activity 16.2 for half of the students

- A copy of Activity 16.3 for half of the students

(Internet access required)

PROCEDURE

1. Introduce the topic of changes in the economy over time. It is common knowledge that Americans have sometimes fallen on hard times, when jobs have been scarce and many people struggled to get by. It is also common knowledge that Americans in other times have benefitted from widespread prosperity. But what might account for these changes, and how could we foresee whether bad times or good times might be coming our way? This lesson will focus on those questions.

2. **Display Slide 16.1.** By reference to the slide's contents, reiterate the point that the economy has ups and downs over time. Economists call this up-and-down activity the *business cycle*. Review the phases of the business cycle, using the definitions and explanations provided on Slide 16.1. Point out that the overall activity of the economy is measured on the vertical axis. GDP is a good proxy for overall economic activity. Time is measured along the horizontal axis. The dotted line shows that GDP rises over time despite the fluctuations of the business cycle. In fact, GDP grew at an average rate of about 3.5 percent per year from 1960 to 2003.

(Note: For information about actual business cycles in U.S. history, visit the website of the National Bureau of Economic Research: www.nber.org/cycles.html. The NBER is the organiza-

tion that officially decides when recessions begin and end. Although many textbooks define a recession as a period when GDP falls for two consecutive quarters, the official NBER definition is "a recession is a period of significant decline in total output, income, employment, and trade, usually lasting from six months to a year, and marked by widespread contractions in many sectors of the economy." Economists do not have an official definition of the difference between a recession and a depression, except to say that a depression is a very severe recession.)

3. Explain that the stock market, like the broader economy, has ups and downs over time. These fluctuations are reflected in changing stock prices, and they are driven by supply and demand. For example, if the demand for stock increases or the supply decreases, prices will rise. If the supply increases or demand decreases, stock prices will fall. These changes in supply and demand largely reflect changes in investor expectations.

4. Explain that changes in stock prices have many important consequences, and not only for billionaires. Changes in stock prices can affect the broader economy or the business cycle, as shown in Slide 16.1. **Ask:** If you had a stock portfolio that used to be worth $500, but is now worth $2,500, how would you react? Or, if the stock used to be worth $10,000 and it is now worth $1,000, how would you react?

(If stocks go up in value, people might decide to sell some of their stock to take a profit, or they might gain confidence about the economy and decide to take out a loan to buy a new car or put an addition on their house. Relate these activities to the business cycle: increased consumption means more sales for businesses. Improved sales encourage

suppliers to produce more, helping to fuel an expanding economy. Increases in stock prices increase the value of companies, and companies may spend more as their value increases. Decreased spending can lead to a contraction in economic activity, or worsen a contraction already in effect.)

5. **Display Slide 16.2.** Discuss the four points on the slide and the definition of *leading economic indicators*. From an economist's point of view, stock prices affect future GDP mainly by changing people's consumption and investment spending. Remind the students that *economic investment* refers to spending by businesses on capital goods. Capital goods are used to produce other goods, so more capital goods lead to increased GDP.

6. Direct the students to the fourth point on Slide 16.2. Introduce the topic of economic forecasting. Stock prices are often a leading indicator of economic activity. Leading indicators suggest what is going to happen to the economy in the future because they tend to move in advance of overall economic activity. **Display Slides 16.2 and 16.3** and use them to explain why higher stock prices may indicate higher GDP in the future.

7. Ask the students why many people (consumers, savers, business owners and managers, politicians) would like to know what will happen in the economy in the future. Why would it be helpful to be able to forecast turning points in the business cycle?

(Knowledge about the future of the economy would help people make plans today. For example, if we knew that the economy would expand in the near future, creating more jobs, consumers would be more likely to take out loans to

buy cars or houses because they would be less likely to worry about losing their jobs and having trouble repaying their loans. They might decide to buy stocks or bonds if they knew the financial markets would improve. Business owners and managers might decide to expand their businesses because they would expect higher sales. Politicians might expect higher tax receipts derived from higher incomes and business profits, and they might be encouraged to change current tax or spending policies based on this information.)

8. Tell the students that some economists try to make economic forecasts, or predictions, of what will happen to the economy in the future. But economic forecasting is not a precise or exact science. In fact, there are several jokes on this topic. The late, famous economist Paul Samuelson once quipped, "Economists have predicted nine of the last five recessions." One problem for forecasters is that they must try to assess too many variables interacting and changing all at one time in the economy. Another is that making accurate forecasts requires predicting sometimes unpredictable human behavior.

9. Explain further that economic forecasting is not only difficult; it is also complex:

   - There are different types of forecasts, focused on different targets. For example, forecasts are made for GDP, prices, interest rates, unemployment rates, and sales and profits for specific businesses.

   - There are different forecasting methods. For example, some economists use complicated mathematical models to make their forecasts while others rely on leading indicators or surveys.

- The Conference Board, a private economics research group, provides information on 10 key leading indicators, including stock prices, every month. Conference Board researchers have found that these 10 variables tend to rise and fall in advance of upturns and downturns in GDP. Using different weights for different variables, researchers compute an index of leading economic indicators that is widely reported in the news media. Economists often use this index, and the leading indicators that make it up, to forecast changes in GDP for periods six to nine months in the future.

  Note: for more information on the 10 key leading indicators and for the latest press release on the index of leading indicators from The Conference Board, go to www.conference-board.org.

10. Tell the students that they will now try their hand at economic forecasting, using actual information from the 10 leading economic indicators supplied by The Conference Board. **Distribute a copy of Activity 16.1** to each student. Go over the list of indicators it presents, discussing why each of these might help people to predict future changes in GDP. Note that when most of the 10 indicators go up, it is expected that GDP will go up in the future. However, when average weekly initial claims for unemployment go up, GDP is expected to go down in the future (The Conference Board inverts this indicator when computing its index). Most of the 10 leading indicators and their relation to GDP can be explained by the information given in Activity 16.1. You will not want to spend much time on indicator 9, a technical measurement of bond market conditions that is difficult to ex-

plain. (Students or teachers who want to pursue this indicator may search the internet for the term "yield curve" for more information.)

11. Organize the class into groups of four or five students each. Come as close as you can to an even number of groups. **Distribute copies of Activity 16.2** to half of the groups and copies of **Activity 16.3** to the other groups. Tell the students that the activities contain actual information from The Conference Board about leading indicators from two different dates in history. The information about the current state of the economy is taken from the *Survey of Current Business*, a monthly publication by the Bureau of Economic Analysis, from the relevant months. (This publication is available online at www.bea.gov/scb.) When the students have made their forecasts, you will tell them, in procedure 14, the date of their information and what really did happen six months after that date. Then they can determine whether their forecasts were accurate.

12. Read over the instructions in the boxes at the top of Activities 16.2 and 16.3 (they are the same on both activities) with the students. Tell the students to read the information from the leading indicators carefully and to prepare a GDP forecast. Each group should choose one person to be its spokesperson. He or she will give a convincing one-to-two minute speech explaining the group's forecast and the reasons for it. Give the students about 15 minutes to prepare their forecasts and presentations. Circulate among the groups to answer questions as they are working.

13. When the groups have finished, call on them to present their forecasts, beginning with those who had Activity 16.2. Discuss the differences among the forecasts from the different groups. Then

call for the presentations from the groups that had Activity 16.3, and discuss the differences in their forecasts.

(Students should point out that some of the leading indicators provide conflicting information, and different groups had different opinions about what was most important. Explain that this is a common problem with economic forecasting, highlighting one reason why such forecasts—even from some of the best economists—are often inaccurate. Predicting the future is very difficult.)

14. After discussion, announce that the information in Activity 16.2 was from February of 2008. Up to that point, the economy had been expanding since the fourth quarter of 2001. However, by the third quarter of 2008 the United States had fallen into its worst recession since the Great Depression. GDP would decline by almost 4 percent in the third quarter of the year and by almost 9 percent in the fourth quarter. The accurate forecast for Activity 16.2 would have predicted that the economy would take a turn for the worse, culminating in a bad recession.

15. The information from Activity 16.3 was from January of 1997. Up to that point, the economy had been expanding for almost six years, and it continued to expand until March of 2001. From July until September (the third quarter) of 1997, the dates for their forecasts, GDP grew at an annual rate of 4.2 percent. The accurate forecast for Activity 16.2 would have predicted significant growth.

CLOSURE

16. To review key points about the business cycle and the role of the stock market in the business cycle, **again display Slides 16.1 and 16.2.** Display internet articles about leading indica-

tors, forecasting, and business cycles; briefly discuss the articles. Encourage the students to look and listen for announcements of economic indicators in the news and to keep informed about trends in economic activity.

ASSESSMENT
Multiple-Choice Questions

1. The peak and trough of the business cycle are similar because

   a. they are both periods of high inflation.
   b. *they are both turning points.*
   c. they are both periods of high unemployment.
   d. they are both low points for the economy.

2. Economists have found that stock prices tend to

   a. *rise before overall GDP rises.*
   b. rise at the same time GDP rises.
   c. rise after GDP rises.
   d. remain very steady over time, not rising or falling.

3. When stock prices go up, this usually results in

   a. increased consumption and decreased investment in the economy.
   b. decreased consumption and increased investment in the economy.
   c. decreased consumption and decreased investment in the economy.
   d. *increased consumption and investment in the economy.*

4. Which statement is true regarding leading economic indicators?

   a. They all go up at the same time.
   b. *Some go up while others are going down.*
   c. They all go down at the same time.
   d. They always correctly predict what will happen in the economy.

Constructed-Response Items

1. List the phases of a typical business cycle. Describe what happens during an expansion phase and a contraction phase.

   (The phases are expansion, peak, decline or contraction, and trough. During an economic expansion, people spend more and businesses invest more, leading to more production, increased GDP and economic growth. More jobs are available and unemployment decreases. The increased demand may lead to increased prices, and interest rates may rise. In a period of contraction, business activity slackens; spending, investment, GDP, and employment rates go down, and prices and interest rates may fall.)

2. Explain how increases in stock prices may lead to future growth in the economy.

   (Answers should include the following: When stock prices go up, stockholders are wealthier. They may spend more, leading to higher future production of goods and services. Increases in stock prices increase the value of corporations. Thus businesses may increase investment in capital goods, leading to business expansion and economic growth.)

Gen i Connection

Mission 14 of the Gen i Revolution game allows students to try their hand at making economic forecasts. The mission's introduction says that political leaders from several countries have heard about Gen i's success in battling economic distress and would like the organization's insight on the next round of economic forecasts. The political leaders are meeting at an undisclosed location, to which the operative has been invited. In this mission's 4-1-1 tutorial, students learn about the phases of the business cycle and gain experience working with leading economic indicators. Students complete the mission by choosing forecasts for the United States, Japan, and Brazil from multiple-choice lists.

Gen i Reflection

In Mission 14 of the Gen i Revolution you helped government leaders of the United States, Brazil, and Japan under hypothetical economic conditions. Now, considering the real economic conditions of the United States today, what do you think is more likely—economic recession, economic stability, or economic expansion? Explain your answer.

ACTIVITY 16.1
TEN LEADING ECONOMIC INDICATORS

1. **Average weekly hours, manufacturing**

   Manufacturing workers are usually hired to work longer hours when their employers plan to hire more workers in the future. They usually work fewer hours when employers plan to lay off workers in the future.

2. **Average weekly initial claims for unemployment insurance**

   When more workers apply for unemployment compensation for the first time, this signals that there will be more layoffs in the future. When fewer new claims are filed, this signals fewer layoffs in the future.

3. **Manufacturers' new orders for consumer goods and materials**

   More new orders for consumer goods mean that firms will be producing more consumer goods in the future. Fewer new orders mean fewer consumer goods will be produced in the future.

4. **Vendor performance diffusion index**

   This measures the speed at which companies receive materials from their suppliers. Slower deliveries indicate increases in demand for materials. When this index goes up (or down), it signals that production in the economy will go up (or down) in the future.

5. **Manufacturers' new orders for non-defense capital goods**

   More new orders for capital goods mean that firms will be producing more capital goods in the future. Fewer new orders mean fewer capital goods will be produced in the future.

6. **Building permits for new private housing units**

   When more building permits are issued, construction of houses will go up in the future. Fewer building permits mean fewer houses will be constructed in the future.

7. **Stock prices, 500 common stocks**

   The S&P 500 stock index reflects price changes for a broad selection of common stocks. Changes in the stock index can reflect the general feelings of investors about the future of the economy.

8. **Money supply, M2**

   The M2 money supply includes currency, checking account deposits, and small savings deposits. If the money supply goes up faster than inflation, banks lend more and the economy can expand in the future. If not, the economy may contract.

9. **Interest rate spread, 10-year Treasury bonds less federal funds**

   This is the difference between interest rates on long-term and short-term investments. Because the Federal Reserve Board has some control over the short-term federal funds rate, it is thought to indicate the intent of monetary policy. It rises when the economy may expand in the future and falls when the economy may contract in the future. When it has been negative, it has been a strong indicator of an on-coming recession.

10. Index of consumer expectations

This index reports results of a monthly survey asking consumers whether they think the economy will improve in the future. If the index goes up, consumers are optimistic and may purchase more goods and services. It goes down if consumers are pessimistic.

ACTIVITY 16.2
TRY YOUR HAND AT ECONOMIC FORECASTING

Congratulations, your firm has been hired to make an important economic forecast. Your job is to predict what will happen to GDP in the economy six to nine months from now. You will base your decision on information you have today about leading economic indicators and the current economic situation. Carefully analyze the information and select one of the following three options:

    a. the economy will experience significant growth,

    b. the economy will be sluggish, without significant growth but without a recession, or

    c. the economy will take a turn for the worse, and a recession is coming.

Prepare a one-to-two minute persuasive speech supporting your forecast. Use evidence from the leading indicators to convince the class that your forecast will prove to be accurate.

This is what you know today:

It is February XXXX. The Bureau of Economic Analysis announced today in the *Survey of Current Business* that real GDP increased 0.6 percent in the fourth quarter of last year, down from 4.9 percent in the third quarter. Consumer spending slowed in the fourth quarter, increasing 2.0 percent after increasing 2.8 percent in the third quarter. Inflation accelerated in the fourth quarter, increasing 3.8 percent after increasing 1.8 percent in the third quarter.

The leading indicators (obtained from The Conference Board):

1. **The average weekly hours worked in manufacturing** have been fairly steady over the past several months.

2. **Average weekly initial claims for unemployment** increased in October, fell in November, increased in December, fell in January, and held steady in February.

3. **Manufacturers' new orders for consumer goods** fell in December, but they had increased during September, October, and November.

4. **The vendor performance index** increased in October, fell in November, and then increased in December, January, and February.

5. **Manufacturers' new orders for non-defense capital goods** fell in the past two months.

6. **Building permits for new private housing** fell in October, November, December, January, and February.

7. **The prices of 500 common stocks** rose in October and November, fell in December, rose again in January and then fell in February.

8. **The money supply (M2)** grew steadily over the past five months.

9. **The interest rate spread**, long-term minus short-term rates, has fallen fairly consistently over the past several months.

10. **The index of consumer expectations** fell in November, December, and January but then increased in February.

ACTIVITY 16.3
TRY YOUR HAND AT ECONOMIC FORECASTING

Congratulations, your firm has been hired to make an important economic forecast. Your job is to predict what will happen to GDP in the economy six to nine months from now. You will base your decision on information you have today about leading economic indicators and the current economic situation. Carefully analyze the information and select one of the following three options:

    a.   the economy will experience significant growth,

    b.   the economy will be sluggish, without significant growth but without a recession, or

    c.   the economy will take a turn for the worse, and a recession is coming.

Prepare a one-to-two minute persuasive speech supporting your decision. Use evidence from the leading indicators to convince the class that your forecast will prove to be accurate.

This is what you know today:

It is January **XXXX**. The Bureau of Economic Analysis announced today in the *Survey of Current Business* that real GDP increased 1.6 percent in the third quarter of last year, down from 4.7 percent in the second quarter. Corporate profits increased by $5.4 billion in the third quarter, about half as much as in the second quarter. The U.S. trade deficit continued to increase. The latest figures you have for prices indicate that the annual rate of inflation is about 3 percent.

The leading indicators (obtained from The Conference Board):

1. **The average weekly hours worked in manufacturing** have been fairly steady, at more than 41 hours for the past several months.

2. **Average weekly initial claims for unemployment** increased in September, fell in October and November, and increased in December.

3. **Manufacturers' new orders for consumer goods** fell in December, but they had increased during September, October, and November.

4. **The vendor performance index** fell in September, but it increased in October, November, and December.

5. **Manufacturers' new orders for non-defense capital goods** increased in June and July, fell in August, increased in September and October, and fell in November and December.

6. **Building permits for new private housing** fell in August, September, and October, but they rose in November and December.

7. **The prices of 500 common stocks** have risen consistently since last July.

8. **The money supply (M2)** grew steadily over the past six months.

9. **The interest rate spread,** long-term minus short-term rates, has fallen fairly consistently over the past several months.

10. **The index of consumer expectations** has increased consistently and quite dramatically over the past nine months.

SLIDE 16.1

LESSON 16 - THE STOCK MARKET AND THE ECONOMY:
CAN YOU FORECAST THE FUTURE?

A Business Cycle

A Business Cycle

Expansion   Contraction   Expansion

Output (GDP)

Peak

Trough

Time

- **Expansion:** The economy is growing. GDP, income, and employment increase. Consumption and investment increase. Businesses are expanding. Interest rates may rise. There may be concerns about inflation.

- **Peak:** The high point of the expansion, and also a turning point. After the peak, an economy begins to contract.

SLIDE 16.2

LESSON 16 - THE STOCK MARKET AND THE ECONOMY:
CAN YOU FORECAST THE FUTURE?

A Business Cycle (Cont.)

- **Contraction:** The economy is declining. GDP, income, and employment decrease. Consumption and investment decrease. Business sales decline. Interest rates and prices may fall.

- **Trough:** This is the low point of the contraction, and also a turning point. After a trough, the economy begins to expand.

- **Recession:** A period of significant decline in total output, income, and employment, usually lasting from six months to a year.

SLIDE 16.3

How Do Stock Prices Affect the Economy?

1. Stock prices affect consumption.

Increases in stock prices mean that shareholders are wealthier. Increased wealth leads to increased consumption. Decreases in stock prices means that shareholders are poorer, and this decreases consumption.

2. Stock prices affect investment.

Increases in the price of a stock means that the value of the corporation has increased. This increased value leads to increased investment and business expansion. Decreases in the price of a stock mean that the value of the corporation has decreased. This decreased value may discourage investment and business expansion.

SLIDE 16.4

How Do Stock Prices Affect the Economy? (Cont.)

3. Stock prices affect expectations.

When stock prices increase, investors may feel optimistic about the future of the economy. This optimism may lead to more spending and more production. When stock prices fall, investors may feel pessimistic about the future of the economy. This pessimism may cause them to hold back on spending and production.

4. Stock prices are a leading indicator of economic activity.

A leading indicator is a statistic that often changes in advance of real GDP changes. Persistent increases in stock prices often precede increases in GDP and economic expansion by a few months. Persistent decreases in stock prices often precede declining GDP and recession by a few months.

LESSONS FROM HISTORY: STOCK MARKET CRASHES

LESSON 17
LESSONS FROM HISTORY: STOCK MARKET CRASHES

LESSON DESCRIPTION

The students analyze information about three stock market crashes: 1929, 1987, and 2007. They use the information to make posters that highlight key information about the crashes, including the role played by the Federal Reserve. After presenting their posters to the class, the students discuss ways in which the three events were similar to and different from one another. They also discuss the likelihood of future stock market crashes.

INTRODUCTION

The stock market crashes of 1929 and 1987 were similar in several ways. Both crashes occurred during October, both involved panic selling, and both were affected by the technology of the day. There were important differences as well. For example, in 1929 the economy showed signs of a forthcoming recession, while the economy in 1987 did not. The stock market crash of 2007 resembled the situation in 1929. The latter was followed by a Great Depression; the former, by a deep recession.

But no recession or depression followed the crash of 1987. Why was the crash of 1929 followed by a depression while the crash of 1987 was not? Many economists think that the answer lies in understanding the actions of the Federal Reserve. After 1929 the Fed continued to decrease the money supply and failed to save the banking system from collapse. After 1987 the Fed provided money to banks so that they could continue to make loans; this action probably stopped the panic and prevented more serious problems.

The recession that started in 2007 had its origins in the housing industry. Beginning in the late 1990s, housing prices began to increase at historically high rates. The bubble in housing prices collapsed in 2008, causing widespread economic damage to households and businesses. The stock market began to decline in 2007; it fell further in 2008 and hit bottom early in 2009. The financial sector of the economy nearly collapsed. Unlike the events of 1987, the crisis of 2007–2009 constituted one of the most significant economic events of its time.

CONCEPTS

Causes and effects of the stock market crash of 1929

Causes and effects of the stock market crash of 1987

Causes and effects of the stock market crash that began in 2007

Federal Reserve

Monetary policy

Supply and demand

OBJECTIVES

Students will be able to:

- Develop and present posters about the stock market crashes that occurred in 1929, 1987, and 2007.

- Compare the three crashes, explaining similarities and differences.

- Explain how Federal Reserve policies contributed to different outcomes in the three crashes.

CONTENT STANDARDS
Voluntary National Content Standards in Economics, **2nd Edition**

- **Standard 4:** People usually respond predictably to positive and negative incentives.

- **Standard 7:** Markets exist when buyers and sellers interact. This interaction determines market prices and thereby allocates scarce goods and services.

- **Standard 8:** Prices send signals and provide incentives to buyers and sellers. When supply or demand changes, market prices adjust, affecting incentives.

- **Standard 10:** Institutions evolve and are created to help individuals and groups accomplish their goals. Banks, labor unions, markets, corporations, legal systems, and not-for-profit organizations are examples of important institutions. A different kind of institution, clearly defined and enforced property rights, is essential to a market economy.

National Standards in K-12 Personal Finance Education, 3rd edition

- **Financial Responsibility and Decision Making Standard 5:** Develop communication strategies for discussing financial issues.

- **Saving and Investing Standard 6:** Investigate how agencies that regulate financial markets protect investors.

TIME REQUIRED
75 minutes

MATERIALS
- Activity 17.1 (see Directions below)

  Directions for using Activity 17.1: Make copies of the Activity and cut each copy into 12 sections, as indicated by the dotted lines. You may wish to laminate the copies. The number of copies to make will depend on your class size. For a class of more than 30 students, make three copies before cutting each copy into sections; for a larger class, make more copies. The point is

that **each student must receive only one section of the Activity**. (You may also wish to make one classroom set of the intact Activity for everyone to receive near the end of the lesson.)

- Eight large sheets of construction paper or butcher paper

- Three or four markers for each of the 12 teams

PROCEDURE

1. To introduce the lesson, describe its historical context briefly: the United States experienced stock market crashes in October 1929, October 1987, and October 2007. These crashes were similar to one another in some respects, but there were differences as well. Taken together, the three crashes provide an important focal point for study. What were the key historical events leading up to and following these dramatic events? What role did Federal Reserve policy play in each crash? This lesson addresses those questions.

2. Write the term *Stock Market Crash* on the board. **Ask:** What do you suppose a stock market crash is? What stock market crashes have you studied in school?

(Accept a variety of answers. Students will probably respond, correctly, that when the stock market crashes, stock prices fall steeply. The price declines are sudden and unexpected. Many stockholders see their wealth dwindle as their investments lose value. Some investors are wiped out. Ripple effects of these losses include reduced consumption and reduced investment, with widespread harmful consequences. Some students will have studied the stock market crash of 1929 and the Great Depression that followed. Fewer will know about the events of 1987. Some may know that stock prices took another downturn beginning in 2007,

but they will probably know little about the causes of the downturn or the role played by the Federal Reserve.)

3. Explain that the first step in analyzing the three crashes is to learn more about them. This will require some reading. Randomly **distribute sections of Activity 17.1**. Each student should receive only one section of the Activity. Explain the distribution: there are 12 types of information in the materials you are passing out. For each crash (1929, 1987, and 2007), there is information about the following four issues:

   • What happened?

   • What followed?

   • What caused it?

   • What role did the Federal Reserve play?

   Allow time for the students to read the information presented in the sections of Activity 17.1 that you have distributed.

4. When the students have finished their reading, organize them into teams. To accomplish this, tell the students to find others who have read the same information about the same crash that they have read, and to form teams. For example, all the students who have "The Crash of 1929: What Happened?" will form a team; all who have "The Crash of 1987: What Caused It?" will form a team; and so on. There will be 12 teams in all. Distribute a piece of construction paper or butcher paper and three or four markers to each team. Instruct each team to make a poster informing others about the information on their handouts. The posters should be informative and should present the information clearly. The teams should spend about 15 minutes making the posters. To make the posters, of course, they will need to decide what

information their posters should present, and how that information should be formatted.

5. Ask each group to select a spokesperson to present its poster to the class. To encourage clear comparisons, you may wish to have the groups present in the following order: what happened (in 1929, in 1987, then in 2007), causes (regarding 1929, 1987, then 2007), what followed (after 1929, after 1987, after 2007), and the role of the Fed (in 1929, in 1987, then in 2007). After each poster is presented, tape it onto the board or a wall to make a comparative display.

6. (Optional) **Distribute an intact copy of Activity 17.1** to each student so that everybody can study information that may not be included on the posters.

7. Discuss the following:

   A. What similarities and differences did you note regarding the stock market crashes?

      (Possible answers: all the crashes began in October; the crashes of 1929 and 1987 were affected by limitations of the technology of the day; in 1929 the economy showed signs of a recession, and in 1987 it did not; the 1929 and 1987 crashes involved new trading-volume records for the time; the crash that began in 2007 was similar to the crash of 1929 in that it was followed by a sharp downturn, unlike the crash of 1987.)

   B. How were the causes of the crash of 1929 similar to the causes of the crash of 1987 and 2007? How were the causes different? (Point out that in trying to explain the causes of a stock market crash, the students really are trying to explain why many people decided to sell their stock at the same time, bringing about a massive increase in the supply of stock on the market.)

(Similarities: The situations in 1929 and 1987 involved panic selling, which led to more panic selling. In both cases, stocks were thought to be overvalued because of speculation. And in both cases tight monetary policy by the Fed is thought to be a cause. Differences: Investors feared recession in 1929; investors feared inflation and debt in 1987. Margin buying increased risk in 1929, and the Smoot-Hawley tariff affected trade adversely; programmed computer trading affected market swings in 1987. The situation in 2007 was unique in some respects. Some observers said it was more like watching a slow-motion train wreck than a crash. The decline in stock prices reduced people's wealth, and a recession followed. However, the underlying causes of the recession of 2007 involved changes in lending standards, the lending practices of Fannie Mae and Freddie Mac, the Fed keeping interest rates too low for too long, bundling by financial institutions of home mortgages into mortgage-backed securities that turned out to have uncertain values, and high levels of household debt.)

C. Compare what happened after the crash of 1929 with what happened after the crashes of 1987 and 2007.

(Possible answers: the Great Depression followed the crash of 1929, and no recession or depression followed the crash of 1987. The stock market recovered quickly after 1987, but it took 25 years to recover after 1929. In both cases reforms were implemented in efforts to
prevent further crashes. The "Great Recession" of 2007-2009 followed the beginning of the stock sell-off in 2007. The "Great Recession" itself was followed by sluggish economic growth, further evidence of how much damage was done.)

D. Compare the reaction of the Fed in each of the three cases.

(The Fed appears to have done the wrong thing after 1929 and the right thing after 1987. After 1929 the Fed continued to decrease the money supply and failed to save the banking system from collapse. After 1987 the Fed provided money to banks so that they could continue to make loans; this action probably stopped the panic and prevented more serious problems. While economists continue to debate the actions taken by the Fed to fight the recession of 2007-2009, it is clear that the Fed acted quickly and aggressively to maintain liquidity in the financial system and reduce the damage caused to institutions holding "toxic assets.")

E. Given what you know about these three stock market crashes, do you think there will be more crashes in the future?

(Students may respond that Fed actions and other reforms may or may not prevent further crashes.)

8. Explain that economists agree that forces of supply and demand may lead to future crashes in stock market prices. Stock prices are determined in part by expectations of future stock prices, which are unknown, so there is an element of psychology affecting supply and demand. When investors think stock prices will go up, this optimism increases demand for stock and pushes prices up. Demand may

continue to rise until stock prices are too high for the value of the underlying corporations. This state of affairs is sometimes described as a "speculative bubble" that is bound to burst at some point. The bubble bursts when many investors decide prices have reached a peak and aren't going to rise further. Such thoughts may cause a large increase in the supply of stock offered for sale, causing prices to fall dramatically. Market analysts agree that if many investors want to leave the market at the same time, nothing can really keep the market from falling.

CLOSURE

9. Review the main points of the lesson. **Ask:**

A. How did Fed policy help cause the Great Depression after the stock market crash of 1929?

(The Fed failed to act as the "lender of last resort." Had the Fed increased the money supply to provide money to banks after the crash, it might have prevented the collapse of the banking system, which was a major cause of the Great Depression.)

B. How did Fed policy help prevent a recession after the stock market crash of 1987?

(The Fed acted quickly to ease monetary policy and reassure banks. It reduced a key interest rate and provided money to increase bank reserves.)

C. How did Fed policy help prevent the collapse of the financial system beginning in 2007?

(The Fed took fast and aggressive action to keep liquidity in the financial system by reducing the federal funds rate and opening the discount window. It took unprecedented ac-

tions to reduce the damage caused to those institutions which were holding "toxic assets.")

ASSESSMENT
Multiple-Choice Questions

1. The stock market crash of 1929

   a. was followed by an economic depression.
   b. occurred on a day when most stock prices went up.
   c. was caused by large increases in the money supply.
   d. was the worst one-day fall in stock prices in the twentieth century.

2. The stock market crash of 1987

   a. was followed by an economic depression.
   b. occurred on a day when most stock prices went up.
   c. was caused by large increases in the money supply.
   d. was the worst one-day fall in stock prices in the twentieth century.

3. The stock market crash of 2007

   a. was followed by a deep economic recession.
   b. was followed by relatively rapid economic recovery.
   c. was caused by the collapse of the North American Free Trade Agreement.
   d. was followed by an immediate decrease in government spending.

4. For the stock market crash of 1929 and 1987,

   a. stock prices recovered quickly afterward.
   b. stocks are thought to have been overvalued.
   c. programmed and computer trading is seen to be a cause.
   d. inflation was a persistent problem in the economy at the time.

5. The primary cause of the recession of 2007-2009 most likely was

    a. the international trade war of 2006.
    b. *collapse in the housing market, followed by widespread weakness in financial markets.*
    c. programmed and computer trading.
    d. persistently low money growth, followed by stubbornly high inflation.

Constructed-Response Items

1. How did Federal Reserve policy after the stock market crash of 1929 differ from Fed policy after the stock market crash of 1987? What were some effects of these policy differences?

    (In 1929 the Fed followed a restrictive or tight monetary policy. After the stock market crash, the Fed did not provide money to banks so they could make loans to their customers who had lost money in the crash. These restrictive policies, and the failure to help the banking system, probably led to the Great Depression. After the crash of 1987, the Fed moved quickly to assure banks and the public that it would provide money to help the economy through the crisis. This expansionary monetary policy probably helped the market to recover quickly, preventing a further crisis.)

2. How were the causes of the stock market crash of 1929 similar to the causes of the stock market crash of 1987? How were they different?

    (Both crashes involved panic selling, which led to more panic selling; in both cases stocks were thought to be over-valued because of speculation; tight monetary policy by the Fed is cited as a cause in both cases. Differences include recession fears in 1929 and inflation fears and debt in 1987; the effects of margin buying and the Smoot-Hawley tariff in

1929; and the effects of programmed trading in 1987.)

3. How did Federal Reserve policy in 2007 differ from Fed policy after the stock market crash of 1987?

    (In some ways, actions taken by the Fed in 2007 were similar to those taken in 1987. In 2007, however, the Fed believed that financial collapse was possible. It acted quickly and took actions that were without precedent. It reduced the federal funds rate to a point as low as it could go. It took other actions to restore liquidity. It encouraged banks to borrow money from the Fed. It extended the amount of lending from the Fed beyond the usually overnight basis to up to 30 days, with possible renewal. As the financial crisis worsened, the Fed implemented completely new tools of monetary policy aimed at restoring liquidity. The new tools included the Term Auction Facility, the Term Securities Lending Facility, and the Term Asset-Backed Securities Loan Facility. While the Fed's actions in 1987 and 2007 had similar goals, the actions taken beginning in 2007 were much more aggressive.)

Gen i Connection

In Mission 13 of the Gen i Revolution game, students take a close look at volatility in the stock markets. In this mission, they take on the role of operatives advising Markos Scott, who heads a scholarship fund that did everything right: started early, pursued a buy and hold strategy, and diversified. Yet an entire asset category crashed. In addressing the problem, the students learn about the stock market crashes of 1929 and 1987. They also learn about the real estate bubble of 2001-2007. They work interactively through the 4-1-1 tutorial, comparing the actions taken by the federal government in 1929, 1987, and 2007-2008. They complete the mission by making recommendations from a multiple-choice list on how Markos can weather a crash in the scholarship fund.

Gen i Reflection

Now that you have advised Markos Scott on how to weather a stock market crash in Mission 13, consider this: If you had $100,000 invested in the stock market and saw the value of your investment fall to $50,000, could you take the advice to leave the money invested? Or would you be inclined to take the money out before it fell further? What does your answer say about the "buy low and sell high" idea? Explain your answer.

ACTIVITY 17.1
UNDERSTANDING MARKET CRASHES

Directions for the teacher: Make copies of this activity (for a class of 30, three copies; more copies for a larger class). Cut each copy into 12 sections as indicated by the dotted lines.

✂ -

The Crash of 1929: What Happened?

The stock market crash of October 1929 is often seen as the end of the prosperous 1920s. However, there were many signs that the economy was already on the way down before the crash. The two worst days were October 24, 1929 ("Black Thursday"), and October 29, 1929 ("Black Tuesday"). What happened?

Stock prices increased dramatically in 1928, with the Dow Jones Industrial Average reaching a peak of 381.2 on September 3. Stock prices fell by about 10 percent following this peak, but then rose again by about 8 percent by mid-October. Panic selling appears to have set in on October 23, and on October 24 a record-breaking 13 million shares were traded, compared to an average of 4 million shares per day in September. The technology of the day (telephone and telegraph lines) was not able to keep up with the trading, and the ticker tape ran an hour and a half late. Many sellers did not learn of the prices they received for their trades until later that night. Several of the nation's largest bankers were alerted to the crisis and announced that they were willing to buy stocks above the going prices. The intent of the bankers was to give people confidence in the market and thus prevent panic selling. On October 25, President Hoover also tried to halt panic selling by reassuring people that the "fundamental business of the country—that is, the production and distribution of goods and services—is on a sound and prosperous basis."

Although prices steadied for a few days, panic selling started again on October 28. Nearly 16.5 million shares were traded on October 29, and the downward trend in stock prices continued. Two weeks after the crash, average prices of leading stocks were about half of what they had been in September.

The Crash of 1929: What Followed?

After the stock market crash of 1929, things only got worse. By the end of 1929 the market recovered somewhat, but in general stock prices continued in a downward spiral until 1932. By 1932 average stock prices had fallen more than 75 percent, people had lost an estimated $45 billion in wealth, and the market did not climb back to its 1929 peak level for another 25 years.

Economists do not view the crash of 1929 as a cause of the Great Depression, but they agree that the fall in stock prices made the situation worse. The optimism and hope of the 1920s gave way to feelings of skepticism and uncertainty. Consumers and businesses were less willing and less able to spend money, given their losses and their lack of confidence in the economy. Banks lost vast amounts in the crash also, and they did not have the liquidity they needed to make loans to tide people over until the market recovered. Many banks subsequently failed. The resulting decrease in consumption and investment spending, and an increased desire to hold cash balances outside the banking system, led to a downward spiral of declining production, increased unemployment, and falling prices. The crash on Wall Street also led to stock market crashes around the world: first in London, then in Paris, Berlin, and Tokyo.

Several reforms were implemented after the crash. They were intended to prevent further stock market crashes. The Glass-Steagall Act of 1933 prohibited banks that are members of the Federal Reserve from affiliating with companies whose major purpose is to sell stocks. The Securities Exchange Act of 1934 established the Securities and Exchange Commission (SEC) to protect the public against misconduct in the securities and financial markets. This act also required the Federal Reserve to regulate margin requirements in order to reduce speculation.

The Crash of 1929: What Caused It?

Economists disagree about the causes of the stock market crash of 1929. They agree, however, that there was no single, dominant cause, and that many factors worked together to bring the market down. Here are some opinions:

1. **Margin buying.** People could buy stock by paying as little as 10 percent down on the purchase price, borrowing the other 90 percent. When stock prices fell, stocks soon weren't worth enough to enable people to pay back the loans. People scrambled to sell their stocks before prices fell even further.

2. **Stocks were overvalued.** The rise in stock prices late in the 1920s was caused by speculation and investors trying to find a way to get rich quickly. In October 1929, stock prices were far too high compared to their earnings and dividends, so prices were bound to fall at some point.

3. **Federal Reserve policies.** The tight monetary policy of the Federal Reserve prior to the crash may have led to the crash. The Fed caused interest rates to rise because it wanted to curb speculation in the stock market late in the1920s. This may have led to a decrease in demand for stocks and falling prices.

4. **The Smoot-Hawley Tariff Act.** This act, meant to stimulate U.S. production, imposed high tariffs on imports. Investors were concerned that if the act passed (it did pass in 1930), the profits of exporting companies would fall and other countries would retaliate by refusing to buy U.S. goods. This expectation of lower profits in the exporting sector may have caused people to sell their stocks.

5. **The general state of the economy.** Signs of a recession were evident in 1929 prior to the crash. Production was falling, prices were falling, and personal income was falling. Several prominent public figures stated openly that they thought bad times were ahead. These signs may have spurred stock sell-offs.

6. **Psychological reasons.** When panic sets in, people may react irrationally. When people saw others selling, they worried that they should sell too, before things got worse. This panic selling caused prices to fall—just what people were hoping to avoid.

The Crash of 1929: What Role Did the Fed Play?

Many economists believe that Federal Reserve policies led to the stock market crash of 1929 and were a main cause of the Great Depression that followed. Prior to the stock market crash, in 1928, the Fed decreased the money supply in the economy, in part to try to discourage stock market speculation. This tight monetary policy probably contributed to falling stock prices in 1929, because it made it more difficult for people to borrow money to buy stocks.

The U.S. banking system was in trouble immediately after the crash of 1929. People who lost money in the stock market could not pay back their bank loans, and banks thus did not have money to give to depositors who wanted to make withdrawals from their accounts. The Fed did little to help the banking system out of this crisis. If the Fed had increased the money supply to provide money to banks after the stock market crash, this might have prevented the banking-system collapse that followed. In fact, the Federal Reserve Bank of New York attempted to do this immediately after the crash, but its action was only a temporary measure, and the rest of the Federal Reserve System did not go along.

The money supply continued to fall and interest rates continued to rise in 1930. By not providing money to increase bank reserves, the Fed probably contributed to further declines in stock prices, which continued until 1932. By not providing money to help the banks through the crisis, Fed policies may also have contributed to the collapse of the banking system. Fed policies are therefore one of the main causes of the Great Depression.

The Crash of 1987: What Happened?

The stock market crash of October 1987 occurred during a period of relative prosperity. Real GDP was increasing at an annual rate of 3.4 percent, and the inflation of the early 1980s had been largely contained. The last previous recession ended in 1982, and the next one was years off. Yet the stock market crashed on Monday, October 19, 1987 ("Black Monday"). What happened?

Stock prices had risen dramatically in the first half of 1987, with the Dow Jones Industrial Average reaching a peak of 2,722.44 on August 25. During the next five weeks prices fell by about 8 percent, but then rose again by about 6 percent. Prices fell steadily the following week. But on October 19, stock prices fell more than on any other single day in the twentieth century. The Dow Jones Industrial Average fell a record 508.32 points, closing at 1,738. This represented a one-day drop of 22.6 percent in the value of stocks—nearly double the one-day loss record set during the crash of 1929. Over 604 million shares were traded on the New York Stock Exchange alone, shattering previous volume records. Some of the volume was caused by panic selling, as investors tried to sell before prices fell further. Some of the selling was done automatically by computers programmed to sell if prices fell below certain levels. Phone networks and computers were jammed for hours because of the unprecedented volume of trades, and many people who tried to trade were unable to do so.

Investors lost an estimated $500 billion in share values in that one day. In many ways, this crash amounted to the nation's worst financial crisis since the Great Depression. Losses immediately affected markets around the world, thanks to electronic links and global communication networks.

✂ -

The Crash of 1987: What Followed?

The crash of 1987 is not thought to have caused serious damage to the economy, and its effects were not as bad as had been expected. Despite the dramatic events of October 19, 1987, by the end of 1987 stock prices reached the same level they had held the year before. The market recovered to its 1987 peak levels again in 1989, two years after the crash. Of course, many people who sold stock when the prices were low lost money. The crash of 1987 made it clear that the finances of countries were tied together and economies were becoming more global. All major world markets declined in October 1987.

The crash was not followed by a depression or even a recession. Although it produced the largest one-day drop in stock prices in the twentieth century, several newspapers and officials did not call it a crash, preferring terms such as "market interruption." In the decade that followed, after a brief recession in 1990-1991 following the Gulf War, the U.S. economy entered into a 10-year expansion period, the longest in the twentieth century. Stock prices continued to climb.

Several reforms were implemented after the crash to try to prevent further stock market crashes. Stock exchanges and brokerage firms upgraded their computer systems and added more phone lines to deal with emergencies. Regulators from different securities markets agreed to meet and communicate regularly to coordinate their activities. The main reform was the introduction of circuit breakers in 1988. Circuit breakers automatically halt trading on major exchanges for a time if stock prices fall more than certain amounts. Circuit breakers are designed to stop panic selling by giving investors time to think over their choices when stock prices are falling dramatically.

The Crash of 1987: What Caused It?

Economists disagree about the causes of the stock market crash of 1987. They agree, however, that there was no single, dominant cause, and that many factors worked together to bring the market down.

Here are some opinions:

1. **Inflationary fears.** Many investors were concerned that the inflation of the 1970s and early 1980s would return, and inflationary fears cause interest rates to rise. The long-term rate on some bonds reached a peak of 10.5 percent on the morning of October 19. This may have caused people to sell stock so that they could invest in bonds and other interest-earning assets instead.

2. **Stocks were overvalued.** The rise in stock prices in the 1980s was caused by speculation and investors trying to find a way to get rich quickly. In October 1987, stock prices were far too high compared to their earnings and dividends, so prices were bound to fall at some point.

3. **Federal Reserve policies.** The Federal Reserve's announcement of an increase in the discount rate from 5.5 percent to 6 percent on September 4, 1987, was unnecessary. It may have signaled to people that the Fed thought high inflation was going to return. Investors may have decided to sell their stock because of the Fed's announcement.

4. **Programmed and computer trading.** Large institutional investing companies programmed their computers to order large stock trades automatically when stock prices reached certain levels. As prices fell on October 19, sell orders came in automatically, jamming the system and causing more panic among investors.

5. **A debt-ridden economy.** Both the trade deficit and government budget deficits were increasing rapidly. Investors may have feared that the prices of U.S. stocks would fall relative to foreign stocks. Anxiety over these growing debts in the third quarter of 1987 may have led to the stock sell-off.

6. **Psychological reasons.** Fear and panic played a part in the crash of 1987. When investors saw stock prices falling, they rushed to try to sell their stocks for whatever they could get before prices fell further.

The Crash of 1987: What Role Did the Fed Play?

The stock market crash of 1987 was relatively painless, largely because the Federal Reserve moved quickly to ease monetary policy and reassure banks. These policies probably prevented big declines in consumption and investment spending that might otherwise have been triggered by the loss of wealth from the crash. The fact that no recession followed the crash of 1987 is often attributed to the competent actions of the Fed immediately following the crash.

Because of the large volume of sell orders on October 19, many stock specialists and brokerage firms needed loans, and many investors needed loans to meet margin calls. One of the first things the Fed did was to reassure banks and the public that it would provide enough money to the economy to prevent a crisis in the banking system. On October 20, the day after the crash, the Fed announced that "The Federal Reserve System, consistent with its responsibilities as the nation's central bank, affirmed today its readiness to serve as a source of liquidity to support the financial and economic system." This announcement was intended to reverse the panic that broke out the day before, and it seems to have worked.

The Fed backed up its promises by using open-market operations to cut a key interest rate by 1 percent and by providing money to increase bank reserves. These moves enabled banks to make loans to the businesses and individuals who needed money because of losses they suffered from the decline in value of their stocks. The Fed also kept lines of communication open with financial institutions, and it tried to persuade banks to make loans to their customers to tide them over through the crisis. Once stock prices recovered, people had money to pay back their loans.

The Crash of 2007: What Happened?

The Dow Jones Industrial Average (DJIA), a stock index made up of 30 large U.S. companies, reached a peak on October 9, 2007. Its peak closing value was 14,164.53. Then the sell-off began. By September 29, 2008, the DJIA had a record-breaking drop with a close at 10,365.45. But the worst was not over.

Another stock index called the Standard & Poor's 500 (S&P 500) told a similar story. The S&P 500 tracks the prices of 500 large companies traded on the New York Stock Exchange and the NASDAQ Stock Market. Between October 2007 and March 2009, the S&P 500 lost 55 percent of its value. The S&P 500 did not begin to reverse itself until March 9, 2009.

Like the crash of 1987, the 2007 crash again showed that the finances of many countries were tied together and economies were becoming more global. All major world markets declined during this period.

The Crash of 2007: What Followed?

The collapse of the stock markets eroded the wealth and endangered the long-term plans of many Americans. At the time, people wondered: Was another Great Depression getting started? The answer, it turned out, was "no." But the losses many people sustained were substantial, and recovery would take years.

The downward slide of the economy in 2008-2009 was steep. Unemployment rose to 10 percent, peaking in October 2009. The stock market lost more than half of its value, with the DJIA bottoming out at 6,443.27. The market again proved the wisdom of "buy and hold" and avoiding panic in troubled times. One year after its March 2009 low, the DJIA had recovered to more than 10,000. Two years later, the DJIA had gone beyond 12,000, and on the third anniversary of the market bottom, the DJIA was closing in on 13,000. Someone who panicked and sold in March 2009, on the other hand, would have locked in a 54 percent loss from the October 2007 peak.

Although the stock market recovered from the 2007 crash relatively well, economic activity and unemployment were more stubborn. From its October 2009 peak of 10.0 percent, unemployment had declined only to 8.9 percent in October 2011—two years after peak unemployment and four years after the stock market's highest point before the recession. At its pre-recession best, unemployment had been under 5 percent.

✂ -

The Crash of 2007: What Caused It?

Most economists agree that the downturn in the stock markets beginning in 2007 had its origins in the housing industry. Beginning in the late 1990s, housing prices started increasing at historically high rates. Housing prices continued to increase at a fast pace until 2006. Then interest rates on home loans increased. The result was that a large number of home owners defaulted on their home mortgages. The defaults led to increasing home foreclosures, in which owners were removed because of their inability to pay. This was all made worse by the fact that there was an oversupply of new homes and condominiums on the market, especially in rapidly growing communities such as Phoenix, Las Vegas, and South Florida. While these areas were particularly hard hit by the collapse, few parts of the nation escaped without damage. The housing bubble had popped, and many families and businesses lost nearly everything.

1. **Changing lending standards:** A primary cause of the recession of 2007-2009 was a change in lending standards. Home ownership was widely regarded as a way to bring people of low and moderate income into the middle class. Beginning in the mid-1990s, the federal government encouraged borrowers to take out high-risk loans and purchase homes with little or no down payment. The assumption was that home prices would continue to increase. When the housing price bubble popped, these households quickly learned that they now owed more on their home mortgages than their homes were worth.

2. **Fannie Mae and Freddie Mac:** Two Government Sponsored Enterprises (GSEs) were tied directly to the changing of lending standards. (A GSE is a business that is privately owned and operated but backed by the federal government.) The GSEs involved were the Federal National Mortgage Association ("Fannie Mae") and the Federal Home Loan Mortgage Corporation ("Freddie Mac"). Since the mid-1990s, these two businesses had become dominant players in the home mortgage market. In 1995, they were ordered by the U.S. Department of Housing and Urban Development (HUD) to increase the number of loans they held from low- and moderate-income family households. HUD also required Fannie and Freddie to accept smaller down payments and to offer large loans relative to the amount of income earned by the home buyers. Many of these loans were "subprime" loans, meaning that borrowers had a poor credit history. Fannie Mae and Freddie Mac took on more than $6 trillion of single-family loans from 1992 to 2008. At first, the new loans offered by Fannie and Freddie helped fuel increased demand for housing—driving prices higher. However, when home prices began to decline and interest rates began to rise, these households were unprepared to absorb the losses.

3. **Low interest rate policy of the Federal Reserve:** The nation had faced a recession early in 2001. One result was that the Federal Reserve kept interest rates at historic lows from 2002 until 2004. Some economists argue that the Fed kept rates too low for too long. These low rates further encouraged home owners to take out home mortgages. Many took out home loans called "adjustable rate mortgages," or ARMs. The low interest rates on ARMs made it possible for people to buy more and larger homes. Beginning in 2005-2006, the Fed changed direction and began to increase interest rates. Many home owners—especially those with ARMs—were caught off guard. Their mortgage payments

increased, while their income remained the same. They could no longer afford to make their home payments. Then when housing prices fell, they were left with homes that were "underwater." That is, the total value of what they owed on their homes was greater than the market value of their homes.

4. **International complications and undetected risk:** Financial institutions in other parts of the world wished to benefit from the U.S. boom in housing prices. This made sense if you consider that U.S. home mortgages were historically regarded as among of safest of all investments. Large investment banks such as Goldman Sachs, Lehman Brothers, and Bear Sterns became involved in financial instruments knows as "mortgage-backed securities." Mortgage-backed securities were purchased by institutions around the world, but especially in Europe. At first, these new financial instruments were highly profitable. However, what had gone unnoticed was that many of the home mortgages now in the mix were of substantially higher risk of default due to the decline in lending standards. When housing prices tanked and default rates increased, it became apparent that the new mortgage-backed securities were far more risky than had been imagined. Given their high exposure to this sort of debt, financial institutions began to collapse. The fourth largest investment bank, Lehman Brothers, quickly went out of business. Merrill Lynch, on the verge of failure, was acquired by Bank of America. The problem spread, and Washington Mutual Bank's collapse became the largest bank failure in U.S. history.

5. **High levels of household debt:** Even as incomes were increasing during these years, people were saving less. Personal savings rates were low and sometimes even negative. Rather than saving more, families were taking on greater and greater amounts of debt relative to their ability to pay. Favorable interest rates and declining lending standards provided incentives that encouraged families to take on debt. So did the tax advantages that came with home mortgages and home equity loans. These incentives encouraged families to place more of their debt into housing loans. Those families then were in a weak financial position when the housing price bubble popped.

The Crash of 2007: What Role Did the Fed Play?*

Unlike the stock market crash of 1987, the decline of stocks in 2007 was followed by a deep and painful recession. The recession officially ended in 2009; however, economic growth continued to be sluggish.

The U.S. government moved aggressively in response to the financial crisis. Beginning in February 2007, the Federal Reserve took action to reduce interest rates. The primary interest rate controlled by the Fed is called the federal funds rate. It is the interest rate banks charge one another for loans. In 10 steps, the federal funds rate was taken from 5.25 percent to 0 to 0.25 percent as of December 2008. Practically speaking, the rate could go no lower.

The nation was facing a liquidity crisis. Liquidity is the ability to quickly convert something of value into cash. For example, a savings account has a great deal of liquidity for an individual bank depositor. The depositor can get cash with a quick visit the bank.

Banks in 2007 and other financial institutions needed liquidity. Why? Many were holding large amounts of mortgage-backed securities and similar assets. Overnight, these assets went from being regarded as safe to being regarded as high risk. They became known as "toxic assets." What made them toxic was that their value was unknown. Within bundles of mortgages, some of the loans were based on traditional lending practices and were likely to be repaid. However, others were based on reduced lending standards, and these were in danger of default. But banks and other financial institutions had immediate financial obligations to meet. They had no time to sort out good mortgages from bad mortgages.

The Federal Reserve took action to restore liquidity. Beginning in the summer of 2007, the Fed initiated a number of temporary measures aimed restoring confidence in the credit markets. It encouraged banks to borrow money from the Fed. It extended the amount of lending from the Fed beyond the usual overnight basis to up to 30 days, with possible renewal.

As the financial crisis worsened, the Fed implemented new tools of monetary policy aimed at restoring liquidity.

- The Term Auction Facility (TAF) was announced in late 2007. It provided one- and three-month loans to banks.

- The Term Securities Lending Facility (TSLF) was initiated in 2008. It allowed banks and some other financial institutions to swap less liquid assets for U.S. Treasury securities owned by the Federal Reserve.

- The Term Asset-Backed Securities Loan Facility (TALF) was announced in November of 2008. It was aimed at easing the negative effects of the "toxic assets" held by many financial institutions. It provided loans to U.S. banks and investment funds to purchase high-quality asset-backed securities.

While some of these actions by the Fed will be debated for years to come, it appears that these actions slowed the panic and prevented a complete collapse of the financial system.

*Sources:

Andrew T. Hill and William C. Wood, "It's Not Your Mother and Father's Money Policy Anymore: The Federal Reserve and Financial Crisis Relief," *Social Education* 75 (2), March/April 2011, pp. 76-81.

James D. Gwartney and Joseph Connors, "The Crash of 2008: Causes and Lessons to Be Learned," *Social Education* 73 (2), March/April 2009, pp. 63-67.

LESSON 18

MANAGING RISK

Lesson 18
Managing Risk

LESSON DESCRIPTION

The students are introduced to new applications of the concept of diversification. A teacher-led demonstration offers students the option of accepting a briefcase filled with $150,000 or accepting the results of a double down coin flip. This demonstration sets the stage for students to understand risks involved in the choices we make and how to take steps to reduce risk. Students use the concept of diversification to help them understand how risks can be spread out over different stocks and other assets. By reading a dialogue among hypothetical residents of Valley View Estates, the students learn about insurance as another tool for spreading out risk.

INTRODUCTION

Most people are risk averse. This means that most people dislike bad things happening to them. For a risk-averse person, the pain of losing $1,000 is greater than the pleasure of winning $1,000. Many risk-averse people use diversification as a way of reducing risk. *Diversification* means replacing a single risk—which could be great or small—with a large number of smaller risks. The value of diversification in reducing risk can be readily seen when it comes to buying stocks. Investors who spread stock purchases out among many types of companies can reduce their risk of loss. Diversification can help cushion wide swings in stock prices. In much the same way, diversification is the key concept in understanding how insurance can be used to reduce risk. Insurance products are designed to spread risk out over many different individuals in order to reduce losses involving autos, home, health, and so forth.

CONCEPTS

Diversification

Insurance

Market-price risk

Risk

OBJECTIVES

Students will be able to:

- Explain how people can use diversification to reduce market-price risks when they invest in stocks.

- Explain how people can use diversification to reduce risks associated with personal losses—car, home, and health—through the purchase of insurance.

CONTENT STANDARDS

Voluntary National Content Standards in Economics, **2nd Edition**

- **Standard 2:** Effective decision making requires comparing the additional costs of alternatives with the additional benefits. Many choices involve doing a little more or a little less of something: few choices are "all or nothing" decisions.

- **Standard 4:** People usually respond predictably to positive and negative incentives.

- **Standard 10:** Institutions evolve and are created to help individuals and groups accomplish their goals. Banks, labor unions, markets, corporations, legal systems, and not-for-profit organizations are examples of important institutions. A different kind of institution, clearly defined and enforced property rights, is essential to a market economy.

National Standards in K-12 Personal Finance Education, 3rd edition

- **Financial Responsibility and Decision Making Standard 4:** Make financial decisions by systematically considering alternatives and consequences.

- **Risk Management and Insurance Standard 1:** Identify common types of risks and basic risk management methods.

- **Risk Management and Insurance Standard 2:** Explain the purpose and importance of property and liability insurance protection.

- **Risk Management and Insurance Standard 3:** Explain the purpose and importance of health, disability, and life insurance protection.

TIME REQUIRED
45 minutes

MATERIALS
- Slides 18.1, 18.2, 18.3, 18.4, 18.5, and 18.6

- Consider having a briefcase filled with play money as a prop to be used in Procedure 3.

- One copy of Activity 18.1 for each student

PROCEDURE
1. Tell the students that the purpose of this lesson is to focus on ways of reducing or controlling some of the risks we face in investing. It also deals with ways we can protect ourselves from personal losses involving cars, home, and health. In these efforts, *diversification* is a key concept. Diversification can be used to reduce the risk of loss arising from stock-price volatility. Diversification linked to the purchase of insurance can also be used to reduce the risk of losses involving cars, homes, and health problems.

2. **Display Slide 18.1.** Discuss how day-to-day events may involve risk. **Ask:**

   - How might eating a breakfast sandwich and having a hot drink in a fast-food restaurant be risky?

     (Accept a variety of answers. Students might say that the food might be contaminated or they might burn themselves drinking a hot drink,)

   - How might driving to school be risky?

     (Accept a variety of answers. Risks include having a car accident or being stopped by the police for violating traffic rules and facing penalties or fines.)

   - How might texting or listening to your music during class be risky?

     (Accept a variety of answers. Depending on school rules, teachers might reduce a student's grades, confiscate the electronics involved, send a student to suspension, and so forth.)

   - How might playing tennis after school be risky?

     (Accept a variety of answers. Playing tennis could result in injury—maybe a twisted ankle or a broken arm caused by a nasty fall.)

3. Make the obvious point that life is filled with risks great and small. It is a gamble just to get out of bed in the morning.

4. **Display Slide 18.2.** Imagine that you have a briefcase filled with $150,000 in cash. Pose the two options presented in Slide 18.2 to the class: would they prefer to accept the $150,000 in cash or risk the double or nothing coin flip?

Ask the students to show their preference by raising their hands in favor of one option or the other. Also ask them to comment on their preferences. Most will probably say they would accept the $150,000 and pass on the coin flip. Stress the point that in this matter, they are like most other people—they are risk averse. For people to be risk averse isn't a bad thing; it may mean only that the people in question dislike bad things happening to them—like losing the $150,000. For a risk-averse person, the pain of losing it all in the coin flip is greater than the pleasure of walking away with $150,000. So most people would accept the cash and pass up the coin flip.

5. **Display Slide 18.3**. Briefly discuss what diversification is and how it can be applied in asset allocation, purchasing stocks, and buying insurance. (These ideas are developed more fully in Activity 18.1.)

6. **Distribute Activity 18.1**. Ask the students to read Part 1 and respond to the **Questions for Discussion**. Discuss the answers:

   A. What is diversification?

   (Diversification means replacing a single risk with a large number of smaller risks. It simply echoes to the old adage: "Don't put all your eggs in one basket.")

   B. What is market-price risk?

   (Market-price risk means that you could lose all of your investment if the market price of your asset declines to zero.)

   C. What is diversification as applied to purchasing stocks?

   (Diversification in that context means spreading the risk of stock ownership out over investments in many companies of different sizes, in different sectors, and in different locations.)

7. Refer the students to Part 2 of **Activity 18.1**. Identify four volunteers to play the parts of Tom, Alicia, Sam, and Roland. Read the introductory paragraphs in Part 2. Then ask the four volunteers to come to the front of the room and read the script. When they have finished, turn to the **Questions for Discussion**s for Part 2. **Ask:**

   A. Why is having home insurance important?

   (Home ownership represents the biggest investment many people make. Therefore it also presents the risk of large losses.)

   B. Using the example of Valley View Estates, what is diversification as applied to buying home insurance?

   (Insurance diversification in that context means spreading some of the risks you face out over other insurance policy holders. In the example of Valley View Estates, home owners could spread a potential loss of $100,000 due to a house fire across the 500 residents. When the $100,000 loss is divided among 500 home owners, the cost to each home owner is $200. If each resident paid a relatively small amount, all residents would be protected against having a big loss. The idea of insurance is to diversify risk—to spread it out over many different individuals in order to reduce losses.)

8. **Display Slides 18.4 to 18.6**. Discuss each slide. Briefly explain how the different forms of insurance work.

9. **Ask:** What types of insurance seem to be of particular importance for young people?

(Accept a variety of answers. Students are likely to mention auto insurance as important. For young people about to move from away from home, renter's insurance might also be considered an important protection. Insurance for personal property might also be important. When students consider their clothing, television set, smartphone, computer, sports equipment, and so forth, they might see the value of their personal property adding up to more than they imagined. Others types of protection they might consider include insurance for health, life, and disability.)

CLOSURE

10. Summarize the lesson briefly by reminding the students that life is a gamble. We face all sorts of risks every day.

    A. Simply stated, what does diversification mean?

       (Its meaning can be summarized in the saying, "Don't place all your eggs in one basket." Diversification is a way of reducing risk by placing a large number of small bets rather than a small number of large bets.)

    B. What is diversification as applied to purchasing stocks?

       (Diversification in that context means spreading the risk of stock ownership out over investment in many companies of different sizes, in different sectors, and in different locations.)

    C. What is diversification as applied to insurance?

       (Diversification in that context means spreading some of the risks an individual faces—arising from car accidents, theft, and fire, for example—out over other many other insurance-policy holders.)

ASSESSMENT
Multiple-Choice Questions

1. The meaning of *diversification* is best summarized in which of the following statements?

    a. *Don't place all your eggs in one basket.*
    b. Try to meet people from many backgrounds.
    c. Read different newspapers.
    d. Try different approaches to getting your work done.

2. Market-price risk is

    a. risk related to the place or institution where goods and services are bought and sold.
    b. *risk related to up and down fluctuation in the price of an asset.*
    c. risk related to an investor's order to stop trading due to market volatility.
    d. risk related to the liability of a stockholder in case of a lawsuit.

3. *Asset diversification* refers to investing in

    a. short sells and short covers.
    b. *a variety of assets including stocks, bonds, and mutual funds.*
    c. certificates of deposit.
    d. international stocks including those in Canada, Asia, and South America.

4. The purpose of insurance is to

    a. create a pool of money used by a company to purchase stocks.
    b. buy and sell low-risk investments such as government bonds.
    c. *spread risks out over a large number of people.*
    d. protect investors from unscrupulous lenders.

Constructed-Response Items

1. Jeremy currently has all the money he saved invested in Coca-Cola stock. He is considering how he could become more diversified in his stock holdings. What advice can you give him?

    (There at least three ways that Jeremy could become more diversified. He should consider investing in companies of different sizes—some large companies, some mid-sized companies, and some small companies. He should consider investing in companies in different sectors of the economy—perhaps technology companies, manufacturing companies, pharmaceutical companies, and utility companies. Finally, he should consider investing in companies in different parts of the world.)

2. Imagine an apartment complex with 100 residents. The residents' association wants to offer insurance against theft. Suppose the residents own an average of $200 worth of possessions. Suppose further that on average five of the 100 residents lose their possessions each year to theft. How much would the association have to charge each resident to cover the total expected losses? How could the residents' association use this calculation to diversify risk among the residents?

    (In a typical year, residents would lose a total of $1,000 [$200 x 5 losses]. That $1,000, spread over 100 residents, equals $10 per resident. The association could use this calculation to run an insurance pool. If each resident paid $10 into a pool for personal property insurance, all the residents would be protected from financial loss due to theft of personal possessions. In other words, the risk would be diversified across all the residents.)

Gen i Connection

Mission 6 of the Gen i Revolution game calls on game players to work through an investing decision. If students have not already played the mission, this is a good time to assign it. (The mission was previously mentioned in connection with Lesson 8 as a resource for showing the relationship between risk and return.) In Mission 6, students take on the role of operatives advising Kai, whose wealthy grandmother has given him and each of her grandchildren $10,000 to invest. Kai is planning to go to college and wants to use his gift to help pay for college expenses. Along the way, Kai needs to consider his financial goals, his comfort with risk, and his time horizon. Students work interactively through a 4-1-1 tutorial on risk across different asset classes, from highly safe bank accounts to highly speculative individual stocks. Students conclude the mission by making a recommendation from a multiple-choice list on how Kai should invest the $10,000.

Gen i Reflection

Kai made a decision on how to invest $10,000 from his grandmother in Mission 6 of the Gen i Revolution. If you had $10,000 of your own to invest, in the context of today's market conditions, what assets would you buy? CDs? Stocks? Bonds? Mutual funds? Why?

ACTIVITY 18.1
GET DIVERSIFIED!

Diversification Part 1: Reducing the Risk of Buying Stocks

Diversification means replacing a single risk with a large number of smaller risks. The basic idea is as simple as the old adage, "Don't put all your eggs in one basket." While diversification appears to be a simple idea, however, it has important implications for investing in stocks and in obtaining protection against various personal losses.

All investment choices involve risk. One type of risk is market-price risk. Market-price risk is the risk that you could lose all of an investment if the market price of the asset—say, 100 shares of stock—declined to zero.

One way to reduce market-price risk is to diversify investments across different categories of assets. This is called *asset diversification.* It means spreading your investment funds out over various investment options such as stocks, bonds, and mutual funds.

The concept of diversification can also be applied to buying stocks. If you buy stock in many companies, the risk of losing all of your investment is reduced. Any given set of stocks—such as technology companies—might perform poorly in a given period of time. However, the idea of stock diversification is that a decline in technology stocks would be balanced out by gains within another group of stocks—perhaps stocks in health care companies. Diversification can help cushion investors against wide swings in stock prices.

Possibilities for diversification in stocks include holding stock in companies that differ along these lines:

- **Sizes**—some large companies, some mid-sized companies, and some small companies.

- **Sectors of the economy**—perhaps some technology companies, manufacturing companies, pharmaceutical companies, and utility companies.

- **Locations**—perhaps companies in the United States and in Canada, Europe, Asia, and South America.

Questions for Discussion

A. What is diversification?

B. What is market-price risk?

C. What is diversification as applied to purchasing stocks?

Diversification Part 2: Reducing Risk by Buying Insurance

Market-price risk is only one risk out of many. People routinely face the risk of losses arising from several other sources. They have car accidents and are victims of robberies. Their homes and cars are damaged in hail storms and floods. They suffer from illness and disability, and they die. Buying insurance is one way to reduce the financial losses that follow when these bad things happen.

The Home Owners of Valley View Estates Learn How Insurance Works

This story tells how the residents of Valley View Estates learned about insurance. Valley View Estates is a housing development serving 500 home owners. These homeowners learned that insurance spreads risks out over a group of people. It provides a way of diversifying risk.

Valley View Estates comprises 500 homes, a playground for little kids, a club house, and a swimming pool. It is home to 500 home owners and their families, 99 dogs, 68 cats, and one pet snake that everyone hopes never escapes.

Valley View Estates has a Home Owners' Association that takes responsibility for providing services to home owners—making sure that lawns are watered in the summer, snow is plowed in the winter, and so on.

Tom Mulligan is President of the Home Owners Association. He thinks he has a plan for how Valley View homeowners might be able to save some money. But in order to explain it, he will have to make sure the Board members understand how insurance works.

Tom has called a meeting of Valley View Estates Home Owners Association Executive Board. Serving on the Board with Tom are Alicia, Sam, and Roland.

Tom Calls the Meeting of the Board to Order

Tom: Welcome everyone. Thanks for coming. I have an idea that I think could save Valley View Estates residents a few bucks. Do you mind if I tell you about it?

Alicia: Not at all, Tom. You know I am always interested in saving a few bucks. What's on your mind?

Tom: You know that buying a home is the biggest investment many people ever make. That certainly is true of the good folks living here in Valley View Estates.

Sam: That's true, Tom. Our homes are very important to us. That's why everyone here has homeowners' insurance. They have that insurance to protect themselves against damage or loss from things such as fire, lightning, or theft.

Tom: That's right, Sam. I was wondering about this angle on insurance: if we purchased home owners insurance as a group, could we save some money?

Roland: Tom, could you tell us how homeowners' insurance actually works? I think a lot of our home owners are confused about that. They just pay their insurance bills—I think they are called premiums—without paying much attention to how the whole thing works.

Tom: Sure. Here is how insurance works. Suppose the value of each home in Valley View Estates is $100,000.

Alicia: That sounds about right. Go on.

Tom: Now, remember that kitchen fire last year at the Lees' home? If their home had burned to the ground, they would have lost $100,000. Follow me?

Sam: I do remember. That was awful. But how does homeowner's insurance enter into the picture?

Tom: Well, let's imagine that in a typical year, one Valley View Estates home owner loses a total of $100,000 for the one home fire. If that home is not insured, it would be a financial disaster for the home owner. That home owner would lose just about everything.

Roland: Yes, Tom, and the point?

Tom: There are 500 of us here in Valley View Estates. What if we could spread that $100,000 loss over all the rest of us? When the $100,000 loss is divided among our 500 home owners, the cost to each home owner would be only $200. ($100,000/ 500 = $200.)

Alicia: I get it. If we each paid a relatively small amount of money—say, $200 a year—we would be protected against having a big loss—possibly $100,000. We pool our money together. Maybe keep it safe in a bank. If any one of us has a fire, we are protected against the loss.

Sam: But what happens if there is no fire in one year? I guess that would be good news, but it is like we placed all that money in the pool and got nothing back.

Tom: Another good point. That is why some people—high risk takers—are tempted not to buy insurance. But if something big goes wrong—like their house burns down—they might lose everything.

Roland: Here's another problem that is much worse. What happens if we have more than one fire per year?

Tom: Excellent question, Roland. We would have to build up the money in our pool over time. Things don't always go according to plan. We would need to be prepared for unexpected costs and savings. If there were two home fires in one year, we would need to have enough cash in reserve to pay for those losses, for instance. In good years, when we have no fires, we can save the money and build up the pool.

Alicia: But we would still not be 100 percent safe, right?

Tom: Right. Nothing could make us 100 percent safe. Instead, the idea is to diversify risk, not eliminate it altogether. We could diversify risk by spreading it out over many different individuals. By doing that we could reduce individuals' losses.

Sam: Thanks for that explanation, Tom. It helps a lot. Is that how other insurance plans work?

Tom: Yes. People can buy insurance on all kinds of things in order to reduce risk. Common forms of insurance include insurance for cars, health, and life. Now, here is my plan for saving us some big bucks.

Questions for Discussion

A. Why is having home insurance important?

B. Using the example of Valley View Estates, what is diversification as applied to buying home insurance?

SLIDE 18.1

It's Risky Out There

- What's the risk in
  - Having a breakfast sandwich and a hot drink at a fast-food restaurant before school?
  - Driving to school?
  - Listening to your music or texting friends during class time?
  - Playing tennis after school?

SLIDE 18.2

Flipping Out Over the Cash

- Imagine that I have a brief case filled with $150,000 in cash.
- Option One: You keep the cash.
  - You can have the $150,000 right now! No strings attached.
- Option Two: Double or nothing.
  - Based on a double or nothing coin flip, you can have $0 if you lose the coin toss or $300,000 if you win.
- Which option would you choose?

SLIDE 18.3

Diversification Can Reduce Risk

- **Diversification** means replacing a single risk with a large number of smaller risks.

- **Asset diversification** means spreading your investment funds out over various investment options such as stocks, bonds, and mutual funds.

- **Stock diversification** means spreading stock ownership risks out over many companies of different sizes, in different sectors, and in different locations.

- **Insurance diversification** means spreading some of the other risks you face—arising from car accidents, theft, and fire—out over other insurance policy holders.

SLIDE 18.4

Auto Insurance

- Auto insurance provides financial protection from losses due to an auto accident or other damage.

- Types of auto insurance coverage:

  - **Collision** provides for the repair or replacement of the car damaged in an accident.

  - **Liability** covers the cost of property damage or injuries to others caused by the policy owner.

  - **Comprehensive** covers the cost of damage to an auto as a result of fire, theft, or storms.

SLIDE 18.5

Renters', Health, and Disability

- **Renters' insurance** provides financial protection in case of loss of personal possessions in a rental unit due to theft, fire, water damage, and so forth.

- **Health insurance** provides payment for certain health care costs.

  - Basic health covers office visits, lab work, hospital costs, and routine care up to a certain limit.

  - Major medical provides protection against catastrophic illness.

- **Disability insurance** provides income over a specified period of time when a person is ill or unable to work.

LEARNING, EARNING, AND INVESTING FOR A NEW GENERATION © COUNCIL FOR ECONOMIC EDUCATION, NEW YORK, NY

SLIDE 18.6

Life Insurance

- **Life insurance** provides financial protection to dependents of the policy owner when the policy owner dies.

  - **Term life** offers protection for a specified period of time. If you don't die within that time, you don't get the money (which is a good thing, remember?).

  - **Permanent life** offers protection that remains in effect during the lifetime of the insured and acquires a cash value.

  - Or you can purchase a variable plan which combines both.

LEARNING, EARNING, AND INVESTING FOR A NEW GENERATION © COUNCIL FOR ECONOMIC EDUCATION, NEW YORK, NY

Lesson 19

Investing Internationally

LESSON 19
INVESTING INTERNATIONALLY

LESSON DESCRIPTION

The students examine the costs and benefits of investing in international markets. They learn that some investors gain international exposure by buying shares of U.S. firms that generate revenue from overseas. They learn about currency exchange rates—how to make conversions from one currency to another, why currencies appreciate and depreciate in value, and how the exchange rate for a currency affects the amount of a foreign stock an investor can buy. They learn about the concepts of a strong and a weak dollar and learn who benefits and who is hurt when the dollar is strong or weak.

INTRODUCTION

Many investors rely on international investing to diversify their portfolios and take advantage of growth opportunities in other parts of the world. However, international investing involves risk. Developing nations may experience economic or political instability. Reporting practices are different in different parts of the world; important information may be hard to acquire or understand. And there is a risk associated with currency exchange rates. For most foreign securities, purchases must be made in the currency of the country or region where the company is headquartered. The potential for currencies to change value in international currency markets creates an additional element of risk for investors.

CONCEPTS

Currency markets

Diversification

Exchange rate

Strong and weak dollar

OBJECTIVES

Students will be able to:

- Identify the costs and benefits of international investing.

- Explain how exchange rates can influence the value of an investment.

- Understand the concepts of a strong dollar and a weak dollar.

- Explain how the strength or weakness of the dollar may affect financial transactions.

CONTENT STANDARDS

Voluntary National Content Standards in Economics, **2nd Edition**

- **Standard 2:** Effective decision making requires comparing the additional costs of alternatives with the additional benefits. Many choices involve doing a little more or a little less of something: few choices are "all or nothing" decisions.

National Standards in K-12 Personal Finance Education, **3rd Edition**

- **Financial Responsibility and Decision Making Standard 4:** Make financial decisions by systematically considering alternatives and consequences.

- **Saving and Investing Standard 3:** Evaluate investment alternatives.

TIME REQUIRED

60 minutes

MATERIALS

- Slides 19.1, 19.2, 19.3, 19.4, 19.5, 19.6, and 19.7.

- A copy of Activity 19.1 for each student

PROCEDURE

1. Tell the students that the purpose of this lesson is to consider some of the costs and benefits of investing internationally. The lesson focuses on how changes in the value of currency can affect individual investments.

2. Explain that most countries have stock and bond markets where people can make investments. Refer to Lesson 7, in which students learned about the Tokyo Stock Exchange. Mention that large stock markets also exist in London, England, and in major cities in most other nations.

3. **Display Slide 19.1** and discuss the costs and benefits of investing internationally. Benefits include opportunities for diversification and growth arising from investment in businesses in other nations. Costs include risks that may arise from political instability, earthquakes, tsunamis, nuclear power-plant meltdowns, and so on. (Of course, some risks of this sort may also arise at home.) In addition, some overseas stock markets require less disclosure of information than markets in the United States. Overall, it is harder for investors to obtain information on international companies than domestic companies. These differences can affect the value of international investments.

4. **Display Slide 19.2.** Explain that investors who buy stocks or bonds of corporations in other nations often see benefits, especially in growth and diversification. To obtain these benefits, however, it is not necessary to invest in foreign companies. Investors may achieve benefits of the same sort by buying stocks or bonds from some U.S. companies that do a great deal of business overseas, generating revenue and profits from overseas sales. Show the students that a substantial amount of the revenues of some of America's largest companies come from overseas. Coca Cola and McDonald's are two examples that will be familiar to them.

5. Explain that foreign stocks and bonds are bought in the currencies of the countries in which they are issued. For example, a British company's stock would be bought in English pounds, a Japanese bond in yen, a Mexican company in pesos, and most European mutual funds in euros. When people invest with brokers, brokers can take care of the necessary exchanges, converting one currency to another.

6. Explain that currency is bought and sold like other goods. The price of a currency, like the price of other goods, is established by the interaction of demand and supply. People in other countries demand U.S. dollars when they want to buy U.S. goods and services, stocks, or bonds. People supply U.S. dollars to the currency market when they want other currencies—often pounds, Canadian dollars, pesos, euros, or yen. To obtain foreign currency, you buy it; its price is called the exchange rate. *(Note: If you are teaching an advanced course in which the students are already familiar with supply and demand, you might draw supply and demand curves for the U.S. dollar, with the price represented as the exchange rate. Then demonstrate how a shift in the supply or demand of the currency affects its price).*

7. **Display Slide 19.3.** Tell the students that while this slide may look confusing, it really isn't difficult to understand. The exchange rate between one U.S. dollar and foreign currencies fluctuates daily as supply and demand conditions for the two currencies change. This slide focuses on the exchange rate between dollars and Japanese yen. Show the students how to use

the exchange rate (in this case, 1 dollar = 76.8 yen) to determine how many yen can be purchased for $10,000. Next show them how many shares of a Japanese company they could purchase with $10,000 when the company's stock is priced at 3,800 yen. Now do the opposite example on the bottom of the slide by converting yen to U.S. dollars and buying a stock that is priced in dollars. Explain that transactions of this sort take place every day as Americans purchase investments in foreign currencies and foreigners buy American stocks and bonds.

8. When describing the market for dollars, people often use the terms *strong dollar* and *weak dollar*. These terms may be misleading—suggesting by connotation that a strong dollar is a good thing while a weak dollar is a bad thing. Explain that this is not necessarily the case. **Display Slide19.4.** Explain that the term *strong dollar* means the value of the dollar is rising as compared to other currencies. Explain that the term *weak dollar* means the value of the dollar is falling as compared to other currencies. When the dollar is weak (or strong), some people are helped and some people are hurt. The students soon will see how this works.

9. But first, **display Slide 19.5.** Tell the students that the class once again will use the example of converting U.S. dollars to Japanese yen. By reference to the top part of the slide, show that the dollar is appreciating. This means that dollars have become more valuable and can buy more yen than they could before. Explain the rest of the example as dollars are converted to yen, using the new exchange rate, and then purchase stock in the same Japanese company at a price of 3,800 yen per share. Emphasize that when the dollar appreciates it can buy more foreign currency (yen,

in this example). When this occurs, Americans can buy nine more shares of a Japanese company with same number of dollars (in this case, $10,000). Next move to the bottom of the slide. **Ask** the students what they think will happen when the dollar depreciates. *(The investor will now be able to buy fewer shares of stock in the Japanese company.)* Make the point that when a currency depreciates, it becomes less valuable and can buy fewer units of foreign currency. Follow this example to the end, showing that after the dollar depreciates the investor can buy about 17 fewer shares of the Japanese stock with $10,000.

10. **Display Slide 19.6.** Now that you have shown how an appreciating (stronger) dollar or a depreciating (weaker) dollar affects the purchase of a foreign stock, turn to the question of who benefits and who is hurt as a currency's value changes. Explain that a strong dollar helps some people while hurting others. A strong dollar is good for U.S. consumers and importers. For example, a strong dollar reduces the cost U.S. consumers pay when they buy imported cars or take vacations in another country. Importers in the United States can sell foreign cars at lower prices. American investors also pay less for acquiring securities from other nations when the dollar is strong. But a strong dollar hurts others. When the dollar is strong, imports cost less; American producers then face increased price competition. Manufacturers of American cars, for example, must compete with manufacturers overseas who sell their cars in the United States at prices that look relatively attractive. A strong dollar also means that American goods and services become more expensive for foreign consumers. This hurts American exporters.

11. **Display Slide 19.7.** Review key points and provide additional clarification as necessary. A weak dollar helps some people and hurts others. When the dollar is weak, U.S. producers face less competition from lower-priced imports; at the same time, foreign consumers pay less for American goods and services, which benefits American exporters. However, American consumers and importers are hurt by a weak dollar because prices of foreign goods and services increase. American investors also have to pay more for acquiring securities from other nations.

12. Distribute a copy of Activity 19.1 to each student. Read the directions with the class. Assign them to respond to the questions in parts A, B, and C.

13. Once the students have completed parts A, B, and C, discuss their work and the answers.

    A. *1. $10,000 x (12.8 pesos / $1) = 128,000 pesos; 128,000 pesos / 120 peso per share = 1,066.7 shares of Oil Mexico.*
    2. $10,000 x (14.5 pesos / $1) = 145,000 pesos; 145,000 pesos / 120 pesos per share = 1208. 3 shares of Oil Mexico.
    3. The dollar appreciated (or got stronger). In part 2, one dollar can buy more pesos than it could in part 1.

    B. *1. €10,000 x ($0.9 / €1) = $9,000; $9,000 / $100 per share = 90 shares of Apple Pie, Inc.*
    2. €10,000 x ($0.8 / €1) = $8,000; $8,000 / $100 per share = 80 shares of Apple Pie, Inc.
    3. The euro depreciated (or got weaker). In part 2, one euro can buy fewer dollars than it could in part 1.

    C. *1. $10,000 x (¥300 / $1) = ¥3,000,000; ¥3,000,000 / ¥3,000 per share = 1,000 shares of Chop Sticks, Inc.*
    2. $10,000 x (¥260 / $1) = ¥2,500,000; ¥2,500,000 / ¥3,000 per share = 833.3 shares of Chop Sticks, Inc.
    3. The dollar depreciated (or got weaker). In part 2, one dollar can buy less yen than it could in part 1.

CLOSURE

14. Explain that many investors seek to diversify their investments by investing in international markets. **Ask:** What are two ways in which investors can accomplish this goal? Which one involves an extra risk?

    (Investors can diversify their investments by buying stock in foreign companies sold on international stock exchanges. Investors can also diversify their investments by buying stocks in U.S. companies that make large amounts of their revenue from overseas. Changes in the value of the currency caused by movements in currency exchange markets make the former method riskier. These changes do not affect investors who invest in domestic firms.)

ASSESSMENT
Multiple-Choice Questions

1. Which of the following is a good reason for investors to invest in foreign markets?

    a. To earn a guaranteed return on investment
    b. To illegally avoid U.S. taxes
    c. To gain dual foreign and U.S. citizenship
    d. *To diversify their investment portfolios*

2. The exchange rate between the U.S. dollar and the yen was 80 yen per one dollar. Now it changes to 90 yen per one dollar. In this example, the dollar

   a. weakened with respect to the yen.
   b. *strengthened with respect to the yen.*
   c. didn't change with respect to the yen.
   d. increased the cost of goods imported from Japan.

3. The exchange rate between the U.S. dollar and the yen was 80 yen per one dollar. Now it changes to 70 yen per one dollar. In this example, the dollar

   a. *weakened with respect to the yen.*
   b. strengthened with respect to the yen.
   c. didn't change with respect to the yen.
   d. did not affect the cost of goods imported from Japan.

4. Which of the following groups benefits from a stronger dollar?

   a. U.S. consumers
   b. U.S. investors who invest internationally
   c. U.S. importers
   d. *All of the above*

Constructed-Response Items

1. Your grandfather notices from his research that many foreign bonds offer investors higher rates of return than most bonds sold in U.S. bond markets. He is ready to invest his money in foreign bonds. What factors would you advise him to consider before he makes this purchase?

   (Answers should include the risk of changing currency values, potential for instability in the overseas region, and issues that might arise because of different accounting standards.)

2. A friend tells you that a strong dollar is always good. Is your friend right?

   (No. Some Americans benefit from a strong dollar while others do well when the dollar is weaker. A strong dollar is generally good for U.S. consumers, U.S. investors who invest internationally, and U.S. importers. However, a weak dollar tends to help U.S. producers, foreign consumers, and U.S. exporters.)

Gen i Connection

Although the Gen i Revolution game does not have a mission specifically devoted to international investing, there are some indirect links. Game mission 14, "Forecasting the future," can be assigned here if it has not already been used with Lesson 16. In this mission, students make forecasts for the economies of Brazil, Japan, and the United States. The mission helps students learn about links between the stock market and the economy in general; the inclusion of Brazil and Japan makes the focus international. In mission 6, the 4-1-1 tutorial on "Risk and Return" provides useful background for the emphasis in Lesson 19 on the added risks of international investing. Note also that Gen i Revolution's treatment of diversification in multiple missions gains new relevance when students recognize that international investing is an effective method of diversifying risk.

Gen i Reflection

Gen i Revolution missions consistently stress the theme of diversifying to reduce risk. Adding international stocks can help investors diversify. Yet many investors shy away from buying international stocks or mutual funds. If you had money to invest, would you put some of it into international stocks or mutual funds? Why or why not? If you answered "yes," in which countries would you be most interested in investing, and why? Explain your answer.

ACTIVITY 19.1
CASE STUDIES OF INTERNATIONAL INVESTING

Directions: In the three cases below, investors are buying foreign stocks and bonds. Read the cases and respond to the questions. First, determine how many shares of the foreign corporation's stock can be purchased with $10,000 before and after the exchange rate changes. Then, in the blanks supplied, write *appreciate* or *depreciate* to tell whether the dollar is appreciating (becoming stronger) or depreciating (becoming weaker) compared to the foreign currency.

A. Susie wishes to purchase shares in the Mexican company, Oil Mexico. This company's stock sells on the Mexican Stock Exchange for 120 pesos per share.

    1. When the exchange rate is 12.8 pesos per 1 U.S. dollar, how many shares of Oil Mexico can Susie buy with $10,000? Show your work. _____

    2. When the exchange rate is 14.5 pesos per 1 U.S. dollar, how many shares of Oil Mexico can Susie buy with $10,000? Show your work. _____

    3. Did the U.S. dollar *appreciate* or *depreciate* with respect to the peso between question 1 and question 2? _____

B. Hans is a European investor. He wishes to purchase shares in the U.S. company, Apple Pie, Inc. This company's stock sells on the New York Stock Exchange for 100 dollars per share.

    1. When the exchange rate is 0.9 dollars per 1 euro, how many shares of Apple Pie, Inc. can Hans buy with 10,000 euros? Show your work. _____

    2. When the exchange rate is 0.8 dollars per 1 euro, how many shares of Apple Pie, Inc. can Hans buy with 10,000 euros? Show your work. _____

3. Did the euro *appreciate* or *depreciate* with respect to the dollar between question 1 and question 2? _____

C. Benny wishes to purchase shares in the Japanese company, Chop Sticks, Inc. The company's stock sells on the Tokyo Stock Exchange for 3,000 yen per share.

1. When the exchange rate is 300 yen per 1 dollar, how many shares of Chop Stocks, Inc. can Benny buy with $10,000? Show your work. _____

2. When the exchange rate is 250 yen per 1 dollar, how many shares of Chop Sticks, Inc. can Benny buy with $10,000? Show your work. _____

3. Did the U.S. dollar *appreciate* or *depreciate* with respect to the yen between question 1 and question 2? _____

SLIDE 19.1

The Benefits and Costs of Investing Internationally

- **Benefits**
  - *Diversification:* Investors can spread risk by owning stocks or bonds of foreign businesses
  - *Growth:* Some foreign businesses may be growing faster than domestic businesses; this may be especially true for emerging markets

- **Costs**
  - *Currency risk:* Exchange-rate changes may mean losses or gains
  - *Instability:* Businesses in emerging markets may experience unexpected economic or political changes
  - *Accounting standards:* Some markets in other countries require less disclosure of information
  - *Taxes:* International investments may be taxed differently than domestic investments

SLIDE 19.2

International Revenue for Selected U.S. Companies

Company Name	Description	2010 Revenues	2010 percentage of revenues from international markets
Coca-Cola	Soft Drinks	$35 Billion	75%
McDonald's	Fast Food	$24 Billion	60%
Pfizer	Pharmaceuticals	$43 Billion	55%
Procter and Gamble	Consumer Products	$79 Billion	32%

SLIDE 19.3

Exchange Rate Examples

- Converting dollars to yen
  - 1 U.S. dollar = 76.8 Japanese yen
  - A Japanese company's stock sells for 3,800 yen per share
  - How many shares can be purchased with $10,000?
  - $10,000 x (76.8 yen/$1) = 768,000 yen
  - 768,000 yen/3,800 yen per share = 202.1 shares
- Converting yen to dollars
  - 1 yen = 0.01 U.S. dollar
  - A U.S. company's stock sells for $80 per share
  - How many shares can be purchased with 1,000,000 yen?
  - 1,000,000 yen x ($0.01/yen) = $13,022
  - $13,022/$80 per share = 162.8 shares

SLIDE 19.4

Strong Dollar, Weak Dollar

- What is a strong dollar?
  - The value of the dollar rises compared to another currency, or more than one other.
  - More foreign currency is necessary to purchase U.S. dollars.
  - The value of the dollar is appreciating.

- What is a weak dollar?
  - The value of the dollar falls compared to another currency, or more than one other.
  - More U.S. dollars are necessary to purchase foreign currency.
  - The value of the dollar is depreciating.

SLIDE 19.5

Exchange Rate Changes

- Dollar appreciates
  - Before appreciation: 1 U.S. dollar = 76.8 Japanese yen
  - After appreciation: 1 U.S. dollar = 80.5 Japanese yen
  - $1 buys more yen
  - $10,000 x (80.5 yen/$1) = 805,000 yen
  - 805,000 yen/3,800 yen per share = 211.8 shares (202.1 when dollar was "weaker")
- Dollar depreciates
  - Before depreciation: 1 U.S. dollar = 76.8 Japanese yen
  - After depreciation: 1 U.S. dollar = 70.5 Japanese yen
  - $1 buys less yen
  - $10,000 x (70.5 yen/$1) = 705,000 yen
  - 705,000 yen/3,800 yen per share = 185.5 shares (202.1 when dollar was "stronger")

SLIDE 19.6

Strong Dollar Impact

- Who is helped by a strong dollar?
  - U.S. consumers: they pay less for foreign goods and services.
  - U.S. investors who invest in companies in other nations: they pay less for foreign currency.
  - U.S. importers: they can sell imported goods and services at lower prices.

- Who is hurt by a strong dollar?
  - U.S. producers: they are competing with lower-priced imports.
  - Foreign consumers: U.S. goods and services are more expensive for them to purchase.
  - U.S. exporters: American goods and services become more expensive for foreign consumers.

SLIDE 19.7

Weak Dollar Impact

- Who is helped by a weak dollar?

  - U.S. producers: they are competing with higher-priced imports.

  - Foreign consumers: U.S. goods and services are less expensive for them to purchase.

  - U.S. exporters: American goods and services become less expensive for foreign consumers.

- Who is hurt by a weak dollar?

  - U.S. consumers: they pay more for foreign goods and services.

  - U.S. investors who invest in companies in other nations: the price of foreign currency increases.

  - Foreign exporters: the prices of foreign goods and services are higher.

THE LANGUAGE OF FINANCIAL MARKETS

LESSON 20
THE LANGUAGE OF FINANCIAL MARKETS

LESSON DESCRIPTION

This lesson provides a vocabulary review with an interactive Quiz Bowl game to reinforce students' knowledge of financial terms used in previous lessons. The students work in small groups to make flash cards to display these financial terms. The terms are grouped in five categories: **Buying and Selling in the Market; Exchanges and Indexes; People in Financial Markets; Stocks, Bonds, and Mutual Funds; Technical Terms**. Each group of students begins by reviewing the terms in one category. Then the students pass their flash cards from group to group until everyone has had an opportunity to review all of the terms. The lesson concludes with a Language of Financial Markets Quiz Bowl game.

INTRODUCTION

Financial markets exist to transfer the savings of individuals and institutions to others who may have a productive use for these funds. Financial markets have played a significant role in fostering economic growth around the world. Examples are numerous and diverse: financial markets help entrepreneurs start new enterprises and they assist large companies engaged in international trade. Financial markets allow ordinary individuals to manage risk, put saved funds to work, and earn returns on their savings. For most people, understanding these dynamics requires new learning. In the course of studying and understanding the main topics in this book—learning, earning and investing—students have in effect learned a new language. Some terms used in this language are names of financial institutions and forms of investment. Some crystallize the results of careful analyses, carried out by academic and pro-

fessional specialists, of basic concepts and principles as they apply to personal finance. Students who become comfortable using these terms will approach media reports of financial information with greater depth of understanding, and they will approach their own decisions about matters of personal finance with enhanced knowledge and skill.

CONCEPTS

Bond

Mutual fund

Stock

Stock market

OBJECTIVES

Students will be able to:

- Recognize and match definitions to corresponding terms commonly used in financial markets.

- Explain the meaning of financial terms used in business discussions and news articles.

CONTENT STANDARDS

Voluntary National Content Standards in Economics, 2nd Edition

- **Standard 10:** Institutions evolve and are created to help individuals and groups accomplish their goals. Banks, labor unions, markets, corporations, legal systems, and not-for-profit organizations are examples of important institutions. A different kind of institution, clearly defined and enforced property rights, is essential to a market economy.

National Standards in K-12 Personal Finance Education, **3rd Edition**

- **Financial Responsibility and Decision Making Standard 2:** Find and evaluate financial information from a variety of sources.

- **Saving and Investing Standard 2:** Explain how investing builds wealth and helps meet financial goals.

- **Saving and Investing Standard 4:** Describe how to buy and sell investments.

TIME REQUIRED

90 minutes

MATERIALS

- Slides 20.1 to 20.63 (Note: To use the Quiz Bowl game interactively, you will need to have this PowerPoint running on a computer and projector. The file is available at http://lei.councilforeconed. org).

- One copy of Activity 20.1 for each student

- Note cards and one marker for each of five groups

- A copy of Activity 20.2 for the Language of Financial Markets Quiz Bowl leader (usually the teacher)

- A copy for each student of a recent news article about financial markets and/or a copy for each student of Activity 20.3

- Optional: Prizes for the Language of Financial Markets Quiz Bowl

PROCEDURE

1. Explain to the students that in previous lessons they have learned so many new terms about finance and investing that, in some ways, they have learned a new language. This lesson allows them to review their knowledge of these terms and compete in a Quiz Bowl game.

2. **Display Slide 20.1.** Give the students a few moments to look over the terms displayed. Explain that students will review the terms in small portions—that is, a few at a time.

3. Distribute a copy of **Activity 20.1** to each student. Randomly divide the class into five groups of equal size. Distribute note cards and markers for making flash cards. Assign each of the five groups a set of terms from **Slide 20.1**.

4. Tell the students to write a term on one side of each flash card and the definition of the term on the other side. When the groups have prepared their flash cards, ask them to quiz one another within their group to practice learning the terms and definitions.

5. Once you think all the students have had a chance to learn the terms within their group, ask the students to pass their cards to the next group: Group 1 to Group 2; Group 2 to Group 3; Group 3 to Group 4; Group 4 to Group 5; and Group 5 to Group 1. After an appropriate period of time rotate once more and continue this process until all the students have had an opportunity to learn the terms from the five groups.

6. Now you are ready to conduct the Language of Financial Markets Quiz Bowl.

   A. **Display Slide 20.2.** Appoint a student to act as Quiz Bowl scorekeeper. Explain the scorekeeper's responsibilities briefly. Point out that Slide 20.2 will be used to keep score in the Quiz Bowl game.

   B. Tell the students that, in their groups, they will compete in the Quiz Bowl. **Display Slide 20.3** on the screen. The answers to the questions or statements on the screen will be terms from Slide 20.1. The note cards and sheet of terms from the activity should now be put away.

C. Ordinarily the teacher will serve as Quiz Bowl leader, but this is also a job that may be allocated to a visiting administrator or classroom guest. The Quiz Bowl leader's job is to use a copy of **Activity 20.2** to ask the questions as the groups choose categories from Slide 20.3. (Having a separate scorekeeper frees the Quiz Bowl leader to handle the game flow from question to question.)

D. To get started, call on a student from Group 1 to select a category and point value. (Point values are indicated by numbers in the columns on Slide 20.3.) The leader may then click on that point value in the PowerPoint and it will change to a screen with the question on it.

E. Read the statement associated with the group's choice and give the group a couple of minutes to consult with their partners and answer.

F. Once the group provides an answer, the Quiz Bowl leader may click on the question in the power point and it will reveal the correct answer.

G. The teacher judges whether the answer is correct. If the term is correctly defined, the scorekeeper enters the points on the team's score, using Slide 20.2. If the term is not correctly defined, the scorekeeper takes away that number of points on Slide 20.2 and the teacher discusses the correct answer. The leader may then click on the "return to game board" button at the bottom of the slide to move to the next team's selection.

H. The leader calls on a student from Group 2 to select a category and point value and proceeds in this manner until all of the questions have been answered correctly (each group will get to try five terms).

I. The teacher declares the group that earned the most points the winner. Optional: Award prizes (or extra credit) to members of the winning team.

7. Look back on the Quiz Bowl Game. Review key terms as necessary. In particular, focus on terms that the teams struggled with in the Quiz Bowl Game, or those in which they seemed to take a special interest.

CLOSURE

8. Bring to class several recent news articles that use some of the terms featured in the lesson. Read excerpts from the news articles out loud. Ask the students to infer which term is being discussed and to explain each term in their own words or by using the definitions they have just reviewed. You may also supplement actual news stories with a simulated story available in Activity 20.3. If you choose to do this, **distribute a copy of Activity 20.3** to each student and ask students to fill in the missing terms *[(1) Dow Jones Industrial Average, (2) New York Stock Exchange, (3) S&P 500 Stock Index, (4) NASDAQ, (5) Bond, (6) Mutual Fund, (7) Dividend]*. Discuss the extent to which the students believe that their understanding of these terms helps them to read and understand economic and financial topics in the news.

9. Tell the students that learning technical terms of the sort they have reviewed in this lesson is sometimes compared to learning a new language—

Spanish, say, or German. Ask them to comment on this comparison, drawing on their own experience as foreign-language learners insofar as possible. Can they identify ways in which the two areas of new learning are alike? Different? Discuss their responses.

ASSESSMENT
Multiple-Choice Questions

1. Which of the following is a capital gain?

   a. A car owner sells her used car to a dealer for more than she expected to receive.
   b. A shipping clerk gets a raise from $10 an hour to $12 an hour.
   c. An investor buys Intel Corp. stock for $30 and sells it for $21.
   d. *An investor buys Intel Corp. stock for $21 and sells it for $30.*

2. Assume that the Dow Jones Industrial Average was at 10,000 at the beginning of the year. If it gains seven percent in the first quarter of this year, it becomes

   a. 17,000.
   b. 10,070.
   c. *10,700.*
   d. 10,007.

3. If you purchased 87 shares of Nike stock and the price was $75 per share, you just spent

   a. *$6,525.*
   b. $8,700.
   c. $7,500.
   d. $6255.

4. Which of the following is a stock exchange?

   a. *NYSE*
   b. DJIA
   c. IPO
   d. AAA

Constructed-Response Items

1. Explain the difference between common stock and preferred stock.

   (Common stocks represent shares of ownership in a corporation. There is no guarantee that common stocks will hold their value or pay a dividend. Preferred stocks also represent shares of ownership; however, preferred stocks guarantee a dividend that will be paid to stockholders before a common stock dividend is paid.)

2. When people ask, "How did the market do today?" they usually have one indicator in mind. What is the indicator and why is it important?

   (When people discuss how the market is doing, they are typically talking about the Dow Jones Industrial Average [the Dow, or the DJIA]. The DJIA is an index of 30 of the largest corporations traded on the stock exchanges. It is the most commonly used stock market indicator in the United States.)

Gen i Connection

Teachers using the Gen i Revolution online game will find that the most important terms from this lesson have been taught across a variety of Gen i missions. Students seeking review of terms within the Gen i Revolution game may note that terms are taught in each mission's 4-1-1 or tutorial section, and in the glossary available from each mission's toolbar. This lesson is intended as a review, to be used before the culminating print lesson in this volume, Lesson 21, and the culminating Gen i mission, Mission 15.

Gen i Reflection

This lesson mentions a comparison between learning the language of financial markets and learning a foreign language. Generally speaking, do you think it is easier to learn **financial terms** from an in-class lesson or from a computer game? Would you learn a **foreign language** more easily from in-class lessons or a computer program? Explain your answer.

ACTIVITY 20.1
THE LANGUAGE OF FINANCIAL MARKETS: DEFINITIONS

AMEX: The acronym stands for American Stock Exchange, formerly an independent market but now part of the New York Stock Exchange; the AMEX's new name is NYSE Amex Equities.

Bond: A debt investment in which an investor lends money to an entity (corporate or governmental) that borrows the money for a defined period of time at an agreed interest rate. Bonds are used by companies, municipalities, states, and the U.S. and foreign governments to finance various projects and activities.

Broker: A professional trader who buys and sells stocks for individuals and institutional customers.

Buying on margin: Buying stock by paying only a percentage of the purchase price (typically 50 percent) and borrowing the balance from a broker. If the buyer can sell the stock at a higher price than she or he paid for it, the amount of the loan can be repaid (plus interest and commission) and the buyer can keep the profit. However, if the stock price falls, the buyer must repay the loan (plus interest and commission) and suffer a loss.

Capital gain: A profit realized from the sale of property, stocks, or other investments.

Commission: A percentage of a stock trade (a buy or sell) paid by a customer to a stockbroker.

Common stock: An ownership share or shares of ownership in a corporation. A common stock offers no guarantee that it will hold its value or pay dividends.

Dealer: Someone who buys and sells stocks from his or her own accounts or the accounts of the firm he or she represents. Some dealers also act as brokers.

Dividend: A share of a company's profits paid to shareholders.

Dow Jones Industrial Average (DJIA): Often referred to as "the Dow" or "the Dow Jones Average," it is one of the oldest and most commonly quoted measures of stock-market performance. The averages it reports are calculated by reference to 30 large, well-known firms.

Growth stock: The stock of a firm that is expected to do well—to have above-average increases in revenues and earnings. Growth stocks often pay no dividend, but the stockholder gains if the price of the stock increases (grows).

Income stock: A stock that pays dividends regularly.

Index fund: A mutual fund that seeks to match the composite investment performance of a large group of stocks or bonds such as those represented by the Standard & Poor's 500 Composite Stock Index.

Initial public offering (IPO): The first sale of stock by a private company to the public.

Institutional investor: An organization (an insurance company or pension fund, for example) that invests in the stock market for clients.

Investment bank: An institution that participates in the primary markets for the sale of newly issued stocks and corporate and government bonds.

Liquidity: The ease with which savings or investments can be turned into cash.

Mutual fund: A company that pools money from investors and uses it to buy stocks or bonds on the investors' behalf. Mutual funds provide diversification and professional management for investors.

NASDAQ Stock Market: Founded in 1971, this stock market is the world's largest in terms of trading volume. The NASDAQ is the home to many technology stocks, including Apple, eBay, Intel, and Yahoo!

New York Stock Exchange (NYSE): The oldest stock exchange in the United States, founded in 1792. Following a 2007 merger with the European stock exchange Euronext, the NYSE has been operated by a parent company, NYSE Euronext Inc.

Over-the-counter market (OTC): A network of securities dealers connected by a computer network to buy and sell stock without a centralized trading floor. The stocks often represent new companies, and the stock prices are relatively low.

Ponzi scheme: An investment fraud that holds no real assets, paying off existing investors by using funds from new investors.

Preferred stock: An ownership share in a corporation with a guaranteed dividend that is paid before any dividends are paid on common stock.

Price: The market value of anything being offered for sale.

Return (rate of return): Money earned from an investment. The money could be profits, interest, appreciation, or a combination of these.

Risk: The chance of losing money on an investment.

Short selling: A stock transaction that allows an investor to make money on a stock expected to fall in value. This transaction involves the immediate sale of shares not owned by the seller, who expects to buy them back later at a lower price.

S&P 500 Stock Index: The acronym stands for the Standard and Poor's 500 Stock Index. The index includes 500 large and varied stocks.

Stockholder: A person who owns stock; sometimes called a shareholder.

Stock split: The division of a firm's outstanding shares of stock into a higher number of shares. A stock split often occurs when the price of a stock is considered too high by a corporation. The purpose is to lower the price of the stock to attract more buyers.

ACTIVITY 20.2
PROMPTS AND CORRECT ANSWERS FOR QUIZ BOWL GAME (RESERVED FOR TEACHER USE)

(Note to the teacher: The boldface headings shown below correspond to column headings used on Slide 20. 3. Point values, also shown on Slide 20.3, are indicated here by the numbers preceding each listed item.)

Invest in This

10: A debt investment in which an investor lends money to an entity (corporate or governmental) that borrows the money for a defined period of time at an agreed rate of interest. **(Bond)**

20: An ownership share or shares of ownership in a corporation. **(Common stock)**

30: A company that pools money from investors and uses it to buy stocks or bonds on the investors' behalf. **(Mutual fund)**

40: The stock of a firm that is expected to do well—to have above-average increases in revenues and earnings. These stocks often pay no dividend, but the stockholder gains if the price of the stock increases. **(Growth stock)**

50: An ownership share in a corporation with a guaranteed dividend that is paid before any dividends are paid on common stock. **(Preferred stock)**

Potent Investments

10: Buying stock by paying only a percentage of the purchase price (typically 50 percent) and borrowing the balance from a broker. **(Buying on margin)**

20: A mutual fund whose objective is to match the composite investment performance of a large group of stocks or bonds such as those represented by the Standard & Poor's 500. **(Index fund)**

30: An investment fraud that holds no real assets, paying off existing investors by using funds from new investors. **(Ponzi scheme)**

40: The chance of losing money on an investment. **(Risk)**

50: A stock transaction that allows an investor to make money on a stock expected to fall in value. This transaction involves the immediate sale of shares not owned by the seller, who expects to buy them back later at a lower price. **(Short selling)**

Index or Exchange

10: The acronym stands for American Stock Exchange, formerly an independent market but now part of the New York Stock Exchange. **(AMEX)**

20: One of the oldest and most commonly quoted measures of stock-market performance. The averages it reports are calculated by reference to 30 large, well-known firms. **(Dow Jones Industrial Average)**

30: Founded in 1971, this stock market is the world's largest in terms of trading volume and is the home to many technology stocks including Apple, eBay, Intel, and Yahoo! **(NASDAQ Stock Market)**

40: The oldest stock exchange in the United States, founded in 1792. Merged in 2007 with the European stock exchange Euronext. (**New York Stock Exchange**)

50: The acronym stands for the Standard and Poor's 500 Stock Index. The index includes 500 large and varied stocks. (**S&P 500 Stock Index**)

Earn It

10: A profit realized from the sale of property, stocks, or other investments. (**Capital gain**)

20: A percentage of a stock trade (a buy or sell) paid by a customer to a stockbroker. (**Commission**)

30: A share of a company's profits paid to shareholders. (**Dividend**)

40: The market value of anything being offered for sale. (**Price**)

50: Money earned from an investment. The money could be profits, interest, appreciation, or a combination of these. (**Return**)

Who Am I?

10: A professional trader who buys and sells stocks for individuals and institutional customers. (**Broker**)

20: Someone who buys and sells stocks from his or her own accounts or the accounts of the firm he or she represents. Some of these people also act as brokers. (**Dealer**)

30: An organization (an insurance company or pension fund, for example) that invests in the stock market for clients. (**Institutional investor**)

40: An institution that participates in the primary markets for the sale of newly issued stocks and corporate and government bonds. (**Investment bank**)

50: A person who owns stock; sometimes called a shareholder. (**Stockholder**)

Financial Markets Potpourri

10: A stock that pays dividends regularly. (**Income stock**)

20: The first sale of stock by a private company to the public. (**Initial public offering**)

30: The ease with which savings or investments can be turned into cash. (**Liquidity**)

40: A network of securities dealers connected by a computer network to buy and sell stock without a centralized trading floor. (**Over-the-counter market**)

50: The division of a firm's outstanding shares of stock into a higher number of shares, often occurring when the price of a stock is considered too high by a corporation. The purpose is to lower the price of the stock to attract more buyers. (**Stock split**)

ACTIVITY 20.3
THE LANGUAGE OF FINANCIAL MARKETS NEWS STORY

Stock Market Rallies

Stocks rallied today on good news about the U.S. economy.
The (1)_____, an index of 30 large company stocks, rose
sharply. The nation's oldest stock market, the (2)_____, saw
higher prices prevail. And the broader (3)_____ also rose
as the majority of the 500 stocks in this index made gains.
The (4)_____ stock market also rallied as technology stocks
surged.

Adam Smith, chief economist at Edinburgh Investments, said
"Many investors are moving their money out of (5)_____
and into stocks as the interest rates these investments pay
have been low." When asked how investors of modest means
can get involved in the stock market, Smith suggested
they consider buying (6)_____, as they typically invest in
many different stocks allowing investors to diversify their
portfolios during this bull market.

Income stocks also made gains as companies increased their
(7)_____ , sharing their profits with investors. Smith
expressed hope that this rally would continue next week,
but he worried that investors may sell stocks and take their
(8)_____ as profits.

SLIDE 20.1

LESSON 20 - THE LANGUAGE OF FINANCIAL MARKETS

The Language of Financial Markets: Terms

Buying and Selling in the Market
- Buying on Margin
- Commission
- Ponzi Scheme
- Price
- Short Selling

Exchanges and Indexes
- Dow Jones Industrial Average (DJIA)
- NASDAQ Stock Market
- New York Stock Exchange (NYSE)
- Over-the-Counter Market
- S&P 500 Stock Index

People in Financial Markets
- Broker
- Dealer
- Institutional Investor
- Investment Bank
- Stockholder

Stocks, Bonds, and Mutual Funds
- Bond
- Common Stock
- Initial Public Offering (IPO)
- Index Fund
- Mutual Fund
- Preferred Stock

Technical Terms
- Capital Gain
- Dividend
- Growth Stock
- Income Stock
- Liquidity
- Risk
- Return
- Stock Split

LEARNING, EARNING, AND INVESTING FOR A NEW GENERATION © COUNCIL FOR ECONOMIC EDUCATION, NEW YORK, NY

SLIDE 20.2

LESSON 20 - THE LANGUAGE OF FINANCIAL MARKETS

The Language of Financial Markets: Quiz Bowl Score Sheet

Group	Score
1	
2	
3	
4	
5	

LEARNING, EARNING, AND INVESTING FOR A NEW GENERATION © COUNCIL FOR ECONOMIC EDUCATION, NEW YORK, NY

SLIDE 20.3

The Language of Financial Markets: Quiz Bowl Game Board

Invest in This	Potent Investments	Index or Exchange	Earn It	Who Am I?	Financial Markets Potpourri
10	10	10	10	10	10
20	20	20	20	20	20
30	30	30	30	30	30
40	40	40	40	40	40
50	50	50	50	50	50

SLIDE 20.4

Invest in This:

A debt investment in which an investor lends money to an entity (corporate or governmental) that borrows the money for a defined period of time at an agreed interest rate.

Click to Check

SLIDE 20.5

LESSON 20 - THE LANGUAGE OF FINANCIAL MARKETS

The correct answer is...

Bond

10

Return to Game Board

LEARNING, EARNING, AND INVESTING FOR A NEW GENERATION © COUNCIL FOR ECONOMIC EDUCATION, NEW YORK, NY

SLIDE 20.6

LESSON 20 - THE LANGUAGE OF FINANCIAL MARKETS

Invest in This:

An ownership share or shares of ownership in a corporation.

Click to Check

LEARNING, EARNING, AND INVESTING FOR A NEW GENERATION © COUNCIL FOR ECONOMIC EDUCATION, NEW YORK, NY

SLIDE 20.7

LESSON 20 - THE LANGUAGE OF FINANCIAL MARKETS

The correct answer is...

Common Stock

20

Return to Game Board

LEARNING, EARNING, AND INVESTING FOR A NEW GENERATION © COUNCIL FOR ECONOMIC EDUCATION, NEW YORK, NY

SLIDE 20.8

LESSON 20 - THE LANGUAGE OF FINANCIAL MARKETS

Invest in This:

A company that pools money from investors and uses it to buy stocks or bonds on the investors' behalf.

Click to Check

LEARNING, EARNING, AND INVESTING FOR A NEW GENERATION © COUNCIL FOR ECONOMIC EDUCATION, NEW YORK, NY

SLIDE 20.9

LESSON 20 - THE LANGUAGE OF FINANCIAL MARKETS

The correct answer is...

Mutual Fund

30

Return to Game Board

LEARNING, EARNING, AND INVESTING FOR A NEW GENERATION © COUNCIL FOR ECONOMIC EDUCATION, NEW YORK, NY

SLIDE 20.10

LESSON 20 - THE LANGUAGE OF FINANCIAL MARKETS

Invest in This:

The stock of a firm that is expected to do well—to have above-average increases in revenues and earnings. These stocks often pay no dividend, but the stockholder gains if the price of the stock increases.

Click to Check

LEARNING, EARNING, AND INVESTING FOR A NEW GENERATION © COUNCIL FOR ECONOMIC EDUCATION, NEW YORK, NY

SLIDE 20.11

LESSON 20 - THE LANGUAGE OF FINANCIAL MARKETS

The correct answer is...

Growth Stock

40

Return to Game Board

LEARNING, EARNING, AND INVESTING FOR A NEW GENERATION © COUNCIL FOR ECONOMIC EDUCATION, NEW YORK, NY

SLIDE 20.12

LESSON 20 - THE LANGUAGE OF FINANCIAL MARKETS

Invest in This:

An ownership share in a corporation with a guaranteed dividend that is paid before any dividends are paid on common stock.

Click to Check

LEARNING, EARNING, AND INVESTING FOR A NEW GENERATION © COUNCIL FOR ECONOMIC EDUCATION, NEW YORK, NY

SLIDE 20.13

LESSON 20 - THE LANGUAGE OF FINANCIAL MARKETS

The correct answer is...

Preferred Stock

50

Return to Game Board

LEARNING, EARNING, AND INVESTING FOR A NEW GENERATION © COUNCIL FOR ECONOMIC EDUCATION, NEW YORK, NY

SLIDE 20.14

LESSON 20 - THE LANGUAGE OF FINANCIAL MARKETS

Potent Investments:

Buying stock by paying only a percentage of the purchase price (typically 50 percent) and borrowing the balance from a broker.

Click to Check

LEARNING, EARNING, AND INVESTING FOR A NEW GENERATION © COUNCIL FOR ECONOMIC EDUCATION, NEW YORK, NY

SLIDE 20.15

LESSON 20 - THE LANGUAGE OF FINANCIAL MARKETS

The correct answer is...

Buying on Margin

10

Return to Game Board

SLIDE 20.16

LESSON 20 - THE LANGUAGE OF FINANCIAL MARKETS

Potent Investments:

A mutual fund whose objective is to match the composite investment performance of a large group of stocks or bonds such as those represented by the Standard & Poor's 500.

Click to Check

SLIDE 20.17

LESSON 20 - THE LANGUAGE OF FINANCIAL MARKETS

The correct answer is...

Index Fund

20

Return to Game Board

LEARNING, EARNING, AND INVESTING FOR A NEW GENERATION © COUNCIL FOR ECONOMIC EDUCATION, NEW YORK, NY

SLIDE 20.18

LESSON 20 - THE LANGUAGE OF FINANCIAL MARKETS

Potent Investments:

An investment fraud that holds no real assets, paying off existing investors by using funds from new investors.

Click to Check

LEARNING, EARNING, AND INVESTING FOR A NEW GENERATION © COUNCIL FOR ECONOMIC EDUCATION, NEW YORK, NY

SLIDE 20.19

LESSON 20 - THE LANGUAGE OF FINANCIAL MARKETS

The correct answer is...

Ponzi Scheme

30

Return to Game Board

SLIDE 20.20

LESSON 20 - THE LANGUAGE OF FINANCIAL MARKETS

Potent Investments:

The chance of losing money on an investment.

Click to Check

SLIDE 20.21

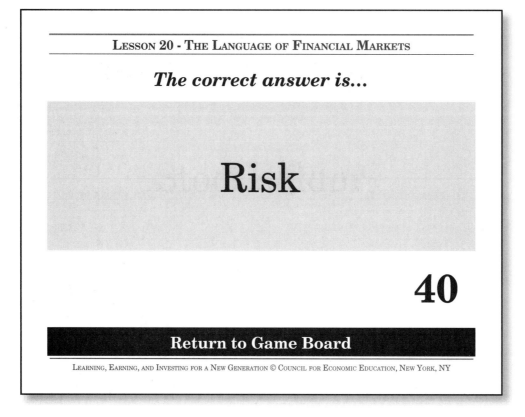

LESSON 20 - THE LANGUAGE OF FINANCIAL MARKETS

The correct answer is...

Risk

40

Return to Game Board

LEARNING, EARNING, AND INVESTING FOR A NEW GENERATION © COUNCIL FOR ECONOMIC EDUCATION, NEW YORK, NY

SLIDE 20.22

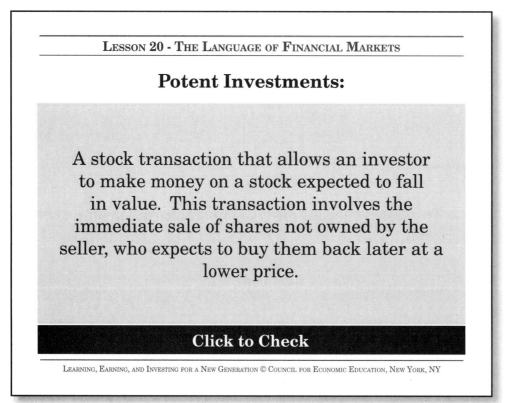

LESSON 20 - THE LANGUAGE OF FINANCIAL MARKETS

Potent Investments:

A stock transaction that allows an investor to make money on a stock expected to fall in value. This transaction involves the immediate sale of shares not owned by the seller, who expects to buy them back later at a lower price.

Click to Check

LEARNING, EARNING, AND INVESTING FOR A NEW GENERATION © COUNCIL FOR ECONOMIC EDUCATION, NEW YORK, NY

SLIDE 20.23

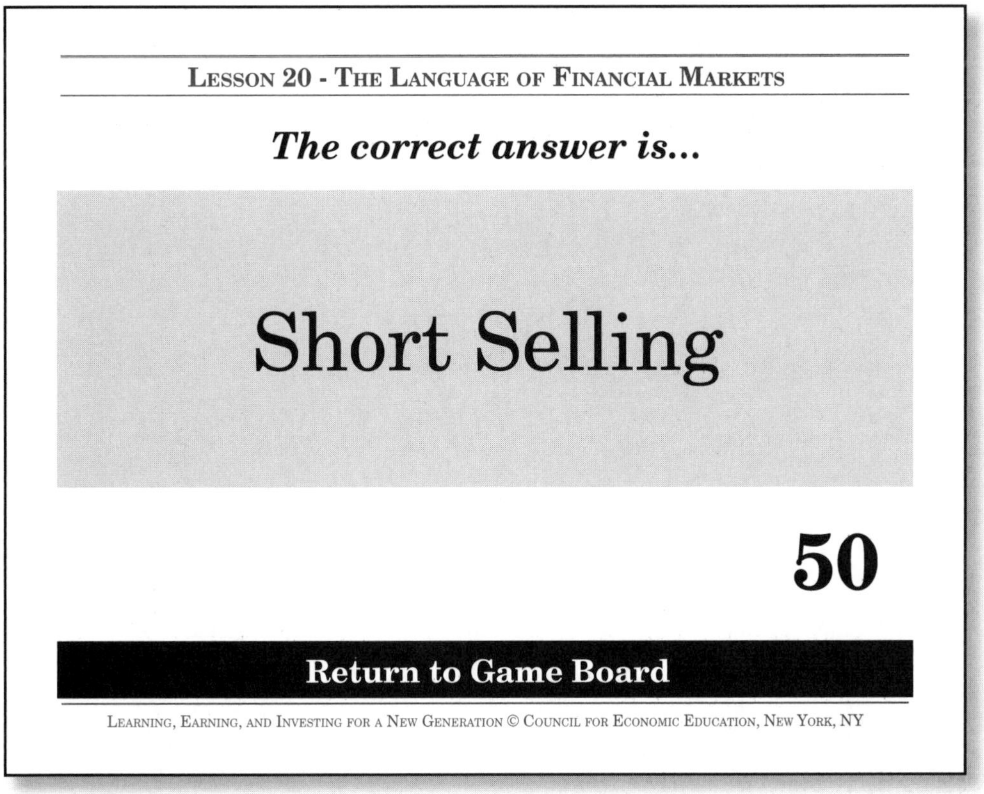

LESSON 20 - THE LANGUAGE OF FINANCIAL MARKETS

The correct answer is...

Short Selling

50

Return to Game Board

SLIDE 20.24

LESSON 20 - THE LANGUAGE OF FINANCIAL MARKETS

Index or Exchange:

The acronym stands for American Stock Exchange, formerly an independent market but now part of the New York Stock Exchange.

Click to Check

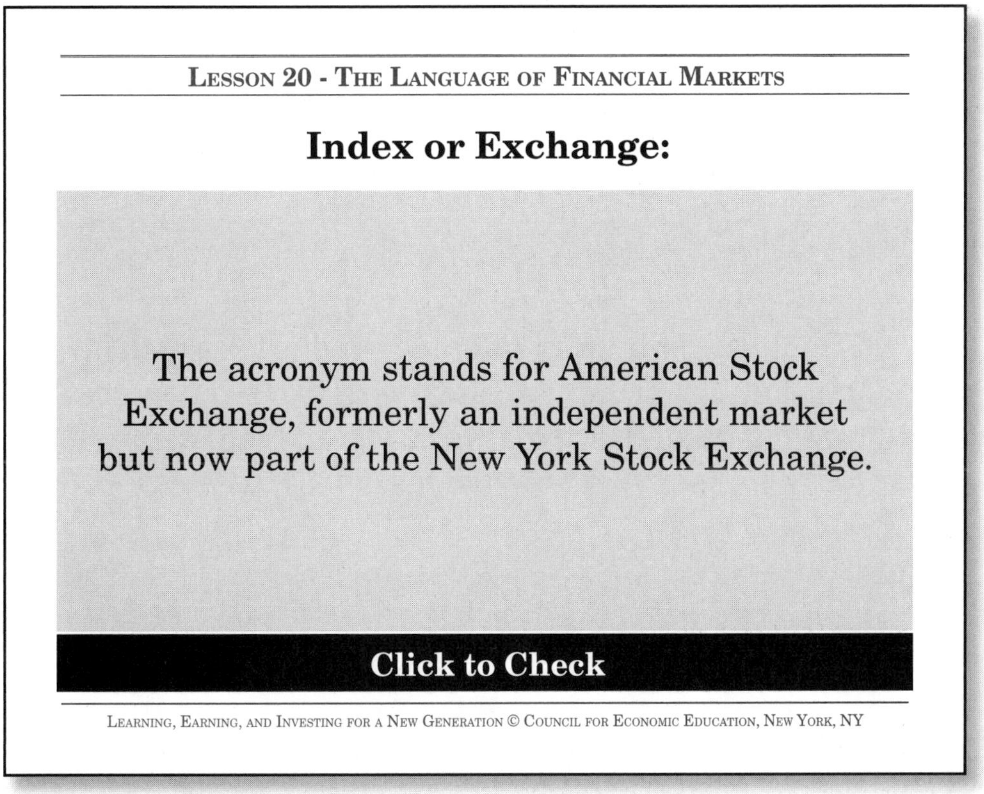

SLIDE 20.25

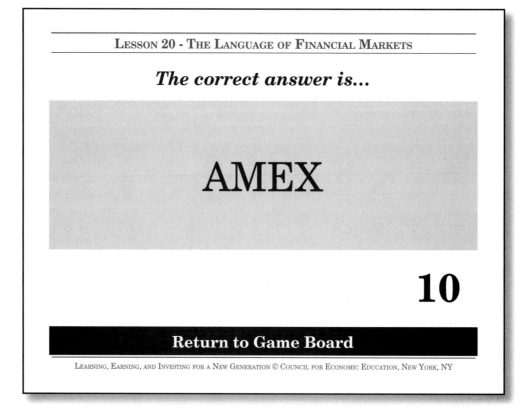

SLIDE 20.26

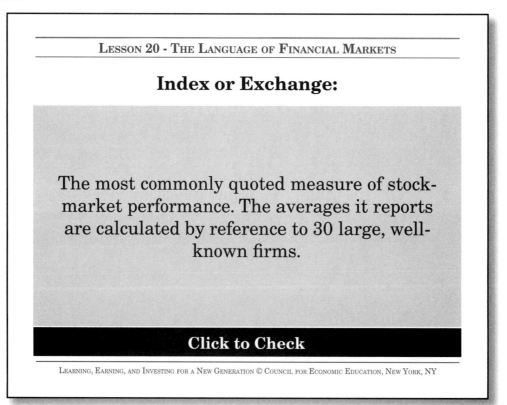

SLIDE 20.27

LESSON 20 - THE LANGUAGE OF FINANCIAL MARKETS

The correct answer is...

Dow Jones Industrial Average

20

Return to Game Board

SLIDE 20.28

LESSON 20 - THE LANGUAGE OF FINANCIAL MARKETS

Index or Exchange:

Founded in 1971, this stock market is the world's largest in terms of trading volume and is the home to many technology stocks including Apple, eBay, Intel, and Yahoo!

Click to Check

SLIDE 20.29

LESSON 20 - THE LANGUAGE OF FINANCIAL MARKETS

The correct answer is...

NASDAQ Stock Market

30

Return to Game Board

LEARNING, EARNING, AND INVESTING FOR A NEW GENERATION © COUNCIL FOR ECONOMIC EDUCATION, NEW YORK, NY

SLIDE 20.30

LESSON 20 - THE LANGUAGE OF FINANCIAL MARKETS

Index or Exchange:

The oldest stock exchange in the United States, founded in 1792. Merged in 2007 with the European stock exchange Euronext.

Click to Check

LEARNING, EARNING, AND INVESTING FOR A NEW GENERATION © COUNCIL FOR ECONOMIC EDUCATION, NEW YORK, NY

SLIDE 20.31

LESSON 20 - THE LANGUAGE OF FINANCIAL MARKETS

The correct answer is...

New York Stock Exchange

40

Return to Game Board

SLIDE 20.32

LESSON 20 - THE LANGUAGE OF FINANCIAL MARKETS

Index or Exchange:

The acronym stands for the Standard and Poor's 500 Stock Index. The index includes 500 large and varied stocks.

Click to Check

SLIDE 20.33

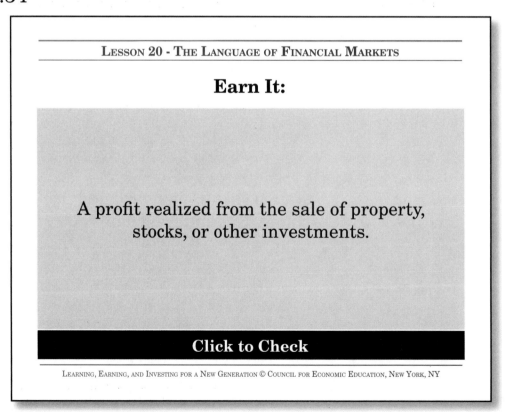

SLIDE 20.34

LESSON 20 - THE LANGUAGE OF FINANCIAL MARKETS

Earn It:

A profit realized from the sale of property, stocks, or other investments.

Click to Check

SLIDE 20.35

The correct answer is...

Capital Gain

10

Return to Game Board

SLIDE 20.36

Earn It:

A percentage of a stock trade (a buy or sell)
paid by a customer to a stockbroker.

Click to Check

SLIDE 20.37

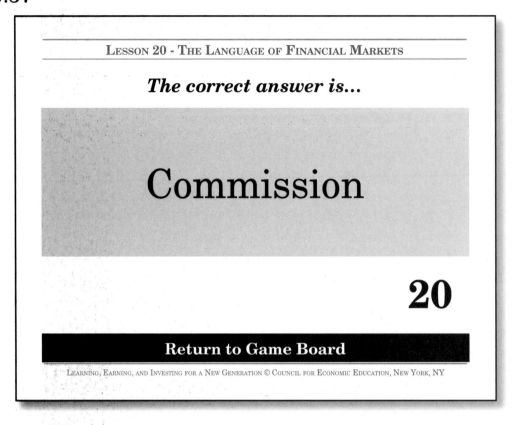

SLIDE 20.38

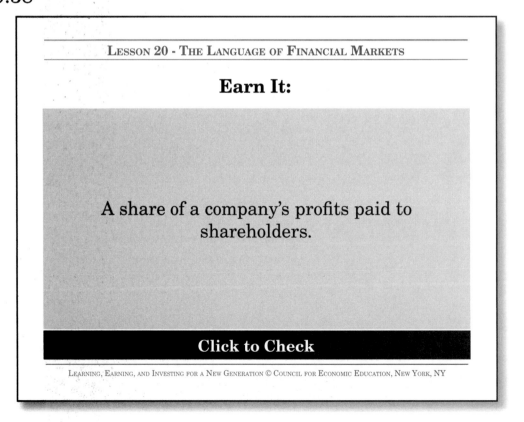

SLIDE 20.39

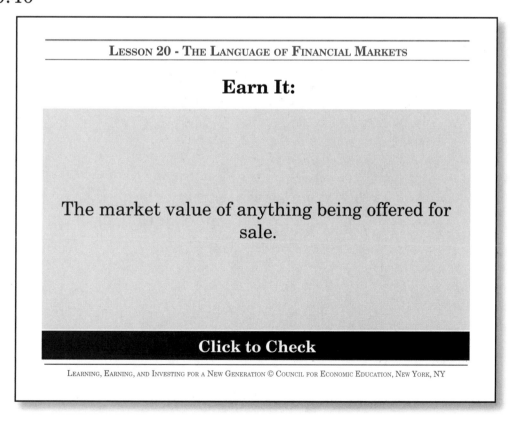

SLIDE 20.40

LESSON 20 - THE LANGUAGE OF FINANCIAL MARKETS

Earn It:

The market value of anything being offered for sale.

Click to Check

LEARNING, EARNING, AND INVESTING FOR A NEW GENERATION © COUNCIL FOR ECONOMIC EDUCATION, NEW YORK, NY

SLIDE 20.41

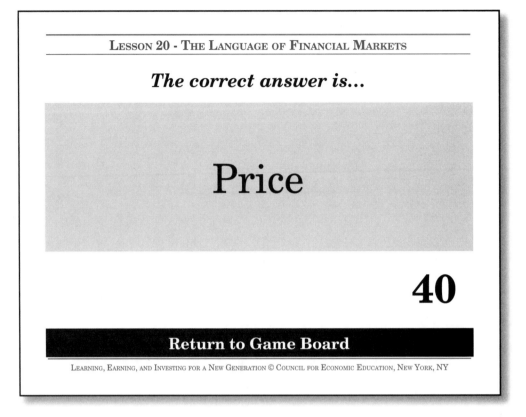

SLIDE 20.42

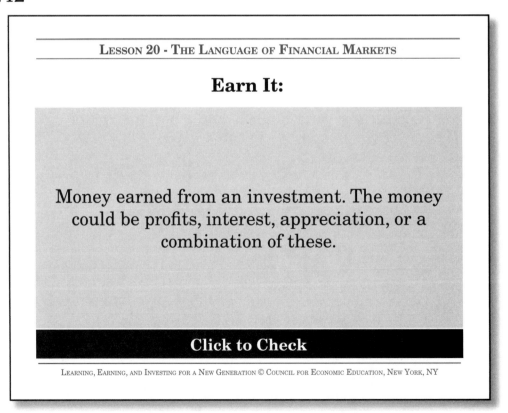

SLIDE 20.43

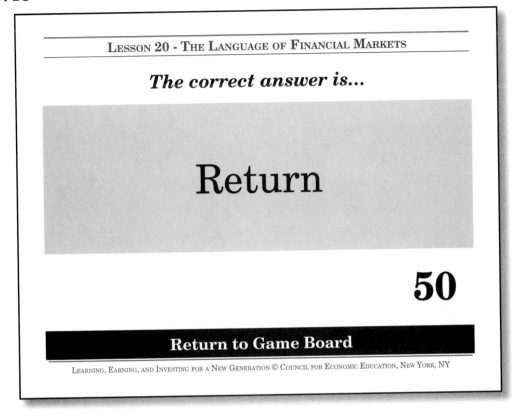

SLIDE 20.44

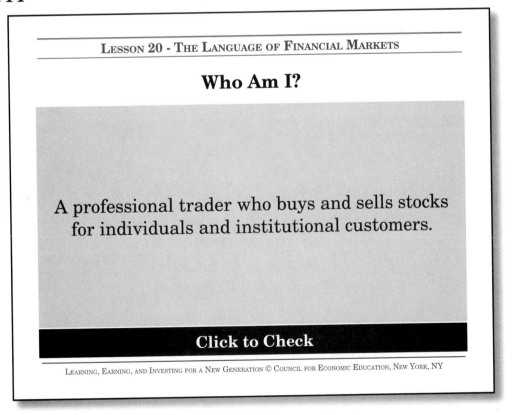

SLIDE 20.45

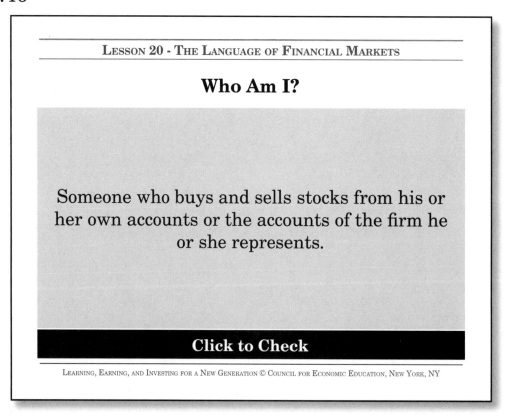

LESSON 20 - THE LANGUAGE OF FINANCIAL MARKETS

The correct answer is...

Broker

10

Return to Game Board

LEARNING, EARNING, AND INVESTING FOR A NEW GENERATION © COUNCIL FOR ECONOMIC EDUCATION, NEW YORK, NY

SLIDE 20.46

LESSON 20 - THE LANGUAGE OF FINANCIAL MARKETS

Who Am I?

Someone who buys and sells stocks from his or her own accounts or the accounts of the firm he or she represents.

Click to Check

LEARNING, EARNING, AND INVESTING FOR A NEW GENERATION © COUNCIL FOR ECONOMIC EDUCATION, NEW YORK, NY

SLIDE 20.47

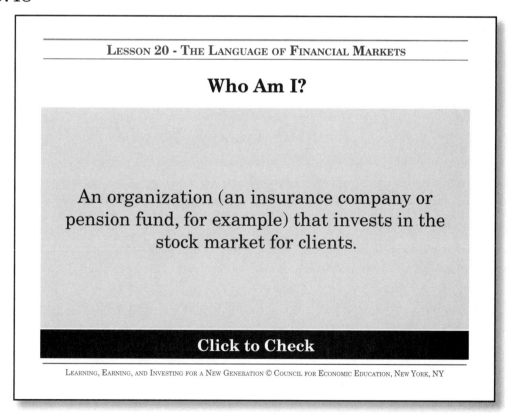

LESSON 20 - THE LANGUAGE OF FINANCIAL MARKETS

The correct answer is...

Dealer

20

Return to Game Board

LEARNING, EARNING, AND INVESTING FOR A NEW GENERATION © COUNCIL FOR ECONOMIC EDUCATION, NEW YORK, NY

SLIDE 20.48

LESSON 20 - THE LANGUAGE OF FINANCIAL MARKETS

Who Am I?

An organization (an insurance company or pension fund, for example) that invests in the stock market for clients.

Click to Check

LEARNING, EARNING, AND INVESTING FOR A NEW GENERATION © COUNCIL FOR ECONOMIC EDUCATION, NEW YORK, NY

SLIDE 20.49

LESSON 20 - THE LANGUAGE OF FINANCIAL MARKETS

The correct answer is...

Institutional Investor

30

Return to Game Board

LEARNING, EARNING, AND INVESTING FOR A NEW GENERATION © COUNCIL FOR ECONOMIC EDUCATION, NEW YORK, NY

SLIDE 20.50

LESSON 20 - THE LANGUAGE OF FINANCIAL MARKETS

Who Am I?

An institution that participates in the primary markets for the sale of newly issued stocks and corporate and government bonds.

Click to Check

LEARNING, EARNING, AND INVESTING FOR A NEW GENERATION © COUNCIL FOR ECONOMIC EDUCATION, NEW YORK, NY

SLIDE 20.51

LESSON 20 - THE LANGUAGE OF FINANCIAL MARKETS

The correct answer is...

Investment Bank

40

Return to Game Board

LEARNING, EARNING, AND INVESTING FOR A NEW GENERATION © COUNCIL FOR ECONOMIC EDUCATION, NEW YORK, NY

SLIDE 20.52

LESSON 20 - THE LANGUAGE OF FINANCIAL MARKETS

Who Am I?

A person who owns stock; sometimes called a shareholder.

Click to Check

LEARNING, EARNING, AND INVESTING FOR A NEW GENERATION © COUNCIL FOR ECONOMIC EDUCATION, NEW YORK, NY

SLIDE 20.53

LESSON 20 - THE LANGUAGE OF FINANCIAL MARKETS

The correct answer is...

Stockholder

50

Return to Game Board

LEARNING, EARNING, AND INVESTING FOR A NEW GENERATION © COUNCIL FOR ECONOMIC EDUCATION, NEW YORK, NY

SLIDE 20.54

LESSON 20 - THE LANGUAGE OF FINANCIAL MARKETS

Financial Markets Potpourri

A stock that pays dividends regularly.

Click to Check

LEARNING, EARNING, AND INVESTING FOR A NEW GENERATION © COUNCIL FOR ECONOMIC EDUCATION, NEW YORK, NY

SLIDE 20.55

LESSON 20 - THE LANGUAGE OF FINANCIAL MARKETS

The correct answer is...

Income Stock

10

Return to Game Board

LEARNING, EARNING, AND INVESTING FOR A NEW GENERATION © COUNCIL FOR ECONOMIC EDUCATION, NEW YORK, NY

SLIDE 20.56

LESSON 20 - THE LANGUAGE OF FINANCIAL MARKETS

Financial Markets Potpourri

The first sale of stock by a private company to the public.

Click to Check

LEARNING, EARNING, AND INVESTING FOR A NEW GENERATION © COUNCIL FOR ECONOMIC EDUCATION, NEW YORK, NY

SLIDE 20.57

LESSON 20 - THE LANGUAGE OF FINANCIAL MARKETS

The correct answer is...

Initial Public Offering

20

Return to Game Board

LEARNING, EARNING, AND INVESTING FOR A NEW GENERATION © COUNCIL FOR ECONOMIC EDUCATION, NEW YORK, NY

SLIDE 20.58

LESSON 20 - THE LANGUAGE OF FINANCIAL MARKETS

Financial Markets Potpourri

The ease with which savings or investments can be turned into cash.

Click to Check

LEARNING, EARNING, AND INVESTING FOR A NEW GENERATION © COUNCIL FOR ECONOMIC EDUCATION, NEW YORK, NY

SLIDE 20.59

LESSON 20 - THE LANGUAGE OF FINANCIAL MARKETS

The correct answer is...

Liquidity

30

Return to Game Board

LEARNING, EARNING, AND INVESTING FOR A NEW GENERATION © COUNCIL FOR ECONOMIC EDUCATION, NEW YORK, NY

SLIDE 20.60

LESSON 20 - THE LANGUAGE OF FINANCIAL MARKETS

Financial Markets Potpourri

A network of securities dealers connected by a computer network to buy and sell stock without a centralized trading floor.

Click to Check

LEARNING, EARNING, AND INVESTING FOR A NEW GENERATION © COUNCIL FOR ECONOMIC EDUCATION, NEW YORK, NY

SLIDE 20.61

LESSON 20 - THE LANGUAGE OF FINANCIAL MARKETS

The correct answer is...

Over-the-Counter Market

40

Return to Game Board

LEARNING, EARNING, AND INVESTING FOR A NEW GENERATION © COUNCIL FOR ECONOMIC EDUCATION, NEW YORK, NY

SLIDE 20.62

LESSON 20 - THE LANGUAGE OF FINANCIAL MARKETS

Financial Markets Potpourri

The division of a firm's outstanding shares of stock into a higher number of shares. The purpose is to lower the price of the stock to attract more buyers.

Click to Check

LEARNING, EARNING, AND INVESTING FOR A NEW GENERATION © COUNCIL FOR ECONOMIC EDUCATION, NEW YORK, NY

SLIDE 20.63

LESSON 20 - THE LANGUAGE OF FINANCIAL MARKETS

The correct answer is...

Stock split

50

Return to Game Board

LESSON 21

PLANNING YOUR FINANCIAL FUTURE

LESSON 21
PLANNING YOUR FINANCIAL FUTURE

LESSON DESCRIPTION

This lesson provides students with a review and an opportunity to apply many of the concepts presented in earlier lessons. The students examine different sorts of risk that come with various investments, and they learn about their own tolerance for risk. They apply their knowledge in an activity in which they act as financial advisers, offering financial advice in four cases.

INTRODUCTION

Risk is inherent in all investments. The possibilities include risk of principal, market risk, interest-rate risk, and inflation risk. Investments also offer the prospect of rewards. Some investments—such as savings accounts—involve low levels of risk and low potential rewards. Other investments—such as growth stocks—involve higher levels of risk and higher potential rewards. Investors need to make choices about the risk-reward ratio with which they are comfortable.

CONCEPTS

Bond

Certificate of deposit

Diversification

Liquidity

Money market account

Mutual funds

Principal

Rate of return

Risk

Savings account

Stocks

OBJECTIVES

Students will be able to:

- Identify the key elements of prudent financial planning, including setting financial goals and developing a saving and investing plan.

- Recognize how tolerance of investment risk can influence saving and investment plans.

- Examine the investment needs of four people in different financial situations and make recommendations.

CONTENT STANDARDS

Voluntary National Content Standards in Economics, **2nd Edition**

- **Standard 1:** Productive resources are limited. Therefore, people cannot have all the goods and services they want; as a result, they must choose some things and give up others.

- **Standard 2:** Effective decision making requires comparing the additional costs of alternatives with the additional benefits. Many choices involve doing a little more or a little less of something: few choices are "all or nothing" decisions.

National Standards in K-12 Personal Finance Education, **3rd edition**

- **Financial Responsibility and Decision Making Standard 4:** Make financial decisions by systematically considering alternatives and consequences.

- **Planning and Money Management Standard 6:** Develop a personal financial plan.

- **Risk Management and Insurance Standard 1:** Identify common types of risks and basic risk management methods.

- **Saving and Investing Standard 1:** Discuss how saving contributes to financial well-being.

- **Saving and Investing Standard 2:** Explain how investing builds wealth and helps meet financial goals.

- **Saving and Investing Standard 3:** Evaluate investment alternatives.

TIME REQUIRED

90 minutes

MATERIALS

- Slides 21.1, 21.2, 21.3, and 21.4

- One copy of Activities 21.1, 21.2, and 21.3 for each student

PROCEDURE

1. Explain that in this lesson the students will use basic principles of investing to give advice to hypothetical clients about how to manage their investments. This exercise will help prepare the students to make their own investment decisions.

2. Tell the students to imagine that there is a board on the floor, eight feet long and four inches wide. **Ask:**

   A. Who would be willing to walk the length of the board for $10?

   (Many students would.)

   B. If we were to raise the board off the floor to a height of 30 or 40 feet, how many of you would walk the length of it for $10? For $100? For $1,000?

   (You may need a big payout to entice students to say they would walk the board at these heights.)

   C. Suppose the board were stretched between two skyscrapers. How much money would it take to get you to try to walk across it then?

   (No takers, except for jokers in the class.)

   D. It's the same board at any height. Why does it require more money to get you to walk across the same board at different heights?

   (The higher the risk, the greater the potential reward must be.)

3. Explain that the same point holds true for investments. Generally, the more uncertain the future value of an asset, the higher the potential rate of return must be. For uncertain or higher-risk investments, the prospect of a higher return is needed to induce investors to take the risk.

4. **Display Slide 21.1.** Discuss the four kinds of risk, one by one. Provide clarification and examples as necessary.

5. **Display Slide 21.2.** Explain that the investment choices shown at the bottom of the pyramid are the safest in one respect: They present little risk of loss of principal. But these choices present another risk—the risk that returns may not keep pace with inflation. Moving up each step on the pyramid brings a prospect of higher rewards in rate of return along with higher risks of loss of principal.

6. **Display Slide 21.3.** Briefly explain that Slide 21.3 lists the elements of a complete financial plan. Tell the students that they will make use of this list today in a simulation activity. In this activity they will act as financial planners, helping their clients develop savings and investment plans.

7. **Distribute Activity 21.1.** Explain that this questionnaire is similar to ones used by financial planners as they

seek to determine their clients' risk tolerance. They use data from these questionnaires to help their clients make investment decisions that fall within their overall tolerance for investment risk. After the students have completed the questionnaire.

Ask: Which range of return would make you the most comfortable?

(Discuss the students' answers. Encourage the students to use economic reasoning as well as personal inclinations in explaining their answers.)

8. **Distribute Activity 21.2 and display Slide 21.4.** Explain that when financial planners work with clients, an early step in the process is to understand each client's goals and current finances. Discuss why each point is an important element for people seeking to offer informed financial advice.

9. **Distribute copies of Activity 21.3** to the class. Tell the students that they are going to act as financial planners and offer advice to four hypothetical clients. Organize the class into groups of four or five students each. Each group represents a financial planning firm. Explain that the planners' clients will be people in various financial situations; the best plan for one may not be suitable for others. Read the directions for Parts 1 and 2 of Activity 21.3 to make sure the students understand how they are to make recommendations for their clients.

10. Provide time for the students to read the four cases and formulate their recommendations. Then ask a student from each group to explain the group's advice for Dan and Sue. **Ask:** What was the most important goal for Dan and Sue? What do you recommend? Do others have other recommendations? Repeat this procedure for each group.

Case 1

Client	Percent in stocks	Percent in bonds	Percent in cash
Dan and Sue	30%	20%	50%

(Answers may vary. Dan and Sue want to reduce their debt and get started saving for college expenses and retirement. For the short term, their best alternative is to reduce expenses and try to deposit their savings in cash accounts. They should use the cash they save to pay off debt and to establish an emergency fund. Soon after their debt is reduced, they should shift tactics. Over the long term, they have time for their savings to earn more. As they become more stable financially, they should invest portions of their savings in stocks as a way of providing for long-term goals.)

Case 2

Client	Percent in stocks	Percent in bonds	Percent in cash
Shannon	25%	25%	50%

(Answers may vary. Shannon should do her best to put $25 per month into her 401(k) plan; otherwise she will lose the employer's $300 annual match. She should also try to save as much as she can. Most of her $1,000 should go into a cash account, in case she needs it for emergencies. This is important because she has little money saved, has little job security, and is solely responsible for her young son. Thus, although she is young, Shannon can't afford much risk. She should find the highest rates of return available while still maintaining liquidity. If possible, she should seek more education or training—to enhance her human capital—so that she can qualify for a higher-paying job.)

Case 3

Client	Percent in stocks	Percent in bonds	Percent in cash
Jennifer	70%	20%	10%

(Jennifer can afford more risk because she has no dependents; she is young and has time to recover from declines in the market; she has a stable job; she has paid off her student loans; and she has some assets and savings beyond what she should hold for emergencies. Though her age and financial situation might allow her to take more risks, those factors could be offset by personal factors if Jennifer had a low tolerance for risk. However, since Jennifer does rock climbing and paragliding for fun, she probably has a high tolerance for risk. In that case, one might think stocks would be the first choice, probably growth stocks, since current income from dividends is less important at this point in Jennifer's life than capital gains. If Jennifer doesn't want to hold individual stocks, she might find growth mutual funds or aggressive growth mutual funds to be a better choice. She will also want to reduce her risk by diversifying within those stock holdings or mutual funds. And Jennifer might want to include some bonds in her portfolio, to reduce her risk further through diversification.)

Case 4

Client	Percent in stocks	Percent in bonds	Percent in cash
Antonio and Maria	70%	20%	10%

(Although they have significant savings and good incomes, Antonio and Maria will not want to make high-risk investments. Since they are near retirement, they cannot rely on having a long time to recover from declines that might occur in the market. They

will probably want to reduce their risk by diversifying. Most people in their situation would likely hold the bulk of their investments in mutual funds, income stock, and bonds. However, Antonio's hobby is researching stocks and following financial markets, so he and Maria might prefer buying individual stocks and might be willing to hold a combination of assets that includes some growth stocks along with income stocks. Because of their incomes, Antonio and Maria are probably in a high tax bracket. As a result, tax-exempt municipal bonds might also be attractive to them.)

CLOSURE

11. Review the lesson, using the following questions:

    A. What are some of the alternatives people can consider when saving or investing?

       (Growth stocks, income stocks, mutual funds, bonds, savings accounts, tax-exempt municipal bonds.)

    B. What are some criteria that people consider in deciding where to invest their money?

       (Liquidity, rate of return, the relationship of risk to reward, safety of principal.)

    C. What are the different types of risk?

       (Losing purchasing power to inflation, losing principal when stock prices fall, losing principal when the market value of bonds falls [when bonds are sold before maturity], and losing value on investments that go bad because of market conditions.)

    D. What are some factors that determine people's investment choices?

       (Age, income, risk tolerance, amount of savings, amount of debt, knowl-

edge of markets, willingness and ability to engage in research, number of dependents.)

ASSESSMENT
Multiple-Choice Questions

1. The ability to convert an asset to cash quickly is called

    a. criteria.
    b. *liquidity.*
    c. a risk factor.
    d. asset management.

2. Which of the following alternatives is the most liquid?

    a. Investments in government bonds
    b. Investments in common stocks
    c. *Deposits in savings accounts*
    d. Certificates of deposit (CDs)

3. Which of the following has had the highest rate of return over time?

    a. Government bonds
    b. *Common stock*
    c. Savings accounts
    d. Certificates of deposit

4. Which of the following best assures the safety of the principal invested?

    a. Growth stock
    b. Mutual funds
    c. Money market funds
    d. *An FDIC-insured savings account*

Constructed-Response Items

1. Imagine that your friend received a surprise gift of $20,000. Your friend decides to invest the money and asks you what factors should determine people's investment choices. How do you respond?

    (Accept a variety of answers. The best answers will include references to age, income, debt, risk tolerance, amount of savings, knowledge of markets, willingness and ability to do research, and number of dependents.)

2. Describe the relationship between risk and reward, and describe the different types of risk.

    (Generally, the greater the reward, the greater the risk. Types of risk include losing purchasing power to inflation, losing principal when stock prices fall, losing principal when the market value of bonds falls [when bonds are sold before maturity], and investments falling in value because of market conditions.)

Gen i Connection

Mission 15 of the Gen i Revolution game takes students through an interactive exercise similar to Activity 21.3 in Lesson 21. In mission 15, students are operatives advising the Red Roosters on how to conduct a financial planning workshop. They work through a 4-1-1 tutorial on identifying different types of risk and the questions individuals should consider when seeking investment advice. The tutorial also addresses helping Jen and Ryan make investment choices according to their financial goals. Having practiced with the cases of Jen and Ryan, and having worked through other questions, the students conclude by providing advice to three different sets of clients. Higher points are awarded for choices that match clients' goals and preferences more closely.

Gen i Reflection

In Gen i Revolution mission 15, you helped the Red Roosters with their financial planning workshop. This provided a brief simulation of what it would be like to work as a financial planner. Based on what you know, would you like to pursue a career as a financial planner at some time in the future? What might you find most satisfying about such a career? What might cause you to lose sleep at night?

ACTIVITY 21.1
ASSESSING YOUR TOLERANCE FOR INVESTMENT RISK

Directions: Each of the following statements presents a situation in which you are asked to decide how comfortable you are with the risk involved. Read each of statements and circle the response that you think best reflects your comfort level.

1. You and a friend are participating in a stock market game. You both have noticed that the share prices of some companies can move a lot, up or down, in any given day. Your friend says: "When it comes to investing, it's scary world out there." When you think about investing your own money, which of the following phrases most likely comes to mind?

   a. Very worried about losses
   b. Uncertain, but ready to plan for investing
   c. Welcoming of a new investment opportunity
   d. Excited about a new investment adventure

2. Imagine that you received a surprise gift of $20,000. You decide to invest the money. Which alternative do you think is best for you over the long term?

   a. Deposit the money in a savings account, a money market account, or a similar safe investment.
   b. Invest it in safe, high-quality bonds or bond mutual funds.
   c. Invest it in stocks or stock mutual funds.
   d. Invest it in very high-risk bonds or stocks.

3. As you are planning to invest the $20,000, your financial adviser explains where your account total might be after one year. Which range would make you the most comfortable?

   a. $19,000 to $21,000
   b. $17,000 to $23,000
   c. $13,000 to $27,000
   d. $10,000 to $30,000

4. Imagine that you reached a decision about how to invest the $20,000 gift. How do you think you would feel afterward?

   a. Worried
   b. Satisfied
   c. Hopeful
   d. Excited

5. For the last five years, your $20,000 investment has returned an average of 8 percent per year. However, it loses 16 percent over the next year. What would you wish to do?

   a. Sell all of the investment.
   b. Sell half of the investment.
   c. Hold onto the investment as it is.
   d. Buy more of the same investment.

Question for Discussion

- The questions above reflect levels of investment risk. If you most often circled "A," you are very risk averse. If you most often circled "B," you are moderately risk averse. If you most often circled "C," you are willing to take moderate risks. If you most often circled "D," you are willing to take larger risks. Which answers did you provide most often? Why?

ACTIVITY 21.2
QUESTIONS FOR CLIENTS

Directions: The following questions are designed to help you obtain important information about your clients. This information can help you provide sound financial advice.

1. **How much does the client have in savings?** Everyone should have some liquid savings in order to handle emergencies. A person with more savings may be willing to assume more risk.

2. **Is the client able to save some money each month without borrowing?** People who are able to save each month are living within their incomes.

3. **Is the client responsible for people who are financially dependent?** Having liquid savings to handle emergencies is especially important for people with dependents. People with no dependents and many years until retirement may be willing take more risks.

4. **How much risk is the client willing to take in order to pursue a higher rate of return?** Some people can tolerate no risk. Others are willing to take some risk with some of their savings in hopes of earning a higher rate of return. Remember the rule of 72 and the difference a higher rate of return makes. Also consider the risks and rewards associated with holding bonds. Some investors consider bonds safe, since the rate of return is known and, barring default, the principal will be returned. However, there is risk. If a bond is sold before maturity, the bond holder will not get the full principal back if market interest rates are higher than they were when the bond was purchased.

5. **How close is the client to retirement?** As retirement approaches, investors have fewer years to recover from a loss and will likely assume less risk.

6. **Does the client expect his or her savings to generate income?** Some investors, especially retirees, count on interest from savings and bonds or the dividends from stocks to provide income. These savers will be looking for high rates of interest and/or high, dependable dividends.

7. **Is the client primarily hoping for growth?** People who don't need additional current income but want the value of their investment to grow for future use may prefer growth stocks—ones that go up in price, yielding annual returns.

ACTIVITY 21.3
INVESTMENT CASE STUDIES

Part 1: Investment Alternatives

Directions for Part 1: Imagine that you are a financial planner—someone who gives advice to clients regarding their overall investment strategies, in return for a fee. Your goal is to recommend the investment strategies that best fit the financial situation and goals of your clients.

Carefully read each of the three criteria listed below and the three investment alternatives that follow. Make use of the criteria and your understanding of the investment alternatives in developing your specific advice for each client. For each client, include your top three recommendations about what percentage of his or her investment dollars should be placed in each category. So, for example, you might recommend that a client place 60 percent of his or her investment dollars in stocks, 30 percent in bonds, and 10 percent in cash.

Three Criteria. Here are three criteria that financial planners and their clients may consider in making investment decisions. These criteria don't automatically determine any investment decision, but they are helpful points of reference.

- *Liquidity: Liquidity* refers to how quickly an investment can be converted to cash. For example, stocks and bonds are nearly liquid forms of investments because they can be sold any day. However, there is market-price risk involved. The stock price may be lower than the purchase price. Cash—such as money held in a savings account—is more liquid. A savings account depositor may withdraw money from savings at any time, without penalty.

- *Protection of the principal: Protection of the principal* refers to risk that some or all of the investment may be lost. Such a loss might occur when stocks lose value in a market downturn (a case of market risk) or when a bond is sold before maturity at a time when interest rates have gone up (a case of interest-rate risk).

- *Estimated rate of return: Estimated rate of return* refers to the expected annual gain on an investment. Investments with low rates of return—such as money held in cash—may appear to be very safe, but their returns may be below the level of inflation. In such a case, the saver suffers a loss in the form of reduced purchasing power.

Three Investment Alternatives (Set against the Three Criteria)

1: Investment in Stocks

Types of investment in stocks	Provides liquidity?	Provides protection of the principal?	Estimated rate of return?
Growth stocks	Yes	No	10 %
Income stock	Yes	No	3 %
Aggressive growth-stock mutual funds	Yes	No	10%
Income stock mutual funds	Yes	No	3 %

2: Investment in Bonds

Types of investment in bonds	Provides liquidity?	Provides protection of the principal?	Estimated rate of return?
Tax-exempt municipal bonds	Yes	Yes	2%
Top-rated government bonds	Yes	Yes	2%
Top-rated corporate bonds	Yes	Yes (but less than government bonds)	4%

3: Investment in Cash

Types of investment in cash	Provides liquidity?	Provides protection of the principal?	Estimated rate of return?
Savings account	Yes	Yes (insured by FDIC)	1%
Certificate of deposit	Yes	Yes	1%
Money market account	Yes	Yes	1%

Part 2: What's Your Best Advice?

Directions for Part 2: Read and discuss the following four cases. Recommend what percentage of savings each client should place in each of the three investment alternatives. Then explain your recommendations.

Case 1: Dan and Sue Wilson

Dan and Sue, ages 29 and 28, are trying to get ahead financially. Dan earns $40,000 a year. Sue is a stay-at-home mom looking after their pre-school child. They would like to buy two "big ticket" items (a new house and a car), but those purchases will have to wait until they are more financially stable. Their primary objective now is to reduce debt and save more money. They have $3,000 in savings. They owe $4,000 in credit-card debt. They would also like to begin saving for college expenses and retirement. How would you advise Dan and Sue to manage their savings?

Client	Percent in stocks	Percent in bonds	Percent in cash
Dan and Sue			

Why?

Case 2: Shannon

Shannon, age 26, is a sportscaster for a small television station. A single mom with a six-year-old son, she gets by on an income of $25,000. With careful budgeting, she has managed to save $1,000. Her employer will match her savings in a 401(k) plan, up to $25 per month. She has worked at the station for two years; she has health insurance but no job security. How would you advise Shannon to manage her savings?

Client	Percent in stocks	Percent in bonds	Percent in cash
Shannon			

Why?

Case 3: Jennifer

Jennifer is 34 years old. She has no dependents and lives in a townhouse worth $120,000. Her monthly payments on the townhouse are $770. She works as a sales representative for a pharmaceutical company, earning $65,000 per year, and she has a company car. She has managed to save $12,000; she would have more money in savings, but until recently she has been concentrating on paying off her student loans; she did pay them off two years ago. She enjoys her work and feels appreciated by her employer. She has good benefits, including health insurance, a retirement plan, and profit sharing. She hopes to stay with this company. She spends her free time rock climbing and paragliding. How would you advise Jennifer to manage her savings?

Client	Percent in stocks	Percent in bonds	Percent in cash
Jennifer			

Why?

Case 4: Antonio and Maria

Antonio, age 55, earns $73,000 per year as a computer administrator; his wife Maria, age 56, earns $90,000 per year as the Vice President of Human Resources for a large firm. They have two grown children and four grandchildren. In addition to a $300,000 home, they own two cars, a sailboat, and a summer cottage at the beach. Both have full retirement benefits at work, and both hope to retire in five years. They have savings of $500,000. Antonio enjoys reading financial magazines, analyzing companies, and following his investments.

Client	Percent in stocks	Percent in bonds	Percent in cash
Antonio and Maria			

Why?

SLIDE 21.1

LESSON 21 - PLANNING YOUR FINANCIAL FUTURE

A World of Risk

- **Risk of principal:** The risk that some of all of the original deposit or investment may be lost.

- **Market risk:** The risk that the forces of supply and demand or unforeseen events may affect the value of an investment.

- **Interest-rate risk:** The risk that interest rates will change. An investor, for example, might hold a fixed-rate investment, such as a bond. If the bond holder decides to sell the bond before maturity and market interest rates are higher than what the bond is earning, the price of the bond will be lower.

- **Inflation risk:** The risk that the return on an investment will not keep pace with inflation, and the saver's purchasing power will fall.

SLIDE 21.2

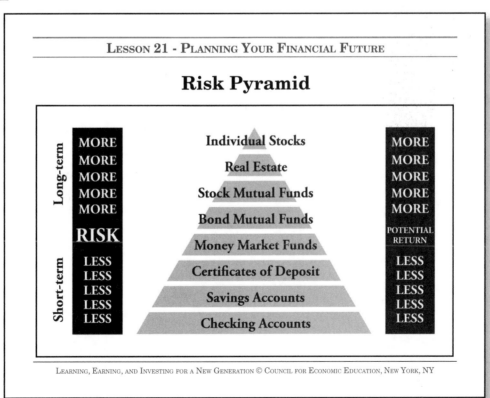

SLIDE 21.3

Elements of a Financial Plan

- Financial goals
- Net worth statement
- Income and expense statement
- Insurance plan
- Saving and investment plan

SLIDE 21.4

Important Things to Know about Your Clients

- How much does the client have in savings?
- Is the client able to save some money each month without borrowing?
- Is the client responsible for people who are financially dependent?
- How much risk is the client willing to take in order to pursue a higher rate of return?
- How close is the client to retirement?
- Does the client expect his or her savings to generate current income?
- Is the client primarily hoping for growth?
- Would the client benefit from tax-deferred or tax-exempt investments?

If you are participating in a short-term contest such as The Stock Market Game® or SMS® Stock Market Simulation, you may find these tips helpful:

First, understand that the only sure way to "win" a stock market game is to win educationally, by learning about economics, markets, and personal financial skills that will help you manage your money better.

But let's say you're focused on getting a higher portfolio value in a stock market game. That's a lot of the fun of the competition, after all. Here's what you do:

1. ***Understand that stock market games are different from investing in real life.*** In real life, you're investing real money, usually for long-term goals such as paying for education. In the game, you're investing play money for a quick payoff, typically 10 weeks. The importance of this: You have to take a lot of risk to win.

2. ***Make sure you invest all, or almost all, of your computer money.*** Cash can't match the return available in the market, so don't leave your money in cash balances.

3. ***Look for stocks that are likely to go up and down a lot.*** Older, more established companies are not usually as good for this as are newer companies. High-priced stocks usually move around less than low-priced (below $10 per share) stocks. When a company is mentioned as a takeover target, it may see major swings in its price. Buying that stock is risky, but you have to take risk to win in a 10-week game.

4. ***Don't be too late.*** Stocks move very quickly in response to news, so don't count on making any money on something that happened last week.

5. ***Check carefully for errors before submitting your trades.***

6. ***Don't buy too many different stocks.*** The more different stocks you own, the more likely it is that you'll earn just about the "market" rate of return. But to win the game, you want to beat the market, not match the market.

7. ***Hold the winners!*** If you have a stock that has made large gains and the end of the game is approaching, do not sell the stock. You will be charged a commission on the sale. But if you just leave the stock alone, its full value will be counted in your portfolio at the end of the game.

8. ***Read the first principle again.*** The game is not like real life, so remember to buy and hold sound investments when you're investing your real money.

These hints are based on "The Stock Market Game: Classroom Use and Strategy," by William C. Wood, Sharon L. O'Hare, and Robert L. Andrews in *The Journal of Economic Education,* Vol. 23, No. 3 (Summer 1992): pp. 236-246.

This glossary provides definitions for words and terms as they are used in financial markets. Some of the words and terms have other meanings in everyday usage (*load, principal,* or *speculation,* for example). The glossary does not address these other meanings.

Alternative: One of two or more choices or courses of action in a given situation.

American Stock Exchange (AMEX): A stock exchange that originated in New York City, often trading in securities of younger and smaller firms. (Renamed NYSE Amex Equities in 2009 after its acquisition by NYSE Euronext, the owner of the New York Stock Exchange.)

Asset: Something of monetary value owned by an individual or an organization.

Bankruptcy: The financial status of an individual or a firm legally judged to have debts that exceed assets and thus unable to pay its bills. Formal bankruptcy may result in reorganization of the firm or it may require liquidation and distribution of proceeds to creditors. Stock listings typically add the letter "Q" to the symbol of a bankrupt company—for example, AAMRQ for American Airlines (which was represented by AAMR before its bankruptcy).

Bear and **bear market:** A bear is an investor who believes that a security's price or security prices in general will go down. A bear market is an extended period of price decline for a security or the securities market in general. (Compare **Bull, Bull market**.)

Benefit: Monetary or non-monetary gain. (See also **Cost, Cost/benefit analysis**.)

Blue chip stock: A high-quality, low-risk stock. The term usually refers to stock in nationally known companies that have been profitable for a long time.

Bond: A certificate of indebtedness issued by a governmental unit or a corporation, promising to repay borrowed money to the lender at a fixed rate of interest and at a specified time.

Bond fund: An investment company that invests in debt securities; may specialize in certain bond categories, such as corporate or municipal, short-term or long-term.

Bond rating: The grading of a bond by reference to the bond issuer's ability to make interest and principal payments as specified in the terms of the bond. The three major rating services—Fitch, Moody's, and Standard & Poor's—use Aaa as their highest rating and grade down through Bs and Cs.

Broker: A professional trader who buys or sells stocks for individuals and institutional customers. (See also **Dealer, Discount broker, Full-service broker**.)

Bull and **bull market:** A bull is an investor or analyst who believes that the price of a security or security prices in general will rise. A bull market is an extended period of rising prices for a security or the securities market in general. (Compare **Bear, Bear market**.)

Business cycles: Fluctuations in the overall rate of national economic activity with alternating periods of expansion and contraction; these vary in duration and degrees of severity; usually measured by real gross domestic product (GDP). (See also **Expansion, Peak, Contraction, Trough**.)

Buying on margin: Buying securities by paying only a percentage (a margin) of the purchase price and borrowing the remainder. The loan is usually arranged by the investor's broker. (See also **Margin requirement**.)

Capital gain: A profit realized from the sale of property, stocks, or other investments.

Capitalization: A measure of the value of a corporation. It is calculated by multiplying the number of the company's outstanding shares by the stock price. Corporations are often referred to by their level of capitalization such as large cap, medium cap, or small cap.

Capital goods: Goods that people use in their work to make other goods. Buildings, tools, machines and other equipment are capital goods.

Certificate of deposit (CD): A receipt issued by a bank to a person depositing money in an account (a CD account) for a specified period of time—often six months, one year, or two years. CD accounts pay interest at specified, fixed rates; banks ordinarily impose penalties for early withdrawals from CD accounts.

Choice: A decision made or a course of action taken, given two or more alternatives. (See also **Alternative, Scarcity**.)

Circuit breaker: The automatic response (usually a halt or slowdown) in activity at a securities exchange in response to certain occurrences in trading. Designed to reduce market volatility, circuit breakers were instituted following sharp market downturns in October 1987 and October 1989.

Closing price: The price of a stock reported at the end (close) of a trading day.

Command economy: An economy in which most economic issues of production and distribution are resolved through central planning and control. (Compare **Market economy**.)

Commission: A percentage of a stock trade (a buy or sell) paid by a customer to a broker.

Common stock: An ownership share or shares of ownership in a corporation. A common stock offers no guarantee that it will hold its value or pay dividends. (Compare **Preferred stock**.)

Competition: Attempts by two or more individuals or organizations to acquire the same goods, services, or productive and financial resources. Consumers compete with other consumers for goods and services. Producers compete with other producers for sales to consumers.

Compound interest: Interest paid on the principal (see **Principal**) and on interest earned previously. (Compare **Simple interest**.)

Consumption: Spending by households on goods and services; the process of buying and using goods and services.

Contraction: A time of declining activity in the business cycle, marked by decreases in GDP, income, employment, investment, and consumption. (See also **Business cycle**.)

Corporate bond: A bond issued by a corporation. (See also **Bond, Municipal bond, U.S. savings bond**.)

Corporation: A legal entity owned by shareholders whose liability for the firm's losses is limited to the value of the stock they own. (Compare **Partnership, Sole proprietorship**.)

Cost: An amount that must be paid to obtain something. (See also **Opportunity cost**.)

Cost/benefit analysis: A process of examining the advantages (benefits) and disadvantages (costs) of each alternative in arriving at a decision.

Coupon: The annual interest paid on a bond, usually stated in terms of the rate paid on a bond's face value. For example, a nine percent coupon $1,000 bond would pay its owner $90 in interest annually up to maturity. (See also **Coupon bond, Coupon rate of return**.)

Coupon bond: A bond that pays interest at regular intervals, with a final payment that includes the original principal when the bond matures. (See also **Zero-coupon bond**.)

Coupon rate of return: See **Coupon**.

Credit: The ability of a customer to obtain goods or services before payment, based on an agreement to pay later.

Credit card: A small, specially coded plastic card issued by a bank or other organization, authorizing the cardholder to purchase goods or services on credit.

Credit rating: An evaluation of a borrower's ability to meet financial obligations. (See also **Bond rating**.)

Currency market: A foreign exchange market in which the currency of one nation (such as the United States) can be used to purchase the currency of another nation (such as Mexico). (See also **Exchange rate**.)

Debt: Money owed to somebody else—as in *I'm $900 in debt*. Also the state or condition of owing money—as in *Jones is always in debt*.

Dealer: Someone who buys and sells stocks from his or her own accounts or the accounts of the firm he or she represents. Some dealers also act as brokers. (See also **Broker**.)

Debt financing: Obtaining funds by issuing bonds. (Compare **Equity financing**.)

Demand: The quantity of a good or service that customers are willing and able to buy at all possible prices during a period of time.

Depression: A severe, prolonged contraction in economic activity. The most famous example is the Great Depression of the 1930s. (See also **Great Depression, Recession**.)

Discount broker: An individual or firm that charges lower commissions than full-service brokers charge for certain services. Discount brokers typically provide only limited advice to investors. (See also **Full-service broker**.)

Disposable income: The money a person has left to spend or save after taxes and other required deductions have been taken out of his or her gross pay. (See also **Gross pay, Net pay**.)

Diversification: Spreading investment funds out over various investment options (stocks, bonds, mutual funds and money market accounts, for example) in an effort to reduce risk.

Dividend: A share of a company's net profits paid to stockholders.

Dividend reinvestment plan (DRIP): A plan that allows stockholders to reinvest dividends automatically in additional shares of the company's stock.

Dow Jones Industrial Average (DJIA): One of the oldest and most widely quoted measures of stock market performance; also called the Dow. The average is calculated by reference to the share prices of 30 large, well-known firms.

Economic forecasting: Predicting what will happen to the economy in the future, often by reference to leading economic indicators. Forecasts may focus on GDP, prices, interest rates, employment, and other variables. (See also **Leading economic indicators**.)

Economic investing: Purchasing capital goods—computers, delivery trucks, or office buildings, for example—to be used in producing goods and services in the future.

Equilibrium price: A price at which the quantity demanded by buyers equals the quantity supplied by sellers; also called the market-clearing price.

Equities: Stocks, both common and preferred—as in *I prefer to invest in equities rather than bonds*.

Equity financing: Obtaining funds by issuing stock. (Compare **Debt financing**.)

Exchange rate: The price of one nation's currency in terms of another nation's currency.

Expansion: A time of growth in the business cycle, marked by increases in GDP, income, employment, investment, and consumption. (See also **Business cycle**.)

Face value: For a bond, the dollar amount on which interest is calculated; also the amount paid to the bondholder at maturity. Also known as par value.

Federal Deposit Insurance Corporation (FDIC): The federal agency that insures deposits at commercial banks, savings banks, and savings associations in the United States.

Federal funds rate: The interest rate banks pay when they borrow funds overnight from other banks.

Federal Reserve: The central bank of the United States. Also called the Fed. Its main function is controlling the money supply through monetary policy. (See also **Monetary policy**.)

Finance charge: The cost of credit, including interest and transaction fees.

Financial institutions: Banks, credit unions, pension funds, insurance companies, mutual funds, and other organizations that act as intermediaries, enabling savers and borrowers to engage in transactions.

Financial markets: Markets for the exchange of financial capital and credit. Most often, these are markets in which investors buy and sell stocks and bonds.

Full-service broker: An individual or firm that provides a wide range of services to investors, including research and advice. (Compare **Discount broker**.)

Fundamental analysis: Analysis of security values by reference to basic factors such as earnings, balance sheet variables, and management quality. (Compare **Technical analysis**.)

Goal: Something a person or organization plans to achieve in the future; an aim or desired result. Financial planners often classify goals according to the time it would take individuals to save the money needed to attain them:

- **Short-term goals:** Goals that might be attained within two months.

- **Medium-term goals:** Goals that might be attained in two months to one year.

- **Long-term goals:** Goals that require three years or more to attain.

Government failure: Policy and budget choices by government officials that result in inefficiency; in cases of government failure, regulation may not suffice to solve a market problem as intended.

Great Depression: A time of deep, prolonged recession in the United States (and elsewhere) during the 1930s. Output fell drastically; unemployment soared; banks failed; and many individuals experienced deprivation and hardship. (See also **Depression, Recession**.)

Gross domestic product (GDP): The market value of all goods and services produced in a nation in a calendar year. When this figure is adjusted for inflation, it is referred to as real GDP.

Growth fund: An investment company whose major objective is long-term capital growth. (Compare **Income fund**.)

Growth stock: The stock of a firm that is expected to have above-average increases in revenues and earnings. Growth stocks often sell at high price-earnings ratios and are subject to wide swings in price. (Compare **Income stock**.)

Hedge fund: An investment fund focusing on a specific type of investment strategy, normally having a limited number of investors. Hedge funds tend to be subject to less regulation and fewer restrictions than many other investments, such as mutual funds.

Human capital: The health, education, experience, training, and skills people bring to their work. People invest in human capital when they give up something of value now to increase their human capital—for example, by completing an apprenticeship training program or a program of studies in nursing.

Incentive: Any reward or benefit (such as money, advantage, or good feeling) that motivates people to do something—as in *Tax provisions in the new forest-management program give landowners an incentive to take good care of the trees on their property*.

Income: Money received for work performed or from investments; may include salaries, wages, fees, dividends, bonuses, interest payments.

Income fund: An investment company that concentrates on bonds, preferred stocks, and common stocks that pay dividends, thus seeking to maximize current income (rather than growth) for investors. (Compare **Growth fund**.)

Income stock: A stock that pays dividends regularly; associated with firms that have stable earnings and operate in a mature industry. (Compare **Growth stock**.)

Index fund: A mutual fund whose objective is to match the composite investment performance of a large group of stocks or bonds such as those represented by the Standard & Poor's 500 Composite Stock Index.

Inflation: A rise in the general or average price level of all the goods and services produced in an economy.

Initial public offering (IPO): A company's first sale of stock to the public.

Insider trading: The illegal buying or selling of securities on the basis of information not available to the general public.

Institutional investor: A financial intermediary (a mutual fund or a pension fund, for example) that invests in the securities markets for clients.

Insurance: A practice or arrangement whereby a company provides a guarantee of compensation for specified forms of loss, damage, injury, or death. People obtain such guarantees by buying insurance policies, for which they pay premiums. The process allows for the spreading out of risk over a pool of insurance policyholders. Specific types of insurance include the following:

- **Home owners' insurance:** Provides financial protection from damage or loss to a home from hazards such as fire, lightning, or theft.

- **Auto insurance:** Provides financial protection from losses caused by accidents or other mishaps. *Collision insurance* provides for the repair or replacement of the car damaged in an accident. *Liability* covers the cost of property damage or injuries to others caused by the policy owner. *Comprehensive* covers the cost of damage to an auto as the result of fire, theft, or storms.

- **Renters' insurance:** Provides financial protection in case of loss of personal possessions in a rental unit due to hazards such as theft, fire, and water damage.

- **Health insurance:** Provides payment for certain health care costs. Basic health insurance covers office visits, lab work, hospital costs, and routine care up to a certain limit. Major medical insurance provides protection against catastrophic illness.

- **Disability insurance:** Provides income over a specified period of time when a person is ill or unable to work.

- **Life insurance:** Provides financial protection to dependents of the policy owner when the policy owner dies.

Interest: Money paid by borrowers, at a particular rate (See **Interest rate**) for their use of the money they have borrowed. Also, money paid by financial institutions to depositors.

Interest rate: The price paid for using someone else's money, expressed as a percentage. Also, the rate (expressed as a percentage) at which financial institutions pay money to depositors.

Investing: Spending money with the expectation of making a financial gain. Investment possibilities include stocks, bonds, mutual funds, real estate, and other financial instruments or ventures. (See also **Economic investing**.)

Investment bank: An institution that participates in the primary markets for the sale of newly issued stocks and corporate and government bonds.

Investment, financial: A decision to forgo benefits today in an effort to increase future wealth or satisfaction over time. (See also **Investing**.)

Junk bond: A high-risk, high-yield bond, unrated or rated lower than Bbb.

Law of demand: An economic principle stating that as the price of a good or service rises (or falls), the quantity of that good or service that people are willing and able to buy during a certain period of time falls (or rises). In other words, quantity demanded goes down when prices rise; quantity demanded goes up when prices fall.

Law of supply: An economic principle stating that as the price of a good or service that producers are willing and able to offer for sale during a certain period of time rises (or falls), the quantity of that good or service supplied rises (or falls). In other words, quantity supplied goes up when prices rise; quantity supplied goes down when prices fall.

Leading economic indicators: Economic variables such as unemployment claims, manufacturers' new orders, stock prices, and new plant and equipment orders that tend to change before real output changes. (See also **Economic forecasting**.)

Limit order: An investor's order to a broker, instructing him or her to execute a transaction (to buy or sell a security) only at a specified price (the limit) or better.

Limited liability: The liability of a firm's owners (in the case of a lawsuit, for example) for no more money than they have invested in the business. Thus, a stockholder can lose no more than he or she has paid for shares of ownership, regardless of the firm's financial obligations. Limited liability is one of the major advantages of organizing a company as a corporation. (See also **Corporation**.)

Liquidity: The ease with which an asset can be converted to cash. For example: money held in a checking account is a liquid asset; real estate is far less liquid

Load: A sales charge investors must pay to acquire certain assets—shares in many mutual funds, for example. Also called front-end load or sales load. (See also **Load fund**.)

Load fund: A mutual fund with shares sold at a price that includes a sales charge, or load—typically four to nine percent of the net amount invested. (See also **Load**.)

Margin requirement: The minimum portion of the purchase price for a new security that an investor must pay in cash. Margin requirements are determined by the Federal Reserve Board. (See also **Buying on margin**.)

Market: A place, institution, or technological arrangement by means of which goods and services are bought and sold.

Market economy: An economy that relies on a system of interdependent market prices to allocate goods, services, and productive resources, and to coordinate the diverse plans of consumers and producers, all of them acting according their self-interest. (Compare **Command economy**.)

Market failure: In financial transactions, unintended shifting of costs or unexpected risks that result from influences such as deception and fraud. More generally, market failure is the systematic overproduction or underproduction of some goods and services that occurs when producers or consumers do not have to bear the full costs of transactions they undertake.

Market order: An investor's order to a broker for immediate execution of a trade at the best price available when the order reaches the marketplace. (Compare **Limit order**.)

Maturity or **maturity date:** The date on which payment of a financial obligation is due. For a bond, the maturity date is the date on which the bond issuer must pay the face value of the bond to the bond holder.

Monetary policy: Changes in the supply of money and the availability of credit, initiated by a nation's central bank (in the United States, by the Fed) to promote price stability, full employment, and economic growth. (See also **Federal Reserve**.)

Money market fund: A fund restricted by law to investing in the short-term money market. These funds provide low risk and low returns, but they maintain their investment value. (See also **Mutual fund**.)

Municipal bond: A bond issued by a city, county, state, or other political entity. Interest paid on most municipal bonds is exempt from federal income taxes and often from state and local taxes as well. (Compare **Bond, Corporate bond, U.S. savings bond**.)

Mutual fund: A pool of money used by a company to buy various assets—including stocks, bonds, or money market instruments—on behalf of its shareholders. Mutual fund investments provide investors with diversification and professional management.

NASDAQ Stock Market: An electronic marketplace enabling buyers and sellers to get together via computer and hundreds of thousands of miles of high-speed data lines to trade stocks.

Net asset value per share (NAV): A valuation of an investment company's shares, calculated by subtracting any liabilities from the market value of the firm's assets and dividing the difference by the number of shares outstanding. In general, NAV is the price an investor would receive when selling shares back to a fund.

New York Stock Exchange (NYSE): The oldest stock exchange in the United States, founded in 1792.

NYSE Amex Equities: A stock exchange that originated in New York City, often trading in securities of younger and smaller firms. (Formerly referred to as the American Stock Exchange; renamed NYSE Amex Equities in 2009 after its acquisition by NYSE Euronext, the owner of the New York Stock Exchange.)

No-load fund: An investment company in which shares are sold directly to customers at net asset value, without a sales charge. (See also **Load**, and compare **Load fund**.)

Odd lot: A trading unit of fewer than 100 shares of stock. To buy one share or seven shares, for example, is to buy an odd lot. (Compare **Round lot**.)

Open market operations: The buying and selling of government bonds by the Federal Reserve to control bank reserves and the money supply; an important monetary policy tool. (See also **Monetary policy**.)

Opportunity cost: The second-best alternative (or the value of that alternative) that must be given up when scarce resources (time or money, for example) are used for one purpose instead of another.

Over-the-counter market (OTC): A widespread aggregation of dealers who make markets in many different securities, trading through computer networks. Virtually all government and municipal bonds and most corporate bonds are traded in the OTC market.

Over-the-counter stock: A stock not listed on an exchange and traded only in the OTC market.

Par value: For a bond, the dollar amount on which interest is calculated, and the amount paid to the bondholder at maturity. Also known as face value.

Partnership: A business owned by two or more people who share the firm's profits and losses. (Compare **Corporation, Sole proprietorship**.)

Pay yourself first: A principle of personal financial management that emphasizes making saving a priority over spending. Individuals "pay themselves first" when they save or invest some money from every paycheck before they buy consumer goods.

Peak: A high point in the expansion phase of the business cycle, and also a turning point. After the peak, the economy begins to contract. (See also **Business cycle**.)

Ponzi scheme: An investment fraud that holds no real assets, paying off existing investors by using funds from new investors.

Portfolio: A collection of savings and investments held by an individual or an institution. The more diversified the portfolio, the more likely it is that the investor will earn the same return as the market. (See also **Diversification**.)

Preferred stock: An ownership share with a guaranteed dividend that is paid before any dividends are paid on common stock. (Compare **Common stock**.)

Price: Regarding securities, the dollar amount at which a security trades.

Price earnings (P/E) ratio: The current price of a stock divided by the current (or sometimes the projected) earnings per share of the issuing firm. A high P/E ratio generally indicates that investors expect the firm's earnings to grow.

Primary market: The market in which new securities are offered for sale for the first time. Investment banks buy shares of stocks directly from corporations that issue them and sell these shares to others. (Compare **Secondary market**.)

Principal: An original amount of money invested or lent.

Productive resources: Natural resources, human resources, capital resources, and entrepreneurship used to make goods and services.

Prospectus: A document related to a new securities offering, intended to provide investors with information that will help them decide whether to buy the security. The prospectus will ordinarily describe the proposed business plan and related information, including financial data, a summary of the firm's business history, a list of its officers, a description of its operations, and notification of any pending litigation.

Recession: A decline in the rate of national economic activity, usually measured by a decline in real GDP for at least two consecutive quarters (i.e., six months). (See also **Contraction**.)

Return: Earnings from an investment, usually expressed as an annual percentage. (See also **Yield**.)

Revolving credit: Credit that is automatically renewed as debts are paid off or paid down.

Reward: The potential gain that may come from investing in a security. (See also **Risk-return relationship**.)

Risk: The chance of losing money on an investment. Risk arises from variability in returns. The greater the potential variability (in stock prices, for example), the greater the risk. (See also **Risk-return relationship**.) Risk is sometimes classified according to the sources of variability:

- **Currency risk:** The risk that returns to be paid in foreign currency will be affected adversely by exchange-rate changes.

- **Inflation risk:** The risk that returns (on money kept in a certificate of deposit, for example) will not keep pace with inflation

- **Interest-rate risk:** The risk that returns will not keep pace with rising interest rates.

- **Market risk:** The risk that forces of supply and demand might affect the value of an investment adversely.

- **Risk of principal:** The risk that some or all of an investor's original deposit or investment might be lost.

Risk-return relationship: As applied to investments: the greater the risk, the greater the potential reward. For example: savings accounts offer depositors very low risk but also low rates of interest; growth stocks are much riskier, but they offer a potential for big gains. (See also **Risk**.)

Role of government: Government activity in establishing a framework or "rules of the game" for economic life. In financial markets specifically, the government's role has included enforcing property rights and correcting market failures.

Round lot: The standard unit of trading in a particular type of security. For stocks, a round lot is 100 shares or a multiple of 100 shares. (Compare **Odd lot.**)

Rule of 72: A mathematical rule used to approximate the number of years it will take for an investment to double in value when interest is compounded. The number of years is calculated by dividing 72 by the annual rate of return. For example, savings deposited in an account paying interest at an annual rate of four percent will double in 72 divided by 4, or 18, years.

S & P 500: The Standard & Poor's 500 Stock Index. An index made up of 500 stock prices to provide a broad indicator of stock price movements.

Save: To set money aside for future use; to divert money from current spending to a savings account or another form of investment.

Saving: The act of consuming less than disposable income (income after taxes) and setting the remainder aside; savings are measured as disposable income minus consumption spending.

Savings account: An interest-bearing account at a financial institution.

Scarcity: The condition that exists because human wants exceed the capacity of available resources to satisfy those wants; also a situation in which a resource has more than one valuable use. The problem of scarcity faces all individuals and organizations, including firms and government agencies. (See also **Choice.**)

Secondary market: A market in which stocks can be bought and sold once they are approved for public sale; for example, the New York Stock Exchange. (Compare **Primary market.**)

Securities and Exchange Commission (SEC): The federal agency that administers U.S. securities laws; established under the Securities Exchange Act of 1934.

Securities index: A statistical composite that measures changes in financial markets. The Dow Jones Industrial Average (DJIA) is the most commonly known securities index. (See also **DJIA.**)

Security: A certificate attesting to a stockholder's ownership shares in a firm, or a bondholder's creditor relationship with a corporation or a governmental unit.

Selling short: To sell short, the buyer borrows shares he or she does not own from a broker. The buyer orders the shares to be sold and takes the money from the sale. Then the buyer waits for the stock price to fall. If the price does fall, the buyer buys the shares at the lower price, pays the broker's commission and any fees, and gains a profit. Selling short is risky; if the stock price increases, the buyer loses money.

Shareholder: An individual or organization that owns common stock or preferred stock. Also called a stockholder.

Shift in demand: A change in one or more of the determinants of demand including consumers' tastes, the number of consumers in the market, consumers' incomes, the prices of related goods, and consumer expectations. A change in demand causes the demand curve to shift to the right or left.

Shift in supply: A change in one or more of the determinants of supply including resource prices, technology, taxes and subsidies, prices of other goods, price expectations, and the number of sellers. A change in supply causes the supply curve to shift to the right or left.

Short cover: Buying a security in order to repay a loan of borrowed stock, concluding a short sale. (See also **Selling short, Short sale**.)

Short sale: A sale of securities not owned by the seller; the seller hopes to buy them back later at a lower price. (See also **Selling short**.)

Shortage: The situation that arises when the quantity demanded of a product exceeds the quantity supplied. Shortages generally occur when a price is set below the equilibrium price. (See also **Equilibrium price**; compare **Surplus**.)

Simple interest: Interest paid on the initial investment only; calculated by multiplying the investment principal times the annual rate of interest times the number of years. (Compare **Compound interest**.)

Sole proprietorship: A business owned by one person. The sole proprietor receives all the profits of the business and is responsible for all of its debts. Many businesses in the United States are sole proprietorships. They are usually small businesses—for example, neighborhood barber shops, gift shops, family farms. (Compare **Corporation, Partnership**.)

Specialist: A member of a securities exchange who makes trades only in one or more designated securities; a "market maker" in the designated security or securities, assigned by the exchange to maintain an orderly market in his or her area of trading.

Speculation: High-risk investment practices. Speculators take above-average risks—buying something on the basis of its potential selling price—in expectation of gaining above-average returns, generally during a short time period.

Stock: An ownership share or shares in a corporation. (See also **Common stock, Preferred stock**.)

Stock certificate: A document attesting to ownership of shares of stock.

Stock market: A market in which the public trades stock that someone already owns.

Stock market crash: A sudden, steep decline in stock prices, prompting many stockholders to sell their shares out of fear that prices will continue to fall. Examples include the crash of October 1929 and the crash of October 2008.

Stock split: The division of the outstanding number of shares into a higher number of shares. The market price per share drops proportionately.

Stock symbol: The letter or sequence of letters used to identify a security. The stock symbol for ExxonMobil, for example, is XOM.

Stockholder: An individual or organization that owns common stock or preferred stock. Also called a shareholder.

Strong dollar: A situation in which the U.S. dollar has a high or rising value compared with other nations' currencies. (Compare **Weak dollar**.)

Supply: The quantity of a good or service that producers are willing and able to offer for sale at each possible price during a period of time.

Surplus: The situation that arises when the quantity supplied of a product exceeds the quantity demanded. Surpluses generally occur when a price is set above the equilibrium price. (See also **Equilibrium price**; compare **Shortage**.)

Technical analysis: The study of relationships among market variables to gain insight into the supply of and demand for securities. The market variables used include price levels, trading volume, and price movements. (Compare **Fundamental analysis**.)

Ticker: An automated quotation system on which security transactions are reported after they occur on an exchange floor. (See also **Ticker tape**.)

Ticker tape: The narrow, continuous roll of paper on which stock transactions were recorded before electronic technology made the old recording system obsolete. The term now refers to the flow of prices appearing on tickers out of brokerage firms. (See also **Ticker**.)

Trade deficit: A negative trade balance—that is, a balance in which a nation's imports are of greater value than its exports.

Trading volume: The number of shares of a stock traded on a given trading day, expressed in multiples of 100.

Treasury bonds: Longer-term (compared to **treasury bills**), interest-bearing bonds issued by the U.S. Treasury.

Trough: A low point in the business cycle, and also a turning point. After a trough, the economy begins to expand. (See also **Business cycle**.)

U.S. savings bonds: Securities issued by the U.S. Treasury in relatively small denominations for individual investors. (See also **Bond**.)

Venture capital: A pool of funds, typically contributed by large investors, from which allocations are made to young, small companies that have good growth prospects but are short of funds. (See also **Venture capital fund**.)

Venture capital fund: An investment company that invests its shareholders' money in new business ventures that are risky but potentially very profitable. Shareholders in the fund are known as venture capitalists.

Weak dollar: A situation in which the U.S. dollar has a low or falling value compared with other nations' currencies. (Compare **Strong dollar**.)

Yield: Earnings from an investment, usually expressed as an annual percentage. (See also **Return**.)

Zero-coupon bond: A bond that pays all its interest and principal at the bond's maturity. An investor's income from a zero-coupon bond comes solely from the bond's appreciation in value.